THE WE[ST] YORKSH[IRE] MOORS

by Christopher Goddard

the dogs on Dog Hill

For Dolly, Eric and those before us who
trespassed as a matter of principle

Published by Northern Heritage Publications
an imprint of Jeremy Mills Publishing Limited

113 Lidget Street
Lindley
Huddersfield
West Yorkshire
HD3 3JR

www.jeremymillspublishing.co.uk

First published 2013
Text and images © Christopher Goddard

ISBN 978-1-906600-99-0

CONTENTS

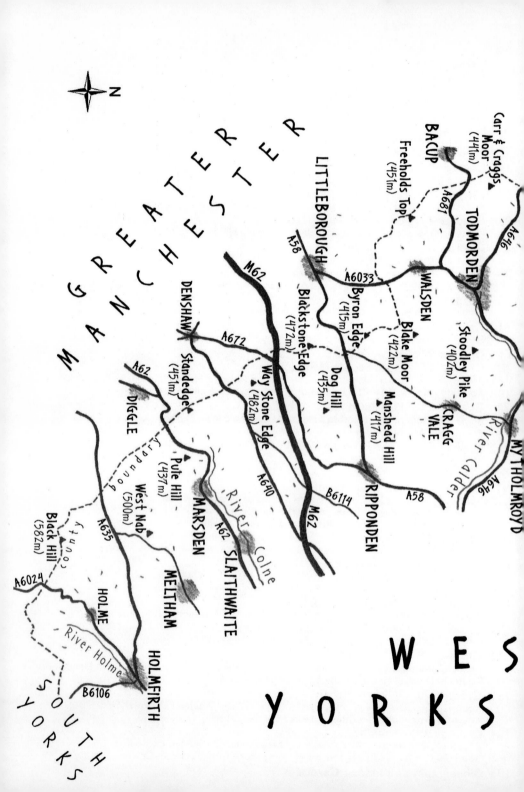

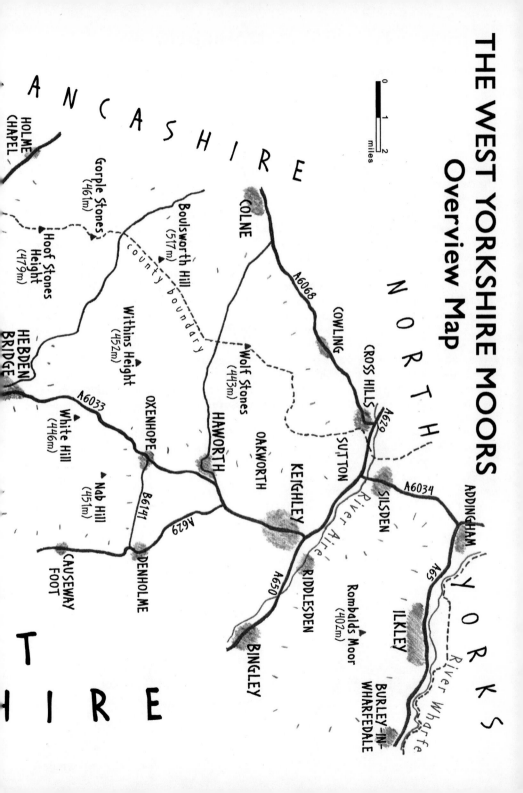

THE WEST YORKSHIRE MOORS
Overview Map

L A N C A S H I R E

N O R T H

Y O R K S

E S T

S H I R E

0
1
2
miles

HOLME CHAPEL

Gorple Stones (461m)

Hoof Stones Height (479m)

Boulsworth Hill (517m)

county boundary

COLNE

A6068

COWLING

CROSS HILLS

A629

Withins Height (452m)

Wolf Stones (443m)

HEBDEN BRIDGE

A6033

White Hill (446m)

OXENHOPE

HAWORTH

OAKWORTH

KEIGHLEY

SUTTON

SILSDEN

A6034

ADDINGHAM

A65

River Aire

Nab Hill (451m)

B6141

A629

RIDDLESDEN

Rombalds Moor (402m)

ILKLEY

River Wharfe

CAUSEWAY FOOT

DENHOLME

A650

BINGLEY

BURLEY-IN-WHARFEDALE

THE WEST YORKSHIRE MOORS

*'And the moors were always there, and the horizon never without its
promise. No Bruddersford man could be exiled from the uplands and
blue air; he always had one foot on the heather...'*
(J.B. Priestley, from *Bright Day*)

Think of West Yorkshire and you think of soot-blackened mills and grimy chimneys, and
the moorlands whose dark features they echo; peat groughs, burnt heather and rough grit.
The two have always been linked, the one providing plentiful water for the other, the
towns stretching as far up every watercourse as possible. For the people of West
Yorkshire (and of Sheffield and Manchester), the closeness of the moors has long been a
chance to get out of the smoke and breathe fresh air. From towns across the South
Pennines, you can walk straight up into the hills – it needn't be an expedition, a holiday, or
a day off, the moors are always right there.

Though the days of the 'dark satanic mills' are gone, we're nostalgic for that very
atmosphere in the crumbling mills and lonely moorland ruins of West Yorkshire today. We
take to the moors in search of signs of this past, and so often when you get there it seems
that you have the whole moor to yourself. Yet when you come back and talk to other
people, you realise that they too wander the moors in the same spirit. But where were
they? And whose feet have tramped such well-worn tracks across the hills? This is the
enigma of the moors – the sense of isolation that pervades these apparently empty spaces,
and yet the proximity of your fellow man, both past and present. There are ancient
settlements, boundary markers, abandoned farmsteads and industrial ley-lines at every
turn, while all the time the thrum of modernity rises to these heights – valley life, pylons,
the M62.

The endless grey horizons that stretch ahead of you at the top of the roads across
Cock Hill, Holme Moss or Windy Hill are all that some people want to see. Sit in the car
for a few minutes, perhaps get out for a blast of chill wind, then drive on. The moors,
though, are harder work than that; the more you give, the more they return. Sometimes
you have to walk all day to appreciate them, to get a sense of what it was you came out
here for. What I have tried to do with this book is give you more inspiration for exploring
these moors and more ways of discovering their secrets.

Dove Stones on Boulsworth Hill

Beginnings

When I moved to Hebden Bridge, one of the first things I did was to yomp up the nearest hills so I could look out over the valley and get a sense of where I was; first High Brown Knoll, then Stoodley Pike. What I found remarkable on both Midgley Moor and Erringden Moor was the failure of the map to convey the paths across these moors. For anyone who holds Ordnance Survey maps in as high esteem as I do, it is a shock when they let you down. The map shows public footpaths where there are just swathes of heather and bog, and then you stumble across a fine path (like the one along Sheep Stones Edge) that is not shown at all. Although there is little the OS can do about the vagaries of the historical network of Public Rights of Way, I found the usually reliable black dashed lines[1] letting me down as well. The consequence is that in many places you are forced to navigate by base geographical features (contours, watercourses, crags, etc) alone. While this may be a good navigational exercise, I felt there was an opportunity to map these moors more accurately.

So I set to work on Midgley Moor and Wadsworth Moor, following every last sheeptrack to see if it would reach a satisfactory conclusion or an interesting feature, and recording what I found. In truth, it is the kind of thing I have been doing since I was a boy. The woods around our house on the edge of Sheffield were mapped and remapped with names being given to every lost quarry and mine-working. On holidays in Greece, I was appalled at the standard of the maps and worked to create a decent plan of Kassiopi and its surrounding coastline. Finding a new path and committing it to the map was what drove me on in these endeavours. My mother said I was born a good century too late and should have been out exploring and mapping the world in the age of empire. Yet the exploring I like to do need not be particularly exotic, rather it just has to be somewhere new – and you can discover new things around the corner from your house every day. Exploring is also not linear, but nearly always leads me round in circles as I am desperate not to miss anything. Indeed this is the only way to make a good map. So, finally, after years of amateur map-making, I felt as if I'd hit upon a project to which I could dedicate my passion for exploring the minutiae of the world outside my door.

It is over six years later and those original maps of Wadsworth Moor have been consigned to the dustbin, but they set in motion the work in this book, which has very much morphed as I have gone along. I squeezed in time between jobs surveying Public Rights of Way and National Trails, though there were many occasions when it felt like a busman's holiday. I was lucky, though, that my work included walking each of the 2500km of paths in both Kirklees and Calderdale during this period, and slowly a fuller picture of West Yorkshire's moorland landscape emerged. Aware that obvious comparisons would be made with Wainwright's style, I never looked at his Lakeland books while producing my maps. When I finally did I was shocked at how much detail mine had in comparison, something that will hopefully be useful to anyone exploring the smaller paths and features of the moors; whether a fell-runner tracing a tiny path across a barren moor or an antiquarian seeking out a remote ancient stone. Yet the beauty of maps is that they are merely suggestive and there are always blank spaces on them yet to be explored.

---

[1] These feint black 'peck' lines are found on 1:25,000 maps, often underneath the thicker green dashes that mark Public Rights of Way. Forget the pretty colours all over the map, these black dashes and the solid black lines indicating fences and walls are often the only things you really need to find your way. These trusty companions have led me up obscure Lakeland fells and guided me through the other-worldly landscape of the Rhinogs in North Wales, as well as alerting me to the possibility of a Right of Way being purely notional (beware when there are no black dashes beneath the green line you are intending to walk!).

My West Yorkshire Moors

The West Yorkshire Moors are not a commonly used designation but, for the purpose of this book, they cover the large section of the South Pennines that falls within the modern county of West Yorkshire. West Yorkshire (as opposed to the West Riding of Yorkshire) was only created in 1974, though it makes a lot of sense in terms of both landscape and the natural watershed. Saddleworth was part of the old West Riding, but is on the other side of the Pennines and its inhabitants speak with a Lancashire dialect. The county boundary also used to run through the middle of Todmorden, which is still home to the Lancashire 2nd XI cricket team. Yet it would be nonsense to include the Saddleworth Moors or exclude the moors west of Todmorden, so I have decided to use the watershed as being the true boundary[2] between West Yorkshire and Lancashire/Greater Manchester – we all know it is the hills that truly separate the roses.

I have divided the moors of West Yorkshire by their high points, despite the fact that many of these are unmarked and little known. Perhaps tops like Way Stone Edge, Carr & Craggs Moor and Withins Height deserve to be better known; after all the former is the highest top in Calderdale and the latter the highest in Bradford, yet all are largely unrecognised. I also decided that 400 metres made a natural cut-off point, meaning that the lower heaths of Norland Moor, Baildon Moor and the Chevin would not be included in this book despite containing areas of access land. All of these are actually very easy commons to explore and have few of the access and navigation problems associated with the higher grouse moors.

I have identified a total of fifty high points in West Yorkshire broadly using the Hewitt[3] classification (see list on Page v). The bulk of the lower tops (which are not included in this book) are either inaccessible or unremarkable (or both), but a few may be worth seeking out. Baildon Moor, Castle Hill and the Chevin are already well-known, but Cheese Gate Nab, Gallows Pole Hill and Meltham Cop are also fine prominences (even if not all are legally accessible). Soil Hill, above Causeway Foot, is another anomaly – it is over 400 metres high, but contains no access land and has a scruffy quarried summit, so I have left it out. It can be easily reached by public footpaths if you wish to complete the set and offers fine views over Bradford.

However, before the Victorians sought to conquer every corner of their world, the peaks were largely ignored, particularly in plateau country such as this. Consequently summits were rarely named, moors simply being known locally as the Great Moor, or else distinguished by parish[4]. Where the moorlands had specific names they were often associated with local folklore, such as Rombalds Moor. The first detailed map of the area was Christopher Saxton's map of Yorkshire in 1577, in which he records only 'Blakeston Edge' and 'Gorpill Hill'. For years Saxton's maps were largely copied, until Thomas Jefferys' map of 1771 added far more detail, especially on the high ground; this saw the addition of 'Rombalds Moor', 'Wool Stones' (Wolf Stones), 'Crowell End' (Crow Hill), 'Hamilton Hill' (Black Hameldon), 'Alderman Stones' (Holder Stones), 'Standedge' and others.

Despite having been active in the south of England for fifty years, the Ordnance Survey's first one-inch (to the mile) map of Yorkshire was published in 1841, but only included the

---

[2] Thus, the tops of both Boulsworth Hill and Blackstone Edge are assumed to stand on the true boundary, though they are stranded in Lancashire by the existing boundary (the latter admittedly by only a few metres).

[3] Hewitts are high points in England and Wales over 2,000 feet with a prominence of thirty metres (or 100 feet) from the surrounding ground. As there are no peaks in West Yorkshire that meet this criteria, I have simply dropped the minimum height to 200 metres.

[4] For example, Wadsworth Moor makes little topographical sense, comprising two separate moors on different sides of Crinsworth, unless taken in the context of the parish of Wadsworth.

eastern part of the county. The western half of West Yorkshire followed in 1843, but it was not until 1858 that the one-inch map of the northern part of the county was published. By then, the remarkable six-inch (to the mile) maps of the whole country had been published – it is to these that we owe so much of our mapping information. While of tremendous value in preserving names we now have little other reference to (like Ogden Spa on Nab Hill, Cheetham Lad on Manshead Hill or Lads Grave on Blackstone Edge), these maps doubtless also erased or bastardised many others. Local names interpreted by surveyors became effectively fixed in stone and little has been changed since – indeed these maps are instantly recognisable in a way that so many earlier maps aren't.

It is impossible to go back and restore many of the earlier names of these places as they were always so fluid, with pronunciations and spellings varying wildly from one valley to the next and from one generation to the next. For example, Too To Hill on Warley Moor is thought to be a poor attempt to understand someone's pronunciation of Toad Hole Hill, but it would be equally foolish to reinstate the latter on a whim. Many names are also interchangeable, like *law* and *lowe* (and sometimes *lad*), or *hoar* and *hare*. However, I have tried to restore some generic local spellings, such as *delf*, *dike* and *sike* (as opposed to the classical delph, dyke and syke). In many cases, names on the map have lost their original meaning and had suffixes like bridge, dean and gate unnecessarily added when the dialect words *hebble*, *-den* and *rake* already suffice. The word *stoop*, originally a stone marking a track in bad weather, has come to refer to any vertical stone and is used as an abbreviation of gate-stoop.

Pule Hill rising above Haigh Clough

As a consequence of all this, the accurate naming of the tops of West Yorkshire is fraught with difficulty, if not downright impossible, and I am happy to stand corrected for future editions. There are defined tops that appear never to have been satisfactorily named, such as that I have called **Freeholds Top**. From the Spodden Valley side, the top occurs above an area called Freeholds and at the end of Trough Edge, but neither Freeholds Top nor Trough Edge End would have been familiar to anyone from the Walsden Valley side, where it is the top of Inchfield Moor. And, on a 1786 map of Lancashire, it is marked as High Houses Moor, a name now entirely lost. So take your pick; I went with its name in Alan Dawson's list of Marilyns[5]. **Gorple Hill** is another top that is yet to be given a satisfactory name. I rejected Hameldon, Standing Stone Height and Birkin Clough Head, and had decided upon taking its name from nearby Gorple Stones to refer to the high point, when I discovered Saxton's 1579 record of Gorpill Hill. Although this has long since fallen out of use, I have resurrected it in the absence of anything else.

---

[5] The Marilyns are another classification for listing hills in the British Isles, only including those with a prominence of 150m. Of the West Yorkshire Moors, only Black Hill, Boulsworth Hill and Freeholds Top qualify.

List of High Points in West Yorkshire
(over 200m and with a prominence of at least 30m or 100ft)

1	Black Hill	Kirklees	582m	Chapter 1, p1
2	Boulsworth Hill	Lancashire/Calderdale	517m	Chapter 4, p25
3	West Nab	Kirklees	500m	Chapter 18, p131
4	Way Stone Edge	Calderdale/Kirklees	482m	Chapter 17, p123
5	Hoof Stones Height	Calderdale	479m	Chapter 10, p63
6	Blackstone Edge	Lancashire/Calderdale	472m	Chapter 2, p11
7	Gorple Hill	Calderdale	467m	Chapter 9, p59
8	Freeholds Top	Calderdale	454m	Chapter 8, p51
9	Withins Height	Bradford/Calderdale	452m	Chapter 20, p149
10	Nab Hill	Bradford	451m	Chapter 12, p79
11	Standedge	Kirklees	451m	Chapter 15, p107
12	White Hill	Calderdale	446m	Chapter 19, p137
13	Wolf Stones	Bradford	443m	Chapter 21, p161
14	Carr & Craggs Moor	Calderdale	441m	Chapter 6, p39
15	Shooters Nab	Kirklees	437m	Chapter 18, p131
16	Pule Hill	Kirklees	437m	Chapter 13, p89
17	Dog Hill	Calderdale	435m	Chapter 7, p45
18	Blake Moor	Calderdale	422m	Chapter 3, p17
19	Manshead Hill	Calderdale	417m	Chapter 11, p73
20	Byron Edge	Calderdale	415m	Chapter 5, p33
21	Soil Hill	Calderdale	403m	GR077313
22	Stoodley Pike	Calderdale	402m	Chapter 16, p113
	Rombalds Moor	Bradford	402m	Chapter 14, p93
24	Worts Hill	Kirklees	391m	GR059155
25	Cheese Gate Nab	Kirklees	385m	GR174066
26	Crow Hill	Calderdale	383m	GR019229
27	Wholestone Moor	Kirklees	380m	GR078167
28	Worlds Hill	Bradford	350m	GR023418
29	Black Moor	Bradford	339m	GR044351
30	Swales Moor	Calderdale	332m	GR087276
31	Edge End Moor	Calderdale	321m	GR975253
32	Swinny Knoll	Kirklees	309m	GR124097
33	Harrop Edge	Bradford	306m	GR095347
34	Meltham Cop	Kirklees	303m	GR092119
35	Harden Moor	Bradford	298m	GR070392
36	Haw Cliff	Kirklees	296m	GR165100
37	Gallows Pole Hill	Calderdale	291m	GR056209
38	Bradshaw Moor	Bradford	287m	GR037397
	Old Lindley Moor	Calderdale	287m	GR091184
40	The Chevin	Leeds	282m	GR200442
	Baildon Hill	Bradford	282m	GR141401
42	Castle Hill	Kirklees	268m	GR152140
43	Emley Moor	Kirklees	265m	GR220129
44	Fixby Ridge	Kirklees	263m	GR125199
45	Beacon Hill	Calderdale	260m	GR103252
46	Chellow Heights	Bradford	259m	GR117353
47	Pool Hill	Kirklees	239m	GR248088
48	Billing Hill	Leeds	233m	GR217392
49	Idle Hill	Bradford	228m	GR164373
50	Westgate Hill	Leeds	223m	GR202296
51	Woodhall Hills	Leeds	201m	GR201354

Using This Book

This book, much like Wainwright's, is divided into chapters for each of the summits in West Yorkshire over 400m. For each summit, there are detailed maps of all the moorland within their scope that is designated as access land. These maps are designed to be used as a base for inspiration and for exploring places and paths off the beaten track. I have striven for a high degree of relative accuracy (i.e. the features and paths marked should be useful in finding nearby marked features), but it should be noted that the Ordnance Survey 1:25,000 Explorer Maps still have both a greater absolute accuracy and more detail[6].

The boundaries of my maps were initially defined by the boundaries of access land, but I soon realised the need to extend the maps in places to reach roads or known places. There are also pockets of non-access land and useful linking sections that had to be included too, with the consequence that not everything I've mapped should be assumed to be legally accessible. These maps should be used alongside OS 1:25,000 maps, which show the boundaries of access land and should be considered essential if you get into bother or need to call for help.

For those who like a guide, I have included a series of prescribed routes, each exploring new pastures and ways opened up since the CRoW Act of 2000. Some of these routes intentionally follow feint sheeptracks or intermittent quad tracks, or cross rough pathless ground to reach summits or other places of interest. Particular care should be taken on these sections and, where possible, alternative routes are included for those who wish to stay on more obvious tracks. But, above all, the book should give you the confidence to freely explore these beautiful open spaces right on our doorstep.

Great Bride Stones on Hoof Stones Height

---

[6] There is nothing more detailed than the contour lines that portray every lump of ground and feint streambed. This was something I quickly acknowledged would have to be omitted, though I have tried to draw out the most striking slopes.

THE GEOLOGY OF THE WEST YORKSHIRE MOORS

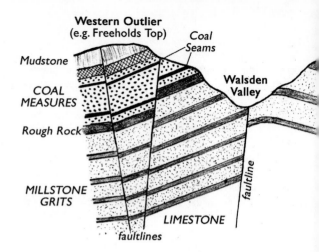

The broad geology of the West Yorkshire Moors is no different from the rest of the Pennines. Running the length of the hills is a broad anticline, an upward fold in the earth's surface that has its oldest rocks at its centre. Different rocks are exposed in different areas, but the overall shape is the same. In the South Pennines, the anticline is steeper in the west than the east, so the moorland plateaus tend to shelve gently down to the east and present steep faces like Blackstone Edge, Boulsworth Hill and Standedge to the west. The oldest rock is the limestone characteristic of both the White Peak and Yorkshire Dales, but in the South Pennines it is not exposed. Where it has been mined in the hushings across the north-western slopes of Boulsworth Hill and Wolf Stones, it represents glacial deposits brought down from the Dales. Elsewhere the limestone lies beneath the surface, covered by successive layers of shale, sandstone and, in places, coal measures.

Virtually all of the rock across the West Yorkshire Moors is of the Carboniferous period, formed between 300 and 360 million years ago. The limestone was formed on a sea floor from the accumulated shells of marine organisms. Subsequently, the land was raised closer to the surface of the sea, with the consequence that sand and mud brought down by rivers were deposited on the shallower sea floor. As sea levels fluctuated over time, these formed alternating layers of thick soft shale and dense hard sandstone. The sandstone in the Pennines is particularly coarse, containing quartz and feldspar, and is known as Millstone Grit. The numerous narrow layers of gritstone laid down across the area are of different ages and have different characteristics; from the oldest Pendleian grit, through Kinderscoutian grit to Marsdenian grit, there are many individual layers with local names (Gorpley Grit, Pule Hill Grit, Todmorden Grit and Warley Wise Grit), but the most common are the youngest beds, Huddersfield White Rock and Rough Rock. It is the latter, coarse and rough to the touch due to its higher feldspar content, that is most often quarried throughout the county because it weathers particularly slowly. In the faces of these quarries is revealed the layering of the rock; in between each narrow band of hard sandstone are the soft shales that end up stacked all around the quarries.

In the late Carboniferous period, the area (and actually much of Europe) became a warm, vegetation-rich swamp with sea levels fluctuating enough that the vegetation was submerged every so often and covered with layers of mud and stone. It is this vegetation which formed the rich coal seams exposed on either side of the Pennines, and found in localised pockets on the moors themselves (particularly west of Todmorden). These coal-bearing strata are known as the coal measures and contain various types of stone other than coal. Some of the older coal measures formed ironstone and the Elland flags, both

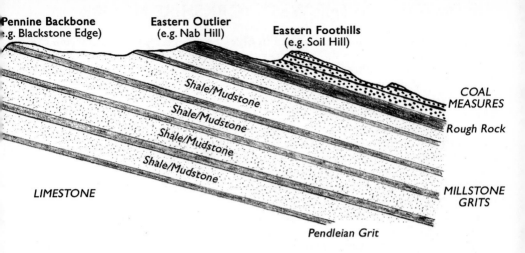

Pennine Backbone (e.g. Blackstone Edge)

Eastern Outlier (e.g. Nab Hill)

Eastern Foothills (e.g. Soil Hill)

COAL MEASURES

Rough Rock

Shale/Mudstone

Shale/Mudstone

Shale/Mudstone

Shale/Mudstone

LIMESTONE

MILLSTONE GRITS

Pendleian Grit

of which have been quarried from an early time; the latter formed the building stone for most of West Yorkshire's towns.

The Pennine anticline was thrust upwards subsequent to all this activity and gradually eroded by ice and water to leave the great moorland plateaus and steep-sided valleys that we are familiar with today. The coal measures have long been eroded almost entirely from the surface of the land and the limestone left below even the deepest valleys. Thus, the bulk of the West Yorkshire Moors is carved from a succession of shales and grits. And it is this geology that is responsible for the often perplexing distribution of water on the moors. In places, apparent basins can be completely dry, yet in others, innocuous slopes turn into unlikely quagmires. Beneath the tussocky grass is the answer to these apparent anomalies.

However, the region is not homogenous, faultlines having further complicated the picture. The Craven Faults (roughly along the line of the Aire Gap) form the divide between the gritstone-based South Pennine moors and limestone-based Dales. A significant faultline also runs through Todmorden, with the land to the west (including Freeholds Top and Carr & Craggs Moor) slipping far further than that to the east and bearing very different characteristics. These moors have more in common with the West Pennine Moors (of which they were once politically part) with coal deposits and shale lain on top of the millstone grit. However, numerous smaller faults here fractured the coal seams into such short sections that where exposed they were only suitable for small and often temporary mining operations.

The last Ice Age reshaped most of the surface features of Northern England as glaciers advanced across the Pennines from the north-west. Although much of the high ground remained clear of ice except at the very height of the Ice Age, Rombalds Moor was entirely glaciated and the valleys of the South Pennines were defined by the glaciers and their subsequent retreat. While Airedale and Wharfedale were scoured by the glaciers themselves, Calderdale and the Colne/Holme Valleys were eroded as the bulk of the meltwater poured east, scouring deeper valleys and leaving a familiar terrace halfway up the moorsides at the level of the previous valley. Many of the odd lumps on the high ground in the north-west of the county (like Harbour Hill, Wycoller Ark and Hitching Stone Hill) were also formed by the glacial meltwater channels that poured across the watershed as the levels of glacial lakes to the west rose. Glacial moraine and erratics are most common in this area of the county too, and have proved important sources of lime, chert and iron in areas where there was otherwise none.

THE HISTORY OF THE WEST YORKSHIRE MOORS

The moorland we see today – like much of our island – is certainly not 'natural' and the rare landscape it represents is the product of thousands of years of climatic and human development. While the history of West Yorkshire, especially that associated with the Industrial Revolution, has been written many times over, that of its wastes is usually only covered in passing. I have tried here to compose a historical evolution of the moors themselves and a chronicle of humankind's interaction with this particular environment since we first stepped foot on it over 10,000 years ago.

Flint shards have been found across the high ground of the South Pennines from Ickornshaw Moor to West Nab, and the greatest concentration of microliths found anywhere in the country was in the area near Pule Hill. People speak of finding flints by the handful in places where the top layer of peat was removed. The oldest of these date from the Mesolithic era (from circa 8000BC) when the majority of the land was covered in dense forest. This had developed after the last Ice Age at altitudes up to approximately 1300ft, leaving only the highest tops in this area covered in heathland. The bracken across Ilkley Moor is an indication that there was previously woodland here, and indeed the whole of Rombalds Moor would have been forested. The earliest settlements on this high ground are likely to have been the summer encampments of hunter-gatherers who migrated with the animals they hunted and the plants they gathered, and the fragments of knapped flint from making blades are the only thing they left behind.

The clearing of the forests came steadily and in waves, most likely driven by a combination of climate changes and population growth. Deforestation probably began during the Neolithic era (from circa 3000BC), by which time sea levels had risen sufficiently for Britain to have become an island. Man began to settle on land and domesticate plants and animals, at first in the form of small clearings in the forest that were abandoned after a few years for regeneration. But, as the population began to rise, the uplands in particular were cleared to provide grazing land as the thin topsoil here would originally have been very rich. Throughout the Bronze Age it is likely these moors were used for widespread grazing of livestock, as well as burial grounds which were set apart from the settlements. This is borne out by the range of prehistoric sites to be found; Rombalds Moor, in particular, is famed for its burial sites, stone circles and proliferation of rock art, but similar ceremonial sites can be found less densely scattered across the rest of the county's moors. There is also evidence of similar Iron Age settlements and enclosures on the high ground.

It is thought that between 1500-500BC the climate became steadily colder and wetter (closer to that of today) and, during the Iron Age, people had to retreat from the high ground. By then, the moorland landscape we are familiar with today would have been largely developed. Once the trees had been removed and the ground grazed, what nutrients there were quickly leached out of the soil. Continued grazing gave the soil little chance to recover and it became steadily more acidic with the wetter climate, leaving the denuded hilltops to develop into blanket bog. Although the moors may still have been suitable for summer grazing, the settlements moved further down the hillsides, causing further forest to be cleared for agriculture, pasture and timber harvesting for the smelting of iron. Only on Castle Hill in Huddersfield, which is significantly lower than the Pennine moors, is there evidence of the sort of hilltop forts typical of the Iron Age, early ramparts and ditches for enclosing stock and dwellings being more commonplace.

The first trackways are likely to have followed the high ground as it was the easiest to traverse – the valley bottoms were dense swamps that were often impassable. Eric Cowling coined the name Rombalds Way for an ancient trackway along the northern edge of Rombalds Moor, suggesting it may even have been part of an earlier trade route between Ireland and Europe while these lands were still connected. Roman roads in the area often followed the same routes, linking the fort at Ilkley (Olicana) and camps at Castleshaw, Slack (near Outlane) and Littleborough with major centres like York, Manchester and Ribchester.

But the Romans had relatively little impact on the area, especially those living in the remote corners of the hills, who continued to speak a Brythonic tongue and worship Celtic deities. After the departure of the Romans, the kingdom of Elmet was established and stretched across the whole of the modern county of West Yorkshire (at its largest probably extending into South Yorkshire). Elmet was possibly defined by a tribal kinship that had survived through the Roman era and was something of an outlier from the surviving kingdoms of the Britons along the west coast[7]. Elmet had been at the heart of the earlier Celtic kingdom of Brigantia, which covered the whole of the north of England and worshipped the deity Brigid (hence the many Bridestones in Yorkshire). Elmet only fell in 617 with the invasion of its stronghold in Barwick-in-Elmet by the Anglo-Saxons of Northumbria. But its native Celtic people probably survived long into the Middle Ages in enclaves in the more remote valleys. Names like Walshaw, Walsden, and Britland Edge Hill are likely to refer to these alien inhabitants (Walsh, like Welsh, meant foreigner), and British Camps are found marked on many early maps. It is said that shepherds on the moors still used old Celtic numerals in the twentieth century when counting sheep.

Little is known of changes through the Middle Ages, though the place-names of the area reflect Anglo-Saxon, Norse and Norman occupation. After the Norman Conquest, large feudal estates were given control of the majority of the land and large swathes of what is now moorland were enclosed from the thirteenth century as huge deer parks. The Forest of Sowerbyshire covered the majority of Erringden, Sowerby and Warley and was the hunting ground of the Lords of Wakefield *(see page 119 for more details on the Erringden Deer Park)*, as was the Forest of Holme. The area around Marsden was part of the hunting ground of the Lords of Pontefract, and there were numerous well-known hunting forests on the Lancashire side of the hills – Rossendale, Pendle, Trawden and Bowland. As their names suggest, these areas were still partly forested and home to wild boar, stags and deer. High ground was also used for cow pasture, with vaccaries set up across the area and overseen by tenants of the manor. These large cattle ranches had demarcated summer and winter grazing grounds and many of the boundary ditches remain etched into the moorsides. Names ending in -*tonstall* are almost unique to Sowerbyshire and indicate the existence of a former vaccary, while *booth* often refers to the wooden hut the herdsman (or boothsman) lived in.

The Little Ice Age – the steady cooling of the European climate that began in the twelfth century – and the Black Death (as well as other diseases among livestock) are thought to have temporarily reversed the trend of diminishing forest cover around the fourteenth century. However, as the climate improved and the population recovered, the enclosure of land continued apace from the sixteenth century onwards. The deer parks were dispaled as the owners of the estates realised there was more money in renting land for farming than using it for hunting. Rough ground was cleared of stones using graving spades, then limed and enclosed in fields for grazing. This 'winning from the moor' is evident in many of the place-names seen commonly across the high ground, such as Reaps, Intake, Hey and New Bricks. Impoverished squatters were also known to settle on the moorland fringes, before eventually being drawn into the manorial tithe system. As demand for land grew, enclosure reached further and further up the moorsides; the soft water was good for bleaching fleeces and the alternating bands of shale and grit meant there were fresh springs at all levels up the hillsides.

Sheep farming and the wool and cotton trades were the main sources of income on the South Pennine hills. However, such was the paltry income to be made on these poor

---

[7] In fact Elmet was ruled by the kingdom of Gwynedd for a time, despite there being a significant Saxon kingdom in between the two.

soils that wool was spun and cloth weaved in the same farms in order to make a decent living (see Page 65 for information on traditional laithe houses and the dual economy). Small scale quarrying was another way of supplementing incomes and led to the pattern of small delfs across the hillsides. In places the surface coal seams were mined, often on a very small scale, such was the fractured localised nature of many of these measures – one of these is still operating at Greens Clough on the edge of Carr & Craggs Moor.

The moorlands were still frequently used for transporting goods, both out of a necessity to cross the hills and a desire to avoid the wetter ground. The network of packhorse trails and drovers' roads had developed ever since animals were first used to cart goods along the prehistoric trackways, but the first Highways Act in 1555 required that roads be kept in a state of repair by each parish, initially using statute labour and later by payment of Highway Rates. The stone causey (short for causeway) tracks that are familiar across the South Pennines were a way of negotiating the boggy ground that many of the routes crossed. Wealthy clothiers who relied on these routes sometimes left money for the provision of bridges, and fine arched examples are still to be found in many remote locations (like Lumb Bridge in Crimsworth Dean, Oxygrains Bridge in Booth Dean or Eastergate Bridge near Marsden). Even with the arrival of turnpikes in the mid-eigteenth century, many still chose to use the old free routes across the tops and the packhorse routes were actually at their busiest around this time. In fact the era of turnpikes was very short lived, due to the arrival of the railways; most never paid their way for their subscribers, but they did lay out the routes of a lot of the modern trans-Pennine roads.

The high-water mark for moorland occupation occurred during the Napoleonic Wars in the late eighteenth and early nineteenth century, when the high price of corn led to land being enclosed in the furthest reaches. A series of Parliamentary Enclosure Acts provided a legal framework for landowners to enclose common land in order to provide food or grain, which were suddenly in great shortage. Most of the large regular fields, straight tracks and long drainage dikes on the moorside date from this era, though the Cotton Famine caused a further spate of enclosures in the 1870s in areas that relied on cotton. In the scramble for land, many commoners exchanged their rights for tiny parcels of useless land on the moorland fringe. Though the high moorland was never enclosed, the Lords themselves often acquired large lots on the high moor and common rights of turbary (collecting peat for personal use) and grazing were eventually lost, effectively allowing much of it to be privatised. Rombalds Moor illustrates the rather haphazard way the wastes ended up being designated. In places where the moor was part of an urban district (like Ilkley, Burley and Bingley), the wastes became urban common and rights were enshrined, but in rural districts they remained private (hence access issues on Hawksworth and Morton Moors) – and this had a huge impact on access until recent years.

The Industrial Revolution – the mechanisation of the spinning and weaving processes and the subsequent development of large steam-powered mills, canals and railways – had brought more people down to the valleys and established the large towns of the area. It also led to a steady decline in the cottage weaving industry and consequently that of hill farming; as already mentioned, many remote farms could not survive on sheep farming alone. Further depopulation of whole valleys and hillsides was caused by building reservoirs to provide clean drinking water for the towns. Some farms were drowned, but most were forced out of business by the ban on grazing any gathering grounds introduced in 1905. Areas like those around Widdop, Withens Clough and Top Withens emptied completely. The fear of polluted drinking water, and in particular a typhoid epidemic, meant the water corporations were as guilty as anyone for prohibiting

peat stacks on Ickornshaw Moor

access for many years (while all the time leasing their land to shooting interests). As long as reservoirs, tunnels and railways were being built, forests planted and power lines, conduits and roads laid, the moorsides were alive with activity and the shanty towns of the navvies who worked on them. Once they left, buildings lay abandoned across the moors and they reverted to being the playground of the wealthy.

Game had been hunted on these estates since the Norman Conquest, but it was only during the nineteenth century that the red grouse became popular. George Fisher, gamekeeper of Walter Spencer-Stanhope of Barnsley, is credited with inventing grouse shooting as we know it around 1805, with the birds being driven by beaters towards a stationary shooter. Interestingly a similar method, called bow and stable, had been used in the medieval deer parks, with herds being driven towards archers. Allied to improving shotguns and the royal approval bestowed on the sport by Queen Victoria, this gave the moorland its greatest commercial asset. In some places (such as Meltham and Warley) the Lords of the Manor held the hunting, hawking and fishing rights across the wastes; in others they were held by local freeholders (such as Marsden, Oxenhope and Haworth, the latter having been enclosed since the sixteenth century). In Ickornshaw, local freeholders have fiercely guarded their shooting rights on the moor to this day; in 1892, when butts were erected on Ickornshaw Moor by gamekeepers from an adjacent estate, shooting was interrupted on the Glorious Twelfth by villagers converging on the moor and tearing them down. But most freeholders (and many Lords) let out their shooting rights or sold them on to wealthy mill-owners or, later, the water corporations.

Gamekeepers were employed and the moorland managed explicitly to maximise red grouse numbers; the heather it feeds on has to be carefully maintained by rotational burning over a period of seven to twenty-five years to prevent birch scrub woodland developing. Gamekeepers weren't the first to do this – it has been suggested that the original Mesolithic hunter-gatherers of the area used a similar system of regular burning on the high ground – but their actions have had a significant impact on the moorland landscape. Initially there were various clashes between farmers or shepherds and gamekeepers where the same land was being used for different purposes, but eventually most moorland rights were acquired by those interested in shooting. Resentment existed among commoners no longer allowed even to collect bilberries on the moor; in Haworth, moorland was deliberately set on fire where grouse were nesting; and in Marsden two gamekeepers were killed in 1903. These battles continue to this day, with the Ban the Burn campaign seeking restrictions on heather burning and the drainage of blanket bogs after a series of serious floods in the Calder Valley in 2012.

The Victorians, who were notoriously fond of the benefits of the fresh air and natural spas provided by the moorlands of West Yorkshire, created the leisure industry as we know it today. Those areas that were publicly accessible – such as Ilkley Moor, Shipley Glen, and the Wessenden Valley – became increasingly popular with all classes and, by the late-nineteenth century, horse-drawn bus services ran up onto the moors. During the Edwardian era, epic walking contests were a popular part of local galas, and long distance cycling wagers were commonly settled. As the twentieth century progressed, pony clubs, sailing clubs, and fell races were established to capitalise on the area's natural resources. Although it would take until the 1970s for the landscape to be officially recognised, the Clean Air Acts from 1956 steadily improved the image of the South Pennines to the point today that it is a popular holiday destination. Its appeal lies in a mix of its much-altered but still ostensibly 'natural' landscape and the preserved industrial heritage that weaves its way through every facet of modern West Yorkshire. Though much of it is hard to trace with any certainty, the moorland bears the scars of its history. Its haggard face is worn with many lines; tracks, ditches and ruins etched in its impenetrable expression for thousands of years, followed, altered and abandoned as history heaps upon itself.

ACCESS TO THE MOORS

"He called me a louse and said, Think of the grouse
Well I thought but I still couldn't see
Why old Kinder Scout and the moors round about
Couldn't take both the poor grouse and me"

(Ewan MacColl, from the song *Manchester Rambler*)

Even ten years ago, it would not have been possible to publish a book such as this. Wainwright got away with it partly because it was in a different era and partly because much of the Lakeland fells were already common land. Access to the moors of the South Pennines has always been more contentious and their ownership and use by grouse shooters make them more akin to the deer hunting estates of the Scottish Highlands. While the Marsden Moors and parts of Rombalds Moor can be considered to be in public ownership, the bulk of West Yorkshire's moors are private estates and had limited access beyond sporadic rights of way before 2000. I grew up in Sheffield long after the age of the mass trespasses, and so was used to roaming freely across the moors of the Dark Peak. When I made it into West Yorkshire, I scrambled up onto West Nab only to be faced with 'Private: No Access' daubed across rocks on the moor beyond. It probably didn't stop me, but it was odd to find such attitudes to public access still prevalent. So we in West Yorkshire have particular reason to be thankful for the Countryside and Rights of Way Act (CRoW) passed in 2000. It is far from perfect in terms of the 'right to roam', but it has given us the chance to legally explore many of the lost corners of the county.

Access Land

The main purpose of the CRoW Act was to open up over 900,000 hectares of land across England and Wales (over 6% of the total area) as Open Access land[8]. This included all registered common land and all land defined as 'open country' by a Countryside Agency survey. Anything considered to be mountain, moor, heath or down can now be identified by pale yellow shading on all new 1:25,000 OS maps. There is little that can be defined as mountain in West Yorkshire and obviously no down, but moor and heath are both prevalent. Moor refers to 'rough unimproved acid grassland', including areas of blanket bog, bare peat and rocky outcrops. Heath is 'characterised by natural ericaceous dwarf shrubs' such as heather, gorse, bilberry and bracken. Both are 'usually of an open character' and the bulk of the West Yorkshire Moors fit nicely into these categories. It is only around the fringes that definitions become stretched and anomalies crop up, often creating parcels of frustratingly excluded land that you need to cross to reach a road, path or further section of access land. It is worth noting that 'agriculturally semi-improved grassland' is explicitly excluded, explaining why enclosures apparently covered in reeds and scrub are not always included as access land. In other places, however, there are clear errors where land has been incorrectly characterised. Reviews of the maps of open country are scheduled every ten years to allow these to be corrected, but the first review in England appears to have been deferred indefinitely.

---

[8] Often called and indeed signed as Access Land, although this is not an official designation.

Even within the land that has been mapped as 'open country', there are numerous exclusions; any land covered by buildings (including those under construction) or their immediate curtilage; land within 20m of a dwelling or building used for housing livestock; land used as a garden, golf course, aerodrome or railway; ploughed or cropped land; land used for active quarrying; land classed as Miltary Lands. Landowners are also allowed to restrict access to any access land for up to 28 days in a year by prior application (though this is not permitted on Christmas Day, Good Friday, or any Bank Holiday or summer weekend day). In other cases exclusions are imposed by the local authority or Secretary of State to protect flora, fauna, geological features or scheduled ancient monuments.

I have tried to sum up the access restrictions at the beginning of each chapter and, apart from the danger area on Shooters Nab, most of them relate to dogs *(see separate section overleaf)*. If you plan to go off the beaten track, you may want to check the website **www.countrysideaccess.gov.uk** for up-to-date information.

So what are we allowed to do on access land? The CRoW Act states that 'Any person is entitled to enter and remain on any access land for the purposes of open-air recreation, if and so long as he does so without breaking or damaging any wall, fence, hedge, stile or gate'. This sounds reasonable, though there are a number of further exclusions: driving a vehicle, riding a bike, using a boat, bathing, lighting fires, shooting, fishing, camping, para-gliding, playing organised games, intentionally damaging wildlife (including foraging), using a metal detector, or disrupting any legal activity *(see Page 50 for a full list of excluded activities)*. If you engage in any of these, you lose your rights of access and are treated as a trespasser – as a consequence you are not allowed on the same landowner's land within 72 hours. It is here that the CRoW Act has got some of its bad press; it fails to define 'open-air recreation' beyond this series of exclusions and creates a law by which pursuits such as swimming in mountain streams and collecting edible wild plants are considered trespass. However, we are talking about civil trespass rather than criminal trespass (which occurs only when illegally crossing railway lines or military land); as such, costs can be claimed by the landowner only where damage can be proven. As always, one hopes that common sense prevails and, as long as you respect the owners and users of the land *(see Grouse Shooting section overleaf)*, you might reasonably be free to swim here or there.

As well as defining access land, the CRoW Act states that 'means of access' (gaps, stiles, gates, bridges) should be provided both onto and within areas of access land where 'necessary for giving the public reasonable access to that land in exercise of the right conferred above'. This is a more contentious issue, as it relies on the local authority to negotiate 'means of access' with landowners, or give notice to them where obstructions are considered to have been created. With new fences springing up all the time and local authorities' resources stretched, it is becoming harder to ensure reasonable easement across access land. This is particularly difficult when you consider that you are considered a trespasser if you cause any damage to walls or fences; while no-one sets out to damage a wall, there are times when you are left with no option but to climb them, and occasionally a stone or two may be loosened. It is obvious that one should use gates and stiles where they exist, but there are numerous places in this book where existing paths have been cut off by fences and ad-hoc stiles have been erected by locals. If you come across these instances, I recommend you contact the appropriate local authority (Leeds, Bradford, Calderdale or Kirklees Metropolitan Borough Councils).

Public Rights of Way

All of the previous section on access land has no relevance to Public Rights of Way, whose legal status is enshrined in separate legislation. Whatever anyone tells you, the legal right to 'pass and repass along the way' always exists on a Public Right of Way unless there is a local authority sign informing of a closure for a dated period – in this case, an alternative route is usually suggested. I have not distinguished Public Rights of Way in my book, but they are clearly marked in green on all 1:25,000 OS maps. One of the problems, and a reason why I started creating this book in the first place, is that many of the mapped moorland Public Rights of Way are historical remnants (and in some cases complete anomalies). Try to trace many of them and you'll find nothing on the ground but rough tussocks; in other cases the old track is long disused and densely overgrown, while there is a perfectly serviceable path 100m away. The law says you can walk along these notional Public Rights of Way across the heart of the moor even when there are access land restrictions, yet you're not permitted to do so along the frequented path nearby. Most walkers are probably happily unaware of these anomalies, and in the end common sense should prevail anyway. However, if challenged when on restricted access land, then use the existence of a nearby Public Right of Way to assert your legal right to pass (ask if they'd rather you walk on that line).

Dogs

Though Yorkshire could be considered 'Dog's Own Country', dogs present something of a problem when accessing its moorland expanses. I researched much of this book with dear Dolly who, as those who knew her will attest, was nothing if not always under close control, but there were many days and times of year when I had to reluctantly leave her at home. The South Pennines is a SSSI (Site of Special Scientific Interest) because of its blanket bogs and important habitats for various nesting birds; while walker's boots may have more impact on the former, rampaging dogs are very good at turfing birds out of their nests.

As a rule, unless clearly stated, dogs are allowed on all access land, but must be kept on a 'short lead' (meaning of fixed length and not more than 2m) when in the vicinity of livestock and during the ground nesting bird season (March 1st – July 31st). The same should be respectfully applied on Public Rights of Way, though the law states only that a dog should be 'on a lead or otherwise under close control' when in an enclosure with sheep. It is an offence to allow a dog to chase livestock, but the landowner may shoot the dog only if it is the only reasonable way to prevent it from worrying or harming livestock.

There are large areas of access land from which dogs are excluded at all times and others where they are excluded between March 1st – July 31st; in these cases dogs are still permitted on all Public Rights of Way but nowhere else. See the access restrictions at the beginning of each chapter for information on specific moors, and **www.countrysideaccess.gov.uk** for up-to-date access restrictions.

Grouse Shooting

As much of West Yorkshire's moorland is owned by various estates with grouse shooting rights, this is the most likely source of confrontation between landowner and walker. Certain estates very much begrudge the concession of access rights to their treasured

the gamekeeper

grounds, while there are plenty of nearby residents who can't stand the idea of shooting animals for sport. I'm not here to discuss the rights and wrongs of grouse shooting or its moorland management techniques, but rather the legalities and practicalities of sharing the moor when there is shot in the air.

Firstly, I will restate that Public Rights of Way will never be closed for shooting – your legal right remains at all times. But that doesn't mean there won't be shooting near or even across Public Rights of Way, just that it will be the responsibility of those shooting to keep an eye on any users of these paths and ensure that they are not endangered by their activity. If necessary, they should wait while you pass, but it may be polite to wait for them if they are in the middle of a shoot.

The CRoW Act does, however, allow the landowner to 'restrict access at their discretion in certain circumstances' for up to 28 days a year (as explained earlier). Five day's notice will usually be required, but if only a small area of land is affected or the restriction is in place for less than four hours, then only two hours' notice is required. Thus it can often be impossible to ascertain whether an area of moorland is definitely accessible. It is worth noting, though, that red grouse may only be shot between August 12th and December 10th and the shoots themselves are very brief. In my experience, encounters with shooting parties have been very civilised, even when I've had a dog with me. My advice is to respect all other users of the moor as long as they are being reasonable.

ACCESS SUMMARY

• Open Access land is not always legally accessible – restrictions and exclusions may be in place. Follow local signage as long as it is clear and dated.

• Unless a specific diversion is in force, Public Rights of Way are always legally accessible, even when access land restrictions and exclusions are in place.

• Dogs are excluded from large areas of the West Yorkshire Moors, especially between March 1st – July 31st. Check before setting off and follow local signage.

• Dogs are always allowed on Public Rights of Way and are not required to be on leads, just under close control, but it is advisable to keep dogs on leads in the vicinity of livestock and during the ground-nesting bird season.

• Respect all other users of the moor, especially those with guns(!), but don't be intimidated.

Lanshaw Lad boundary stone on Rombalds Moor

The moorlands tended to be the most contentious parts of any parish boundaries, often being treated as shared commons or having undefined boundaries. As a result, many of the boundary disputes centred on the moors, such as that between Haworth and Trawden which resulted in the summit of Boulsworth Hill being entirely in Lancashire. As there were few natural features, boundary stones became a particularly common sight in West Yorkshire during the 18th and 19th centuries after the Enclosure Acts parcelled up the remaining common land. Boundary perambulations became increasingly common too, though they had taken place in many parishes and manors in Rogation week since the Middle Ages. The practice is thought to be based on ancient crop-blessing ceremonies and the term *rogation* relates to a divine blessing. As the term 'beating the bounds' suggests, these rituals became increasingly about asserting the parish's boundaries and defining its community.

CHAPTER 1 - BLACK HILL

Height: 582m

Grid Ref: SE078047

Map Sheet: OL1 (The Dark Peak)

Access: No dogs on Cook's Study Hill and Snailsden Pike End (east of boundary fence) at any time.

Public Transport: Regular bus and/or train service to Marsden and Holmfirth. Bus 314 runs from Huddersfield to Holme.

Black Hill is comfortably the highest peak in West Yorkshire, though it is usually considered to be more a part of the Peak District than the South Pennines. The name is very apt as its vast peaty plateau was famous as a bane of Pennine Way walkers. These days stone walkways cross the peat, but Black Hill retains its formidable air. The summit crests above a massive expanse of moorland that starts above Marsden and continues round to Ramsden Clough, while also taking in large sections of moorland in Greater Manchester, Derbyshire and South Yorkshire.

The whole of the moor is within the Peak District National Park, the only part of West Yorkshire that is, so it is very accessible and popular. The valleys around Digley, Ramsden Clough and the Wessenden Reservoirs are the busiest, but elsewhere people tend to disappear into the endless mosses of Black Hill.

Ramsden Clough and Ruddle Clough Knoll

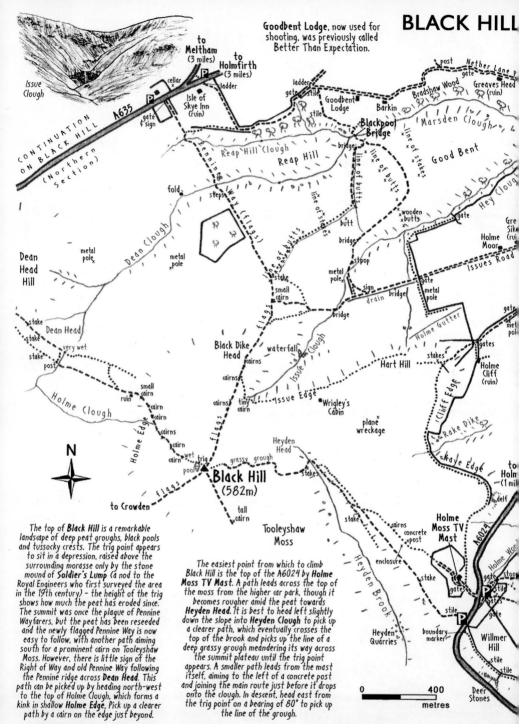

Goodbent Lodge, now used for shooting, was previously called Better Than Expectation.

to Meltham (3 miles)

to Holmfirth (3 miles)

Issue Clough

A635

CONTINUATION ON BLACK HILL (Northern Section)

cellar

ladder

Isle of Skye Inn (ruin)

gate & sign

ladder

ladder

gate stile

stile

Goodbent Lodge

Barkin

Bradshaw Wood

post

Nether Lane

gate

Greaves Head (ruin)

Marsden Clough

Blackpool Bridge

bridge

Reap Hill Clough

Reap Hill

Pennine Way (flags)

fold

steps

line of stakes

line of butts

line of butts

Good Bent

Hey Clough

gate

Gre Sik (rui)

Holme Moor

Issues Road

line of butts

line of butts

butt

wooden butts

Dean Clough

metal pole

metal pole

stake

small cairn

bridge

stpost

metal pole

sign

drain bridge

gate

metal pole

Dean Head Hill

bridge

Holme Gutter

gate

met pol

stake

stake

stake

Dean Head

very wet

post

ruin

small cairn

cairn

cairn

cairns

cairn

cairn

cairn

Holme Edge

wet pool

trig

flags

flags

flags

Black Dike Head

cairns

cairns

cairns

tiny cairn

waterfall

Issue Clough

Issue Edge

Wrigley's Cabin

plane wreckage

Hart Hill

stakes

Holme Cliff (ruin)

Cliff Edge

Rake Dike

Kaye Edge

to Holm (1 mil)

delf

Heyden Head

grassy grough

stakes

Black Hill (582m)

to Crowden

tall cairn

Tooleyshaw Moss

Heyden Brook

stake

cairns

concrete post

enclosure

stake

Holme Moss TV Mast

gate

gate

stile

gates

A6024

Holme Woo

stoop

P

P

stile

gate

Heyden Quarries

boundary marker

Willmer Hill

stile

stile

Deer Stones

The top of **Black Hill** is a remarkable landscape of deep peat groughs, black pools and tussocky crests. The trig point appears to sit in a depression, raised above the surrounding morasse only by the stone mound of **Soldier's Lump** (a nod to the Royal Engineers who first surveyed the area in the 19th century) - the height of the trig shows how much the peat has eroded since. The summit was once the plague of Pennine Wayfarers, but the peat has been reseeded and the newly flagged Pennine Way is now easy to follow, with another path aiming south for a prominent cairn on Tooleyshaw Moss. However, there is little sign of the Right of Way and old Pennine Way following the Pennine ridge across **Dean Head**. This path can be picked up by heading north-west to the top of Holme Clough, which forms a kink in shallow **Holme Edge**. Pick up a clearer path by a cairn on the edge just beyond.

The easiest point from which to climb Black Hill is the top of the A6024 by **Holme Moss TV Mast**. A path leads across the top of the moss from the higher car park, though it becomes rougher amid the peat towards **Heyden Head**. It is best to head left slightly down the slope into **Heyden Clough** to pick up a clearer path, which eventually crosses the top of the brook and picks up the line of a deep grassy grough meandering its way across the summit plateau until the trig point appears. A smaller path leads from the mast itself, aiming to the left of a concrete post and joining the main route just before it drops onto the clough. In descent, head east from the trig point on a bearing of 80° to pick up the line of the grough.

The **plane wreckage** at the heart of the moss above Wrigley's Cabin is that of a Canadian Sabre which crashed during an exercise in 1954. There are other wrecks on Black Hill too; that of a Swordfish at Heyden Head and a pair of Meteors that ploughed into Sliddens Moss a mile south-west of the summit, the latter having a particularly impressive array of debris.

The fenceline heading south-east along the county boundary from Holme Moss can be followed via a feint path as far as **Britland Edge Hill**. Thereafter it is more difficult and you ar as well to try to pick up one of the small landrover tracks alon the side of **Ramsden Clough** to the slight saddle to the nort (though beware these may not last as long as this book).

0   400   metres

N

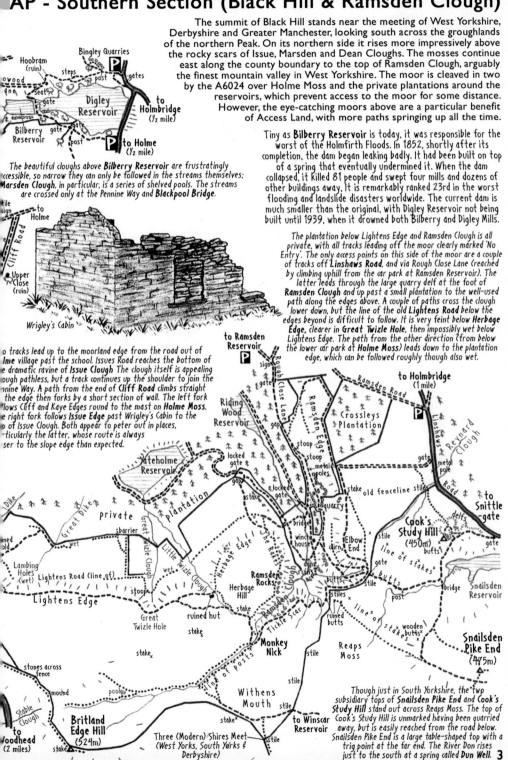

AP - Southern Section (Black Hill & Ramsden Clough)

The summit of Black Hill stands near the meeting of West Yorkshire, Derbyshire and Greater Manchester, looking south across the groughlands of the northern Peak. On its northern side it rises more impressively above the rocky scars of Issue, Marsden and Dean Cloughs. The mosses continue east along the county boundary to the top of Ramsden Clough, arguably the finest mountain valley in West Yorkshire. The moor is cleaved in two by the A6024 over Holme Moss and the private plantations around the reservoirs, which prevent access to the moor for some distance. However, the eye-catching moors above are a particular benefit of Access Land, with more paths springing up all the time.

Tiny as **Bilberry Reservoir** is today, it was responsible for the worst of the Holmfirth Floods. In 1852, shortly after its completion, the dam began leaking badly. It had been built on top of a spring that eventually undermined it. When the dam collapsed, it killed 81 people and swept four mills and dozens of other buildings away. It is remarkably ranked 23rd in the worst flooding and landslide disasters worldwide. The current dam is much smaller than the original, with Digley Reservoir not being built until 1939, when it drowned both Bilberry and Digley Mills.

*The beautiful cloughs above **Bilberry Reservoir** are frustratingly inaccessible, so narrow they can only be followed in the streams themselves; **Marsden Clough**, in particular, is a series of shelved pools. The streams are crossed only at the Pennine Way and **Blackpool Bridge**.*

*The plantation below Lightens Edge and Ramsden Clough is all private, with all tracks leading off the moor clearly marked 'No Entry'. The only access points on this side of the moor are a couple of tracks off **Linshaws Road**, and via Rough Close Lane (reached by climbing uphill from the car park at Ramsden Reservoir). The latter leads through the large quarry delf at the foot of **Ramsden Clough** and up past a small plantation to the well-used path along the edges above. A couple of paths cross the clough lower down, but the line of the old Lightens Road below the edges beyond is difficult to follow. It is very feint below Herbage Edge, clearer in **Great Twizle Hole**, then impossibly wet below Lightens Edge. The path from the other direction (from below the lower car park at Holme Moss) leads down to the plantation edge, which can be followed roughly though also wet.*

o tracks lead up to the moorland edge from the road out of lme village past the school. Issues Road reaches the bottom of e dramatic ravine of **Issue Clough** The clough itself is appealing ough pathless, but a track continues up the shoulder to join the nnine Way. A path from the end of **Cliff Road** climbs straight the edge then forks by a short section of wall. The left fork lows Cliff and Kaye Edges round to the mast on Holme Moss, e right fork follows Issue Edge past Wrigley's Cabin to the p of Issue Clough. Both appear to peter out in places, ticularly the latter, whose route is always ser to the slope edge than expected.

*Though just in South Yorkshire, the two subsidiary tops of **Snailsden Pike End** and **Cook's Study Hill** stand out across Reaps Moss. The top of Cook's Study Hill is unmarked having been quarried away, but is easily reached from the road below. Snailsden Pike End is a large table-shaped top with a trig point at the far end. The River Don rises just to the south at a spring called **Dun Well**.*

3

BLACK HILL MAP

An excessively waymarked route has been created around **Butterley Reservoir** and is a very pleasant walk, though it offers little chance to explore further. 'Walking the Wild Wood' can be joined in **Netherley** by dropping down from the playing fields and following a path along the edge of the plantation. The promising-looking path along the reservoir shore itself has a fence across that must be negotiated.

A circuit of **Swellands Reservoir** can also be made using a number of feint tracks. A couple of paths strike off north from the end of the dam, the driest crossing **Good Hill** to the track above **Carr Clough**. Another follows the old drain around the hillside, but can be difficult to join below the dam due to wet ground.

to Marsden (2 miles)
CONTINUATION ON STANDEDGE (p 111)
CONTINUATION ON PULE HILL (p 90-1)
to Netherley (¼ mile)

golf cours

Gilberts Cottage

marker stone

Mount Bar

Mount Road

Carr Clough

falls

Great Western Inn

A62

marker stone

sign

marker stone

drain

Old Bridge House (site of)

Redbrook Reservoir

bridge

Warcock Hill

marker stone

cutting

bridge

stake

remains of stile

plank

drain

Butterley Clough

sailing club

Floating Light Inn (former)

to Delph (2 miles)

to Diggle (1 mile)

signs

gate & sign.

P

gate

blocked gate

sign

bridge

gate

stiles

stiles

line of thin stakes

sign

stile

stiles

stile

stiles

stile

flags

gate

stile

Good Hill

stile

rough pile of stones

stile

ruined grouse butts

ruin

wet

bridge

Swellands Reservoir

easies crossi point o drain

pool

ruin

gap

Brun Clough

Brun Clough Reservoir

Round Hill

muddy

muddy

wet

gate

wet

Black Moss Reservoir

bridges

ventilation shaft

quarry

ruin

Higher Knoll

Diggle Edge

ruin

bridge

bridge

Blakel

North Clough

Little Black Moss Reservoir

pool

cairn

stile

bridge

drain

stake

flagstones

Black Moss (or Blakely Moss)

B.R.A.

An alternative to following the Pennine Way from **Black Moss Reservoir** down to the Brun Clough car park heads left just beyond the far end of the dam, following a broad grassy depression (and occasional vehicle track) around the hillside. It is muddy in places, but drops down to a track near the Standedge Tunnel ventilation shaft below **Brun Clough Reservoir**.

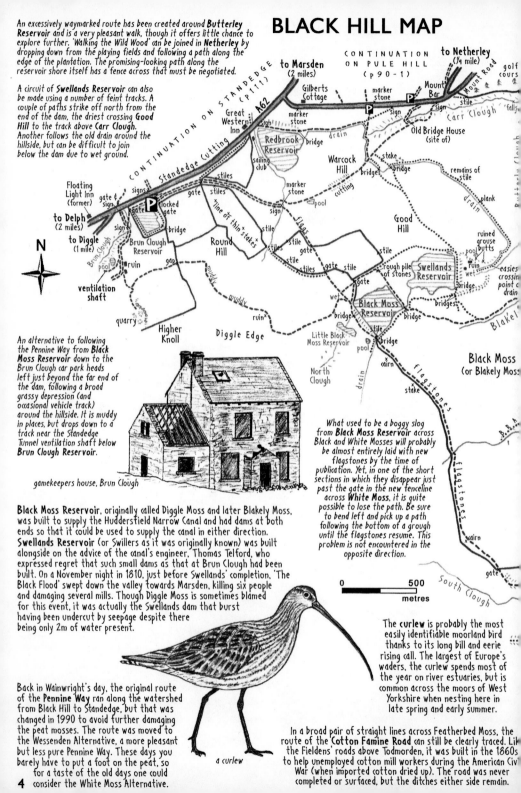

gamekeepers house, Brun Clough

What used to be a boggy slog from **Black Moss Reservoir** across Black and White Mosses will probably be almost entirely laid with new flagstones by the time of publication. Yet, in one of the short sections in which they disappear just past the gate in the new fenceline across **White Moss**, it is quite possible to lose the path. Be sure to bend left and pick up a path following the bottom of a grough until the flagstones resume. This problem is not encountered in the opposite direction.

flagstones

cairn

0   500
metres

South Clough

gate

Black Moss Reservoir, originally called Diggle Moss and later Blakely Moss, was built to supply the Huddersfield Narrow Canal and had dams at both ends so that it could be used to supply the canal in either direction. **Swellands Reservoir** (or Swillers as it was originally known) was built alongside on the advice of the canal's engineer, Thomas Telford, who expressed regret that such small dams as that at Brun Clough had been built. On a November night in 1810, just before Swellands' completion, 'The Black Flood' swept down the valley towards Marsden, killing six people and damaging several mills. Though Diggle Moss is sometimes blamed for this event, it was actually the Swellands dam that burst having been undercut by seepage despite there being only 2m of water present.

The **curlew** is probably the most easily identifiable moorland bird thanks to its long bill and eerie rising call. The largest of Europe's waders, the curlew spends most of the year on river estuaries, but is common across the moors of West Yorkshire when nesting here in late spring and early summer.

Back in Wainwright's day, the original route of the **Pennine Way** ran along the watershed from Black Hill to Standedge, but that was changed in 1990 to avoid further damaging the peat mosses. The route was moved to the Wessenden Alternative, a more pleasant but less pure Pennine Way. These days you barely have to put a foot on the peat, so for a taste of the old days one could consider the White Moss Alternative.

a curlew

In a broad pair of straight lines across Featherbed Moss, the route of the **Cotton Famine Road** can still be clearly traced. Lik the Fieldens' roads above Todmorden, it was built in the 1860s to help unemployed cotton mill workers during the American Civ War (when imported cotton dried up). The road was never completed or surfaced, but the ditches either side remain.

4

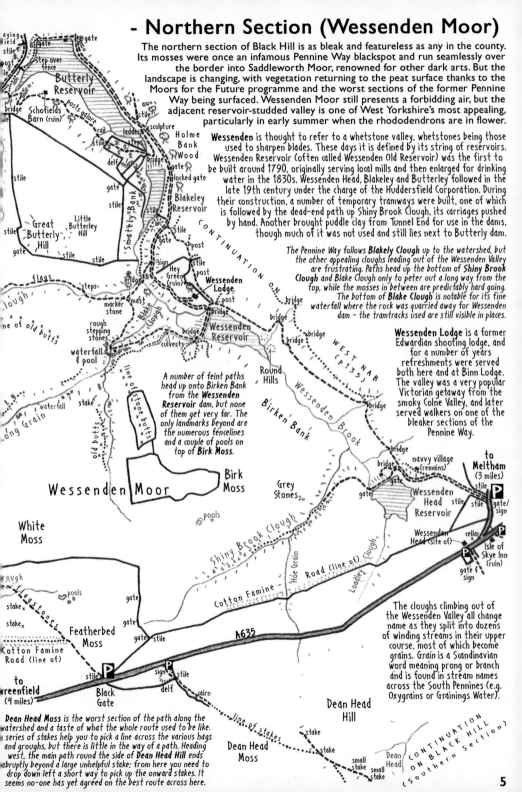

The northern section of Black Hill is as bleak and featureless as any in the county. Its mosses were once an infamous Pennine Way blackspot and run seamlessly over the border into Saddleworth Moor, renowned for other dark arts. But the landscape is changing, with vegetation returning to the peat surface thanks to the Moors for the Future programme and the worst sections of the former Pennine Way being surfaced. Wessenden Moor still presents a forbidding air, but the adjacent reservoir-studded valley is one of West Yorkshire's most appealing, particularly in early summer when the rhododendrons are in flower.

Wessenden is thought to refer to a whetstone valley, whetstones being those used to sharpen blades. These days it is defined by its string of reservoirs. Wessenden Reservoir (often called Wessenden Old Reservoir) was the first to be built around 1790, originally serving local mills and then enlarged for drinking water in the 1830s. Wessenden Head, Blakeley and Butterley followed in the late 19th century under the charge of the Huddersfield Corporation. During their construction, a number of temporary tramways were built, one of which is followed by the dead-end path up Shiny Brook Clough, its carriages pushed by hand. Another brought puddle clay from Tunnel End for use in the dams, though much of it was not used and still lies next to Butterly dam.

The Pennine Way follows **Blakely Clough** up to the watershed, but the other appealing cloughs leading out of the Wessenden Valley are frustrating. Paths head up the bottom of **Shiny Brook Clough** and Blake Clough only to peter out a long way from the top, while the mosses in between are predictably hard going. The bottom of **Blake Clough** is notable for its fine waterfall where the rock was quarried away for Wessenden dam - the tramtracks used are still visible in places.

Wessenden Lodge is a former Edwardian shooting lodge, and for a number of years refreshments were served both here and at Binn Lodge. The valley was a very popular Victorian getaway from the smoky Colne Valley, and later served walkers on one of the bleaker sections of the Pennine Way.

A number of feint paths head up onto Birken Bank from the **Wessenden Reservoir** dam, but none of them get very far. The only landmarks beyond are the numerous fencelines and a couple of pools on top of **Birk Moss**.

The cloughs climbing out of the Wessenden Valley all change name as they split into dozens of winding streams in their upper course, most of which become grains. Grain is a Scandinavian word meaning prong or branch and is found in stream names across the South Pennines (e.g. Oxygrains or Grainings Water).

Dean Head Moss is the worst section of the path along the watershed and a taste of what the whole route used to be like. A series of stakes help you to pick a line across the various hags and groughs, but there is little in the way of a path. Heading west, the main path round the side of **Dean Head Hill** ends abruptly beyond a large unhelpful stake; from here you need to drop down left a short way to pick up the onward stakes. It seems no-one has yet agreed on the best route across here.

5

to Meltham (3 miles)

to Greenfield (4 miles)

CONTINUATION ON WEST NAB (p135)

CONTINUATION ON BLACK HILL (Southern Section)

ROUTE 1: BLACK HILL AND RAMSDEN CLOUGH FROM HOLMBRIDGE

Distance: 10 miles (16.5km)

Ascent: 480m

Difficulty: Moderate

Parking: Limited street parking in Holmbridge. Free car parks at Digley Reservoir or Holme Moss.

Public Transport: Bus 314 runs from Huddersfield/Holmfirth to Holmbridge, bus H7 runs from Holmfirth only.

Character: A beautiful route and possibly the finest circuit of West Yorkshire's highest peak. Despite crossing Black Hill's barren peat mosses by less popular routes, there are clear paths throughout - only the section from Holme Moss to Black Hill needs any real care. Elsewhere the route takes in the drama of Ramsden and Marsden Cloughs and the charms of Digley Reservoir.

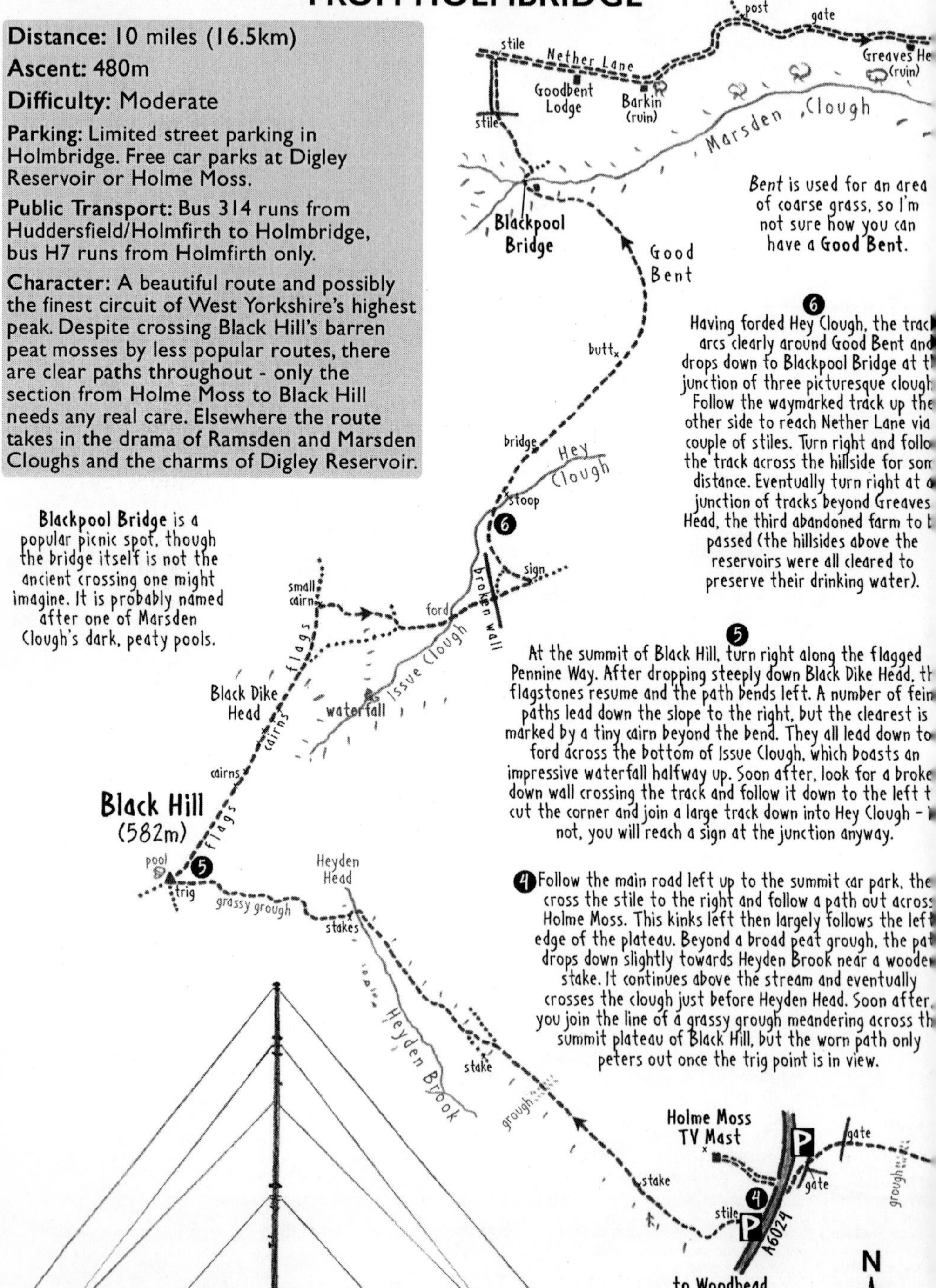

Blackpool Bridge is a popular picnic spot, though the bridge itself is not the ancient crossing one might imagine. It is probably named after one of Marsden Clough's dark, peaty pools.

Bent is used for an area of coarse grass, so I'm not sure how you can have a *Good Bent.*

6 Having forded Hey Clough, the track arcs clearly around Good Bent and drops down to Blackpool Bridge at the junction of three picturesque cloughs. Follow the waymarked track up the other side to reach Nether Lane via a couple of stiles. Turn right and follow the track across the hillside for some distance. Eventually turn right at a junction of tracks beyond Greaves Head, the third abandoned farm to be passed (the hillsides above the reservoirs were all cleared to preserve their drinking water).

5 At the summit of Black Hill, turn right along the flagged Pennine Way. After dropping steeply down Black Dike Head, the flagstones resume and the path bends left. A number of feint paths lead down the slope to the right, but the clearest is marked by a tiny cairn beyond the bend. They all lead down to ford across the bottom of Issue Clough, which boasts an impressive waterfall halfway up. Soon after, look for a broken down wall crossing the track and follow it down to the left to cut the corner and join a large track down into Hey Clough – if not, you will reach a sign at the junction anyway.

4 Follow the main road left up to the summit car park, then cross the stile to the right and follow a path out across Holme Moss. This kinks left then largely follows the left edge of the plateau. Beyond a broad peat grough, the path drops down slightly towards Heyden Brook near a wooden stake. It continues above the stream and eventually crosses the clough just before Heyden Head. Soon after, you join the line of a grassy grough meandering across the summit plateau of Black Hill, but the worn path only peters out once the trig point is in view.

to Woodhead
(2 miles)

N

Black Hill
(582m)

Holme Moss TV Mast

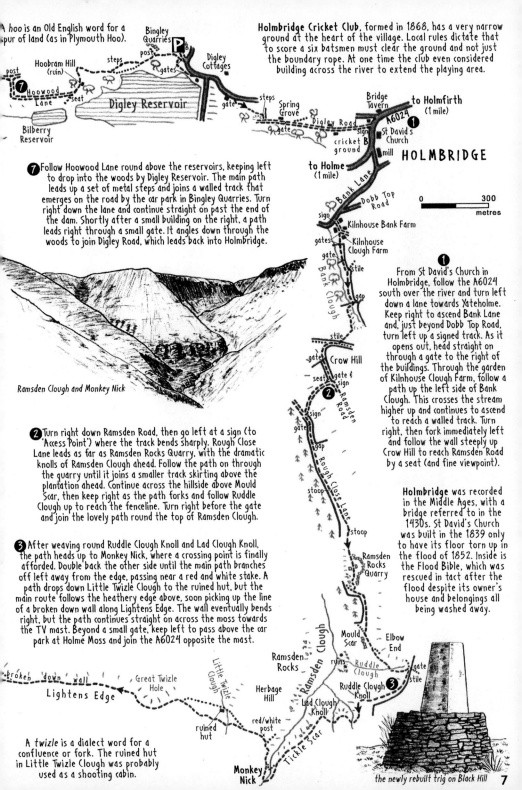

hoo is an Old English word for a spur of land (as in Plymouth Hoo).

Holmbridge Cricket Club, formed in 1868, has a very narrow ground at the heart of the village. Local rules dictate that to score a six batsmen must clear the ground and not just the boundary rope. At one time the club even considered building across the river to extend the playing area.

7 Follow Hoowood Lane round above the reservoirs, keeping left to drop into the woods by Digley Reservoir. The main path leads up a set of metal steps and joins a walled track that emerges from the car park in Bingley Quarries. Turn right down the lane and continue straight on past the end of the dam. Shortly after a small building on the right, a path leads right through a small gate. It angles down through the woods to join Digley Road, which leads back into Holmbridge.

Ramsden Clough and Monkey Nick

2 Turn right down Ramsden Road, then go left at a sign (to 'Access Point') where the track bends sharply. Rough Close Lane leads as far as Ramsden Rocks Quarry, with the dramatic knolls of Ramsden Clough ahead. Follow the path on through the quarry until it joins a smaller track skirting above the plantation ahead. Continue across the hillside above Mould Scar, then keep right as the path forks and follow Ruddle Clough up to reach the fenceline. Turn right before the gate and join the lovely path round the top of Ramsden Clough.

3 After weaving round Ruddle Clough Knoll and Lad Clough Knoll, the path heads up to Monkey Nick, where a crossing point is finally afforded. Double back the other side until the main path branches off left away from the edge, passing near a red and white stake. A path drops down Little Twizle Clough to the ruined hut, but the main route follows the heathery edge above, soon picking up the line of a broken down wall along Lightens Edge. The wall eventually bends right, but the path continues straight on across the moss towards the TV mast. Beyond a small gate, keep left to pass above the car park at Holme Moss and join the A6024 opposite the mast.

A *twizle* is a dialect word for a confluence or fork. The ruined hut in Little Twizle Clough was probably used as a shooting cabin.

1 From St David's Church in Holmbridge, follow the A6024 south over the river and turn left down a lane towards Yateholme. Keep right to ascend Bank Lane and, just beyond Dobb Top Road, turn left up a signed track. As it opens out, head straight on through a gate to the right of the buildings. Through the garden of Kilnhouse Clough Farm, follow a path up the left side of Bank Clough. This crosses the stream higher up and continues to ascend to reach a walled track. Turn right, then fork immediately left and follow the wall steeply up Crow Hill to reach Ramsden Road by a seat (and fine viewpoint).

Holmbridge was recorded in the Middle Ages, with a bridge referred to in the 1430s. St David's Church was built in the 1839 only to have its floor torn up in the flood of 1852. Inside is the Flood Bible, which was rescued in tact after the flood despite its owner's house and belongings all being washed away.

0 — 300 metres

the newly rebuilt trig on Black Hill

7

ROUTE 2: BLACK HILL AND WESSENDEN VALLEY FROM MARSDEN

Distance: 12½ miles (20km)

Ascent: 450m

Difficulty: Strenuous

Parking: Various street parking in Marsden. Free car parks at Black Gate or Wessenden Head.

Public Transport: Buses 182/183/184/185 run from Huddersfield to Marsden (with 184 continuing to Oldham).

Character: A long tramp across Wessenden Moor to the Black Hill plateau that utilises both the old and new routes of the Pennine Way. While the path across the mosses is boggy and indistinct in places, it is a far cry from its former glories and on a good day offers a fine high level circuit of the moor. From the summit, the descent is on firm paths throughout as it winds down the delightful Wessenden Valley back to civilisation.

Bank Bottom Mills form a giant complex of weaving sheds along the bottom end of Wessenden Brook – such is their scale, they represent Marsden's most dominant landmark. The bottom of the Wessenden Valley had been a warren of smaller mills throughout the 19th century and the name 'Bank Bottom' originally referred to two older mills slightly upstream; the higher mill (known locally as Top Bank) was lost beneath Butterly's dam wall and the lower mill demolished soon after. Under the Crowther family, the present site of Bank Bottom developed in the early 20th century and, at their height the mills covered 14 acres and employed nearly 2000 people. During World War I, it was a major source of troops' blankets and George V visited in 1918 in recognition of this service. In 1931, the mills' philanthropic owner John Edward Crowther shot himself at the height of the Depression and the whole village is said to have mourned. Bank Bottom Mills only closed down in 2003, when the last 244 jobs at the site went.

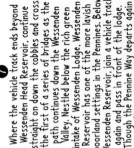

one of the many black rabbits in the fields by Holme Bank Wood

① Following the A62 west out of Marsden, turn left into Fall Lane (signed towards Marsden Golf Club). Pass the first of a series of large mills and continue straight on at the mini-roundabout, starting to climb up Binn Road. After less than 100m, bear right before the Marsden Industrial Society building on a track heading between (and in places under) the towering buildings of Bank Bottom Mills.

② Where the track emerges below Butterly Reservoir, head straight on across the overflow channel into some woods and then steeply up some steps (which also look suspiciously like a spillway). Turn right at the top to reach Mount Road in Netherley. Head straight across into Netherley Drive, then bear right up a tarmac track past Spout Ing. Reaching Old Mount Road, double back left for a few metres to a narrow path signed up to the right. Follow this steadily up the side of a wall to reach the edge of the moor at a gate just beyond a large barn.

③ Turn left upon reaching the large track across the hillside. This rejoins Old Mount Road by its junction with Mount Road. Head straight across the junction, following a signed path down into Carr Clough. The path follows the far side of the clough briefly before heading off across the moss on the line of the Coach Road. Follow this until you meet the Pennine Way at a small stream; double back left to ascend Good Hill via the flagstones.

Both Mount Road and the Standedge Trail across Warcock Hill follow the amended line of the second turnpike road across Standedge. Otherwise known as the Coach Road, it was built in two stages in 1791 and 1815, the original turnpike having been built some fifty years earlier up Old Mount Road and across the foot of Pule Hill. When the third turnpike road was built in 1839 along what is now the A62 and up through the Standedge Cutting, the Coach Road was ... [text trimmed]

⑦ Where the vehicle track ends beyond Wessenden Head Reservoir, continue straight on down the cobbles and cross the first of a series of bridges as the path continues down the Wessenden Valley. Nestled below the rich green intake of Wessenden Lodge. Wessenden Reservoir has one of the more lavish moorland settings in the Pennines. Below Wessenden Reservoir, join a vehicle track again and pass in front of the lodge. Though the Pennine Way departs again soon after, continue along the track ...

MARSDEN

to Huddersfield (7 miles)

New Inn
Fire Station
butcher
Marsden Industrial Society
Marsden Sports Hall
Binn Road

NETHERLEY

Bank Bottom Mills
Bank Top gate
Farm
Butterly Reservoir
Gate House
Barn
Old Mount Road
Mount Road
Spout Ing

sculpture
Holme Bank Wood
Wessenden Road
former rocking stone
Blakeley Reservoir
sign
Wessenden Lodge
post
bridge
Wessenden Reservoir
Round Hills
bridge
bridge
Leygill Clough
bridge

Warcock Hill
Good Hill
marker stone
flags
gate
Black Moss Reservoir
Little Black Moss Reservoir
pool
bridge
Carr Clough

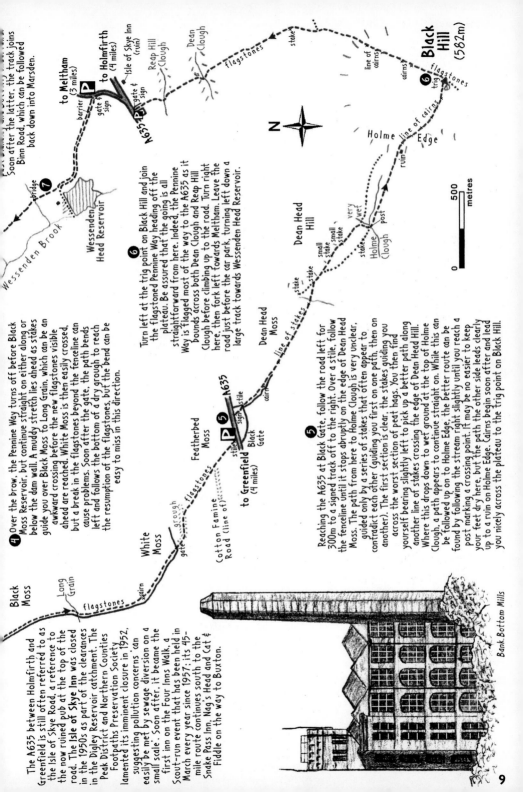

to Meltham (3 miles)

to Holmfirth (4 miles)

Isle of Skye Inn (ruin)

barrier | gate & sign | gate & sign | **A635** | **P**

Black Hill (582m)

trig

flagstones

line of cairns

Reap Hill Clough

Dean Clough

line of cairns

cairns

N

Holme Edge — line of cairns

ruin

flagstones

7 bridge

Wessenden Head Reservoir

Wessenden Brook

500 metres
0

Dean Head Hill

stake | small stake | small stake

very wet

Holme Clough post

stake

Holme Clough

6

Dean Head Moss

line of stakes

stake | stake | stake

cairn

5 **A635** **P** signs | stile

stile | stile | Black Gate

Featherbed Moss

to Greenfield (4 miles)

Cotton Famine Road (line of)

gate | grough

flagstones

White Moss

grough

flagstones

Black Moss

Long Grain

flagstones × cairn

Bank Bottom Mills

Soon after the latter, the track joins Binn Road, which can be followed back down into Marsden.

4 Over the brow, the Pennine Way turns off before Black Moss Reservoir, but continue straight on either along or below the dam wall. A muddy stretch lies ahead as stakes guide you over Black Moss to Long Grain, which can be an awkward crossing before the new flagstones visible ahead are reached. White Moss is then easily crossed, but a break in the flagstones beyond the fenceline can cause problems. Soon after the gate, the path bends left and follows the bottom of a dry grough to reach the resumption of the flagstones, but the bend can be easy to miss in this direction.

The A635 between Holmfirth and Greenfield is still often referred to as the Isle of Skye Road, a reference to the now ruined pub at the top of the road. The Isle of Skye Inn was closed in the 1950s as part of the clearances in the Digley Reservoir catchment. The Peak District and Northern Counties Footpaths Preservation Society lamented its imminent closure in 1952, suggesting pollution concerns 'can easily be met by sewage diversion on a small scale'. Soon after, it became the first inn on the Four Inns Walk, a Scout-run event that has been held in March every year since 1957; its 45-mile route continues south to the Snake Pass Inn, Nag's Head and Cat & Fiddle on the way to Buxton.

6 Turn left at the trig point on Black Hill and join the flagstoned Pennine Way heading off the plateau. Be assured that the going is all straightforward from here. Indeed, the Pennine Way is flagged most of the way to the A635 as it bounds across both Dean Clough and Reap Hill Clough before climbing up to the road. Turn right here, then fork left towards Meltham. Leave the road just before the car park, turning left down a large track towards Wessenden Head Reservoir.

5 Reaching the A635 at Black Gate, follow the road left for 300m to a signed track off to the right. Over a stile, follow the fenceline until it stops abruptly on the edge of Dean Head Moss. The path from here to Holme Clough is very unclear, guided only by a series of stakes that often appear to contradict each other (guiding you first on one path, then on another). The first section is clear, the stakes guiding you across the worst section of peat hags. You then find yourself bearing slightly left to pick up a better path along another line of stakes crossing the edge of Dean Head Hill. Where this drops down to wet ground at the top of Holme Clough, a path appears to continue straight on. While this can be followed up on to Holme Edge, the better route can be found by following the stream right slightly until you reach a post marking a crossing point. If may be no easier to keep your feet dry here, but the path on the other side leads clearly up to a ruin on Holme Edge. Cairns begin soon after and lead you nicely across the plateau to the trig point on Black Hill.

9

The **cloudberry** (or dwarf mulberry) is a type of raspberry that is found on northern acid uplands. Though it is not common in this country, it can occasionally be found as a ground-hugging mat of crinkly green leaves, particularly around Black Hill. Leo H Grindon talks about the Isle of Skye Road in 1882; "It is hereabouts that the cloudberry, that most artistic of northern fruits, never seen and unable to exist upon lower levels, is for our own neighbourhood, so plentiful. When ripe, so thick is the spread of rosy amber that the spectacle is most bright and pretty, the ground seeming strewed with white-heart cherries".

When it blooms, the cloudberry has small white flowers, after which it develops a distinctive edible orange fruit that is particularly high in Vitamin C. Across West Yorkshire, the names of Cloud Berry Farm, Cloudberry Way and Cloudberry Knoll demonstrate its proliferation in the past. It was also known as knotberry or knoutberry (see Knotberry Moor in Derbyshire and Great Knoutberry Hill in North Yorkshire), though there is some debate as to the origins of this name. It may refer to a *knott* (as in a crag), to King Knut who is said to have been saved by eating them, or simply to the knotted nature of the fruit itself.

CHAPTER 2 - BLACKSTONE EDGE

Height: 472m

Grid Ref: SD972163

Map Sheet: OL21 (South Pennines)

Access: No restrictions.

Public Transport: Littleborough is on main bus and train routes. Bus 528 runs from Halifax to Littleborough via Blackstone Edge Reservoir. Bus 900 runs from Hebden Bridge to Ripponden via Blackstone Edge Reservoir & B6138.

Blackstone Edge is a fine summit, its trig perched on one of the rocky castellations that peer down on the A58. Lancastrians will justifiably claim this peak as their own as its imposing wall of rock looks west over Littleborough and Rochdale, yet its summit stands atop the Pennines and it cradles the basin of Green Withens on its Yorkshire flank. Blackstone Edge is a name that appears on the earliest maps of the Pennines, as Blakestone Edge on Saxton's sixteenth century map. It has been suggested that the name referred to a boundary marker no longer present rather than the natural rock itself (which is only black thanks to industrial pollution), but it could also derive from *bealach*, a Celtic word for a pass or way from one district to another.

The proximity of Dog Hill and Byron Edge means there is little area to Blackstone Edge, but what there is is largely covered in scattered rock. The quantity of stone hereabouts is demonstrated by the lines of cairns up the Pennine Way and the fact that monoliths and stone circles on the hill are almost impossible to distinguish. With main roads crossing the Pennines either side, Blackstone Edge is easily accessed and rarely quiet, though when Daniel Defoe crossed Blackstone Edge in his 'Tour Through the Whole Island of Great Britain' in 1727, he likened the Pennines to the Andes and feared for his life in inclement weather.

The wall of Blackstone Edge

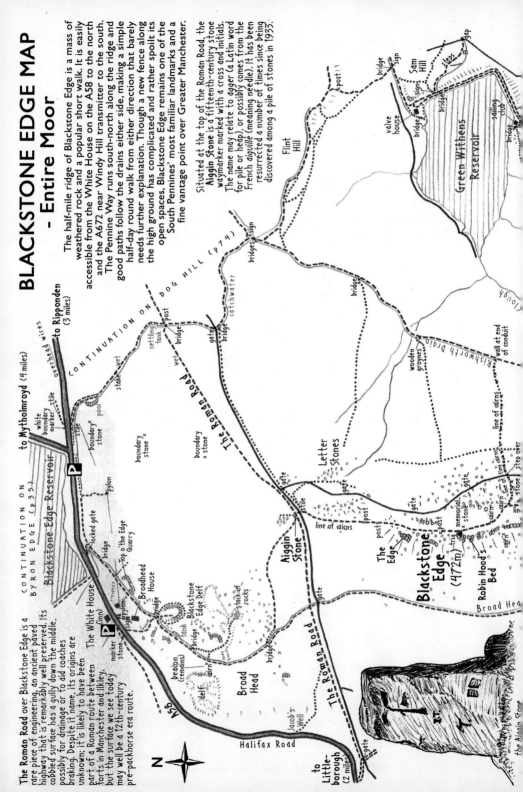

BLACKSTONE EDGE MAP
- Entire Moor

The half-mile ridge of Blackstone Edge is a mass of weathered rock and a popular short walk. It is easily accessible from the White House on the A58 to the north and the A672 near Windy Hill transmitter to the south. The Pennine Way runs south-north along the ridge and good paths follow the drains either side, making a simple half-day round walk from either direction that barely needs further explanation. Though a new fence along the high ground has complicated and rather spoilt its open spaces, Blackstone Edge remains one of the South Pennines' most familiar landmarks and a fine vantage point over Greater Manchester.

Situated at the top of the Roman Road, the Aiggin Stone is a fifteenth-century stone waymarker marked with a cross and initials. The name may relate to agger (a Latin word for pile or heap), or possibly comes from the French aiguille (meaning needle). It has been resurrected a number of times since being discovered among a pile of stones in 1933.

The Roman Road over Blackstone Edge is a rare piece of engineering, an ancient paved highway that is remarkably well preserved. Its cobbled surface has a gully down the middle, possibly for drainage or to aid coaches braking. Despite its name, its origins are unknown; it is likely to have been part of a Roman route between forts in Manchester and Ilkley, but the surface we see today may well be a 12th-century pre-packhorse era route.

Hanging Rocks

bridge
bridge
bridge

Linsgreave Drain

stile & sign

to Ripponden (4 miles)

Rocking Stone

depot

Lads Grave Clough

M62 (Junction 22)

CONTINUATION ON WAY (Western section - p126)

shallow peat shelf

Redmires

wet

gate

very wet

tiny cairn

gate

gate

gate

Redmires Moss

Longden End Brook

f cairns

Sun End

balanced stones

tiny cairn

cairn

groyne-like barriers

bridge

bridge

Drain

to Hoar Edge & Hollingworth Lake

The eastern flank of Blackstone Edge is less dramatic, but its grassy slopes are crossed by a number of smaller paths. A useful sheeptrack sets off from a bridge over the conduit by the old sailing club at **Green Withens Reservoir** and can be followed all the way up to the path along Rishworth Drain (see Route 3 for more details). Several other paths head up the edge from Rishworth Drain, though rarely are the gates in the new fenceline below the summit in the right place: the most clear route follows a line of cairns to the summit, but others make for the **Letter Stones** or **Sun End** only to peter out. If you're lucky you may find my camera here, lost in this maze of tussocky tracks on a snowy day.

Slippery Moss

bridge

gate

cairn

gate

cairn

cairn

Lads Grave (site of)

sign

sign

footbridge

M62

crags

Rook Stones Hill

gate

post

mast

Windy Hill transmitter

sign

P

to Denshaw (2½ miles)

Redmires Moss was once renowned for being the boggiest stretch of the Pennine Way – some feat indeed! – and was marked on older maps as Stakes in the Moss. Its recent surfacing, though, means it is a straightforward tramp to the motorway. The Pennine Way continues south past the mast on Windy Hill, but another useful path follows the motorway down to a conduit in Lads Grave Clough.

pool

to Hollingworth Lake (3 miles)

0 300
metres

The names of **Blackstone Edge and Robin Hood's Bed** tend to be used somewhat interchangeably to refer to the rough rocks scattered across the crest of the ridge. Blackstone Edge itself is the wall of vertical black rock rearing up at the northern end of the ridge, while Robin Hood's Bed is the cloven hoof of towering rock just south of the parapet on which the trig point stands. These latter rocks form a pair of pillars of which Robin Hood's Bed is the higher and more intriguing. The rock tower is riven with great cracks that make it hard to reach: perhaps Robin was thought to have lain in the natural cradle on top, which is eroded rather like a paw. It is most likely that he replaced earlier folklore about a character who is said to have hurled a rock now known as Robin Hood's Quoit across the other side of Littleborough.

With the Pennine Way running along its length, the paths on Blackstone Edge are largely obvious. The only alternative on its west side is a path following **Broad Head Drain** (mostly dry) with good views of the crags above. The path continues round to the west, passing over **Hoar Edge** and dropping down towards Hollingworth. The only way to get back to the ridge is via a feint path back to the left from a line of wooden groyne-like barriers. The path heads for the balanced stone on the cluster of boulders at **Sun End** but runs out as peat and rock take over – the ground is easy to cross though.

The **Blackstone Edge Gathering** took place on August 1st 1846, when 30,000 Chartists from the industrial towns on both sides of the Pennines gathered near the summit for a rally. Chartism was a working-class movement that sought voting reform, most significantly the right of every man to vote. The event was famously chronicled by the poet Ernest Jones, one of the leading advocates of the Chartist cause who was imprisoned for his sedition.

In 2007, the Rochdale Observer featured an article on the witches of Blackstone Edge. Groups of white-robed women have been seen clambering up Blackstone Edge from the White House on a number of occasions. It has been suggested there is a fertility stone, or some other such mystical site, hidden amid the scattered rocks where they perform rituals, but the group's intentions remain a mystery.

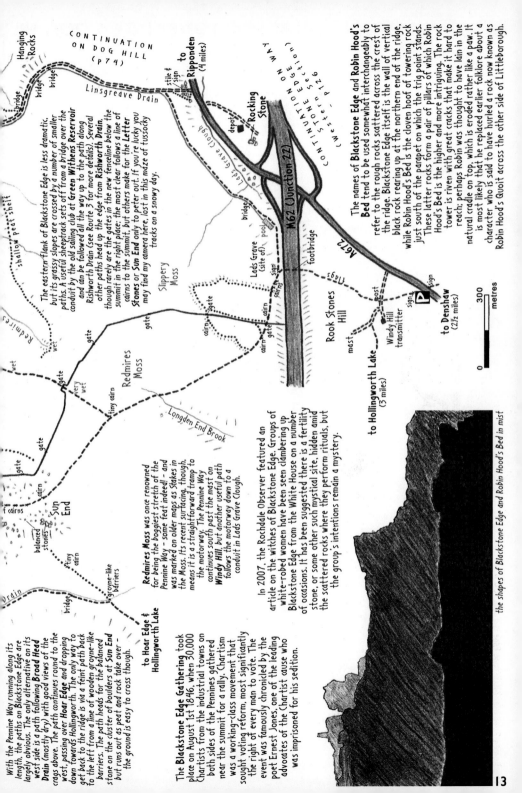

the shapes of Blackstone Edge and Robin Hood's Bed in mist

ROUTE 2: BLACKSTONE EDGE & DOG HILL

N

Blackstone Edge Reservoir

to Mytholmroyd
(4 miles)

boundary marker ×

to Ripponden
(3 miles)

locked gate

sign

P

6

stile

boundary× stone

The White House

P

A58

bridge

*pylon

pool

stake

wet

6 Follow the A58 away from the reservoir and join a track along the side of Rishworth Drain at a stile shortly after the junction. Stay on the drain for some distance, crossing first the line of the Roman Road, then a fenceline. Turn left at a sign towards 'Baitings Resr' immediately before crossing a small bridge and contour across to join another drain round Warm Withens Hill.

Top o'the Edge Quarry

tank

Rishworth Drain

to Little-borough
(2½ miles)

paste

Blackstone Edge Delf

tank

tank

bridge

post

gate

0   300
metres

sign

bridge

cairn
×

Broad Head Drain

delf

5

5 Stay on Broad Head Drain past a number of quarries and beyond the White House. Where it bends sharply back towards the A58, bear right on a grassy track above the road. Stay beside the road as the path becomes smaller and eventually reaches the layby (an alternative starting point for the route).

4 From the trig point, rejoin the broad Pennine Way as it picks its way along the stones of the edge to reach the Roman Road crossing the moor. Head straight across, keeping left of the Aiggin Stone on a path descending to Broad Head Drain (follow this right for 100m to locate a handy bridge).

bridge

Broad Head Drain

Aiggin Stone

stile

The Roman Road

cairn

cairn

cairn

post

Blackstone Edge Reservoir is home to the highest nesting **shelducks** in the country. The shelduck has a distinctive red bill, black head and brown stripe and it breeds in rabbit holes or burrows in the side of the reservoir.

the Edge

a shelduck

Green Withens Reservoir was constructed in the 1890s by the Wakefield Corporation and was later enlarged. Its water is transferred to Spa Clough via a pipe and from there to Ringstone Edge Reservoir via Moss Moor Catchwater. A railway ran up Castle Dean Clough with stone for the dam from Derby Delf and is followed by this route.

post

Blackstone Edge
(435m)

Robin Hood's Bed

cairn

cairns ×

trig

4

post

gate

step over fence

line of tiny cairns

stone shelter

gate

wall at end of drain

wet

3 After a short distance, you'll reach a path contouring across the back of Blackstone Edge. Turn right along this path (wet peat in places) as far as a wall at the start of a conduit, from where a well-cairned path leads left up the hillside. Unfortunately the makers of the new fence failed to notice this path, so you need to use the rocks stacked against the fence to climb it (unless you want to divert to a gate 100m to the right). Continuing up the rockier slope, you soon reach the Pennine Way running right along the ridge to the summit of Blackstone Edge.

Redmires Clough

slight peat

gate

Alternative Route

pathless

wet

3

wet

Alternative
To avoid the pathless section, c⟨...⟩ from Green Withens Reservoir. Af⟨...⟩ where the drain veers off and stay w⟨...⟩ just below the M62. The path contin⟨...⟩ the motorway to reach the Pennine ⟨...⟩ right all the way up on to the t⟨...⟩

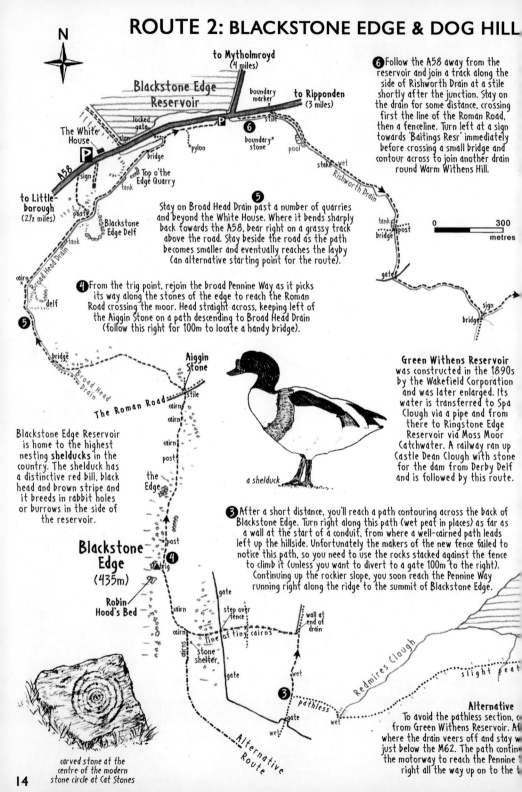

carved stone at the centre of the modern stone circle at Cat Stones

14

FROM OXYGRAINS BRIDGE OR THE WHITE HOUSE

Distance: 6½ miles (10km) **Parking:** Layby on A671 by Oxygrains Bridge, layby on A58 by
Ascent: 350m   Blackstone Edge Reservoir, or free car park below the White House.
Difficulty: Moderate   **Public Transport:** Blackstone Edge Reservoir is on the 528 (Halifax-
Rochdale) and 900 (Hebden Bridge-Huddersfield) bus routes.

Character: Beginning and ending on the moor, this relatively short walk links the natural
neighbours of Blackstone Edge and Dog Hill via Green Withens and Blackstone Edge Reservoirs
and their many drains. Much of the walking is straightforward, but two short pathless sections
across wet ground are used to create a satisfying round (although the longer section can be avoided
by using an alternative route). The route can be started from either Oxygrains Bridge or the White
House, though the former offers the more natural starting point in the valley bottom.

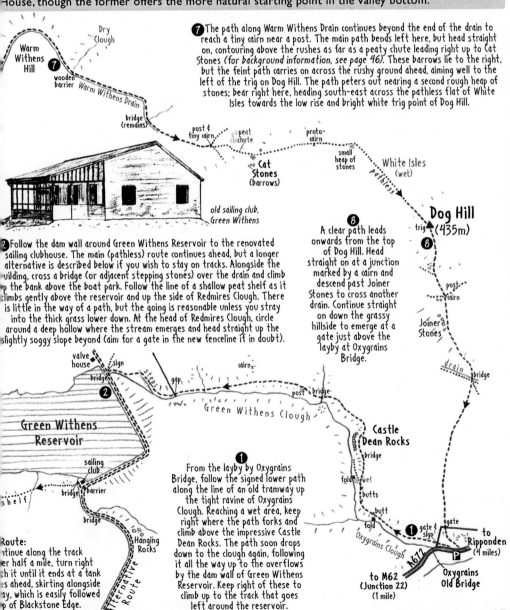

7 The path along Warm Withens Drain continues beyond the end of the drain to
reach a tiny cairn near a post. The main path bends left here, but head straight
on, contouring above the rushes as far as a peaty chute leading right up to Cat
Stones (for background information, see page 46). These barrows lie to the right,
but the feint path carries on across the rushy ground ahead, aiming well to the
left of the trig on Dog Hill. The path peters out nearing a second rough heap of
stones; bear right here, heading south-east across the pathless flat of White
Isles towards the low rise and bright white trig point of Dog Hill.

8 A clear path leads
onwards from the top
of Dog Hill. Head
straight on at a junction
marked by a cairn and
descend past Joiner
Stones to cross another
drain. Continue straight
on down the grassy
hillside to emerge at a
gate just above the
layby at Oxygrains
Bridge.

2 Follow the dam wall around Green Withens Reservoir to the renovated
sailing clubhouse. The main (pathless) route continues ahead, but a longer
alternative is described below if you wish to stay on tracks. Alongside the
building, cross a bridge (or adjacent stepping stones) over the drain and climb
up the bank above the boat park. Follow the line of a shallow peat shelf as it
climbs gently above the reservoir and up the side of Redmires Clough. There
is little in the way of a path, but the going is reasonable unless you stray
into the thick grass lower down. At the head of Redmires Clough, circle
around a deep hollow where the stream emerges and head straight up the
slightly soggy slope beyond (aim for a gate in the new fenceline if in doubt).

1 From the layby by Oxygrains
Bridge, follow the signed lower path
along the line of an old tramway up
the tight ravine of Oxygrains
Clough. Reaching a wet area, keep
right where the path forks and
climb above the impressive Castle
Dean Rocks. The path soon drops
down to the clough again, following
it all the way up to the overflows
by the dam wall of Green Withens
Reservoir. Keep right of these to
climb up to the track that goes
left around the reservoir.

Route:
...ntinue along the track
...er half a mile, turn right
...h it until it ends at a tank
...s ahead, skirting alongside
...y, which is easily followed
...p of Blackstone Edge.

15

THE CIVIL WAR IN THE SOUTH PENNINES

The Civil War reached all corners of the country and the hills of West Yorkshire were no exception. It is often assumed that when Civil War broke out in 1642, most of the manufacturing towns on both sides of the Pennines signed up with the Roundheads. Though they often provided men for the Parliamentary cause, support was far from unanimous and much of the north was still in thrall to the gentry. Rochdale, for example, was divided equally, with the Lord of the Manor being rewarded for his services to the King with the title Baron Byron. Given the opportunity, the Puritan populace generally supported the Parliamentarians, but neighbours fought each other on both sides right up to the Battle of Marston Moor.

Initially much of the fighting in the county took place around Leeds, control of which changed hands more than once. After a West Yorkshire Parliamentarian force was defeated at Adwalton Moor (near Drighlington) in June 1643, a Royalist base was established in Halifax under Sir Francis Mackworth. The rebels fled over the hills to Rochdale, where by now there was a Parliamentary garrison of 800 troops guarding the routes across the Pennines. There were cannons at Blackstone Edge and a sentry station at Bleakedgate to the south. When Royalist cavalry under the Marquis of Newcastle tried to advance on Manchester, the charge floundered in the heather and they beat a hasty retreat.

By the autumn of 1643, the Parliamentarians had established a garrison at Heptonstall; though considerably smaller than Sir Francis Mackworth's force at Halifax, they regularly harrassed them and raided outposts at Sowerby Bridge and Warley. A skirmish is thought to have taken place on the moorland fringe at Slaughter Gap near Mixenden while the Roundheads were returning over the moors from a raid. Gun barrels, locks and flints have been recovered in the area and the site is sometimes referred to as Bloody Field (though it may be that the name Slaughter originally referred to a sloe-tree).

After one sortie, Mackworth responded with a night-time assault on Heptonstall, but in bad weather they were repelled in the Battle of Heptonstall, during which stones were rolled down the Buttress upon the attackers. However, the Heptonstall base was soon abandoned and a large Royalist force burned part of the village in revenge. Haworth suffered similar retaliation for rebel allegiance. Within nine days, though, the Royalists lost Halifax when a force was dispatched from Rochdale, and Mackworth abandoned the area to deal with the advance of the Scots. Royalists were gradually being pushed out of West Yorkshire, and York was under seige, so relief was sent for. A large Royalist army marched into the area, pillaging as it went, and the decisive battle took place at Marston Moor in July 1644. The Parliamentarian victory there effectively ended any Royalist presence in the north of England, though Skipton Castle was surrendered only in 1645 after a three-year siege, and Pontefract Castle (the last northern bastion of the Royalists) finally destroyed in 1649.

the Parliamentary Ensign

CHAPTER 3 - BLAKE MOOR
(aka Little Holder Stones)

Height: 422m

Grid Ref: SD972212

Map Sheet: OL21
(South Pennines)

Access: No restrictions.

Public Transport:
Todmorden and Walsden
are on main Caldervale bus
and train routes. Bus C runs
from Hebden Bridge to Cragg
Vale, with bus 900 continuing
up B6138 to Ripponden.

I have a soft spot for **Blake Moor** as it is forever in the shadow of its near neighbour Stoodley Pike, despite being some 20m higher. The name is probably unfamiliar as the trig point stands on nearby Little Holder Stones and the moorland could equally be referred to as Turley Holes & Higher House Moor or Withens Moor. Yet Blake Moor is the true high point of the fascinating moorland that stretches west from Cragg Vale, east from Walsden and south from the Calder Valley. Its summit plateau is encircled by high-level drains and reservoirs but, despite being crested by numerous intriguing outcrops, it remains a lost peak. Someone recently built a huge cairn on the plateau, yet it is still some way from the true top. While many wander across Langfield Common, or slog across the Pennine Way, Blake Moor stands in quiet isolation. Its name may be a corruption of either black or bleak, both familiar to anyone who has crossed the dark peat expanse of its summit plateau.

The twin stacks of Holder Stones on the plateau of Blake Moor

18

Turley Holes and Higher House Moors naturally look towards Blake Moor and thus provide a number of good routes of approach (though little in the way of paths) leading to the high drains that encircle the summit plateau. Within this ring, Blake Moor is an enchanting warren of peat and heather littered with evocatively-sculpted stones. The twin pikes of Holder Stones stand out from the north-west and Dove Lowe Stones dominate from the south, while the Two Lads is a truly atmospheric place on the north-eastern shoulder of the moor. Before the new peat regeneration fencelines went up, it was one of my favourite areas of feral moorland to explore. It has been tamed a little, but is still well worth exploring from Withens Clough, Sykes Gate or near Blackstone Edge Reservoir.

The main tracks from **Withens Clough Reservoir** head north-west towards Withens Gate, but a couple of feint routes allow direct access onto Blake Moor. The first bears south-east from the gap at the south end of the dam wall and leads beneath the **Buck Stones**. A short scramble brings you onto the edge, which can be followed along to the carefully balanced **Hattering Stone**. The second and easier route is accessed over a stile at the south-west end of the reservoir. The first section is rough until a sheeptrack is picked up crossing the hill to the left then following a branch of **Deep Slade** through the bracken. The path disappears upon reaching the peat wastes beyond a gate in the new fenceline further up.

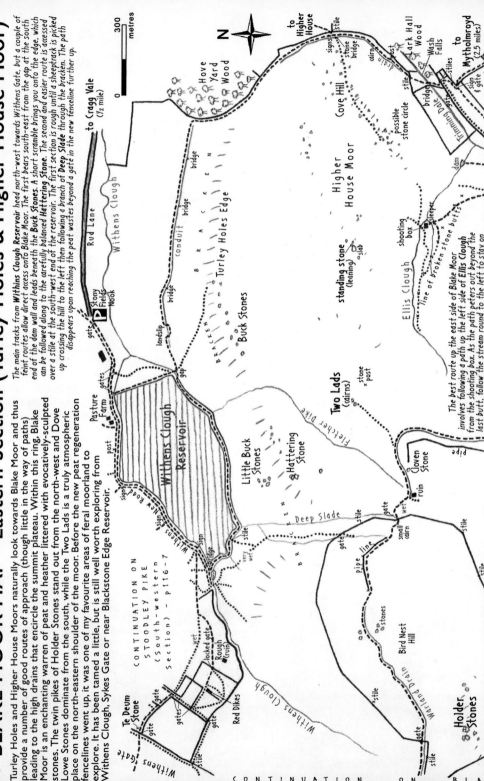

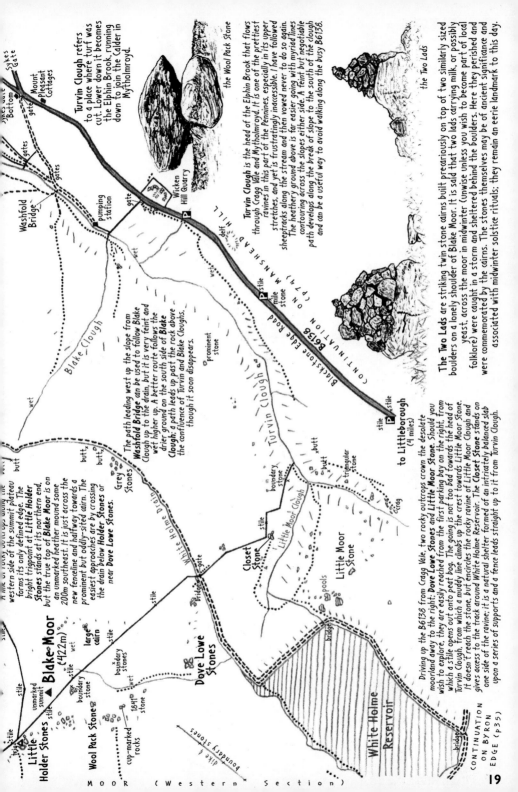

Turvin Clough refers to a place where turf was cut. Lower down it becomes the Elphin Brook, running down to join the Calder in Mytholmroyd.

the Wool Pack Stone

Turvin Clough is the head of the Elphin Brook that flows through Cragg Vale and Mytholmroyd. It is one of the prettiest ravines in this part of the Pennines, especially in its upper stretches, and yet is frustratingly inaccessible. I have followed sheeptracks along the stream and then vowed never to do so again. The heathery ground above is far easier going with myriad lines contouring across the slopes either side. A feint but negotiable path develops along the break of slope to the south of the clough and can be a useful way to avoid walking along the busy B6138.

the Two Lads

The Two Lads are striking twin stone cairns built precariously on top of two similarly sized boulders on a lonely shoulder of Blake Moor. It is said that two lads carrying milk, or possibly yeast, across the moor in midwinter (unwise unless you wish to become part of local folklore) were caught in a storm and sheltered behind the boulders. Here they perished and were commemorated by the cairns. The stones themselves may be of ancient significance and associated with midwinter solstice rituals; they remain an eerie landmark to this day.

Sykes Gate
gate
Mount Pleasant Cottages
Sykes Gate Bottom
gates
gate
gates
gates
Washfold Bridge
pumping station
gate
Wicken Hill Quarry
P
delf
CONTINUATION ON MANSHEAD HILL (274)
Blackstone Edge Road
B6138
mile stone
P stile
wet
wet
wet
to Littleborough (4 miles)
P stile
stile

Blake Clough

The path leading west up the slope from **Washfold Bridge** can be used to follow Blake Clough up to the drain, but it is very feint and wet higher up. A better route follows the drier ground on the south side of **Blake Clough**; a path leads up past the rock above the confluence of Turvin and Blake Cloughs, though it soon disappears.

prominent stone
Grey Stones
butt
butt
butt x
wet

A mile of rocky outcrop along the western side of the summit plateau forms its only defined edge. The bright trigpoint at **Little Holder Stones** stands at its northern end, but the true top of **Blake Moor** is on an unmarked heather mound some 200m southeast. It is just across the new fenceline and halfway towards a prominent but oddly-sited cairn. The easiest approaches are by crossing the drain below **Holder Stones** or near **Dove Lowe Stones**.

sun
▲ Blake Moor (422m)
wet
large cairn
stile
stile
stile
stile
boundary stones
boundary stone
wet
unmarked summit
stile
Little Holder Stones
trig
stile
stile
Wool Pack Stones
1841 stone
boundary stone
cup-marked rocks

CONTINUATION ON BYRON EDGE (p35)

MOOR (Western Section)

Turvin Clough
butt
boundary stone
stile
Little Moor Clough
butt
crag
triangular stone
Closet Stone
stile
gate
Little Moor Stone
pools
Bridge gate
bridge
stile
White Holme Drain
Dove Lowe Stones
bridge
White Holme Reservoir
dike
boundary stones

Driving up the B6138 from Cragg Vale, two rocky outcrops crown the desolate moorland away to the right: **Dove Lowe Stones** and **Little Moor Stone**. Should you wish to explore, they are easily reached from the first parking bay on the right, from which a stile opens out onto peat bog. The going is not too bad towards the head of Turvin Clough, from which a muddy line climbs up the crest towards Little Moor Stone. It doesn't reach the stone, but encircles the rocky ravine of Little Moor Clough and gives access to the track around White Holme Reservoir. The Closet Stone stands on one side of the ravine; it is a natural shelter formed of an intricately balanced slab upon a series of supports and a fence leads straight up to it from Turvin Clough.

19

BLAKE MOOR MAP - Western Section (Langfield Common & Walsden Moor)

Langfield Common is the name given to this varied and fascinating area of moorland that is only part of Blake Moor because of its inability to thrust up a natural highpoint. Coldwell Hill is as close as it gets; a rounded summit at 398m covered in giant flat boulders. The moor is well trodden because of its accessibility from Lumbutts and the Shepherd's Rest, and because of the dramatic edge it presents to the north, which forms a natural arc from Rake End round to Stoodley Pike and offers some of the best views over the Upper Calder Valley. Above the edge, a broad plateau stretches south past Gaddings Dam and the striking tower of the Basin Stone, one of West Yorkshire's most recognisable stones, towards the slopes of Blake Moor itself. The area offers lots of good walking and probably more interest than its popular neighbour, Stoodley Pike.

The current Gaddings Dam was originally Gaddings Dam West, built in the 1830s by the Fielden Brothers. It is said to have been built using convict labour from Manchester, which may explain the existence of Jail Hole nearby. Immediately adjacent was Gaddings Dam East, built thirty years earlier to supply the Rochdale Canal. It was claimed that Lumbutts Mill was being deprived of water by this dam and so a tunnel (still present beneath the hillside) was built from Gaddings Dam West to Lee Dam at Lumbutts. The eastern dam is now empty with a breached wall, but since the western dam was never used for drinking water, swimming off its golden beach was permitted.

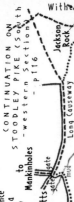

A Noon Stone was traditionally used for timekeeping by casting a particular shadow at midday, but I am confused by a reference to Noon Pike as a boundary marker on a 1786 map of Lancashire. It appears to correlate to Stony Edge.

The Shepherd's Rest only became a pub in 1859. Before that it had been a museum, filled with James Greenwood's collection of curios. The museum's popularity undoubtedly inspired William Butterfield to turn it into a pub.

A number of routes lead up to Langfield Common from the Shepherd's Rest. The main track skirts beneath the impressive crags of Langfield Edge, while a more direct route ascends the flank to Gaddings Dam. The most interesting route, however, weaves through Jail Hole's maze of outcrops and hollows. A grassy quarry path leaves the main track near the stone ruin and winds up to the quarry. A feint path then bears left and ascends the arête (of sorts) to skirt along the edge above and join the path up to Gaddings Dam.

The dam was bought by the Gaddings Dam Group in 2001 to protect its status as the highest beach in England and save it too from being drained.

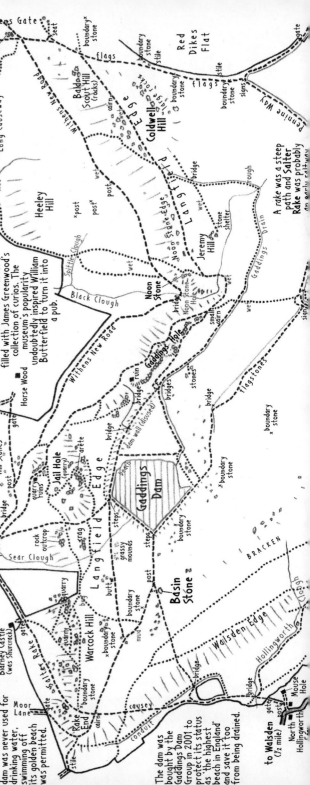

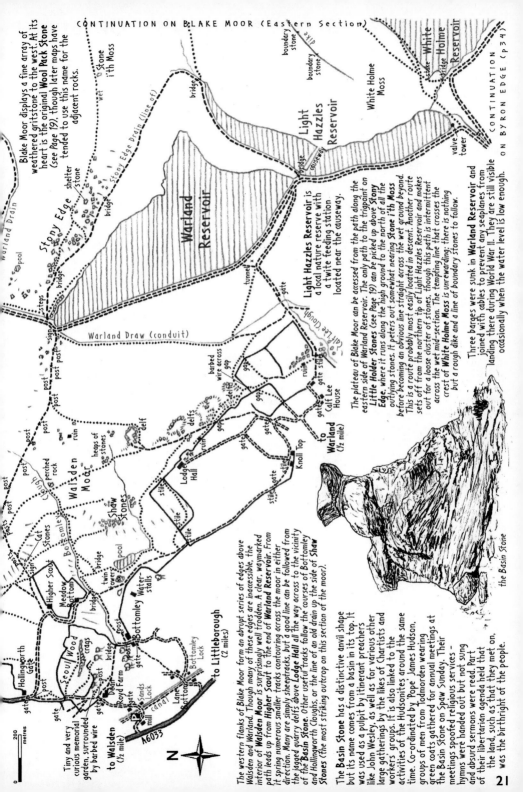

Blake Moor displays a fine array of weathered gritstone to the west. At its heart is the original **Wool Pack Stone** (see Page 19), though later maps have tended to use this name for the adjacent rocks.

Stone i'th Moss

wet

Warland Drain

Stony Edge Drain (line of)

Stony Edge

shelter stone

bridge

bridge

steps

bridge

pool

sign

post

post

post

post

post

post

post

post

post

posts

post

post

sign

club

perched rock

Cat Stones

Higher Scout

Meadow Bottom

bridge

twin towers

Bottomley Clough

bridge

pool

Hollingworth Gate

gate

post

Seouil Wood

crags

Dean Royd Farm

gate

gate

Sands mill

Lane Bottom

A6033

P

gate

gate

bridge

post

Bottomley Lock

Sands Lock

(canal)

Bottomley

Water stalls

to Littleborough (2 miles)

to Walsden (½ mile)

Tiny and very curious memorial garden, surrounded by barbed wire

N

0 200 metres

boundary stone

boundary stone

boundary stone

White Holme Reservoir

lake

bridge

White Holme Moss

Light Hazzles Reservoir

bridge

causeway

valve tower

Warland Reservoir

tunnel

Warland Draw (conduit)

gate

gate

sign

post

post

post

Cat Lee Clough

barbed wire across

gap

gap

gate

gate

gate

gap

gate

gate

ruin

gate

Calf Lee House

gate

stile

stile

ruin

stile

gate

stile

stile

stile

Knoll Top

stile

gate

stile

stile

Lodge Hall

stile

stile

delf

delfs

delf

delf

delfs

ruin

heaps of stones

ruin

Walsden Moor

Shaw Stones

to Warland (½ mile)

Light Hazzles Reservoir is a local nature reserve with a twite feeding station located near the causeway.

The plateau of Blake Moor can be accessed from the path along the eastern side of Warland Reservoir. The only path to the trigpoint on **Little Holder Stones** (see Page 19) can be picked up above **Stony Edge**, where it runs along the high ground to the north of all the outlying stones. It peters out somewhat nearing **Stone i'th Moss** before becoming an obvious line straight across the wet ground beyond. This is a route probably most easily located in descent. Another route sets off from the northern tip of Light Hazzles Reservoir and makes out for a loose cluster of stones, though this path is intermittent across the wet mid-section. The tempting line that crosses the crest of **White Holme Moss** is unrewarding; there is nothing but a rough dike and a line of boundary stones to follow.

Three barges were sunk in **Warland Reservoir** and joined with cables to prevent any seaplanes from landing there during World War II. They are still visible occasionally when the water level is low enough.

the Basin Stone

The western flanks of Blake Moor form an abrupt series of edges above Walsden and Warland. Though many of these edges are inaccessible, the interior of **Walsden Moor** is surprisingly well trodden. A clear, waymarked path leads up from **Higher Scout** to the end of **Warland Reservoir**. From it spring numerous smaller tracks contouring across the moor in either direction. Many are simply sheeptracks, but a good line can be followed from the jagged quarry delfs above **Lodge Hall** all the way across to the vicinity of the **Basin Stone**. Other useful tracks follow the courses of Bottomley and Hollingworth Cloughs, or the line of an old drain up the side of **Shaw Stones** (the most striking outcrop on this section of the moor).

The **Basin Stone** has a distinctive anvil shape but its name comes from a basin in its top. It was used as a pulpit by itinerant preachers like John Wesley, as well as for various other large gatherings by the likes of Chartists and workers' groups. It is also linked to the activities of the Hudsonites around the same time. Co-ordinated by 'Pope' James Hudson, groups of men from Todmorden wearing green coats gathered for annual meetings at the Basin Stone on Spaw Sunday. Their meetings spoofed religious services – hymns were handed out but not sung and absurd sermons were read. Part of their libertarian agenda held that the land, such as that they met on, was the birthright of the people.

21

ROUTE 4: HOLDER STONES & STOODLEY PIKE

Distance: 8 miles (12.5km)

Ascent: 270m

Difficulty: Moderate

Parking: On the roadside near Hinchliffe Arms or on B6138 through Cragg Vale.

Public Transport: Cragg Vale is on the Metroconnect C from Hebden Bridge/Mytholmroyd, and 900 Hebden Bridge-Huddersfield bus routes.

Character: A high-level circuit around Withens Clough that takes in the summits of both Blake Moor and Stoodley Pike. The first section, from Higher House up to the Two Lads, is pathless across rough heather moor and navigation is not straightforward (a compass should be carried). Blake Moor's wild nature contrasts nicely with the well-trodden paths of Stoodley Pike.

The new fenceline around the summit plateau of Blake Moor is part of a large-scale peat restoration project. Heather is being spread across areas of bare peat to prevent this valuable habitat from being washed away and resolve water quality problems in the reservoirs below.

N

6 Turn right and follow one of two parallel paths east from Stoodley Pike Monument to a stile. Where the Pennine Way turns left, continue straight on across the wet ground to a stile leading into Sunderland Pasture Plantation. Turn left at a sign in the middle of the plantation to reach a stile leading onto Bank Top Lane.

The **Te Deum Stone** stands at the top of Withens Gate and is carved with a cross and an inscription 'Te Deum Laudamus', meaning 'We praise Thee, o Lord'. Also known as The Cross or Lord's Stone, it is thought to have been erected in the 1680s by Robert Sutcliffe of Withens. Coffin-bearers heading from Cragg Vale or Withens to Mankinholes and Lumbutts are thought to have rested the coffin on the stone and prayed. Part of the stone has since been chipped off, possibly by a quarryman aiming to damage the cross.

5 Beyond the low ramparts of Coldwell Hill, a path arrives from the left just before a small rocky outcrop. The alternative route (identical to part of Route 20, see page 123) continues straight on to join the main path along the edge to Stoodley Pike but, to stick to our circuit of Withens Clough, turn right here down a feinter path. This aims for the corner of the wall ahead and follows the left side of the wall to the main track across Withens Gate. Turn right through the gate, passing the Te Deum Stone and descending to the next wall; turn left before this and pick up a sheeptrack climbing along the shallow edge above the wall. Through a gap in the next wall, the rocks of Henry Edge can be followed to meet a large track heading up the hill from a gate. Turn left here, the summit of Stoodley Pike and its giant monument soon becoming obvious ahead.

4 Retrace your steps to Warland Drain and rejoin the path along its side. At a sharp kink in the drain, turn right along the flagstoned Pennine Way across Red Dikes Flat.

Holder Stones were originally known as Alder or Alderman Stones, probably referring to the tree found on wet slopes. It has been suggested as the site of ancient remains by a 19th century archaeologist, T James.

3 Turn left up the shoulder from the Two Lads and pick up a feint line leading up to the path along the drain that encircles Blake Moor. Follow this right, passing a ruined shooting box and joining the line of an exposed pipeline beyond the fenceline. The towers of Holder Stones soon loom ahead; to reach them and the trig point beyond, cross the drain where you can and climb up the slope (if the drain full, using the fence may be the best bet). A feint path leads across the worn peat between Holder Stones and Little Holder Stones, but the true summit of Blake Moor stands imperceptibly away to the southeast across the moor and the new fenceline.

Map labels

Dick's Lane · stile · sign · wet · stile · sign

Stoodley Pike Monument · cairn · cairn · cairn

Stoodley Pike (402m) · Sunderlan...

unmarked summit · cairn · cairn · cairn · cairn · post · large cairn

High Stones · ladder · post · gate

alternative route

Long Stoop · Te Deum Stone · gap · Henry Edge · gap · gate

Withens Gate · wet · gate · seat · small cairn · stile

Pennine Way · boundary stone · stile · boundary stone · Coldwell Hill · Red Dikes Flat · boundary stone · signs · gate · gate

Warland Drain · Bird Nest Hill · Pipeline · Deep Slade · cairn · wet · gate

shooting box (ruin) · Cloven Stone

Holder Stones · Little Holder Stones · stile · trig · stile · stile · Blake Moor (422m) · unmarked summit

FROM CRAGG VALE

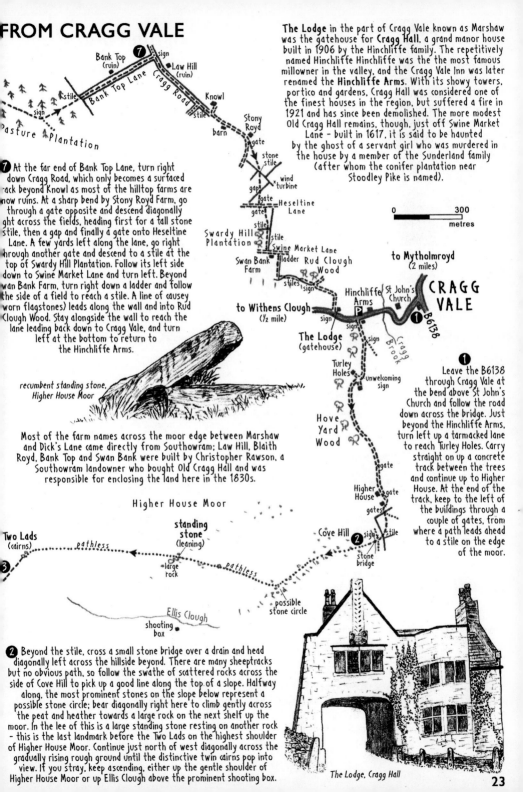

The Lodge in the part of Cragg Vale known as Marshaw was the gatehouse for **Cragg Hall**, a grand manor house built in 1906 by the Hinchliffe family. The repetitively named Hinchliffe Hinchliffe was the the most famous millowner in the valley, and the Cragg Vale Inn was later renamed the **Hinchliffe Arms**. With its showy towers, portico and gardens, Cragg Hall was considered one of the finest houses in the region, but suffered a fire in 1921 and has since been demolished. The more modest Old Cragg Hall remains, though, just off Swine Market Lane - built in 1617, it is said to be haunted by the ghost of a servant girl who was murdered in the house by a member of the Sunderland family (after whom the conifer plantation near Stoodley Pike is named).

7 At the far end of Bank Top Lane, turn right down Cragg Road, which only becomes a surfaced track beyond Knowl as most of the hilltop farms are now ruins. At a sharp bend by Stony Royd Farm, go through a gate opposite and descend diagonally right across the fields, heading first for a tall stone stile, then a gap and finally a gate onto Heseltine Lane. A few yards left along the lane, go right through another gate and descend to a stile at the top of Swardy Hill Plantation. Follow its left side down to Swine Market Lane and turn left. Beyond Swan Bank Farm, turn right down a ladder and follow the side of a field to reach a stile. A line of causey (worn flagstones) leads along the wall and into Rud Clough Wood. Stay alongside the wall to reach the lane leading back down to Cragg Vale, and turn left at the bottom to return to the Hinchliffe Arms.

recumbent standing stone, Higher House Moor

Most of the farm names across the moor edge between Marshaw and Dick's Lane came directly from Southowram; Law Hill, Blaith Royd, Bank Top and Swan Bank were built by Christopher Rawson, a Southowram landowner who bought Old Cragg Hall and was responsible for enclosing the land here in the 1830s.

1 Leave the B6138 through Cragg Vale at the bend above St John's Church and follow the road down across the bridge. Just beyond the Hinchliffe Arms, turn left up a tarmacked lane to reach Turley Holes. Carry straight on up a concrete track between the trees and continue up to Higher House. At the end of the track, keep to the left of the buildings through a couple of gates, from where a path leads ahead to a stile on the edge of the moor.

2 Beyond the stile, cross a small stone bridge over a drain and head diagonally left across the hillside beyond. There are many sheeptracks but no obvious path, so follow the swathe of scattered rocks across the side of Cove Hill to pick up a good line along the top of a slope. Halfway along, the most prominent stones on the slope below represent a possible stone circle; bear diagonally right here to climb gently across the peat and heather towards a large rock on the next shelf up the moor. In the lee of this is a large standing stone resting on another rock - this is the last landmark before the Two Lads on the highest shoulder of Higher House Moor. Continue just north of west diagonally across the gradually rising rough ground until the distinctive twin cairns pop into view. If you stray, keep ascending, either up the gentle shoulder of Higher House Moor or up Ellis Clough above the prominent shooting box.

The Lodge, Cragg Hall

23

OMBROGENOUS BOG: Moors for the Future?

Ombrogenous bogs have dominated large parts of the Pennine uplands for thousands of years. The high rainfall and flat plateaus provide perfect conditions for the generation of peat, which is formed of partially decomposed vegetation, particularly mosses. The word *ombrogenous* refers to these plants, which thrive in wet conditions but rely entirely on rainfall for their water. The result is a very acidic and specialised microclimate in which only a few (often rare) species thrive. Because of this, and the fact that peat is essentially a living organism, the blanket bogs are very sensitive to changes in climate, hydrology, air pollution, grazing and burning.

Peat erosion is now widespread in the South Pennines, possibly an inevitable consequence of climate change. Every time you scramble up a peat hag and the surface gives way, it is obvious just how easy it is to erode peat. In part the erosion of the peat surface is due to its natural ageing, but the rate of degradation has accelerated significantly. The smoke from mills in neighbouring industrial towns, overgrazing and the popularity of walking on the moors have destroyed many plants, particularly the sphagnum mosses that regenerate the peat.

But help is at hand. These blanket bogs are a surprising hive of activity these days, with new fences, pathways, helicopter bags and jute netting appearing all the time. Though this may go against the grain for those who value these moors for their open spaces and solitude, it is all an essential part of protecting and restoring this fragile landscape. Currently the South Pennines are considered to be botanically poor and the Moors for the Future project was launched in 2002 to counter this. Across Blake Moor and Black Hill, many steep peat slopes have been covered with netting to prevent peat from being washed away, and reseeded to encourage surface vegetation to regenerate. The fences are to keep sheep from grazing any new growth that develops and are designed only to be a temporary feature of the moorlands.

CHAPTER 4 - BOULSWORTH HILL
(aka Lad Law)

Height: 517m

Grid Ref: SD930356

Map Sheet: OL21 (South Pennines)

Access: No dogs permitted at any time (except access to summit via Scotch Road or permissive routes from northwest or around Walshaw Dean Reservoirs & on public rights of way). Where permitted, keep dogs on leads between 1st August to 10th December.

Public Transport: Bus 906 runs from Hebden Bridge to Widdop on summer weekends and bank holidays.

Now Boulsworth is technically a Lancastrian hill, but it probably shouldn't be (if we assume the Pennine watershed to be the boundary) and it caps a large area of moorland wilderness within West Yorkshire. **Boulsworth Hill** itself rears up impressively from the northwest (indeed the name is thought to mean 'bull's neck'), but its height is such that it dominates the moorland scene across the northwest of the county. Its summit ridge is studded with numerous rocky outcrops, among which are the legendary Elk and Bison carvings and Druid's Slaughter Stone, which only add to the forbidding air.

Before the Right to Roam legislation of 2000, the whole of Boulsworth Hill was a private grouse moor and access to it had long been a source of contention. Attempts were made to open it up in the 1950s, but these were thwarted over rather ridiculous issues of drinking water purity. So make the most of the opportunity to explore the finest expanse of open heath in the county; though you'll find little in the way of paths across much of the moor, this is great tramping country.

Boulsworth Hill from Greave Clough

The southern slopes of Boulsworth Hill form one of the finest largely untrodden moors in the county; away from the shooting tracks that dominate Greave Clough, Boulsworth is an entrancing desert of heather and weathered rocks. With access restricted by the Savile Estate until 2000, the Access to Boulsworth Campaign fought for many years for public rights across this moor, which is still dominated by its shooting interests.

The altar-shaped stone south-west of the summit is known as the **Druid's Slaughter Stone** and is said to have been used for sacrificial offerings. Certainly neolithic and mesolithic tools have been found high up on Boulsworth Hill. Beneath the rock is carved 'Lad Law The Hill Of Slaughter' and, on the top 'Llad Hloew', adjacent to a natural bowl that could be imagined to hold sacrificial blood. Both are thought to be relatively modern carvings, but the latter may refer to a Celtic word for kill or sacrifice, possibly to Taram, an equivalent of Thor (also found in the name of nearby Thursden valley).

The easiest ascent of **Boulsworth Hill** from the south is by the large track branching off at the top of the Hebden Bridge–Colne road. Known both as the **Oil Track** or **Scotch Road**, this heads a mile into the wilderness before leaving you at a broad open area (the site of the failed oil well). An obvious path from the far left corner ascends the shoulder of Boulsworth Hill, while a couple of feinter paths from the far right corner make directly for the **Dove Stones**. The two can be combined in an easy round; if so, I recommend going via Dove Stones first as this path is hard to locate from above.

Hidden away in steep Black Clough, **Robin Hood's House** may have been a hideaway of Barefoot Harry. He lived at Widdop and his gang of robbers, renowned across West Yorkshire, were said to hide out in Lancashire in times of danger.

The path following the line of **Dove Stones** towards Widdop becomes unclear as it crosses the peat groughs at the top of Tom Groove. The natural line takes you towards the scattered stones of **Grey Stone Hill**, but if you are heading for **the Scout** you are as well to bear south across the peat, cutting straight over to the obvious edge overlooking **Widdop Reservoir**.

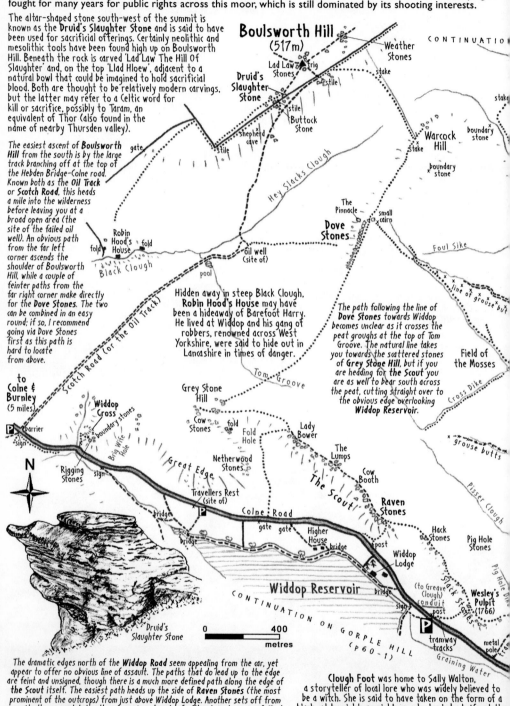

The dramatic edges north of the **Widdop Road** seem appealing from the car, yet appear to offer no obvious line of assault. The paths that do lead up to the edge are feint and unsigned, though there is a much more defined path along the edge of **the Scout** itself. The easiest path heads up the side of **Raven Stones** (the most prominent of the outcrops) from just above Widdop Lodge. Another sets off from opposite the car park below the reservoir and angles for the closest corner of **Slack Stones**. The least clear heads up the depression between **Netherwood Stones** and **Lady Bower** and can be difficult to identify from the road.

Clough Foot was home to Sally Walton, a storyteller of local lore who was widely believed to be a witch. She is said to have taken on the form of a black cat by night; a neighbour who hurled a knife at the cat found Sally to have a bandaged arm the next day. Interestingly she was still buried at Blake Dean Chapel.

Map labels:
Boulsworth Hill (517m)
Weather Stones
CONTINUATIO
Lad Law Stones
trig
stake
stile
Druid's Slaughter Stone
stile
Buttock Stone
stake
boundary stone
shepherd cave
Warcock Hill
stile
boundary stone
gate
stile
The Pinnacle
small cairn
Dove Stones
Foul Sike
Robin Hood's House
fold
fold
oil well (site of)
pool
Black Clough
line of grouse but
Tom Groove
Field of the Mosses
Cross Dike
Grey Stone Hill
to Colne & Burnley (5 miles)
Scotch Road (or the Oil Track)
Widdop Cross
boundary stones
Cow Stones
fold
Fold Hole
Lady Bower
The Lumps
grouse butts
Big Wife Hole
Great Edge
Netherwood Stones
Cow Booth
The Scout
Pisser Clough
N
Rigging Stones
sign
barrier
sign
Travellers Rest (site of)
bridge
Raven Stones
Hack Stones
Pig Hole Stones
Colne Road
gate
gate
Higher House
bridge
post
Widdop Lodge
Pig Hole Clough
Slack Stones
Wesley's Pulpit (1766)
bridge
sign
(to Greave (clough) conduit post
Druid's Slaughter Stone
0   400 metres
Widdop Reservoir
CONTINUATION ON GORPLE HILL (P60-1)
tramway tracks
metal pole
Graining Water

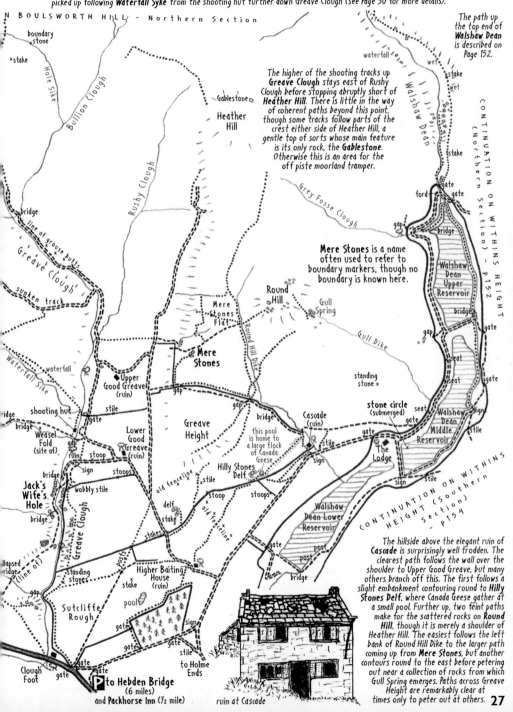

number of large shooting tracks lead up **Greave Clough**, the clearest of which follows the stream's east bank all the way up to the county boundary, here a feint path continues north-east across the heather. If you are heading for the summit of Boulsworth Hill, you may be as well to continue along the line of the stream contouring around **Warcock Hill** to pick up the path between Dove Stones and Boulsworth Hill. An alternative is to branch off the main track earlier, following a sunken shooting track straight up towards **Dove Stones**. Though this eventually peters out, a feint track can soon be picked up following **Waterfall Syke** from the shooting hut further down Greave Clough (see Page 30 for more details).

N BOULSWORTH HILL - Northern Section

The path up the top end of **Walshaw Dean** is described on Page 152.

The higher of the shooting tracks up **Greave Clough** stays east of Rushy Clough before stopping abruptly short of **Heather Hill**. There is little in the way of coherent paths beyond this point, though some tracks follow parts of the crest either side of Heather Hill, a gentle top of sorts whose main feature is its only rock, the **Gablestone**. Otherwise this is an area for the off piste moorland tramper.

Mere Stones is a name often used to refer to boundary markers, though no boundary is known here.

The hillside above the elegant ruin of **Cascade** is surprisingly well trodden. The clearest path follows the wall over the shoulder to Upper Good Greave, but many others branch off this. The first follows a slight embankment contouring round to **Hilly Stones Delf**, where Canada Geese gather at a small pool. Further up, two feint paths make for the scattered rocks on **Round Hill**, though it is merely a shoulder of Heather Hill. The easiest follows the left bank of Round Hill Dike to the larger path coming up from **Mere Stones**, but another contours round to the east before petering out near a collection of rocks from which Gull Spring emerges. Paths across Greave Height are remarkably clear at times only to peter out at others.

Map labels

boundary stone
×stake
Hole Sike
Bullion Clough
×stake
Gablestone
Heather Hill
Rushy Clough
waterfall
Walshaw Dean
wet
×stake
wet
CONTINUATION ON WITHINS HEIGHT (Northern Section) - P152
Grey Fosse Clough
ford
gate
gate
gap
bridge
Walshaw Dean Upper Reservoir
bridge
bridge
line of grouse butts
Greave Clough
sunken track
Mere Stones Flat
Round Hill
Gull Spring
Round Hill Dike
Gull Dike
gap
gate
seat
Waterfall Syke
waterfall
Mere Stones
Upper Good Greave (ruin)
gap
stile
gap
gap
standing stone ×
stone circle (submerged)
seat
Walshaw Dean Middle Reservoir
sign
stile
seat
gate
shooting hut
bridge
gate
Weasel Fold (site of)
Lower Good Greave (ruin)
stoop
Greave Height
gap
gap
Cascade (ruin)
this pool is home to a large flock of Canada Geese
stile
gate
The Lodge
sign
bridge
sign
ruin
stoop
sign
stoops
Hilly Stones Delf
old fenceline
stile
stoop
stoops
CONTINUATION ON WITHINS HEIGHT (Southern Section) - P154
Jack's Wife's Hole
wobbly stile
delf
old fenceline
stake
Walshaw Dean Lower Reservoir
bridge
collapsed bridge (line of)
stake
posts
standing stones
Higher Baiting House (ruin)
stake
pool
gate
gate
post
post
bridge
Sutcliffe Rough
gap
sign
gate
stile
to Holme Ends
Clough Foot
gate
gate
gate
P to Hebden Bridge (6 miles) and Packhorse Inn (½ mile)
ruin at Cascade

27

BOULSWORTH HILL MAP (Northern Section)

I am fully aware that the bulk of this map is in Lancashire and not West Yorkshire, though I prefer to use the true Pennine watershed as the natural boundary between the two counties. However, such are the difficulties in accessing Boulsworth Hill, especially from the Keighley and Haworth side, that I have included the obvious route from Watersheddles and Combe Hill Cross. This follows the ancient bridleway along the foot of the hills past Saucer Hill Clough, an area littered with glacial drift and lime hushings. Apart from the busy northern fringe, this is wild open moorland with a scattering of interesting stone outcrops but little in the way of paths. Its exploration is one of the joys of the new access rights, yet it is laced with the sort of unexpected bog that has you swearing to stick to the path next time.

Across the northern edge of Boulsworth Hill and Wolf Stones, and in places on Rombalds Moor, there are various scars (similar to those at Sheddon Clough) where limestone was mined by **hushing**. The limestone here is not exposed, but represents lines of glacial deposits largely made up of gravel, but with erratics of grit, chert and ironstone. There was just enough limestone, brought down from further north, present in the moraines here to justify its extraction. Hushing describes the effect controlled torrents of water had on the soil, leaving the erratics to be sorted; these hillsides are cut across by various disused dikes and dams for this purpose. There are also the remains of a number of small kilns, used to burn the lime on site and produce quicklime, and the strange conical mounds of waste alongside.

*There are several satisfying routes of ascent of **Boulsworth Hill** from the north. The obvious circuit harks back to pre-CROW access agreements with the Water Board, climbing via the **Abbot Stone** and descending via **Little Chair Stones** to the reservoir near Spoutley Lumb. In those days you could venture no further, but other routes are now accessible up Saucer Hill Clough. Leave the main track that skirts the foot of the moor by the cattle grid leading down to Mean Moss. Beyond the first gate, the best route branches right to reach another gate (sadly locked) and follows a feint track up the west side of the clough to reach **Little Saucer Stones**. If you don't want to climb the gate, continue left to pick up a line of wooden grouse butts that climb nearly all the way to **Great Saucer Stones**.*

Brink Ends Cairn is a small Bronze Age burial cairn in the bracken above Turnhole Clough. It is visible from a small path leading up the bank from the sign above the over-sized new bridge.

A feint path sets off across the moor from Robin Scar only to abandon you near the **Water Cut**, a disused dike that is even harder to avoid than it is to follow.

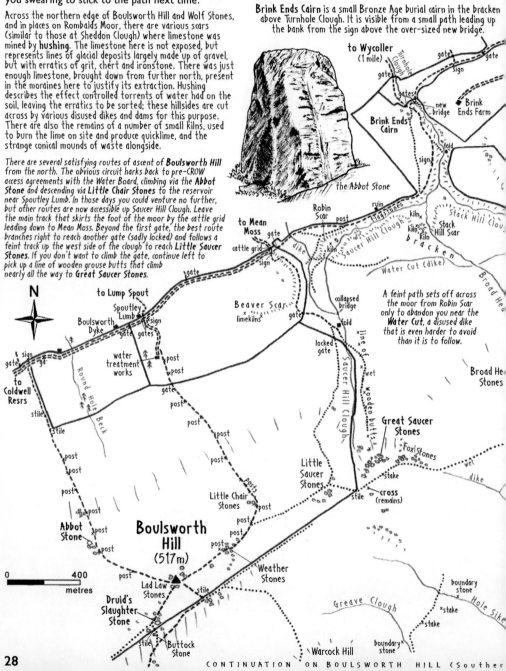

CONTINUATION ON BOULSWORTH HILL (Souther

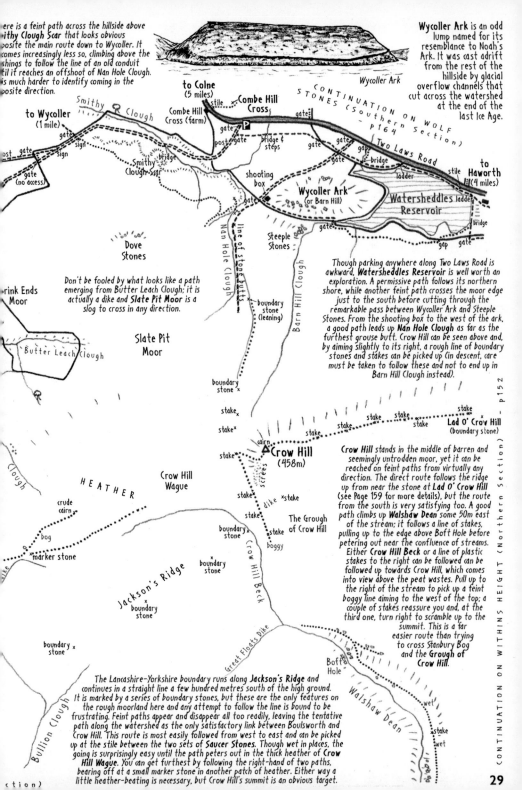

...ere is a feint path across the hillside above ...ithy Clough Scar that looks obvious ...posite the main route down to Wycoller. It ...comes increasingly less so, climbing above the ...shings to follow the line of an old conduit ...til it reaches an offshoot of Nan Hole Clough. ...is much harder to identify coming in the ...posite direction.

Wycoller Ark is an odd lump named for its resemblance to Noah's Ark. It was cast adrift from the rest of the hillside by glacial overflow channels that cut across the watershed at the end of the last Ice Age.

Wycoller Ark

to Colne
(5 miles)

Combe Hill Cross (farm)

Combe Hill Cross

stile

gate

post gate

bridge & steps

to Wycoller
(1 mile)

CONTINUATION ON WOLF STONES (Southern Section) – P 164

Two Laws Road

to Haworth
(4 miles)

Smithy Clough

gate

sign

gate
(no access)

post

gate

Smithy Clough Scar

bridge

gate

gate

gate

gate

gate

gap

bridge

stile

ladder

Watersheddles Reservoir

ladder

bridge

shooting box

gate

gate

gate

gap

gate

Wycoller Ark
(or Barn Hill)

Nan Hole Clough

Steeple Stones

line of stone butts

Dove Stones

Don't be fooled by what looks like a path emerging from Butter Leach Clough; it is actually a dike and **Slate Pit Moor** is a slog to cross in any direction.

...rink Ends Moor

Butter Leach Clough

Slate Pit Moor

Barn Hill Clough

boundary stone (leaning)

boundary stone ×

stake×

stake×

stake×

cairn

stake×

stake ×

stake

stake

stake

stake

Lad O' Crow Hill
(boundary stone)

stake

– P 152

Though parking anywhere along Two Laws Road is awkward, **Watersheddles Reservoir** is well worth an exploration. A permissive path follows its northern shore, while another feint path crosses the moor edge just to the south before cutting through the remarkable pass between Wycoller Ark and Steeple Stones. From the shooting box to the west of the ark, a good path leads up **Nan Hole Clough** as far as the furthest grouse butt. Crow Hill can be seen above and, by aiming slightly to its right, a rough line of boundary stones and stakes can be picked up (in descent, care must be taken to follow these and not to end up in Barn Hill Clough instead).

Crow Hill
(458m)

stake×

H E A T H E R

crude cairn

bog

marker stone

dike

screes

dike

×stake

The Grough of Crow Hill

boundary stone

stake

boggy

Crow Hill Wague

boundary stone

boundary stone

Crow Hill Beck

Jackson's Ridge

boundary stone

boundary stone

Clough

Great Floats Dike

Boft Hole

Walshaw Dean

wet

stake

wet

boundary stone ×

Bullion Clough

Crow Hill stands in the middle of barren and seemingly untrodden moor, yet it can be reached on feint paths from virtually any direction. The direct route follows the ridge up from near the stone at **Lad O' Crow Hill** (see Page 159 for more details), but the route from the south is very satisfying too. A good path climbs up **Walshaw Dean** some 50m east of the stream; it follows a line of stakes, pulling up to the edge above Boft Hole before petering out near the confluence of streams. Either **Crow Hill Beck** or a line of plastic stakes to the right can be followed can be followed up towards Crow Hill, which comes into view above the peat wastes. Pull up to the right of the stream to pick up a feint boggy line aiming to the west of the top; a couple of stakes reassure you and, at the third one, turn right to scramble up to the summit. This is a far easier route than trying to cross Stanbury Bog and the Grough of Crow Hill.

The Lancashire–Yorkshire boundary runs along **Jackson's Ridge** and continues in a straight line a few hundred metres south of the high ground. It is marked by a series of boundary stones, but these are the only features on the rough moorland here and any attempt to follow the line is bound to be frustrating. Feint paths appear and disappear all too readily, leaving the tentative path along the watershed as the only satisfactory link between Boulsworth and Crow Hill. This route is most easily followed from west to east and can be picked up at the stile between the two sets of **Saucer Stones**. Though wet in places, the going is surprisingly easy until the path peters out in the thick heather of **Crow Hill Wague**. You can get furthest by following the right-hand of two paths, bearing off at a small marker stone in another patch of heather. Either way a little heather-beating is necessary, but Crow Hill's summit is an obvious target.

CONTINUATION ON WITHINS HEIGHT (Northern Section)

...ction)

ROUTE 5: BOULSWORTH HILL AND GORPLE HILL FROM WIDDOP

Distance: 7½ miles (12km)

Ascent: 320m

Difficulty: Moderate

Parking: At the car park below the dam of Widdop Reservoir on the Hebden Bridge - Colne road.

Public Transport: The Widdop car park is the terminus of the 906 bus service, which runs from Hebden Bridge six times a day on weekends and bank holidays from April to September.

Character: This route is a rarity in that the entire walk is on open moorland, forming a natural circuit of the hills overlooking Widdop Reservoir. Parts of the walk are undefined (indeed any ascent of Boulsworth Hill from Greave Clough needs careful navigation), but the result is a joyous tramp across the lonely watershed tops of Boulsworth Hill and Gorple Hill. The route can be shortened if needed by following the road (or reservoir shore) back down to Widdop before ascending Gorple Hill.

Access: No dogs on this route.

Shuttleworth Rocks

② Join the main vehicle track up Greave Clough near the shooting hut and follow it briefly up the right bank. However, immediately beyond the first gate, turn left to ford two streams* and follow a feint track up the hillside beyond. The line through the heather peters out as it veers towards Waterfall Sike, but other feint tracks can soon be picked up above the stream. This becomes clearer again as the ground opens out on the heather plain of the Fields of the Mosses and picks up the line of another stream soon after. Follow the right-hand side of this grough up towards the stones on the horizon (even when the path tries to lead you away to the right). Soon after a line of grouse butts, the obvious path branches left across the grough and leads clearly on up to the back of the Dove Stones.

* If Greave Clough is difficult to cross, you can use a small bridge by the shooting hut and follow a feint path up the oppisite bank.

Boulsworth Hill
(517 m)

③ The hills open up at the Dove Stones and present an obvious arc round to the summit of Boulsworth Hill. Join the slightly wet path through the stones, heading right towards the feint lump of Warcock Hill. The path skirts to the left of its summit, whereupon you need to turn left along the obvious green line of a dike across the saddle. The easiest path stays to the left of the dike before curling away from it as it climbs up towards Boulsworth, but there are so many different lines here it is hard to know which one you're on. Aim to reach the fenceline at a rocky outcrop on the edge and cross a stile soon after to reach the trigpoint.

The **Scotch Road** is thought to follow an ancient trackway along the high ground from the Iron Age settlement at Burwain's Camp. It later became a trade route between the Thursden and Worth valleys. The name may relate to an Old English word *scarth* meaning *scarth*, a characteristic of the road. However, I suspect it refers to Scotch pedlars, who roamed the northern uplands in the 18th century selling fabrics, including a cheap cloth known as *Scotch-cloth*. There is also a Scots House in Holme Clough on Black Hill, and Scotchman's Arm near Ponden. More recently it has become known as the **Oil Track**; the track we see today was constructed in 1963, when it was thought there was oil beneath the shales of Hey Slacks Clough. A large drill was installed and a bore over 6,000ft deep sunk, but no oil ever found.

The **Dove Stones** are a great scar of gritstone in one long line facing the higher summit of Boulsworth Hill. It is the most interesting outcrop on the moor with the Pinnacle cast loose at its northern end. The name (previously Dew Stones) is thought to be a bastardisation of Dew Stones (from the gaelic *dubh*, meaning black).

line of dike
stake
stake
Warcock Hill

Lad Law
Stones
trig stile
④
Druid's
Slaughter
Stone
stile

Hey Slacks Clough

line of grouse butts
small cairn
⑤
The Pinnacle
Dove Stones

wet

cross grough here

④ From the trigpoint at Lad Law Stones, head back towards the fenceline in the direction of the distinctively shaped anvil or dragon of the Druid's Slaughter Stone (see *Page 26* for more details). Cross another stile soon after the stone and descend diagonally to reach the main path down into Hay Slacks Clough. Across the stream, join the end of the Scotch Road and follow its gentle grassy crest for a mile to the top of the Widdop road.

the oil well (site of)

pool

Scotch Road (or the Oil Track)

Field of

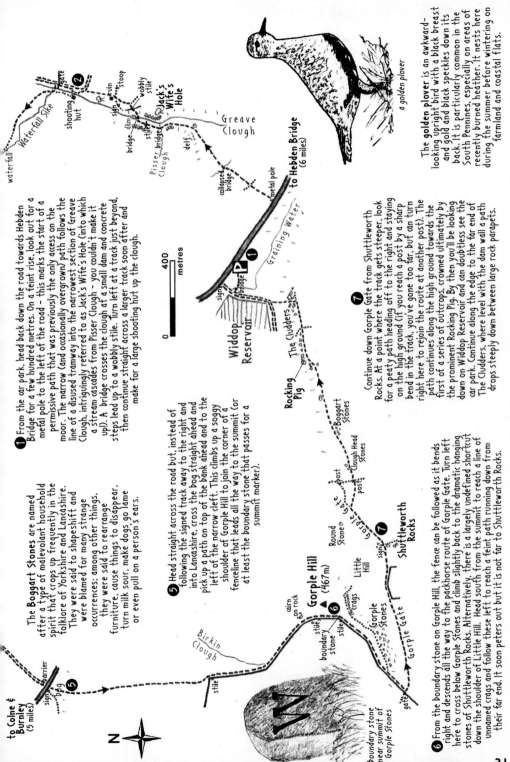

1 From the car park, head back down the road towards Hebden Bridge for a few hundred metres. On a feint rise, look out for a metal pole to the left of the road – this marks the start of a permissive path that was previously the only access on the moor. The narrow (and occasionally overgrown) path follows the line of a disused tramway into the narrowest section of Greave Clough, intriguingly referred to as Jack's Wife's Hole (into which a stream cascades from Pisser Clough – you couldn't make it up). A bridge crosses the clough at a small dam and concrete steps lead up to a wobbly stile. Turn left at a track just beyond, then continue straight across a larger track soon after and make for a large shooting hut up the clough.

5 Head straight across the road but, instead of following the signed track away to the right and into Lancashire, cross the bog straight ahead and pick up a path on top of the bank ahead and to the left of the narrow cleft. This climbs up a soggy shoulder of Gorple Hill to join the corner of a fenceline that leads all the way to the summit (or at least the boundary stone that passes for a summit marker).

7 Continue down Gorple Gate from Shuttleworth Rocks. At a point where the track gets steeper, look for a peaty path heading off to the right and staying on the high ground (if you reach a post by a sharp bend in the track, you've gone too far, but can turn right here to rejoin the route at another post). The path continues along the high ground towards the first of a series of outcrops, crowned ultimately by the prominent Rocking Pig. By then you'll be looking down on Widdop Reservoir and can doubtless see the car park. Continue along the edge to the far end of The Cludders, where level with the dam wall a path drops steeply down between large rock parapets.

The **golden plover** is an awkward-looking upright bird with a black breast and gold and black speckles down its back. It is particularly common in the South Pennines, especially on areas of recently burned heather. It nests here during the summer before wintering on farmland and coastal flats.

a golden plover

The **Boggart Stones** are named after a type of malevolent household spirit that crops up frequently in the folklore of Yorkshire and Lancashire. They were said to shapeshift and were blamed for many strange occurrences; among other things, they were said to rearrange furniture, cause things to disappear, turn milk sour, make dogs go lame or even pull on a person's ears.

6 From the boundary stone on Gorple Hill, the fence can be followed as it bends right and descends all the way to the packhorse route of Gorple Gate. Turn left here to cross below Gorple Stones and climb slightly back to the dramatic hanging stones of Shuttleworth Rocks. Alternatively, there is a largely undefined shortcut down the shoulder of Little Hill. Head south from the summit to reach a line of unnamed crags and follow these left to reach a feint path running down from their far end. It soon peters out but it is not far to Shuttleworth Rocks.

THE ELK & BISON CARVINGS, BOULSWORTH HILL

In 1920, two boys playing in the stones scattered across Boulsworth Hill discovered a pair of carvings on the inside of one of the rocks; one of a running bison and the other possibly of an elk head-on. Many suggest that the only explanation for depictions of North American animals on this Pennine hillside are that they are the work of Native Americans who were touring the area as part of Buffalo Bill's Wild West show. Presented by Bill Cody himself, this mammoth extravaganza filled four trains and employed 400 horses and 100 Native Americans of various tribes. Having spent five months in Manchester in 1887, they later toured the whole country, performing in Keighley in 1903 and Burnley in 1904, but it seems unlikely they would have desecrated the sacred landscape in this way. It has also been suggested that it was the work of Reverend Percival Weldon, who owned part of Boulsworth Hill in the nineteenth century and may have been inspired by the age of scientific discovery to create his own piece of history.

The fact that their origin and age are unknown allows rumours of the carvings being prehistoric to persist. Eight thousand years ago, when Britain was connected to the continent, large aurochs (European bison) roamed the forested landscape and, alongside Irish elks (giant deer), were the principal large animals. It is quite feasible that mesolithic man, whose flint tools have been found on Boulsworth Hill, carved these figures into the nearby rocks. This theory is best supported by the fact that the sun illuminates the carved rock only once a year at midsummer sunrise. However, one look at the carvings is usually enough to say that they really don't look 8,000 years old, and it is thought unlikely they would have existed in isolation.

The Elk & the Bison rock carvings on Boulsworth Hill

Another carving, that of a hawk (or possibly Horus, a hawk-headed Egyptian god), has been found on a rock near Upper Gorple Reservoir. This initially raised similar questions of its origin; though it may be the work of a navvy, it is thought to relate to an early twentieth-century Bradford-based occult group called the Temple of Horrors.

The Boulsworth carvings are located on the side of what could generously be described as a cave - it is possible for an individual to shelter in the hollow between the rocks here - but if you went looking for a cave you would never find it. The location is generally kept secret to protect the small carvings but, even with plenty of advice, it took me five trips to locate it, and only then with the aid of a guide. So by all means go hunting, but prepare to be patient.

CHAPTER 5 - BYRON EDGE

Height: 415m

Grid Ref: SE969190

Map Sheet: OL21 (South Pennines)

Access: No restrictions.

Public Transport: Bus 528 runs between Halifax and Littleborough via Blackstone Edge Reservoir. Bus 900 runs between Hebden Bridge and Ripponden via B6138. Buses 589/590 run between Todmorden and Littleborough via Warland and Summit.

Byron Edge is a gentle rise in the reservoir-studded moor north of the A58 at the White House, its unmarked summit straddling the county boundary like any true Pennine top. Byron Edge is likely named after the Barony of Rochdale whose manor it would have fallen under; they went by the name Lord Byron, the most famous being the renowned romantic poet. Sandwiched between Blackstone Edge and White Holme Reservoirs and a series of drains, it is largely unspectacular and a series of power lines crossing the moordoes little to improve matters. Byron Edge is quickly bypassed on the Pennine Way, but its western flank has its moments where Leach Hill Rocks and the shapely outlier of Snoddle Hill overlook the Chelburn Reservoirs. Despite being part of Greater Manchester, these slopes are easily reached climbing out of Walsden and Warland and offer the most interesting approach to Byron Edge.

Byron Edge and Blackstone Edge from Light Hazzles Edge

CONTINUATION ON BLAKE MOOR (Western Section) - p 21

The rugged rockfaces of **Warland Quarry** can be accessed from a path diagonally up the hillside adjacent to Quarry Cottages by the swing bridge above Warland Upper Lock. You can then scramble up to the top and follow the edge along to **Long Lees Quarry**, though there are a couple of fences across the route. The Access Land extends right down to the canal here, but can be difficult to explore without encountering fences or landowners. (Curiously the apparently similar section of land around **Light Hazzles Quarry** is not access land.

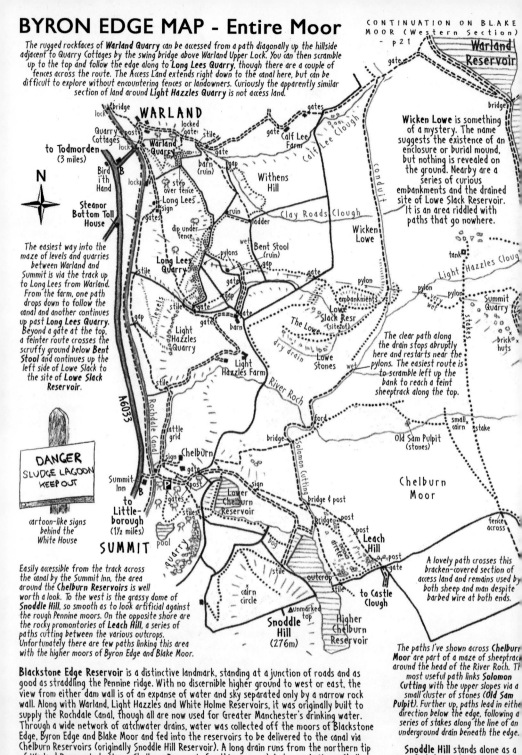

Wicken Lowe is something of a mystery. The name suggests the existence of an enclosure or burial mound, but nothing is revealed on the ground. Nearby are a series of curious embankments and the drained site of Lowe Slack Reservoir. It is an area riddled with paths that go nowhere.

The easiest way into the maze of levels and quarries between Warland and Summit is via the track up to Long Lees from Warland. From the farm, one path drops down to follow the canal and another continues up past **Long Lees Quarry**. Beyond a gate at the top, a feinter route crosses the scruffy ground below **Bent Stool** and continues up the left side of Lowe Slack to the site of **Lowe Slack Reservoir**.

The clear path along the drain stops abruptly here and restarts near the pylons. The easiest route is to scramble left up the bank to reach a feint sheeptrack along the top.

DANGER SLUDGE LAGOON KEEP OUT

cartoon-like signs behind the White House

Easily accessible from the track across the canal by the Summit Inn, the area around the **Chelburn Reservoirs** is well worth a look. To the west is the grassy dome of **Snoddle Hill**, so smooth as to look artificial against the rough Pennine moors. On the opposite shore are the rocky promontories of **Leach Hill**, a series of paths cutting between the various outcrops. Unfortunately there are few paths linking this area with the higher moors of Byron Edge and Blake Moor.

A lovely path crosses this bracken-covered section of access land and remains used by both sheep and man despite barbed wire at both ends.

The paths I've shown across **Chelburn Moor** are part of a maze of sheeptracks around the head of the River Roch. The most useful path links **Solomon Cutting** with the upper slopes via a small cluster of stones (**Old Sam Pulpit**). Further up, paths lead in either direction below the edge, following a series of stakes along the line of an underground drain beneath the edge.

Snoddle Hill stands alone as a perfect dome, its name possibly derived from a dialect word 'snod' (or snood) meaning smooth.

Blackstone Edge Reservoir is a distinctive landmark, standing at a junction of roads and as good as straddling the Pennine ridge. With no discernible higher ground to west or east, the view from either dam wall is of an expanse of water and sky separated only by a narrow rock wall. Along with Warland, Light Hazzles and White Holme Reservoirs, it was originally built to supply the Rochdale Canal, though all are now used for Greater Manchester's drinking water. Through a wide network of catchwater drains, water was collected off the moors of Blackstone Edge, Byron Edge and Blake Moor and fed into the reservoirs to be delivered to the canal via Chelburn Reservoirs (originally Snoddle Hill Reservoir). A long drain runs from the northern tip of Warland Reservoir to Upper Chelburn Reservoir for this purpose, but as only Upper Chelburn Reservoir, along with Hollingworth Lake, still serves to top up the canal, most of the drains across these moors are now dry, acting only as conduits for some useful path links.

34

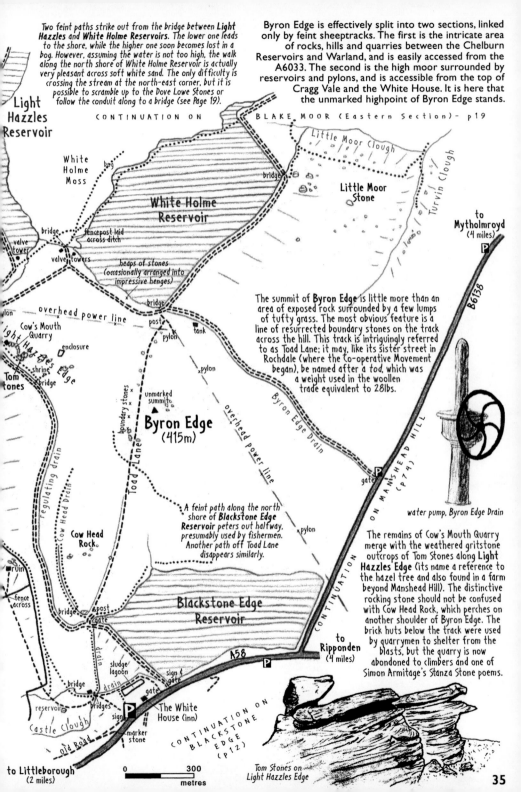

Two feint paths strike out from the bridge between **Light Hazzles** and **White Holme Reservoirs**. The lower one leads to the shore, while the higher one soon becomes lost in a bog. However, assuming the water is not too high, the walk along the north shore of White Holme Reservoir is actually very pleasant across soft white sand. The only difficulty is crossing the stream at the north-east corner, but it is possible to scramble up to the Dove Lowe Stones or follow the conduit along to a bridge (see Page 19).

Byron Edge is effectively split into two sections, linked only by feint sheeptracks. The first is the intricate area of rocks, hills and quarries between the Chelburn Reservoirs and Warland, and is easily accessed from the A6033. The second is the high moor surrounded by reservoirs and pylons, and is accessible from the top of Cragg Vale and the White House. It is here that the unmarked highpoint of Byron Edge stands.

CONTINUATION ON BLAKE MOOR (Eastern Section) - p19

Light Hazzles Reservoir

White Holme Moss

bog

White Holme Reservoir

Little Moor Clough

Turvin Clough

bridge

Little Moor Stone

to Mytholmroyd (4 miles)

B6138

bridge

valve tower

valve towers

fencepost laid across ditch

heaps of stones (occasionally arranged into impressive henges)

overhead power line

bridge

post

tank

pylon

The summit of **Byron Edge** is little more than an area of exposed rock surrounded by a few lumps of tufty grass. The most obvious feature is a line of resurrected boundary stones on the track across the hill. This track is intriguingly referred to as Toad Lane; it may, like its sister street in Rochdale (where the Co-operative Movement began), be named after a *tod*, which was a weight used in the woollen trade equivalent to 28lbs.

Cow's Mouth Quarry

enclosure

Light Hazzles Edge

shrine

bridge

Tom Stones

boundary stones

unmarked summit

pylon

Byron Edge (415m)

Toad Lane

Byron Edge Drain

overhead power line

pylon

gate

ON MANSHEAD HILL (P74)

water pump, Byron Edge Drain

regulating drain

Cow Head Drain

Cow Head Rock

A feint path along the north shore of **Blackstone Edge Reservoir** peters out halfway, presumably used by fishermen. Another path off Toad Lane disappears similarly.

ruin

fence across

bridge

post

gate

drain

sludge lagoon

Blackstone Edge Reservoir

to Ripponden (4 miles)

A58

The remains of Cow's Mouth Quarry merge with the weathered gritstone outcrops of Tom Stones along **Light Hazzles Edge** (its name a reference to the hazel tree and also found in a farm beyond Manshead Hill). The distinctive rocking stone should not be confused with Cow Head Rock, which perches on another shoulder of Byron Edge. The brick huts below the track were used by quarrymen to shelter from the blasts, but the quarry is now abandoned to climbers and one of Simon Armitage's Stanza Stone poems.

bridge

reservoir

Castle Clough

old road

bridges

sign

drain

gate

sign & gate

marker stone

The White House (inn)

CONTINUATION ON BLACKSTONE EDGE (P12)

to Littleborough (2 miles)

0   300
metres

Tom Stones on Light Hazzles Edge

CONTINUATION

ROUTE 6: BYRON EDGE & BLAKE MOOR FROM WARLAND (OR WALSDEN)

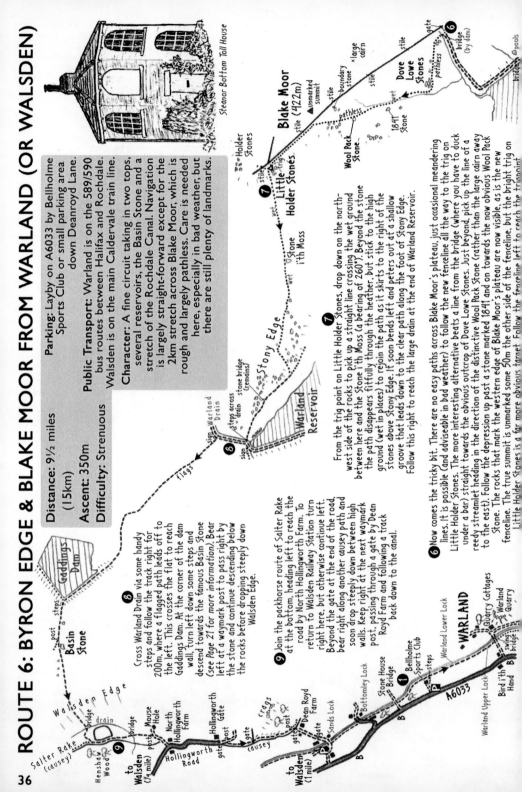

Steanor Bottom Toll House

Distance: 9½ miles (15km)

Ascent: 350m

Difficulty: Strenuous

Parking: Layby on A6033 by Bellholme Sports Club or small parking area down Deanroyd Lane.

Public Transport: Warland is on the 589/590 bus routes between Halifax and Rochdale. Walsden is on the main Caldervale train line.

Character: A fine circuit taking in two tops, several reservoirs, the Basin Stone and a stretch of the Rochdale Canal. Navigation is largely straight-forward except for the 2km stretch across Blake Moor, which is rough and largely pathless. Care is needed here, especially in bad weather, but there are still plenty of landmarks.

---

⑧ Cross Warland Drain via some handy steps and follow the track right for 200m, where a flagged path leads off to the left. This crosses the flat to reach Gaddings Dam. At the corner of the dam wall, turn left down some steps and descend towards the famous Basin Stone (see Page 21 for more information). Bear left at a waymark post to pass right by the stone and continue descending below the rocks before dropping steeply down Walsden Edge.

⑨ Join the packhorse route of Salter Rake at the bottom, heading left to reach the road by North Hollingworth Farm. To return to Walsden Railway Station turn right here, but otherwise continue left. Beyond the gate at the end of the road, bear right along another causey path and soon drop steeply down between high walls. Keep right at the next waymark post, passing through a gate by Dean Royd Farm and following a track back down to the canal.

⑦ From the trig point on Little Holder Stones, drop down on the north-west side of the rocks to pick up a straight line crossing the wet ground between here and the Stone i'th Moss (a bearing of 260°). Beyond the stone the path disappears fitfully through the heather, but stick to the high ground (wet in places) to rejoin the path as it skirts to the right of the stones above Stony Edge. If soon bends left and peters out at a shallow groove that leads down to the clear path along the foot of Stony Edge. Follow this right to reach the large drain at the end of Warland Reservoir.

⑥ Now comes the tricky bit. There are no easy paths across Blake Moor's plateau, just occasional meandering lines. It is possible (and advisable in bad weather) to follow the new fenceline all the way to the trig on Little Holder Stones. The more interesting alternative beats a line from the bridge (where you have to duck under a bar) straight towards the obvious outcrop of Dove Lowe Stones. Just beyond, pick up the line of a reedy streamlet heading in the direction of the distinctive Wool Pack Stone (rather than the large cairn away to the east). Follow the depression up past a stone marked 1841 and on towards the now obvious Wool Pack Stone. The rocks that mark the western edge of Blake Moor's plateau are now visible, as is the new fenceline. The true summit is unmarked some 50m the other side of the fenceline, but the bright trig on Little Holder Stones is a far more obvious target. Follow the fenceline left to reach the trigpoint.

36

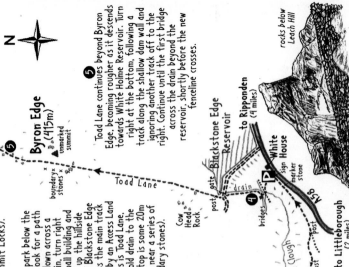

The **Bird i'th Hand** was originally built on the old Calderbrook Road over to Littleborough, though it was then known as the Bird at Calf Holes. When the new turnpike road was opened in 1825 along the line of today's A6033, landlord Henry Rogers had it taken down and rebuilt at its current location to maximise business.

One of the original proposals for the route of a trans-Pennine canal was by the Bolton & Bury Canal Company, who suggested a route linking Chelburn and Ripponden via a 4.8-mile tunnel. In the end a competing company built the **Rochdale Canal**, though it too was planned to have a significant tunnel between Walsden and Sladen. When this was by-passed by a series of locks, it necessitated the building of several reservoirs to supply them with water: Chelburn, Blackstone Edge, White Holme, Light Hazzles, Warland, and Hollingworth Lake (from which water was pumped by steam 45 feet to a 4-mile conduit that linked it to Summit Locks).

① Join the canal (either opposite the Walsden railway station, from the small car park down Deanroyd Lane, or behind the Bellholme Sports Club) and follow it right as far as Warland. Above Warland Upper Lock, cross the canal via a swing bridge and turn immediately right. Follow the track up to Long Lees, where a sign has been turned in the wrong direction. It should point right, through a gate below the second building to join the rough canal-side. Cross a stile and follow a path through a gap in a broken wall before climbing away from the canal a little. Before reaching a beckoning gateway, bend round to the left to find a stile onto a track that leads down to Chelburn.

As is evident from this map, it is entirely possible to follow the canal all the way to the Summit Inn, but I've tried to break up the route and make it more interesting.

② The track reaches a junction below the hamlet of Chelburn; follow the sign along a path that continues opposite. It bends round to the left and joins the track up from the Summit Inn; follow this left up through a gate onto the open moor. Past Lower Chelburn Reservoir, bear left at a signpost and follow the waymarked Pennine Bridleway across a drain and up over Leach Hill. This drops down to a gate and follows a newly-fenced route around the farm at Leach. It emerges on the track beyond the farm (home to the Field of Dreams animal sanctuary); follow the track left all the way to Castle Clough.

③ After crossing the large bridge over Castle Clough, the track turns sharply right, but a small path climbs up the bank to the left and joins the track above. This track soon crosses back over the clough, but bear right just before the bridge and climb steeply up the slope past a series of posts. The path soon joins the steadier gradient of the Old Road, now a surfaced bridleway leading up to the White House.

④ Upon reaching the lower car park below the White House, turn left and look for a path from the far end leading down across a depression. Across the drain, turn right immediately in front of a small building and follow the side of the drain up the hillside beyond to reach the corner of Blackstone Edge Reservoir. Head straight across the main track here and pick up another path by an Access Land post some 20m beyond. This is Toad Lane, which follows the line of an old drain to the top of Byron Edge (the true top is some 20m off to the right of the track near a series of recently re-erected boundary stones).

⑤ Toad Lane continues beyond Byron Edge, becoming rougher as it descends towards White Holme Reservoir. Turn right at the bottom, following a track along the shallow dam wall and ignoring another track off to the right. Continue until the first bridge across the drain beyond the new reservoir, shortly before the new fenceline crosses.

White Holme Reservoir

N

0 400
metres

Byron Edge
▲ (415m)
unmarked summit

Toad Lane

boundary x
stones x

×post
×pylon

bridge

⑤

⑤

Blackstone Edge Reservoir
to Ripponden

gate
post

drain

④

bridges

post

A58

White House
sign
marker stone

Cow Head Rock

to Littleborough
(2 miles)

post

post

Castle Clough

posts

③
bridge
bridges

Castle
bridge

Castle Bungalow
(ruin)

signs
gate

signs & gate

gate

Leach Hill
heap of posts
head of rocks

gates
gates
gate
gate

Higher Chelburn Reservoir

Leach

post

drain
sign
bridge & post

sign

gate

②
Chelburn
sign

Lower Chelburn Reservoir

gate

post
R
B
post

SUMMIT

Summit Inn
B
R

to Littleborough
(1½ miles)

Rochdale Canal

Long Lees Lock

①
Long Lees

stile
sign

Long Lees Mill
(site of)

stile

gate
Withens Hill

stile

gap

rocks below Leach Hill

37

The **Emperor Moth** is found on moorland and heath such as the West Yorkshire Moors, though it is far from common. Indeed my only sighting of one was in the heather near Byron Edge. This sketch is of the female, which is up to 10cm in span and has distinctive peacock eyes on each of its wings and red patches on their tips. The male is smaller with feathered antennae.

CHAPTER 6 - CARR & CRAGGS MOOR
(aka Todmorden Moor)

Height: 441m

Grid Ref: SD894252

Map Sheet: OL21 (South Pennines)

Access: No restrictions.

Public Transport: Todmorden is on Caldervale routes. Buses 65 & 273 run from Todmorden to Bacup via Clough Foot. Buses 589 & 591 run from Todmorden to Burnley via Cornholme and Portsmouth.

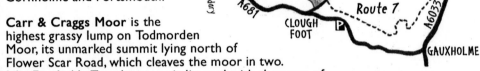

Carr & Craggs Moor is the highest grassy lump on Todmorden Moor, its unmarked summit lying north of Flower Scar Road, which cleaves the moor in two. Like Freeholds Top, the moor is littered with the scars of opencast coal mining and fire clay extraction, which were particularly concentrated along Dulesgate (the A681). It remains scarred to this day by landfill, fly-tipping and the new wind farm, but without the marks of spoil heaps, trial holes, quarries and subsidence, Carr & Craggs Moor would be largely uninteresting. To the north, overlooking Cornholme and Portsmouth, the moor finally breaks into life with the rocky promontories of Eagle's Crag and the Old Woman. The name Carr is likely to come from the Old Norse word *kjarr*, meaning swamp or wet hollow (indeed in Lancashire dialect carr-water was peaty water). This combination of carr and craggs seems to sum up the character of the moor, but is confused somewhat by its recording as 'Carn Crags Moor' on the 1848 map (a mis-spelling or perhaps a suggestion of a Celtic link?).

Carr & Craggs Moor from Stones Lane

Though the top of Carr & Craggs Moor is rather dour, the routes up from **Portsmouth** and **Cornholme** are anything but. A good path starting opposite the Roebuck Inn climbs above the dramatic scar of **Beater Clough** via a former tram road to reach the mine and landfill site at its head. Various paths also climb up **Tower Clough** above Bearnshaw Tower, the most substantial going through the plantation. The others all lead to the ruins of **Flower Scar Farm**, though some are tough going - the best starts at a stile on the first bend above the tower and follows the stream below the plantation before zig-zagging up to the ruins.

Portsmouth was so named by the son of the first landlord of the Roebuck Inn he was a mariner who had been recently stationed on the south coast.

Beater Clough starts off promisingly, a rocky scar rising steeply out of Portsmouth, but halfway up it flattens out and changes name as well as character. **Greens Clough** is very obviously polluted, predominantly by iron oxides from the coal mine workings all across the moor above. Though Hill Top Colliery closed in the 1960s, there is still a small working mine in the clough, a jumble of rusty prefab buildings that represents a one-man drift mine operation. A landfill site occupied the former colliery site and has recently been filled in so it is little more than a fenced off lump at the head of the clough.

a lonk sheep in Cock Hill Wood

A **lonk** is a hardy sheep bred in the South Pennines, its name a corruption of 'lanky'. It has a black and white face and long legs, and is bred for meat and carpet wool.

The top of *Carr & Craggs Moor* is unmarked and unspectacular on a ridge of high ground stretching across from Flower Scar Road. A feint sheeptrack follows this crest, but the easiest way to reach the summit is to follow feint paths along the fence from the top of Tower Clough or the track near Heald Top Farm.

The **Astronomy Centre** was founded in 1982 by former telescope-maker Peter Drew and the three-storey observatory was specially built to be the best-equipped amateur facility in the country. As well as aiming to construct the largest optical telescope in the country, the Astronomy Centre also encourages public interest in astronomy. Thus visitors are welcome on Saturday evenings for a small charge.

Flower Scar Road was a Bronze Age highway between Bacup and Todmorden, but there is little evidence of this now. Fly-tipping along the track reduced the moor to little more than a rubbish dump until it was closed and barriers erected in 2005. Much of the waste has been cleared today thanks to Todmorden Moor Regeneration Trust, but the improvements here are very much a work in progress and there is still plenty of off-roading across Todmorden Moor.

40

Map labels:
to Burnley (5 miles); Roebuck Inn sign; PORTSMOUTH; Portsmouth Mill; overhead power line; Beater Clough; Greens Clough; gate; A646; to Cornholme (½ mile); Shepherd Pile; Carr Road; Carr View; sign; delf; post; stile; Cock Hill Wood; The Old Woman; posts; post; post; bridge & post; pylon; coal mine; locked gate; landfill site; plantation; disused pit; posts; sign; pylon; to Thieveley Pike; Heald Top Farm; gate; gates; pylon; boundary stone; boundary stone; locked gate (no access); stile; colliery (site of); Tower; post; unmarked summit; Carr & Craggs Moor (441m); trial holes; fenced hole; colliery (site of); Flower Scar Road; stone; barrier; barriers; fenced hole; Holden Gate Slack; Todmorden Moor; rushes; fenced hole; Black Edge; White Edge; fenced hole; posts; post; spoil heaps; post; to Bacup (1 mile); Sharney Ford; post; pylon; gap; sheds; pylon; quarry; Saunder Clough; spoil heap; fenced hole; post; very wet; A681; Clough Head Quarry; factory (Sharneyford Works); gate; pool; shed; colliery (site of); pylons; wet; gate; ruin; stile; stile; muddy; gates; gate; Holden Gate; dam; Spring Well; gate; sign; Limers Gate; Astronomy Centre; reservoir; CONTINUATION ON FREEHOLDS TOP (Northern Section) - P52; Dulesgate; to Todmorden (3 miles); Priest Booth

...is obvious, **Bearnshaw Tower** no longer has a tower; it ...parently collapsed in 1860 following frenzied digging beneath it ...r a pot of gold rumoured to be buried there. However, its ...me remains associated with the witch of Bearnshaw Tower, a ...th-century woman who was said to run around in the form of ...white doe or cat. While in doe form, Lady Sybil was hunted by ...r future husband on horseback and cornered on **Eagle Crag**, a ...sion that is still said to haunt the crag (also known as the ...itches' Horse Block) on Hallowe'en. Denied a Christian burial, ...e was laid beneath Eagle Crag along with another mystic, ...other Helston. The name Eagle Crag is thought to have been ...ven it by a passing traveller, it having been previously known ... Bill Knipe, possibly come from the Norse for a projecting rock.

Todmorden Moor is an urban common with rights for common grazing, yet its landscape is entirely shaped by mining, quarrying and landfill. There is little wild peat or heather, just a barren surface that has been subjected to industrial forces. That continues, with the construction of five wind turbines changing the face of the moor yet again, while further opencast mining and landfill developments have been opposed within the last twenty years. Restoration schemes are underway to encourage regeneration of the heath moor, though there have been notable failures in the past. In the 1990s, waste paper pulp was spread across neighbouring Heald Moor as a soil improver, only to form a hard crust that took years to break down. Flower Scar Hill forms the most prominent part of Todmorden Moor, but it is a false top that leads gently up to the true summit of Carr & Craggs Moor.

0   300
metres

The Old Woman is the most prominent of the crags jutting out of the woods above Portsmouth. The name is thought to relate to the mother goddess of the land and weather, known in Gaelic as the Cailleach. It was common for Christians to refer to pagan beliefs as Old Lad, Old Wife or Old Woman.

The most obvious route from Dulesgate onto Todmorden Moor follows **Limers Gate** from Spring Well and is well waymarked through the spoil heaps below White Edge. A smaller path branches off up the side of **Saunder Clough** to reach Flower Scar Road - if in doubt it passes right beneath a pylon. Another path leads up from the top of the heaps and hollows of the large quarry by **Sharneyford Works** (which are best accessed by a track passing above the factory).

Sourhall Cottages have been residences only since 1949, before which they operated as **Sourhall Hospital**. In 1874, upon an outbreak of smallpox in Todmorden, this former mill was converted into an isolation hospital. It later held patients with scarlet fever, typhoid and diptheria and is sometimes referred to as Sourhall Joint Hospital - not because it had anything to do with joints but as it was run jointly between Todmorden and Bacup.

Coal mining developed in the early 19th century with the advent of steam-powered mills and Todmorden Moor was littered with fragmented seams that could be mined from the surface. Each drift mine (often called day holes) was worked by only a few people reaching steadily underground along the seam until it was too dangerous to continue. The coal was removed by carts and a series of tramways operated by boys as young as six. Along **Dulesgate**, the presence of fire-clay also allowed for the making of bricks, and so much of the coal was used to fire the brickworks. The Temperley family owned a large pipeworks at Saunder Clough that made sanitary pipes and covered a large area around the site of the Astronomy Centre.

Map labels:
Stubley Lane (to Cornholme)
Bearnshaw Tower
stile, gate, post
kedk ate
posts, stile, stiles, post
line of posts
Tower Quarry
tile
Height Top
to Cornholme
to Cornholme (½ mile)
Roundfield (ruin)
post, post
wet
Barewise Wood
bridge
A646
Staff of Life Inn
to Todmorden (1½ miles)
bridge, gate
Wet Shaw
Eagle Crag
New Towneley
to Lydgate
gate
Tower Causeway
Clough
post
Flower Scar (ruin)
stile, sign, sign, delf, posts, post
Lower Moor
Lowe Hill
post, post, post, posts
West End
stile
delf, delf
post, post
Dyke Green
stile
wet, signs
Guide Quarry
post, wet, posts
quarry & pool
Dyke (ruin)
gates
arch in ruin
Flower Scar Hill (420m)
boggy, delfs
post, post, post
Higher Woodfield Farm
gate
wet, post
sign
P
Ridge House
Sourhall Cottages
sign
Country Friends (aka The Sourhall)
to Todmorden (1 mile)
SOURHALL
lower Scar Road
Woodfield Top
gate
barn
Acre Nook Clough
Limers Gate
Higher Hanging Shaw
barn
gate, gates
post, post, post
Acre Nook (ruin)
gate, gated, gate
Lower Hanging Shaw
Back o'th' Edge
to Clough Foot
gate
Southall Road
CLOUGH FOOT
The Astronomy Centre

N

41

4 Crossing Tower Clough, the path reaches a stile; turn left before this and follow the fenceline up to another major track. Continue straight across this, following the fence to the top of Carr & Craggs Moor. The unmarked summit is off to the left level with the second boundary stone.

Follow the high ground left here (a bearing of 150°) and hope to pick up a feint sheeptrack aiming for the marker stone at the top of Flower Scar Road.

3 Climb up to join the main track around Lower Moor; follow it right only for a few yards before ascending left around the rim of a flooded quarry delf. At the back, pick up a feint path bearing right across the side of the moor. Aim for a post and bear left by the second of these to angle up the slope on a clear path.

Follow the line of posts all the way to the road (Tower Causeway) and head straight across to join Flower Scar Road, now closed to traffic. This track bends left and starts to climb up towards Flower Scar Hill. Two paths cross the track, marked by posts; 75 yards after the second, turn sharply right onto a feint path following the line of a grassy dike around the face of Flower Scar Hill. Above the dramatic ruins of Flower Scar Farm, fork left and climb slightly towards the head of Tower Clough by the left corner of the plantation.

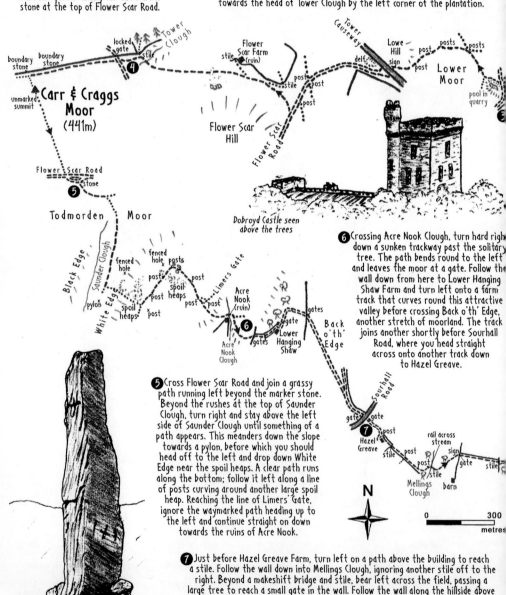

Dobroyd Castle seen above the trees

6 Crossing Acre Nook Clough, turn hard right down a sunken trackway past the solitary tree. The path bends round to the left and leaves the moor at a gate. Follow the wall down from here to Lower Hanging Shaw Farm and turn left onto a farm track that curves round this attractive valley before crossing Back o' th' Edge, another stretch of moorland. The track joins another shortly before Sourhall Road, where you head straight across onto another track down to Hazel Greave.

5 Cross Flower Scar Road and join a grassy path running left beyond the marker stone. Beyond the rushes at the top of Saunder Clough, turn right and stay above the left side of Saunder Clough until something of a path appears. This meanders down the slope towards a pylon, before which you should head off to the left and drop down White Edge near the spoil heaps. A clear path runs along the bottom; follow it left along a line of posts curving around another large spoil heap. Reaching the line of Limers' Gate, ignore the waymarked path heading up to the left and continue straight on down towards the ruins of Acre Nook.

7 Just before Hazel Greave Farm, turn left on a path above the building to reach a stile. Follow the wall down into Mellings Clough, ignoring another stile off to the right. Beyond a makeshift bridge and stile, bear left across the field, passing a large tree to reach a small gate in the wall. Follow the wall along the hillside above Stones Wood and join a clear path straight across the fields beyond. Where the wall ascends steeply, bear right along a slight depression to reach a stile. Follow the top side of a wall beyond and turn left up a muddy track above Friths Farm. This almost immediately opens out into a field, where you turn sharply back to the left, climbing steeply up a grassy depression to a stile into Stones Lane.

42 *the largest of the Stones menhirs*

ROUTE 7: CARR & CRAGGS MOOR AND STONES MENHIRS FROM TODMORDEN

Distance: 7 miles (11.5km)

Ascent: 390m

Difficulty: Moderate

Parking: At the railway station, or bottom of Dobroyd Road (opposite Morrisons).

Public Transport: Todmorden is on the main Caldervale train & bus routes.

Character: Todmorden Moor is invisible from the town, but makes for a natural circuit. The edge of the moor is reached not far above Centre Vale Park before heading for its high point on Carr & Craggs Moor. The walking here is on feint tracks (there is little else) and care is needed in navigation, but none of it is particularly rough or strenuous. The return route takes in the remarkable standing stones at Stones that really ought to be better known.

Centre Vale Park stands on the site of Centre Vale House, a mansion built by Thomas Ramsbotham in the 1820s and later owned by the Fieldens. Carr Barn was one of a number of houses along Lovers Walk and was home to Ruth Stansfield, the weaver who captured John Fielden's heart.

❶ Head left from Todmorden Railway Station down Station Approach and, on the corner, turn left to pass under the railway. As Ridge Road bends left, ascend Ridge Steps straight ahead; at the top, turn soft right onto a cycleway above the houses. Passing through the woods above Centre Vale Park, stay on the tarmac of Lovers Walk until you come to an open area that was the site of Carr Barn; fork left here to reach Siggett Lane.

❷ Turn left up Siggett Lane for 100m, then follow the signed path right steeply up through Ewood Wood. Beyond a fine viewpoint, the path bends left and enters a field; follow its left-hand edge to a grassy lane climbing up to the hamlet of Todmorden Edge. At the road, turn right for a short distance; opposite the last building, a scruffy gate leads into the field to the left and a path follows a wet depression along the side of the wall. Where the wall bends, go right through a gate that is difficult to open and not waymarked. Follow the opposite side of the wall and fence on to the next gate (occasionally tied), where you bear left slightly up the slope towards a gate on the edge of Lower Moor.

Todmorden Edge was an important meeting place for both the Quakers and later the Methodists. It was also the original site of the Todmorden Golf Club.

It is hard to get a glimpse of **Dobroyd Castle**, shrouded as it is by trees, yet it should be one of Todmorden's most striking buildings. It cost more than Todmorden Town Hall and was built in the 1860s by John Fielden, supposedly in response to Ruth Stansfield only agreeing to marry him if he built her a castle. Since his death, it has been used by the Home Office, a private school, a buddhist retreat, and most recently an activity centre.

❽ Turn left up Stones Lane and, before the most prominent standing stone, turn right to skirt around the high wall of Stones Farm. To explore the stones here, head further up Stones Lane or access the fields through a couple of gates (permission should be sought from the landowner). Join the road leading down the hill from Stones Farm as it winds steeply past various houses to a large junction in front of the gate to Dobroyd Castle. Head straight on here down a dead-end track through the woods to reach a railway crossing. Immediately beyond, turn left on a cycle track alongside the railway that soon emerges by Todmorden Station.

The hamlet of **Stones** is named for a reason, yet the three standing stones in the vicinity appear to be somewhat unheralded. The most prominent is a 12-foot monolith standing in a field right next to Stones Lane. Nearby a fragile finger-like stone is thrust up from a millstone on the top of Centre Hill (note there is no legal way to reach this stone). It has been suggested that it was moved up here from the adjacent field to celebrate the Battle of Waterloo and used to have a weather-cock on top. The final stone is somewhat shorter and stands some 300m up Stones Lane in a field to the left. Little is known about the place, but it is a remarkable site .

43

The **twite** is also known as the Pennine finch and the
moors of the South Pennine are its last breeding ground in
England. It is a small brown finch closely related to the
linnet and distinguished by its darker streaks and short
beak. It is a partial migrant, wintering on the coast and
breeding on high ground, amid mature heather and bracken.
There are only around a hundred pairs left in the area and
their habitat is being further threatened by invasive
species and moorland fires. The twite is on the Red List of
Birds of Conservation Concern and much work is being done
to preserve and regenerate both its breeding and feeding
grounds - Carr and Craggs Moor is one of the moors to
have seen the twite's return in recent years.

CHAPTER 7 - DOG HILL

Height: 435m

Grid Ref: SE003171

Map Sheet: OL21
(South Pennines)

Access: No restrictions.

Public Transport: Regular buses to Ripponden from Halifax and Littleborough. Bus 560 runs from Halifax to Rishworth. Bus 900 runs from Ripponden to Hebden Bridge via Blackstone Edge Reservoir & Cragg Vale.

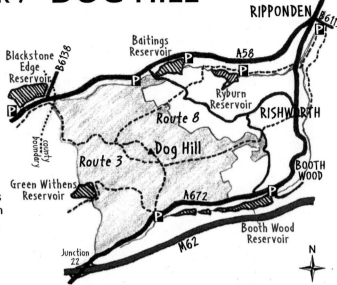

Dog Hill is an outlying eastward spur from neighbouring Blackstone Edge, but forms a satisfying twin with Manshead Hill, the two trigs facing each other across the Upper Ryburn Valley. Both hills are pleasing ascents, with Dog Hill having more varied approaches and being easily accessible from any direction, particularly Rishworth and along the A672. The moor is dominated by reservoirs and the drains that circle the summit plateau, but the quarried knoll of Pike End and the impressive buttresses of Castle Dean Rocks ensure there is plenty of interest. Its obvious-sounding name may refer to one of the black dogs of legend, or simply the more domesticated kind – certainly ours always seemed at home on its summit.

Dog Hill from Green Withens Drain

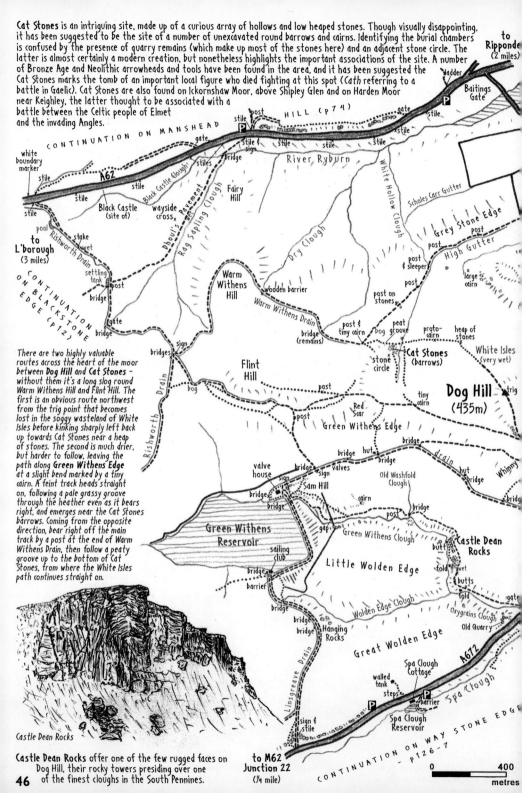

Cat Stones is an intriguing site, made up of a curious array of hollows and low heaped stones. Though visually disappointing, it has been suggested to be the site of a number of unexcavated round barrows and cairns. Identifying the burial chambers is confused by the presence of quarry remains (which make up most of the stones here) and an adjacent stone circle. The latter is almost certainly a modern creation, but nonetheless highlights the important associations of the site. A number of Bronze Age and Neolithic arrowheads and tools have been found in the area, and it has been suggested the Cat Stones marks the tomb of an important local figure who died fighting at this spot (*Cath* referring to a battle in Gaelic). Cat Stones are also found on Ickornshaw Moor, above Shipley Glen and on Harden Moor near Keighley, the latter thought to be associated with a battle between the Celtic people of Elmet and the invading Angles.

to Ripponde (2 miles)

ladder

Baitings Gate

P

CONTINUATION ON MANSHEAD HILL (p74)

post

stile

stile & sign

gate

bridge

stiles

stile

stile

stile

stile

stile

gate

stile

P

River Ryburn

White Hollow Clough

Scholes Carr Gutter

Grey Stone Edge

post

High Gutter

post

post & sleeper

post

large cairn

white boundary marker

stile

A62

stile

stile

Black Castle Clough

Dhoul's Pavement

Rag Sapling Clough

Fairy Hill

Black Castle (site of)

wayside cross

to L'borough (3 miles)

pool

stake

wet

Rishworth Drain

settling tank

post

bridge

gate

bridge

CONTINUATION ON BLACKSTONE EDGE (p12)

Warm Withens Hill

wooden barrier

Warm Withens Drain

Dry Clough

post on stones

bog groove

peat groove

post & tiny cairn

bog

proto-cairn

heap of stones

White Isles (very wet)

bridge (remains)

Cat Stones (barrows)

bridges

sign

stone circle

Flint Hill

Rishworth Drain

bog

post

post

Red Scar

Green Withens Edge

tiny cairn

Dog Hill (435m)

trig

There are two highly valuable routes across the heart of the moor between **Dog Hill** and **Cat Stones** – without them it's a long slog round Warm Withens Hill and Flint Hill. The first is an obvious route northwest from the trig point that becomes lost in the soggy wasteland of White Isles before kinking sharply left back up towards Cat Stones near a heap of stones. The second is much drier, but harder to follow, leaving the path along **Green Withens Edge** at a slight bend marked by a tiny cairn. A feint track heads straight on, following a pale grassy groove through the heather even as it bears right, and emerges near the Cat Stones barrows. Coming from the opposite direction, bear right off the main track by a post at the end of Warm Withens Drain, then follow a peaty groove up to the bottom of Cat Stones, from where the White Isles path continues straight on.

valve house

sign

bridge

sign

valves

bridge

bridge

hut

bridge

drain

hut

bridge

Whinny

bridge

Sam Hill

Old Washfold Clough

cairn

bridge

Green Withens Reservoir

sailing club

gap

Green Withens Clough

post

butt

Castle Dean Rocks

fold

wet

Little Wolden Edge

butts

fold

gate

bridge

barrier

Wolden Edge Clough

Great Wolden Edge

Oxygrains Clough

Old Quarry

bridge

bridge

Hanging Rocks

Linsgreave Drain

Spa Clough Cottage

A672

Spa Clough

walled tank

steps

P

barrier

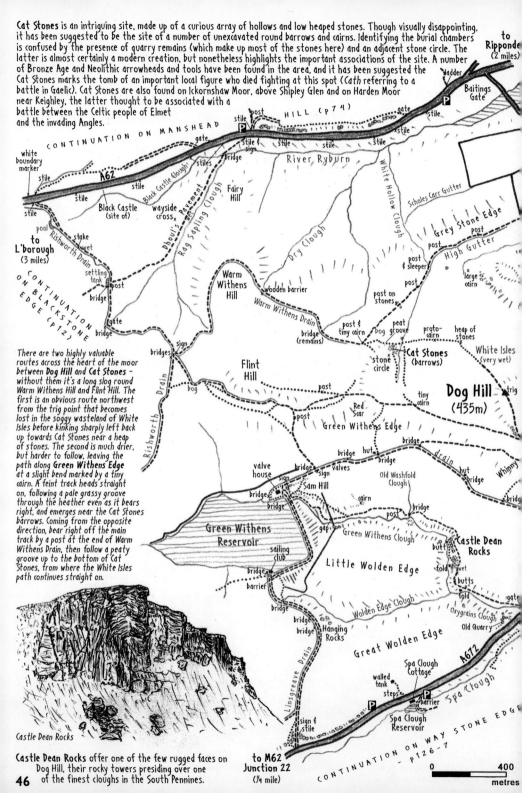

Castle Dean Rocks

sign & stile

P

Spa Clough Reservoir

CONTINUATION ON WAY STONE EDGE – p126-7

Castle Dean Rocks offer one of the few rugged faces on Dog Hill, their rocky towers presiding over one of the finest cloughs in the South Pennines.

to M62 Junction 22 (¼ mile)

46

0   400
metres

DOG HILL MAP - Entire Moor

Dog Hill is the shapely but largely featureless eastward extension of Blackstone Edge with slopes overlooking Ripponden, Rishworth, Baitings and Booth Dean. There are no rights of way between Blackwood Edge in the east and Rag Sapling Clough in the west, which is particularly curious since there are several old packhorse roads crossing the moor - Blackwood Edge Road, Pike End Gate, Dog Hill Road and Henley Road can all still be traced (even if not always walked). There are, however, plenty of paths, the clearest following the drains to the north and south of the high ground or leading from Oxygrains Old Bridge to Green Withens and Dog Hill summit, all of which are permissive routes. There are smaller tracks across the peat heart of the moor, but the tussocky grass flanks are best avoided if you value your ankles.

The jumbled shapes of Lench Holes (Lench is a dialect word for a ledge of rock) form one of the more interesting sides of Dog Hill, yet remain largely inaccessible. From the northeast a feint track follows a level towards them, but crosses a very wet depression; you're probably better cutting across from High Gutter towards an inexplicably large cairn on a hidden shoulder to the west. From Blackwood or Nook End ruins, there are also feint tracks up the hillside. One of these follows the zigzag depression of the old Dog Hill Road and can be recognised in descent by a tyre and a sink perched close together on its edge. All paths in this area appear to lead towards the same cluster of stones, recognisable from Blackwood Edge Road by a prominent triangular rock, but none of them are so obliging as to continue satisfactorily towards the trig point itself.

Rish is an old form of rush and, considering the extent of the squelchy rush-strewn fields below Nook End, Blackwood and Lench House, Rishworth seems well named.

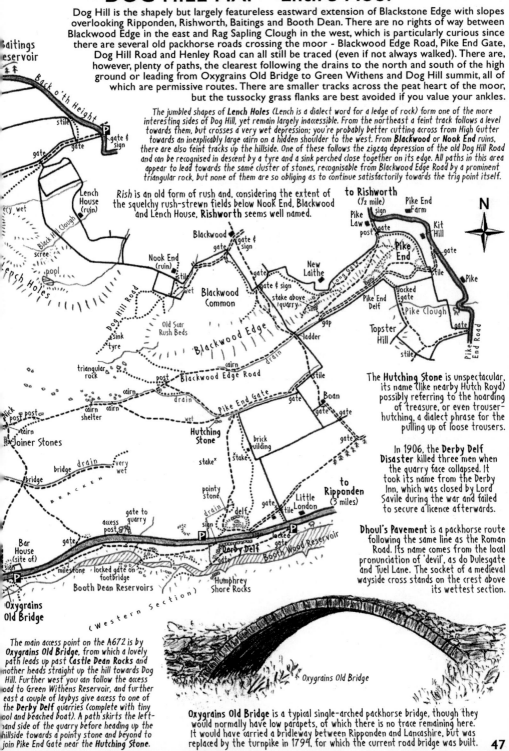

The **Hutching Stone** is unspectacular, its name (like nearby Hutch Royd) possibly referring to the hoarding of treasure, or even trouser-hutching, a dialect phrase for the pulling up of loose trousers.

In 1906, the **Derby Delf Disaster** killed three men when the quarry face collapsed. It took its name from the Derby Inn, which was closed by Lord Savile during the war and failed to secure a licence afterwards.

Dhoul's Pavement is a packhorse route following the same line as the Roman Road. Its name comes from the local pronunciation of 'devil', as do Dulesgate and Tuel Lane. The socket of a medieval wayside cross stands on the crest above its wettest section.

Oxygrains Old Bridge

The main access point on the A672 is by **Oxygrains Old Bridge**, from which a lovely path leads up past **Castle Dean Rocks** and another heads straight up the hill towards Dog Hill. Further west you can follow the access road to Green Withens Reservoir, and further east a couple of laybys give access to one of the **Derby Delf** quarries (complete with tiny pool and beached boat). A path skirts the left-hand side of the quarry before heading up the hillside towards a pointy stone and beyond to join Pike End Gate near the **Hutching Stone**.

Oxygrains Old Bridge is a typical single-arched packhorse bridge, though they would normally have low parapets, of which there is no trace remaining here. It would have carried a bridleway between Ripponden and Lancashire, but was replaced by the turnpike in 1794, for which the current road bridge was built.

47

ROUTE 8: DOG HILL AND RYBURN RESERVOIR FROM RIPPONDEN

Distance: 8½ miles (13.5km)

Ascent: 370m

Difficulty: Moderate

Parking: Free car park in Ripponden on Mill Fold Way (off the B6113). There is also a smaller car park below Ryburn Reservoir, reached from the A58.

Public Transport: Ripponden is on the 528 (to Rochdale), 531, 557 and 560 bus routes from Halifax.

Character: Dog Hill overlooks the upper Ryburn Valley and makes a natural objective from Ripponden or Rishworth. The valley itself is beautifully verdant especially around Ryburn Reservoir, yet also dense with the mills, ponds and railways of its industrial heritage. The route follows the valley out to Rishworth Mill then ascends Dog Hill via Pike End before returning via Ryburn Reservoir. The ground and navigation is largely good, apart from the short stretch across the open moor between Dog Hill and Cat Stones, which can be awkward in bad weather

Beeston Hall Rocks take their name from the farm just up the hillside. It was originally Thrum Hall (after the loose ends of a warp when cloth is cut) and the rocks appear to have been renamed at the same time.

6 Turn right and follow the clear path across the pale grassy northern slopes of the moor. Leave the moor at a gate at the end of High Gutter and follow the walled route down to the road. Turn left then immediately right down the track to Higher Wormald. Pass in front of the building to a gate leading into another walled grassy avenue. By the ruins of New House, turn left steeply down the side of another wall into the upper Ryburn Valley.

St Bartholomew's Church, Ripponden

7 Across the bridge over the River Ryburn, keep right along the stream to pass the ungainly hunks of Beeston Hall Rocks. The path joins the pleasant wooded shore of Ryburn Reservoir and eventually opens out into a field beyond. Turn right down steps beyond a second stile and continue downhill to the left of the dam wall. Bear left halfway down and skirt round a garage to join a cobbled track heading downhill past the new houses of the Ryburn Valley.

Molinia (or purple moor grass) grows across the sides of many of the moors of West Yorkshire and is the bane of the off-piste rambler. What looks like gentle grass from a distance turns out to be hideous tussocks with a penchant for wet ground. But molinia is trouble to the conservationist too, an invasive monoculture whose presence is a sign of overgrazing and excessive burning on peat moorlands.

5 The path continues north-west from the the top of Dog Hill across White Isles. Where it drops down into a peat grough, there is a heap of stones; turn left here and try to pick up another feint path heading across the hillside towards the rough heaps of Cat Stones (a bearing of 265°). The path runs through a peat gully below the right side of the stones (*see Page 46 for background information*) and descends to pick up a feint path across the slope. This soon reaches a stake and tiny cairn on the main path running below the edge.

Dog Hill (435m)

purple moor grass (the dreaded molinia)

N

```
0          300
        metres
```

St Bartholomew's Church in Ripponden is one of two fine churches passed on the route; the other is in the aptly-named hamlet of Godly (which actually refers to a 'good clearing'). The current Gothic Revival building is actually the fourth church built on the site, others having been built in 1464, 1610 and 1736. The second was said to have had a gallery entrance directly from the Old Bridge, but was destroyed by a flood that tore bodies from their graves and washed away the font (which can now be found in the Old Bridge Inn). The Old Bridge Inn claims to be 'probably Yorkshire's oldest hostelry' and can be traced back to 1307.

Ryburn Reservoir, like those at Baitings and Booth Dean, was built by the Wakefield Corporation. It may originally have been named Bogden Reservoir after the clough and mill it inundated. On the slopes above, Hanging Lee Mill (known as Little Britain long before the TV series) was used as a hostel during the reservoir's construction.

Ripponden is an attractive if rather slight town strung out along arterial roads. Its name is a contraction of Ryburn-Dean and it is thought to have developed around a Roman ford.

1 From the centre of Ripponden, either follow the B6113 down across the river or Priest Lane over the adjacent packhorse bridge (Ripponden Old Bridge). Turn left to pass in front of the church; where this lane bends left uphill, turn right to reach the road again. Head straight across into a walled path above a factory. This leads to a bridge, before which you turn right to follow the line of the old railway. Continue under the first bridge, then turn left up some steps before the next to reach Quakers Lane.

An old branch line ran from Sowerby Bridge and terminated at Rishworth Station, whose platforms can still be seen in the woods below Quakers Lane. It opened in 1878 and was originally planned to run through a tunnel towards Rochdale, but the line ceased to be used in 1929.

2 Follow grassy Quakers Lane along the top of the woods, keeping right as it forks to join a track down the hill. Turn left at the bottom to climb up towards Holme House. Pass to the left of the house on a path into the woods and across the meadow beyond. Turn right at a stile to pass round the front of the palatial flats of Rishworth Mill.

The grand edifice of **Rishworth Mill** was a large cotton spinning mill built in 1860 alongside an earlier corn mill. **Slithero Mill** was one of the few mills in the Ryburn Valley that didn't convert to cotton, serving as a fulling mill and later a paper mill. Originally Lower Oakes, its name (also that of a small clough known as Derby Delf) is something of a mystery. Perhaps it is Scandinavian, meaning 'scabbard-howe' (a howe being a Viking burial mound), or perhaps it is just dialect for slippery?

8 The cobbles soon give way to the tarmac of Bar Lane, which winds its way between mill ponds, cottages and expensive new developments all the way to Slithero Bridge. Turn right at the main road, then immediately left down Holme House Lane. Over the bridge, turn left again to pick up a path along the riverside, which can be followed all the way into Ripponden. Stay on the right bank to join the road that passes the car park and reaches the B6113.

3 Turn right up the road from Rishworth Mill and follow the left walkway straight on past the front of the school. Head across the main road and continue straight on up the hill through the hamlet of Godly (the site of Rishworth's church). Ignoring various unwelcoming signs, follow the track up towards Arkin Royd. Reaching the farm, bear left off the track to a small gate above the house, only to have to recross the track almost immediately (the vagaries of public rights of way!). Continue up the fenceline past Upper Arkin Royd and join the track left to reach the road. Head straight across onto another track that reaches the edge of the moor at a stile below Pike End.

4 The track bends first left then right to reach the wall along the top of the ridge; alternatively you can carry straight on at the first bend and follow the edge of Pike End round to rejoin the track. Where the track bends left to a gateway, branch right and aim for a ladder over the wall ahead. Continue straight on up the broad shoulder of Dog Hill, following the sunken line of Blackwood Edge Road even where paths lead off to the right. Follow the posts to reach a cairn just over the crest, where you turn right to climb steadily up to the trig point on Dog Hill.

Pike End

20 THINGS YOU'RE NOT ALLOWED TO DO ON ACCESS LAND

a) drive or ride any vehicle other than an invalid carriage.

b) use a vessel or sailboard on any non-tidal water.

c) have with you any animal other than a dog.

d) commit any criminal offence.

e) light or tend a fire or do any act which is likely to cause a fire.

f) intentionally or recklessly take, kill, injure or disturb any animal, bird or fish.

g) intentionally or recklessly take, damage or destroy any eggs or nests.

h) feed any livestock.

i) bathe in any non-tidal water.

j) engage in any operations of or connected with hunting, shooting, fishing, trapping, snaring, taking or destroying of animals, birds or fish or have with you any engine, instrument or apparatus used for hunting, shooting, fishing, trapping, snaring, taking or destroying animals, birds or fish.

k) use or have with you any metal detector.

l) intentionally remove, damage or destroy any plant, shrub, tree or root or any part of a plant, shrub, tree or root.

m) obstruct the flow of any drain or watercourse, or open, shut or otherwise interfere with any sluice-gate or other apparatus.

n) without reasonable excuse, interfere with any fence, barrier or other device designed to prevent accidents to people or to enclose livestock.

o) neglect to shut any gate or to fasten it where any means of doing so is provided, except where it is reasonable to assume that a gate is intended to be left open.

p) affix or write any advertisement, bill, placard or notice.

q) in relation to any lawful activity which persons are engaging in or are about to engage in on that or adjoining land, do anything which is intended by you to have the effect:

    (i) of intimidating those persons so as to deter them or any of them from engaging in that activity,

    (ii) of obstructing that activity, or

    (iii) of disrupting that activity.

r) without reasonable excuse, do anything which (whether or not intended by him to have the effect mentioned in paragraph (q)) disturbs, annoys or obstructs any persons engaged in a lawful activity on the land.

s) engage in any organised games, or in camping, hang-gliding or para-gliding.

t) engage in any activity which is organised or undertaken (whether by him or another) for any commercial purpose.

(extracted from the Countryside and Rights of Way Act 2000)

CHAPTER 8 - FREEHOLDS TOP
(aka Trough Edge End)

Height: 454m

Grid Ref: SD906219

Map Sheet: OL21 (South Pennines)

Access: No restrictions.

Public Transport: Todmorden and Walsden are on Caldervale routes. Buses 65 and 273 run between Todmorden and Bacup via Clough Foot.

Freeholds Top is another favourite of mine and a rare part of the Pennine ridge that faces more to the east than the west. The summit stands on top of a steep escarpment visible across most of the Upper Calder Valley and offers a fine vantage point in all directions. The ridge, looking naturally to Walsden, shelters in its arms a number of impressively steep cloughs, the most well-known being Gorpley Clough. There are many other corners, though, that are worth exploring on a moor that could all too easily be dismissed (or indeed covered in wind farms, as will soon be happening on Shore Moor). Its names (it is equally often known as Trough Edge End) come from the Spodden Valley side, *freeholds* relating to the slopes above Shawforth that were enclosed from waste in the 16th century and freed from duty to the Lords of the Manor (in this case, Lord Byron).

Freeholds Top from Sour Hall Road in midwinter

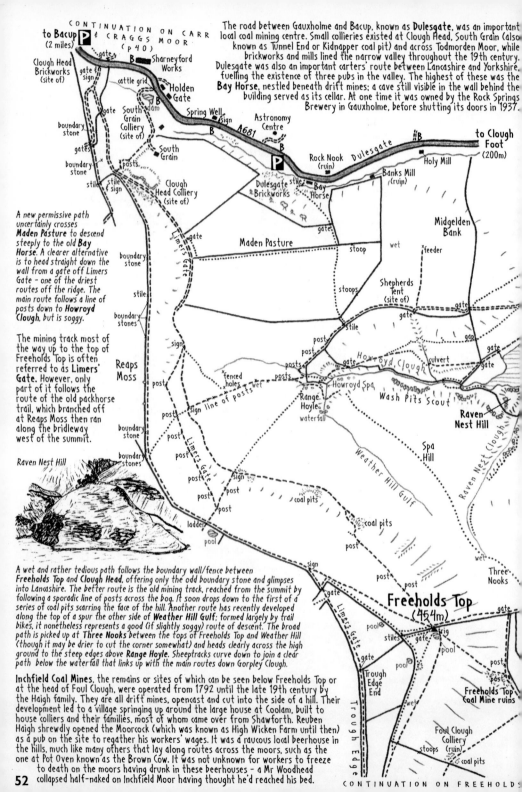

to Bacup (2 miles)

Clough Head Brickworks (site of)

Sharneyford Works

cattle grid

Holden Gate

Clough Head Brickworks (site of)

gate sign

boundary stone

gates

boundary stone

stile

stile & sign

South Grain Colliery (site of)

South Grain

posts

Clough Head Colliery (site of)

Spring Well

sign

A681

B

Astronomy Centre

B

Rock Nook (ruin)

Dulesgate

Holy Mill

B

to Clough Foot (200m)

Banks Mill (ruin)

Dulesgate Brickworks

stile

Bay Horse

Midgelden Bank

gate

Maden Pasture

stoop

wet

feeder

Shepherds Tent (site of)

gate

stoops

gate

boundary stone

stile

stoops

stile

Howroyd Clough

gap

gate

post

culvert

gate

post

gate

Limers Gate

posts

gate

Howroyd Spa

Wash Pits Scout

stile

Reaps Moss

sign

fenced holes

posts

wet

Range Hoyle

Raven Nest Hill

post

sign

line of posts

waterfall

Spa Hill

boundary stone

post

Weather Hill Gulf

Raven Nest Clough

Raven Nest Hill

post

boundary stones

Limers Gate

sign

coal pits

post

post

post

coal pits

post

wet

Three Nooks

ladder

post

sign

pool

post

post

gate

Freeholds Top (454m)

Limers Gate

gate

pool

stiles

trig

gate

gate

Freeholds Top Coal Mine ruins

gate

post

pool

wet

Trough Edge End

Trough Edge

Foul Clough Colliery (ruin)

stoops

coal pits

A new permissive path uncertainly crosses **Maden Pasture** to descend steeply to the old **Bay Horse**. A clearer alternative is to head straight down the wall from a gate off Limers Gate – one of the driest routes off the ridge. The main route follows a line of posts down to **Howroyd Clough**, but is soggy.

The mining track most of the way up to the top of Freeholds Top is often referred to as **Limers' Gate**. However, only part of it follows the route of the old packhorse trail, which branched off at Reaps Moss then ran along the bridleway west of the summit.

The road between Gauxholme and Bacup, known as **Dulesgate**, was an important local coal mining centre. Small collieries existed at Clough Head, South Grain (also known as Tunnel End or Kidnapper coal pit) and across Todmorden Moor, while brickworks and mills lined the narrow valley throughout the 19th century. Dulesgate was also an important carters' route between Lancashire and Yorkshire, fuelling the existence of three pubs in the valley. The highest of these was the **Bay Horse**, nestled beneath drift mines; a cave still visible in the wall behind the building served as its cellar. At one time it was owned by the Rock Springs Brewery in Gauxholme, before shutting its doors in 1937.

A wet and rather tedious path follows the boundary wall/fence between **Freeholds Top** and **Clough Head**, offering only the odd boundary stone and glimpses into Lancashire. The better route is the old mining track, reached from the summit by following a sporadic line of posts across the bog. It soon drops down to the first of a series of coal pits scarring the face of the hill. Another route has recently developed along the top of a spur the other side of **Weather Hill Gulf**, formed largely by trail bikes, it nonetheless represents a good (if slightly soggy) route of descent. The broad path is picked up at **Three Nooks** between the tops of Freeholds Top and Weather Hill (though it may be drier to cut the corner somewhat) and heads clearly across the high ground to the steep edges above **Range Hoyle**. Sheeptracks curve down to join a clear path below the waterfall that links up with the main routes down Gorpley Clough.

Inchfield Coal Mines, the remains or sites of which can be seen below Freeholds Top or at the head of Foul Clough, were operated from 1792 until the late 19th century by the Haigh family. They are all drift mines, opencast and cut into the side of a hill. Their development led to a village springing up around the large house at Coolam, built to house colliers and their families, most of whom came over from Shawforth. Reuben Haigh shrewdly opened the Moorcock (which was known as High Wicken Farm until then) as a pub on the site to regather his workers' wages. It was a raucous local beerhouse in the hills, much like many others that lay along routes across the moors, such as the one at Pot Oven known as the Brown Cow. It was not unknown for workers to freeze to death on the moors having drunk in these beerhouses – a Mr Woodhead collapsed half-naked on Inchfield Moor having thought he'd reached his bed.

CONTINUATION ON FREEHOLDS

The northern side of Freeholds Top is dominated by Gorpley Reservoir and Clough, one of the finest valleys in the South Pennines. Few places have as majestic rock precipices as those on the southern shore of Gorpley Reservoir, while waterfalls nestle in the woods below and at Lange Hoyle above. These steep flanks are in sharp contrast to the wet plateau of Inchfield Pasture and the broad ridge on which the trig point stands. The moor, though, is generally very accessible, with clear paths leading up from Walsden, Gorpley Clough and Dulesgate, as well as more adventurous routes exploring the hillsides in between. Freeholds Top is a natural focal point for the whole moor, all routes appearing to converge there. A striking element of the landscape here are the coal pits and black spoil heaps scattered from Foul Clough Road to Dulesgate, the remains of 19th century drift mines that ensured these moors were once far more populated and busy than they are today.

*If, like me, you are drawn to the rocky scars on the southern side of **Gorpley Reservoir**, there are a couple of options open to you. The best route heads up the left-hand edge of the dam (you'll need to duck down on the reservoir-side to avoid a drain) and follows the shore to the bottom of **Oatley Hill Scar**. A path leads up the wall/fence to a point where many have ducked under the wire and then continues up the edge of the scar. A number of paths lead across the hillside from here towards **Raven Nest Hill**, the lower ones leading to an easy step-over the fence to explore these myriad mesa-like knolls. The best onward route hugs the side of **Raven Nest Clough**; though the path is not clear, the going is not too rough and soon there are peaty sheeptracks picking their way up to Three Nooks. The other path to **Oatley Hill Scar** follows the line of pylons across the hillside from Foul Clough Road. It is intermittent at its high point, but rewards you by emerging above the scar's great edges.*

N

0   300
metres

to Todmorden
(1 mile)

*The rights of way across **Inchfield Pasture** are marked by lines of yellow posts, but a more obvious and drier path passes via **Shaw Stone** (a disappointing outcrop).*

Iron was extracted from exposed ore throughout the Iron, Roman and Dark Ages. A farm called Furnace was submerged beneath **Ramsden Clough Reservoir** and several lumps of cast iron were unearthed nearby. Abraham Newell records cinders of slag iron being evidence of bloomeries in Gorpley Clough, Beaumont Clough and at Jackson Rock. This may also be the source of the names Pot Oven, Red Clough and Reddyshore Scout (near Summit).

Foul Clough Road was built to link the Inchfield Coal Mines with the turnpike - indeed Inchfield Road was known as t'Coil Gate. The continuation past Top-of-All was built in the 1860s during the cotton famine, when workers were kept busy on such apparently aimless projects as these. It was not used until a mine was opened on Ramsden Hill in the 1920s.

to Walsden
(½ mile)

The most obvious route up **Freeholds Top** from Walsden follows **Foul Clough Road** before forking right past the haunting towers of Coolam, and then again to pass the coal mine ruins and climb straight up to the summit. The main alternative leaves Foul Clough Road earlier, at a sign beneath the power lines, and pulls up the side of **Weather Hill** to reach the top.

— the ruins of Coolam

Map labels:
Gorpley Farm, chimney, stile, stile, Stones Wood House, gate, bridge, bridge, waterfalls, Gorpley Mill (ruins), A681, Stoneswood Mill, sign, Dean Farm, gates, Gorpley Clough, bridges, stile, gate gate, electric gate, Howroyd, stile, Water Treatment Works, line of posts, sign, Gorpley Clough Reservoir, gates, step over, step under fence, pylon, Shaw Stone, Oatley Hill Scar, pylon, Inchfield Pasture, fold, line of posts, Naze Road (to Gauxholme), gate, sign, Long Causeway (causey), line of posts, Pasture Side Farm, sign & gate, gate, Oatley Hill, pylon, line of posts, Weather Hill, post, stile, no stile, pylon, sign, sign, delf, line of posts, sign, gate, gate, Brown Road Farm, cattle grid, sign, stoop, Thornsgreese, Pot Oven, feeders, Vicarage (ruin), gate, Higher Ditches, Red Clough, Lower Ditches, stoop, gate, Coolam falls (ruin), Moorcock (ruin), gap, Top-of-All (ruin), Under Clough, Ramsden Clough Reservoir (disused), Foul Clough Road, B stile, P

Ramsden Clough Reservoir was decommissioned in 2003 because there was too much peat in the water. It was subsequently drained, leaving the peculiar grey basin we now see. A private company, Todmorden Water Works Company, built the reservoir in the 1880s and later sold it to the Rochdale Corporation, meaning that Gorpley Clough had to be built to supply Todmorden.

Getting up from **Cranberry Dam** to the **Long Causeway** is not straightforward. The easiest route follows the track up to Horsepasture, then crosses a stile to follow an angled groove across the hillside. In descent this path is easily missed, but can be joined by dropping down from a gap where the Long Causeway reaches the wall. A slightly rougher alternative follows a wall along the side of a steep ravine to the north. Crossing a stile in the clough, climb straight up the steep slope to the right to join the wall; eventually cross it when the ground completely drops away. Otherwise you need to head up towards **Middle Ramsden** to follow paths up the hillside opposite.

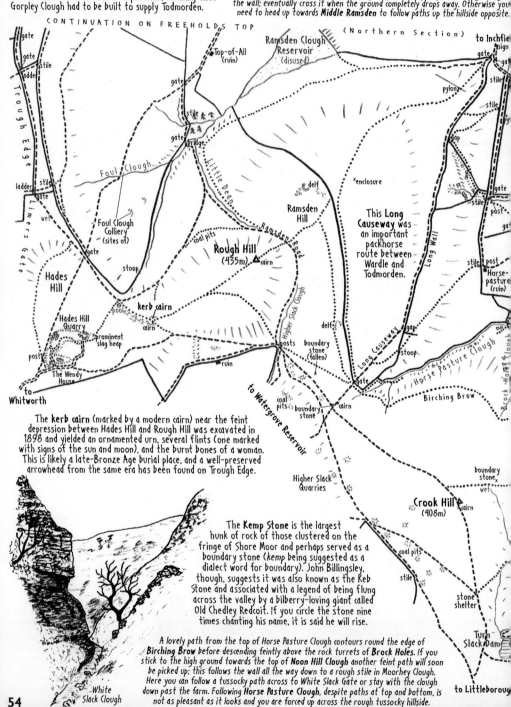

CONTINUATION ON FREEHOLDS TOP (Northern Section)

to Inchfield

Ramsden Clough Reservoir (disused)

Top-of-All (ruin)

Trough Edge

Foul Clough

Little Dean

Foul Clough Colliery (sites of)

Ramsden Hill

Limers Gate

Ramsden Road

Rough Hill (435m) ▲ cairn

coal pits

stoop

Hades Hill

kerb cairn

cairn

pool

Hades Hill Quarry

prominent slag heap

The Wendy House

to Whitworth

ruin

posts

enclosure

delf

This **Long Causeway** was an important packhorse route between Wardle and Todmorden.

Higher Slack Clough

delf

boundary stone (fallen)

Long Wall

Long Causeway

stoop

gate

Horse-pasture (ruin)

post

Horse Pasture Clough

Birching Brow

Brock Holes Clough

to Watergrove Reservoir

coal pits

boundary stone

cairn

The **kerb cairn** (marked by a modern cairn) near the feint depression between Hades Hill and Rough Hill was excavated in 1898 and yielded an ornamented urn, several flints (one marked with signs of the sun and moon), and the burnt bones of a woman. This is likely a late-Bronze Age burial place, and a well-preserved arrowhead from the same era has been found on Trough Edge.

Higher Slack Quarries

boundary stone

wet

Crook Hill (408m) ▲ cairn

coal pits

The **Kemp Stone** is the largest hunk of rock of those clustered on the fringe of Shore Moor and perhaps served as a boundary stone (kemp being suggested as a dialect word for boundary). John Billingsley, though, suggests it was also known as the Keb Stone and associated with a legend of being flung across the valley by a bilberry-loving giant called Old Chedley Redcoit. If you circle the stone nine times chanting his name, it is said he will rise.

stile

stone shelter

Turn Slack Dam

A lovely path from the top of Horse Pasture Clough contours round the edge of **Birching Brow** before descending feintly above the rock turrets of **Brock Holes**. If you stick to the high ground towards the top of **Noon Hill Clough** another feint path will soon be picked up; this follows the wall all the way down to a rough stile in Moorhey Clough. Here you can follow a tussocky path across to White Slack Gate or stay with the clough down past the farm. Following **Horse Pasture Clough**, despite paths at top and bottom, is not as pleasant as it looks and you are forced up across the rough tussocky hillside.

White Slack Clough

to Littleborough

FREEHOLDS TOP MAP - Southern Section (Shore Moor)

The moortops here straggle messily towards Greater Manchester, but they are not without interest. The lonely peat ridges here offer better walking than Todmorden Moor and the cloughs between them are among the most dramatic in the South Pennines. The large basin holding Cranberry Dam is particularly interesting, with a series of rocky scars climbing up to the tops while the shapely canyon of White Slack Clough drops away below. One thing to bear in mind, though, is that virtually this whole area of moorland will soon be the site of a large wind farm. Though plans for three turbines on a site on Reaps Moss just north of Freeholds Top were rejected, Coronation Power are building twelve turbines on Shore Moor and I wouldn't be surprised if more developments followed along this exposed ridge.

White Slack Clough is possibly the most beautiful rocky cleft in the South Pennines, short but amazingly dramatic. Its course can be followed from a stile at the bottom of the quarry above Ramsden Wood, a feint path leading to the lowest of a series of waterfalls. Above this, it is a case of following the course of the stream between rocky turrets until your course is blocked by the secluded higher falls. Another feint path angles up from the lower falls to White Slack Edge with further great views.

None of the routes between Moorhey Flat and the Long Causeway are entirely straightforward. A clear path runs up Moor Bank Clough to the Kemp Stone, then bends left over to Allenden Hill and Fox Stones before descending towards Littleborough. To stay on the high ground, you can look for a rough path heading off to the right near the top of Owler Clough; once on top of Great Hill, a wet scar continues across the peaty hilltop to Stubley Cross and Crook Hills. The alternative is to pick up a feint path north from Fox Stones; this crosses the larger path from Allenden Hill, then bends left around a finely-balanced stack of stones. Here you can bear right up to Great Hill or contour round to join the line of an old conduit leading to Turn Slack Dam.

RAMSDEN WOOD
sign
stile
post
to Walsden
(¼ mile)
post
gate
Jack Wood
post
stile
quarry
Middle Ramsden (ruin)
White Slack Edge
pylon
stile
post
waterfall
large stoop
to Walsden
(¼ mile)
gate
gate
Lower Allescholes
White Slack Gate
blue car
pylon
wet ladder
pylon
stake
Higher Allescholes
to Walsden
(¼ mile)
Stone House Bridge
sign
Rough Stones Farm
gate
shaft
gate
B
A6033
N
stiles
waterfalls
White Slack (ruin)
pylon
pylon
Friezland
post
post
shaft
P
Cranberry Dam
Moor Hey Farm
gate
milestone
sign
shaft
wet
Bird i'th Hand
Noon Hill
locked gate
rough stile
gates
pylon
shaft
posts
pylon
stile
gate
B
to Little-borough
(2½ miles)
Noon Hill Clough
Moorhey Clough
Moorhey Flat
wet causeway
Brock Holes
Ferny Hill
gate
Kemp Stone
Moor Bank Clough
Great Hill
wet
rushes
stoops
Owler Clough
Stubley Cross Hill
peat hag
boundary stone
peat hags
ruin
Allenden Hill
delf
conduit
Blue Pot Clough
heap of stones
heap of stones
gate
to Summit
Fox Stones
Cuckoo Hill
Forest (ruin)

0   300
metres

the Kemp Stone

4 Whichever path you take at the top of Gorpley Clough, it emerges on a track opposite the water treatment works. Despite the presence of paths, access along the immediate shore of Gorpley Clough Reservoir is unclear, so this route goes as close as possible while still providing great views of the scars on the opposite shore. Follow the track right at the water works up to a T-junction, then head left to pass Keepers Lodge at Howroyd. The track climbs from the second gate for 100m; where it bends slightly right, bear left onto a feint path along a grassy level. Passing through a gap in the wall, the path contours round the hillside and aims for the waterfall at the head of Howroyd Clough.

to Bacup (3 miles)

Stones Wood House

Stones Wood

stile

waterfalls   bridge   bridge

Gorpley Mill (ruin)

A681   gate

bridge

electric gate

gate

Howroyd

Water Works

gate & sign   bridges

sign

4

Gorpley Clough

gap

Gorpley Clough Reservoir

3 Continue past Frith's Farm and, at a junction by the ruined building beyond, head straight on into the field. Follow the hillside across and bear slightly left beyond the next wall to reach a metal kissing gate. A lovely path through Stones Wood eventually drops down to the main road, 200m up which is Gorpley Clough car park. Take the gate from the car park and follow a path up the steep ravine, criss-crossing the stream a number of times.

5   quarry   gate   Tramway   (line of)

post   Howroyd Clough   wet

line of posts

Range Hoyle

Wash Pits Scout

Raven Nest Hill

sign

sign   coal pits   coal pits

coal pits

post

Gorpley Clough Reservoir was built in the 1900s and was originally planned to have a twin above. This route joins the line of a railway that ran along the north shore, supplying stone from a quarry at the head of the clough.

5 At the small quarry at the end of the former tramway line, the path bends left across a small stream. At the top of the bank, look for a path right following the line of the stream up to a broken down wall. Head straight on towards the first of a line of posts leading up the soggy moorland slope. Turn left at the old mining track and follow it round the hillside past a number of coal pits. Just before the last of these, fork right to skirt above the scree and join a line of sporadic posts leading across to the summit of Freeholds Top.

posts

gate   trig   pool

Freeholds Top
(454m)   **6**

6 From the trig point, continue along the ridge, forking right around the end of the pool by the summit. The path follows the high ground and soon joins the fenceline that marks the county boundary. Follow this for some distance, passing a couple of stiles before climbing slightly again to reach a gate near the top of Hades Hill. Through the gate, turn left to continue along the fenceline. Where the fence bends round to the left, head straight on past some slight delfs to reach a modern cairn marking the site of an ancient ring cairn. Turn left here, dropping down across a boggy depression to reach the high ground of Rough Hill, marked by another satisfying cairn.

wet

broken wall

stile

Trough Edge

stile

7 From the cairn on Rough Hill, drop down to another depression and turn right, curving round towards Watergrove Reservoir with Greater Manchester beyond. Dropping down to a major junction in Higher Slack Clough, turn left and keep left at a second post, staying above the coal pits to reach a boundary stone on the Long Causeway. Head straight across, climbing steadily on to reach the top of Crook Hill near a small cairn at a bend in the path.

stile

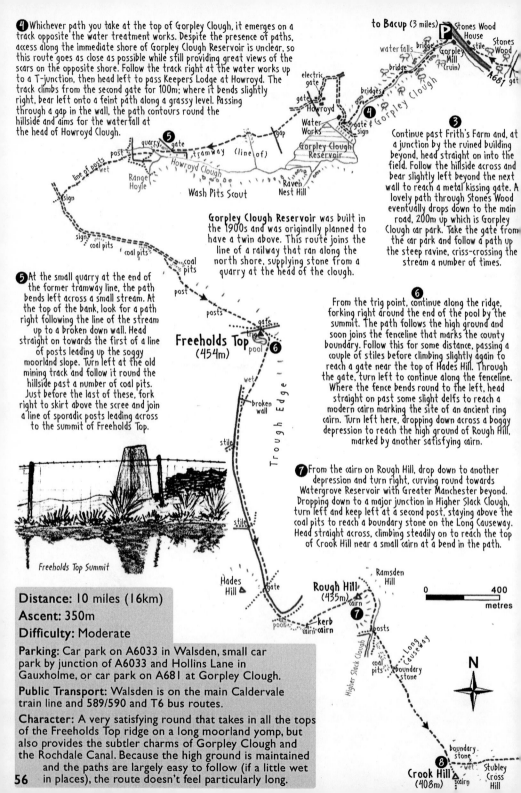

Freeholds Top Summit

Hades Hill   gate

pool   cairn   cairn

Ramsden Hill

Rough Hill
(435m)   **7**

cairn

kerb   posts

0   400
metres

Distance: 10 miles (16km)

Ascent: 350m

Difficulty: Moderate

Parking: Car park on A6033 in Walsden, small car park by junction of A6033 and Hollins Lane in Gauxholme, or car park on A681 at Gorpley Clough.

Public Transport: Walsden is on the main Caldervale train line and 589/590 and T6 bus routes.

Character: A very satisfying round that takes in all the tops of the Freeholds Top ridge on a long moorland yomp, but also provides the subtler charms of Gorpley Clough and the Rochdale Canal. Because the high ground is maintained and the paths are largely easy to follow (if a little wet in places), the route doesn't feel particularly long.

Higher Slack Clough

coal pits   boundary stone

Long Causeway

N

boundary stone   wet   Stubley Cross Hill

8   cairn

Crook Hill
(408m)

ROUTE 9: FREEHOLDS TOP, GORPLEY CLOUGH & SHORE MOOR FROM WALSDEN

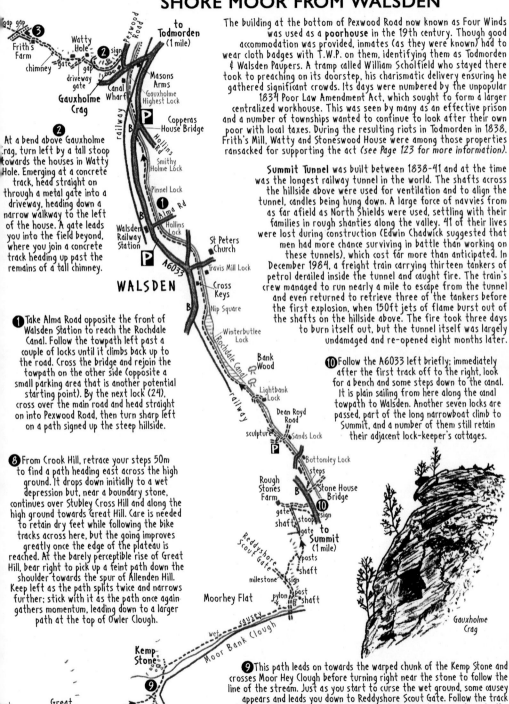

At a bend above Gauxholme Crag, turn left by a tall stoop towards the houses in Watty Hole. Emerging at a concrete track, head straight on through a metal gate into a driveway, heading down a narrow walkway to the left of the house. A gate leads you into the field beyond, where you join a concrete track heading up past the remains of a tall chimney.

The building at the bottom of Pexwood Road now known as Four Winds was used as a **poorhouse** in the 19th century. Though good accommodation was provided, inmates (as they were known) had to wear cloth badges with T.W.P. on them, identifying them as Todmorden & Walsden Paupers. A tramp called William Scholfield who stayed there took to preaching on its doorstep, his charismatic delivery ensuring he gathered significant crowds. Its days were numbered by the unpopular 1834 Poor Law Amendment Act, which sought to form a larger centralized workhouse. This was seen by many as an effective prison and a number of townships wanted to continue to look after their own poor with local taxes. During the resulting riots in Todmorden in 1838, Frith's Mill, Watty and Stoneswood House were among those properties ransacked for supporting the act (see Page 123 for more information).

Summit Tunnel was built between 1838-41 and at the time was the longest railway tunnel in the world. The shafts across the hillside above were used for ventilation and to align the tunnel, candles being hung down. A large force of navvies from as far afield as North Shields were used, settling with their families in rough shanties along the valley. 41 of their lives were lost during construction (Edwin Chadwick suggested that men had more chance surviving in battle than working in these tunnels), which cost far more than anticipated. In December 1984, a freight train carrying thirteen tankers of petrol derailed inside the tunnel and caught fire. The train's crew managed to run nearly a mile to escape from the tunnel and even returned to retrieve three of the tankers before the first explosion, when 150ft jets of flame burst out of the shafts on the hillside above. The fire took three days to burn itself out, but the tunnel itself was largely undamaged and re-opened eight months later.

1 Take Alma Road opposite the front of Walsden Station to reach the Rochdale Canal. Follow the towpath left past a couple of locks until it climbs back up to the road. Cross the bridge and rejoin the towpath on the other side (opposite a small parking area that is another potential starting point). By the next lock (24), cross over the main road and head straight on into Pexwood Road, then turn sharp left on a path signed up the steep hillside.

10 Follow the A6033 left briefly; immediately after the first track off to the right, look for a bench and some steps down to the canal. It is plain sailing from here along the canal towpath to Walsden. Another seven locks are passed, part of the long narrowboat climb to Summit, and a number of them still retain their adjacent lock-keeper's cottages.

8 From Crook Hill, retrace your steps 50m to find a path heading east across the high ground. It drops down initially to a wet depression but, near a boundary stone, continues over Stubley Cross Hill and along the high ground towards Great Hill. Care is needed to retain dry feet while following the bike tracks across here, but the going improves greatly once the edge of the plateau is reached. At the barely perceptible rise of Great Hill, bear right to pick up a feint path down the shoulder towards the spur of Allenden Hill. Keep left as the path splits twice and narrows further; stick with it as the path once again gathers momentum, leading down to a larger path at the top of Owler Clough.

9 This path leads on towards the warped chunk of the Kemp Stone and crosses Moor Hey Clough before turning right near the stone to follow the line of the stream. Just as you start to curse the wet ground, some causey appears and leads you down to Reddyshore Scout Gate. Follow the track left for 200m, then join the Pennine Bridleway as it zigzags down to the line of ventilation shafts above Summit Tunnel. Turn left and pass through a couple of gate before turning right down to the main road.

57

The **ring ouzel** is a migratory mountain thrush closely
related to the blackbird (indeed ouzel is an old name
for the common blackbird). The ring refers to the
white band around is neck; otherwise it is largely black
with a yellow bill. It tends to nest among boulders or
crags and is most likely seen in steep-sided cloughs
like those found around the edge of Freeholds Top,
though it is a particularly shy and skittish bird.

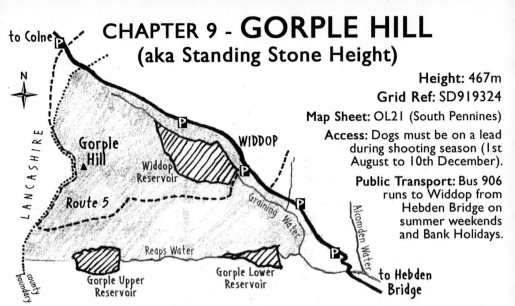

CHAPTER 9 - GORPLE HILL
(aka Standing Stone Height)

Height: 467m

Grid Ref: SD919324

Map Sheet: OL21 (South Pennines)

Access: Dogs must be on a lead during shooting season (1st August to 10th December).

Public Transport: Bus 906 runs to Widdop from Hebden Bridge on summer weekends and Bank Holidays.

Gorple Hill is the wedge of moor squeezed between Widdop and the Gorple Reservoirs and straddling the Lancashire-Yorkshire boundary. Here the Pennines seem like an undulating ridge of hills with Hoof Stones Height and the Black Hameldon ridge rising impressively to the south and Boulsworth Hill to the north. Seen from the east, Gorple Hill is the shapely dome in the middle of the ridge. Though its summit is something of a boggy plateau above the crags of Gorple Stones, it has dramatic rock-scarred faces on many sides and some of the best climbing and bouldering sites in the South Pennines, with the parapets of Cludders Slack towering above the beautiful moorland road between Hebden Bridge and Colne. Gorple Hill is a long way from any real settlement and it is a full day's walk to take in these heights without using the bus or a car up to Widdop. Once here, though, there is plenty of easy moorland walking and the potential for satisfying round routes makes it worthy of a day out.

The name Gorple has been suggested to mean 'upper pile' or even 'bloody pile' (from Anglo-Saxon, possibly referring to the scattered mass of Gorple Stones on the southern face of the hill), but may also come from the Celtic *gor* (moor) and *pwl* (pool) - indeed gorcock is another name for the red grouse. Gorpill Hill was one of the few Pennine hills marked on Saxton's map of 1579 and it is from here I've salvaged the name.

Gorple Hill and the Pennine watershed from Reaps Bottom

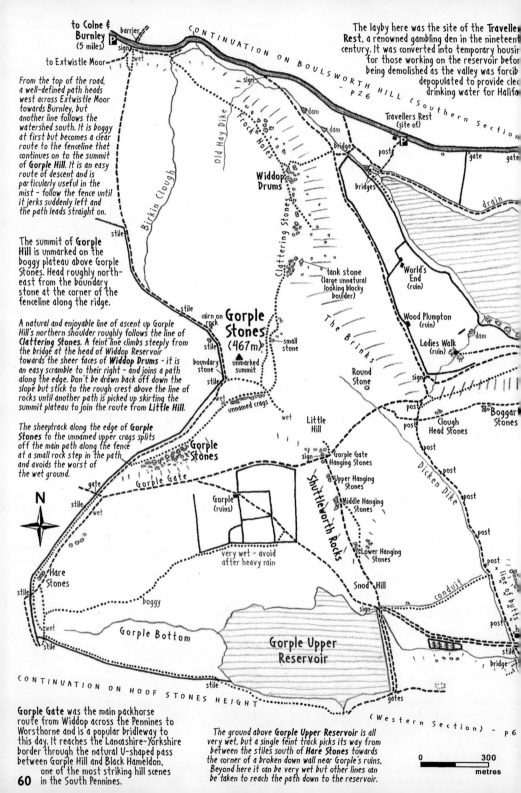

to Colne & Burnley (5 miles)

to Extwistle Moor

CONTINUATION ON BOULSWORTH HILL - P26 (Southern Section)

The layby here was the site of the **Travellers Rest**, a renowned gambling den in the nineteenth century. It was converted into temporary housing for those working on the reservoir before being demolished as the valley was forcibly depopulated to provide clean drinking water for Halifax.

From the top of the road, a well-defined path heads west across Extwistle Moor towards Burnley, but another line follows the watershed south. It is boggy at first but becomes a clear route to the fenceline that continues on to the summit of **Gorple Hill**. It is an easy route of descent and is particularly useful in the mist - follow the fence until it jerks suddenly left and the path leads straight on.

The summit of **Gorple Hill** is unmarked on the boggy plateau above Gorple Stones. Head roughly north-east from the boundary stone at the corner of the fenceline along the ridge.

A natural and enjoyable line of ascent up Gorple Hill's northern shoulder roughly follows the line of **Clattering Stones**. A feint line climbs steeply from the bridge at the head of Widdop Reservoir towards the sheer faces of **Widdop Drums** - it is an easy scramble to their right - and joins a path along the edge. Don't be drawn back off down the slope but stick to the rough crest above the line of rocks until another path is picked up skirting the summit plateau to join the route from **Little Hill**.

The sheeptrack along the edge of **Gorple Stones** to the unnamed upper crags splits off the main path along the fence at a small rock step in the path and avoids the worst of the wet ground.

Gorple Gate was the main packhorse route from Widdop across the Pennines to Worsthorne and is a popular bridleway to this day. It reaches the Lancashire-Yorkshire border through the natural U-shaped pass between Gorple Hill and Black Hameldon, one of the most striking hill scenes in the South Pennines.

The ground above **Gorple Upper Reservoir** is all very wet, but a single feint track picks its way from between the stiles south of **Hare Stones** towards the corner of a broken down wall near Gorple's ruins. Beyond here it can be very wet but other lines can be taken to reach the path down to the reservoir.

Map labels:
barrier · sign · wet · sign · dam · dam · bridge · Travellers Rest (site of) · post · gate · gate · Old Hay Dike · Frock Holes · Widdop Drums · bridges · drain · Clattering Stones · Birkin Clough · stile · World's End (ruin) · tank stone (large unnatural looking blocky boulder) · Wood Plumpton (ruin) · Ladies Walk (ruin) · dam · stile · cairn on rock · **Gorple Stones (467m)** · small stone · The Brinks · boundary stone · unmarked summit · Round Stone · stile · stile · wet · unnamed crags · wet · Little Hill · sign · post · post · Clough Head Stones · Boggart Stones · **Gorple Stones** · Gorple Gate · gate · sign · Gorple Gate Hanging Stones · Upper Hanging Stones · Shuttleworth Rocks · Dicken Dike · post · post · post · stile · wet · Gorple (ruins) · Middle Hanging Stones · post · Lower Hanging Stones · Hare Stones · very wet - avoid after heavy rain · Snod Hill · conduit · line of butts · post · N · stile · boggy · Gorple Bottom · sign · Gorple Upper Reservoir · gates · stile · bridge · wet · stile · CONTINUATION ON HOOF STONES HEIGHT · stile · (Western Section) - P6

0 — 300 metres

60

GORPLE HILL MAP - Entire Moor

Gorple Hill is a well-trodden moor; though its summit is off the beaten track, the rocky fringes above Widdop and Gorple Reservoirs are easily accessed. Most of the moor is strewn with interesting rock features; beyond the well-known Cludders and Shuttleworth Rocks, it is worth seeking out the Widdop Drums, two Round Stones or Gorple Stones.

The collection of rock towers that draw rock-climbers and walkers alike to Widdop are known by many names, from Widdop Rocks to Cludders Slack. In fact, they are **the Cludders** (a *cludder* being a mass of rock) and the slack refers to the gentler slope below. Chief among the rocks of the Cludders is the rocking stone known as the Rocking Pig, which sits atop a narrow vertical slab, the ascent of which is said to be one of the hardest on gritstone in the country. The large boulders on the slack below are also a popular site for bouldering.

Widdop is a contraction of 'wide hope', a *hope* being a hollow in the hills, but the scattered hamlet here was abandoned with the construction of the reservoir. Despite being so remote, there was obviously enough of a population for John Wesley to deem it worth visiting twice, the latter commemorated on a rock by the dam marked J.W. 1766 and known as Wesley's Pulpit. Construction began on the dam in 1871, utilising a horse-drawn tramway along the hillside from Shackleton (a remnant of which can be seen on the raised area opposite the car park, though not on the original line of the tramway). Some 200 navvies worked on the project and were housed in a wooden shanty town, which was known as Navvyopolis and located by Well Hole. The Mayor of Halifax opened the reservoir in 1878, though it is smaller than originally planned as a dam could not satisfactorily be constructed across the narrow Notch.

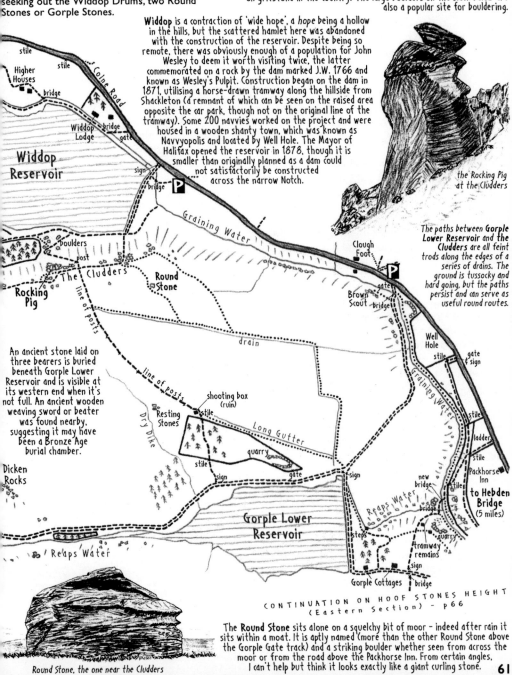

the Rocking Pig at the Cludders

The paths between **Gorple Lower Reservoir** and **the Cludders** are all feint trods along the edges of a series of drains. The ground is tussocky and hard going, but the paths persist and can serve as useful round routes.

An ancient stone laid on three bearers is buried beneath Gorple Lower Reservoir and is visible at its western end when it's not full. An ancient wooden weaving sword or beater was found nearby, suggesting it may have been a Bronze Age burial chamber.

(map labels): stile · Higher Houses · stile · bridge · Colne Road · bridge · gate · Widdop Lodge · sign · bridge · P · Widdop Reservoir · Graining Water · boulders · post · The Cludders · Rocking Pig · line of posts · Round Stone · Clough Foot · P · gate · Brown Scout · bridge · Well Hole · stile · gate & sign · drain · line of posts · Dry Dike · Resting Stones · shooting box (ruin) · stile · Long Gutter · Graining Water · stile · ladder · stile · stile · quarry · Packhorse Inn · Dicken Rocks · stile · sign · gate · sign · new bridge · stile · to Hebden Bridge (5 miles) · Reaps Water · bridge · Gorple Lower Reservoir · quarry · Reaps Water · steps · tramway remains · sign · Gorple Cottages · bridge

CONTINUATION ON HOOF STONES HEIGHT
(Eastern Section) - p66

The **Round Stone** sits alone on a squelchy bit of moor - indeed after rain it sits within a moat. It is aptly named (more than the other Round Stone above the Gorple Gate track) and a striking boulder whether seen from across the moor or from the road above the Packhorse Inn. From certain angles, I can't help but think it looks exactly like a giant curling stone.

Round Stone, the one near the Cludders

FELL RUNNING & RACING

Among those who make fullest use of the moorland spaces opened up since 2000 are the fell runners. While it is of course not a new sport, it is as popular now as its ever been. Certain feint paths that I have been hard pushed to account for turn out to have been worn by hundreds of fell-runners that you see filing across the skylines usually left to the sheep and grouse. It is something I have been drawn to since moving to the area; once you reach the moorland (the difficult bit!), it offers lovely, springy ground and gently undulating slopes and a real sense of escape from the clutter of the valleys far below. It often feels that these moors were made for running on.

Fell running grew out of the Guides Races that were held in the Dales and the Lake District from the early nineteenth century. These races were just some of the trials of strength competed in at local shows and, in hilly country, it made sense to race to the top of the nearest hill and back. Initially, like all sports, it was closely linked to gambling - there are plenty of tales of locals obstructing the leader and influencing the outcome. Similar races doubtless took place at local events in West Yorkshire as well, though none have survived to this day. A fell race is recorded as part of the Lammas Fair that took place at the Hitching Stone in the mid-nineteenth century — men from the villages of Cowling and Sutton charged across the moss and back between the Hitching and Navax Stones.

Fell running only became a sport in the twentieth century with the formation of amateur running clubs and races officially sanctioned by the Amateur Athletic Association. Holmfirth Harriers is the oldest fell running club in the area, having continued since 1907 (although Halifax Harriers is over 125 years old and has a fell running arm); it dwindled like many other clubs in the 1950s and 60s, but it kept going and now has a booming 700-strong membership. Other lapsed clubs re-formed in the 1970s, such as the Harriers of Ilkley, while many new clubs have sprung up since.

West Yorkshire now boasts a very full fell running calendar as more and more people want to take part in events; the average field numbers in the hundreds. The Stoodley Pike Fell Race is possibly the oldest established in the area, a short haul up and down the pike from Lumbutts established in the 1970s. Many others have been running for 25 years, like the Holme Moss Fell Race, the Easter Bunny Runs around Penistone Hill, while the Auld Lang Syne from Haworth on December 31st was established in the early 90s. The area even has its own version of the Bob Graham Round; the South Pennine 39 Trigs is 105 miles long and includes some 20,000ft of ascent, though it has yet to be completed in under 24 hours. The Haworth Hobble (or Wuthering Hike) has been shortened from 44 to 32 miles, but is still an ultra-marathon, likewise the Calderdale Hike. The ultimate test of endurance is The Spine, a seven-day race along the length of the Pennine Way in January each year that brands itself 'Britain's most brutal race'.

CHAPTER 10 - HOOF STONES HEIGHT
(aka Black Hameldon)

Height: 479m

Grid Ref: SD914291

Map Sheet: OL21 (South Pennines)

Access: No access to Hawks Stones during lambing season (5th April to 17th May).

Public Transport: Buses E & 517 run from Hebden Bridge to Colden, Blackshaw Head /Kebcote. Bus CT runs from Todmorden to Cross Stone/Blackshaw Head. Bus 906 runs from Hebden Bridge to Widdop on summer weekends and Bank Holidays.

The trig point at **Hoof Stones Height** crowns a great swathe of moorland, starting at Popples Common near Heptonstall and arcing right round to Bride Stones Moor and Whirlaw Rocks just above Todmorden. The name would appear to be a corruption of Hoar Stones Height – it is marked as Hoat Stones Height on the 1843 map and Hoar Side Moor lies on its east flank. Hoar (sometimes spelt Hoor) Stones, like Hare Stones just to the north, comes from an Old English word *har* relating to a boundary and appears frequently in the South Pennines. The summit ridge, a wall of dark peat that is also referred to as Black Hameldon (evocatively meaning 'black-scarred hill'), forms the county boundary and remains a remote corner of West Yorkshire. Unlike the busy fringe of the moor, its heart is by-passed by the Pennine Way and many other major routes across the moors, yet represents one of the most natural summits in Calderdale with grand views towards Pendle and the Dales.

Hoof Stones Height rising above Reaps Water

63

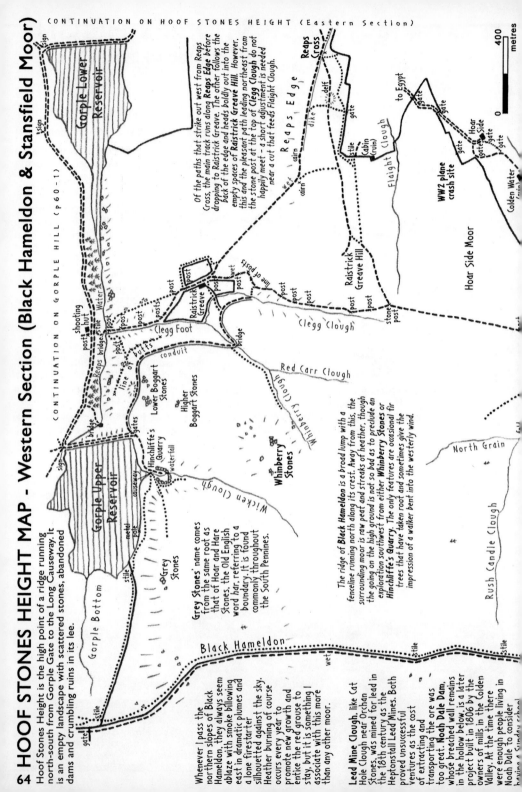

HOOF STONES HEIGHT MAP - Western Section (Black Hameldon & Stansfield Moor)

64 Hoof Stones Height is the high point of a ridge running north-south from Gorple Gate to the Long Causeway. It is an empty landscape with scattered stones, abandoned dams and crumbling ruins in its lee.

400 metres
0

Gorple Lower Reservoir

Reaps Cross

Reaps Edge

to Egypt

delf

dike

cairn

cairn

gate

gate

gate

gate

Hoar Side

Golden Water (ruin)

Of the paths that strike out west from Reaps Cross, the main track runs along **Reaps Edge** before dropping to Raistrick Greave. The other follows the back of the edge and heads boldly out into the empty spaces of **Raistrick Greave Hill**. However, this and the pleasant path leading northeast from the stone post at the top of Clegg Clough do not happily meet - a short adjustment is needed near a cut that feeds Flaight Clough.

gate

stile

Cabin (ruin)

Flaight Clough

Raistrick Greave Hill

WW2 plane crash site

Hoar Side Moor

CONTINUATION ON GORPLE HILL (p 60-1)

shooting hut

post

post

post

post

posts

post

post

post

line of posts

post

post

post

post

post

stone post

post

Water

Reaps bridge

stile

bridge

line of butts

conduit

bridge

Clegg Foot

Raistrick Greave

Clegg Clough

Red Carr Clough

Whinberry Clough

North Grain

sign

sign

sign

post

gate

Lower Boggart Stones

Higher Boggart Stones

Whinberry Stones

bridge

gates

Hinchliffe's Quarry

waterfall

causeway

metal pole

Gorple Upper Reservoir

Grey Stones

stile

Gorple Bottom

Wicken Clough

Grey Stones' name comes from the same root as that of Hoar and Hare Stones, the Old English word *har*, referring to a boundary. It is found commonly throughout the South Pennines.

The ridge of **Black Hameldon** is a broad lump with a fenceline running north along its crest. Away from this, the surrounding moor is raw peat and streaks of heather, though the going on the high ground is not so bad as to preclude an exploration southwest from either **Whinberry Stones** or **Hinchliffe's Quarry**. The only features are occasional fir trees that have taken root and sometimes give the impression of a walker bent into the westerly wind.

Black Hameldon

wet

stile

wet

stile

Rush Candle Clough

Whenever I pass the northern slopes of Black Hameldon, they always seem ablaze with smoke billowing east in dramatic plumes and a lone firestarter silhouetted against the sky. Heather burning of course occurs every year to promote new growth and entice the red grouse to stay, but it is something I associate with this more than any other moor.

Lead Mine Clough, like Cat Hole Clough near Orchan Stones, was mined for lead in the 18th century as the Heptonstall Lead Mines. Both proved unsuccessful ventures as the cost of extracting and transporting the ore was too great. **Noah Dale Dam,** whose breached wall remains in the hollow below, was a later project built in 1806 by the owners of mills in the Golden Valley. At the time there were enough people living in Noah Dale to consider

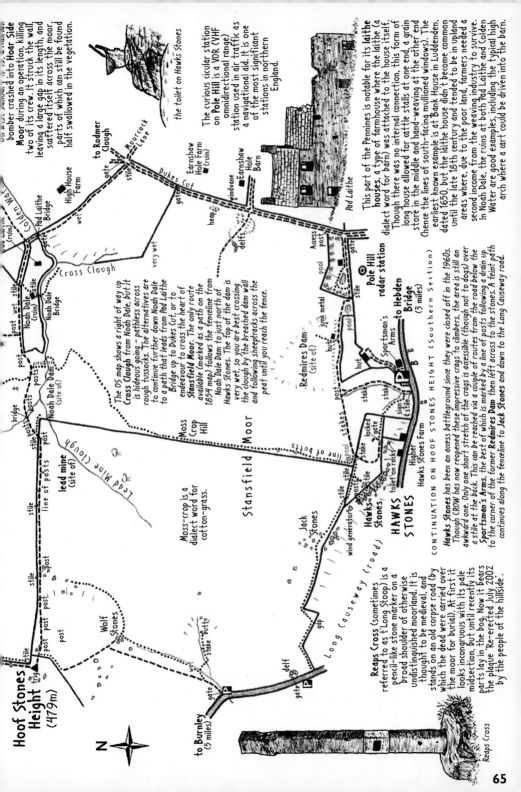

bomber crashed into **Hoar Side Moor** during an operation, killing two of its crew. It struck the wall, leaving a large gap in its length, and scattered itself across the moor, parts of which can still be found half swallowed in the vegetation.

the toilet on Hawks Stones

The curious circular station on **Pole Hill** is a VOR (VHF omnidirectional range) station used in air traffic as a navigational aid. It is one of the most significant stations in northern England.

This part of the Pennines is notable for its **laithe houses**, a type of farmhouse where the laithe (a dialect word for barn) was attached to the house itself. Though there was no internal connection, this form of long house allowed for cattle stalls at one end, a grain store in the middle and hand-weaving at the other end (hence the lines of south-facing mullioned windows). The earliest known example is at Bank House in Luddenden, dated 1650, but the laithe house didn't become common until the late 18th century and tended to be in upland areas where, due to the poor land, farmers needed a second income from the weaving industry to survive. In Noah Dale, the ruins at both **Pad Laithe** and **Golden Water** are good examples, including the typical high arch where a cart could be driven into the barn.

Pad Laithe

The OS map shows a right of way up **Cross Clough** from Noah Dale, but it is hideous going – pathless across rough tussocks. The alternatives are to continue further down Noah Dale to a path that leads from **Pad Laithe Bridge** up to Dukes Cut, or to endeavour to cross the heart of **Stansfield Moor**. The only route available (marked as a path on the 1854 map) follows the fenceline from Noah Dale Dam to just north of Hawks Stones. The top of the dam is very wet, so you are best crossing the clough by the breached dam wall and following sheeptracks across the peat until you reach the fence.

to **Rodmer Clough**

Moorcock Lane

High House Farm

gate stile

Dukes Cut

gate

Earnshaw Hole Farm (ruin)

Earnshaw Hole Barn

windvane

heap

delfs

very wet

Pad Laithe Bridge

gate

gate

Cross Clough

wet

Golden Water

(ruin)

post wet stile

Noah Dale (ruin)

post post stile

Noah Dale Bridge

bridge

stile

posts

post posts

Noah Dale Dam (site of)

stile post

line of posts

Lead Mine Clough

lead mine (site of)

Moss Crop Hill

Moss-crop is a dialect word for cotton-grass.

Stansfield Moor

Access post

gate

pool

Pole Hill radar station

stile

junk metal

pool

hut

Sportsman's Arms

to **Hebden Bridge** (3 miles)

Redmires Dam (site of)

hut

post stake

stake

stakes

sign stile

locked gate

stake

line of butts

pool

stile stake

stile stile

toilet on rocks

posts

Hawks Stones

HAWKS STONES

wind generators

Higher Hawks Stones Farm

Jack Stones

Long Causeway (road)

gap

delf

gate P

gate

to **Burnley** (5 miles)

Reaps Cross (sometimes referred to as t'Long Stoop) is a pencil-like stone marker on a broad shoulder of otherwise undistinguished moorland. It is thought to be medieval, and stands on an old corpse road (by which the dead were carried over the moor for burial). At first it looks incongruous with its pale midsection, but until recently its parts lay in the bog. Now it bears the plaque 'Re-erected July 2002 by the people of the hillside.'

Reaps Cross

Wolf Stones

post post post post

stile post post

post

stile

trig

Hoof Stones Height (479m)

N

CONTINUATION ON HOOF STONES HEIGHT (Southern Section)

Hawks Stones has been an access battleground since they were closed off in the 1960s. Though CROW has now reopened these impressive crags to climbers, the area is still an awkward one. Only one short stretch of the crags is accessible (though not to dogs) over a stile at the back. This can be reached via a couple of routes following the road below the **Sportsman's Arms**, the best of which is marked by a line of posts following a drain up to the corner of the former **Redmires Dam** then left across to the stones. A feint path continues along the fenceline from Jack Stones and down to the Long Causeway road.

stake stake
butt

65

Standing Stone Hill, the highest point on Heptonstall Moor, is a proud lump crowned by a trig point and feels quite separate from Hoof Stones Height, but it is not quite high enough to count as a moor in its own right. On its north side, the picturesque ravine of Blake Dean, where a couple of mountain streams meeting amid the bracken and heather, is one of the most recognisable corners of the South Pennines. This side of the moor is both easily accessible and understandably busy in summer, while paths leading up from Colden and Popples Common tend to peter out in Black Mires.

It is well worth exploring Blake Dean. The lower section, between the road and the top of Hardcastle Crags woodland, is busy with paths. A path along the south bank is slightly rougher going and is accessed by jumping over the low wall just before the bridge on the road in Blake Dean. The higher section, along Graining Water, is more remote but the south bank can be followed fairly easily - only one short section beneath King Common Brinks is at all rough. Although the north bank looks a better bet from the bridge near Reaps Water, a wall soon squeezes the bank in too tightly to follow.

Blake Dean Scout Hostel is part of what remains of a Baptist Chapel built in 1820 and used until 1959. The chapel itself has since been demolished, but not the cottages that served as a Sunday School nor the tiny graveyard squeezed in the elbow of the hairpin bend. So steep is the hillside that it gave rise to the local phrase downstairs to the gallery and upstairs to the bottom, and the graveyard is said to be haunted by the ghost of the green lady, a young woman who fell from the Trestle Bridge in Blake Dean.

The **Gorple Reservoirs** were built between 1927 and 1934, employing 14 steam locomotives on various tracks and inclines (sections of which can still be seen protruding from the moor). The quarries like Reaps Level were dug to find stone for the dams and the scattered remains below the Lower Reservoir include those of the navvies huts.

The stone walls across the Hebden Water near Blake Dean are actually the feet of what was an incredible structure carrying the **Hardcastle Crags Tramway** across the valley. The tramway carried men and materials from the navvies' township at Dawson City (near Heptonstall) to the Walshaw Dean Reservoirs during their construction in the early 1900s. Its line, as well as that of an earlier tramway up to Widdop, can still be seen across New Laithe Moor (the vents show the line of the conduit taking the water to Halifax). The rest of the **trestle bridge**, 105ft of height was made entirely of wood and designed, like Dawson City's wooden shanty, to last just a few years. Though sparks set it on fire on occasion, the teetering bridge never collapsed.

N

*The best line of ascent to the trig point on **Standing Stone Hill** is via the gentle depression of Ling Hollow. A path branches off the Pennine Way near a small pool and cairn, and*

Blake Dean is marked as Black Dean on some OS maps, both possibly referring to the Celtic word bedlach, meaning a pass.

to Hebden Bridge (4 miles)

Widdop Gate

Widdop Road

Hardcastle Crags (National Trust woodland)

Break Hole

New Laithe

vent

bench post

stile

gate

New Laithe Moor

Lipscomb Road

Iron Age enclosure

trestle bridge (remains)

Hebden Water

Widdop

Gypsy Holme

bridge

dike

CONTINUATION ON HEIGHT Section (Southern WITHINS)_p154

Hoar Stones

tramway vent

tramway (line of)

(line of) bridge

stile

gate

posts

post

stile

stile

Alcomden Water

line of posts

stile sign

Holme Ends

Ridge Nook

Old Harry Rocks

stile

gate stoops across stream

Blake Dean Hostel

gate

stile

plantation

post

cairn

cairn

post

stile

cairn

cairn

pool in cairn

CONTINUATION ON HILL (Southern Section) BOULSWORTH - p27

The Ridge

Packhorse Inn

to Widdop (1 mile)

ladder stile

post

Cow Shade Rocks

fold

stile

King Common Brinks

Buck Stones

King Common (ruin)

Standing Stone

Graining Water

stile

drain

bridge

bridge

aerial ropeway support

CONTINUATION ON GORPLE HILL (p61)

stile

new bridge

bridges

tramway remains

sign

Reaps Water

steps

sign

Reaps Cottages

Gorple (ruin)

Reaps Level (quarry)

Reaps Pool

pools

bridge

sign

gate

sign

Gorple Lower Reservoir

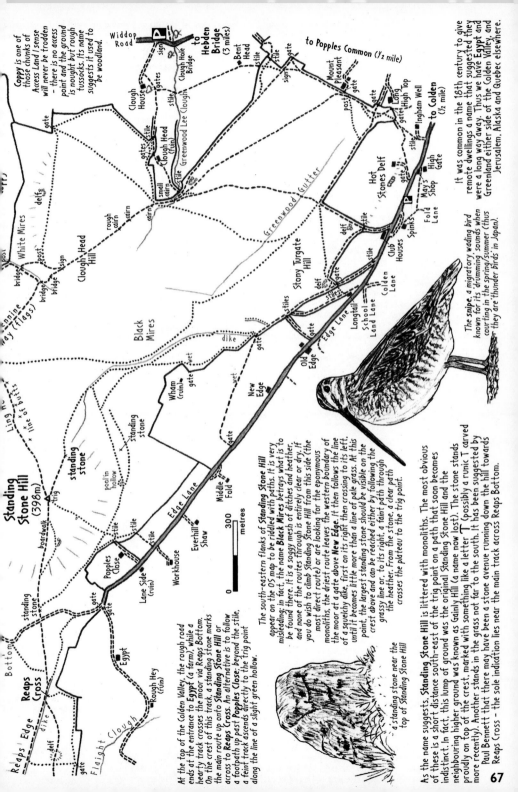

Coppy is one of those chunks of Access Land I sense will never be trodden – there is no access point and the ground is nought but rough tussocks. Its name suggests it used to be woodland.

Map labels:

Widdop Road · P · sign · to Hebden Bridge (3 miles) · to Popples Common (½ mile) · Clough Hole Bridge · gates · stile · Clough House · Greenwood Lee Clough · Clough Head (ruin) · small cairn · cairn · Bent Head · stile · gate · sign post · Mount Pleasant · gate · Long High Top · gate · Ingham Well · to Colden (½ mile) · stile · Hot Stones Delf · High Gate · May's Shop · Fold Lane · delf · Spinks · Club Houses · stile · Colden Lane · Longtail School · Land Lane · stiles · gate · Edge Lane · Old Edge · gate · dike · wet · gate · Wham (ruin) · gate · wet · New Edge · stiles · gate · Black Mires · Standing stone · Pennine Way (flags) · bridge · sign · bridge · White Mires · post · rough cairn · Clough Head Hill · delf · cairn · Greenwood Gutter · Stony Turgate Hill · delf · gate · Ling · line of butts · poolin hollow · standing stone · boardwalk · trig · Standing Stone Hill (398m) · Everhill Shaw · Middle Fold · stile · stile · Popples Close · Lane Side (ruin) · Workhouse · Reaps' Edge · Reaps Cross · Bottom · gate · standing stone · gate · Egypt · Rough Hey (ruin) · Flaight Clough · delf · gate

0 300 metres

At the top of the Colden Valley, the rough road ends at the entrance to **Egypt** (a farm), while a hearty track crosses the moor via **Reaps Bottom**. On the crest of this track, a standing stone marks the main route up onto **Standing Stone Hill** or across to **Reaps Cross**. An alternative is to follow a footpath up past **Popples Close**: beyond the stile, a feint track ascends directly to the trig point along the line of a slight green hollow.

The south-eastern flanks of **Standing Stone Hill** appear on the OS map to be riddled with paths. It is very misleading, in fact, the name **Black Mires** betrays what is to be found there. It is a saggy mesh of ditches and heather, and none of the routes through is entirely clear or dry. If you do wish to climb Standing Stone Hill from this side ('the most direct route') or are looking for the eponymous monoliths, the driest route leaves the western boundary of the moor at a gate above **New Edge**. It then follows the line of a squelchy dike, first on its right then crossing to its left, until it becomes little more than a line of pale grass. At this point, the largest standing stone should be visible on the crest above and can be reached either by following the grassy line or, to its right, a clear path through the heather. From the stone, a clear path crosses the plateau to the trig point.

It was common in the 18th century to give remote dwellings a name that suggested they were a long way away. Thus we have **Egypt** and **Greenland** either side of the Colden Valley, and Jerusalem, Alaska and Quebec elsewhere.

The **snipe**, a migratory wading bird known for its drumming sounds when courting in the spring/summer (thus they are 'thunder birds' in Japan).

As the name suggests, **Standing Stone Hill** is littered with monoliths. The most obvious of these is a short distance south-east of the trig point on a path that soon becomes indistinct. In fact, this lump of ground was the original Standing Stone Hill and the neighbouring higher ground was known as **Gainly Hill** (a name now lost). The stone stands proudly on top of the crest, marked with something like a letter T (possibly a runic T carved more recently). Another stands in the grass not far to the south. It has been suggested by Paul Bennett that there may have been a stone avenue running down the hill towards **Reaps Cross** – the sole indication lies near the main track across Reaps Bottom.

a standing stone near the top of Standing Stone Hill

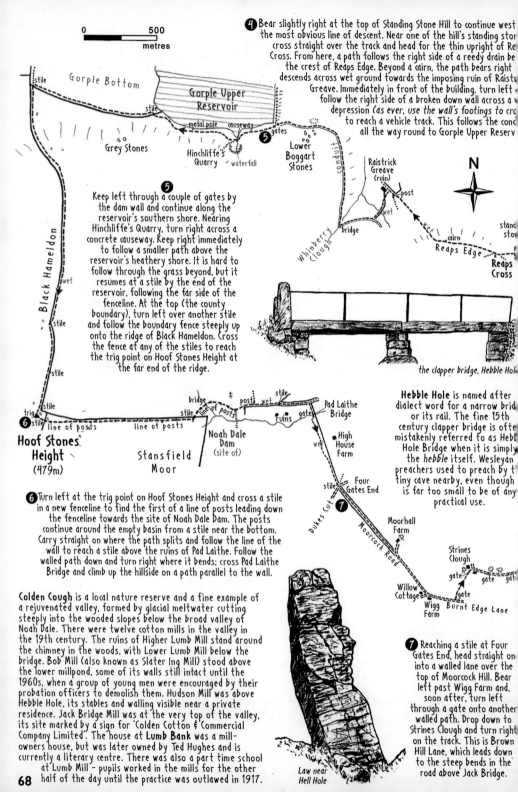

0 500 metres

4 Bear slightly right at the top of Standing Stone Hill to continue west the most obvious line of descent. Near one of the hill's standing ston cross straight over the track and head for the thin upright of Re Cross. From here, a path follows the right side of a reedy drain be the crest of Reaps Edge. Beyond a cairn, the path bears right descends across wet ground towards the imposing ruin of Raistri Greave. Immediately in front of the building, turn left follow the right side of a broken down wall across a depression (as ever, use the wall's footings to cro to reach a vehicle track. This follows the conc all the way round to Gorple Upper Reserv

Gorple Bottom

Gorple Upper Reservoir

stile

stile

metal pole   causeway

Grey Stones

Hinchliffe's Quarry   waterfall

gates

Lower Boggart Stones

Raistrick Greave (ruin)

post

wet

Whinberry Clough

bridge

cairn

Reaps Edge

Reaps Cross

stand ston

N

5 Keep left through a couple of gates by the dam wall and continue along the reservoir's southern shore. Nearing Hinchliffe's Quarry, turn right across a concrete causeway. Keep right immediately to follow a smaller path above the reservoir's heathery shore. It is hard to follow through the grass beyond, but it resumes at a stile by the end of the reservoir, following the far side of the fenceline. At the top (the county boundary), turn left over another stile and follow the boundary fence steeply up onto the ridge of Black Hameldon. Cross the fence at any of the stiles to reach the trig point on Hoof Stones Height at the far end of the ridge.

Black Hameldon

wet

stile

stile

stile

the clapper bridge, Hebble Hol

Hebble Hole is named after dialect word for a narrow brid or its rail. The fine 15th century clapper bridge is ofte mistakenly referred to as Hebb Hole Bridge when it is simply the *hebble* itself. Wesleyan preachers used to preach by t tiny cave nearby, even though is far too small to be of any practical use.

trig   stile

6 stile   line of posts   line of posts

Hoof Stones Height (479m)

bridge   posts   wet   stile

stile   line of posts

ruins   gate

Noah Dale Dam (site of)

Stansfield Moor

Pad Laithe Bridge

High House Farm

wet

stile   Four Gates End

7

Dukes Cut

Moorcock Road

Moorhall Farm

Strines Clough

gate   gate   gate

Willow Cottage   gate

Wigg Farm   Burnt Edge Lane

6 Turn left at the trig point on Hoof Stones Height and cross a stile in a new fenceline to find the first of a line of posts leading down the fenceline towards the site of Noah Dale Dam. The posts continue around the empty basin from a stile near the bottom. Carry straight on where the path splits and follow the line of the wall to reach a stile above the ruins of Pad Laithe. Follow the walled path down and turn right where it bends; cross Pad Laithe Bridge and climb up the hillside on a path parallel to the wall.

Colden Cough is a local nature reserve and a fine example of a rejuvenated valley, formed by glacial meltwater cutting steeply into the wooded slopes below the broad valley of Noah Dale. There were twelve cotton mills in the valley in the 19th century. The ruins of Higher Lumb Mill stand around the chimney in the woods, with Lower Lumb Mill below the bridge. Bob Mill (also known as Slater Ing Mill) stood above the lower millpond, some of its walls still intact until the 1960s, when a group of young men were encouraged by their probation officers to demolish them. Hudson Mill was above Hebble Hole, its stables and walling visible near a private residence. Jack Bridge Mill was at the very top of the valley, its site marked by a sign for 'Colden Cotton & Commercial Company Limited'. The house at **Lumb Bank** was a mill-owners house, but was later owned by Ted Hughes and is currently a literary centre. There was also a part time school at Lumb Mill – pupils worked in the mills for the other half of the day until the practice was outlawed in 1917.

Law near Hell Hole

7 Reaching a stile at Four Gates End, head straight on into a walled lane over the top of Moorcock Hill. Bear left past Wigg Farm and, soon after, turn left through a gate onto another walled path. Drop down to Strines Clough and turn right on the track. This is Brown Hill Lane, which leads down to the steep bends in the road above Jack Bridge.

ROUTE 10: HOOF STONES HEIGHT & STANDING STONE HILL FROM HEBDEN BRIDGE

Distance: 13½ miles (22km)

Ascent: 540m

Difficulty: Strenuous

Parking: At the railway station or car parks in the town centre (pay & display).

Public Transport: Hebden Bridge is on the main Caldervale train & bus routes. Bus E runs from Hebden Bridge to Blackshaw Head via Popples Common and Jack Bridge and can be used to shorten the route.

Character: A substantial walk out of Hebden Bridge, steadily climbing to the summit of Hoof Stones Height on the county boundary via Heptonstall Crags and Standing Stone Hill. The return route drops into Noah Dale, then crosses Moorcock Hill to follow Colden Clough back into Hebden Bridge. Over half the walk follows rough tracks across remote moorland, but the result is a good round route to this distant summit where none is obvious from the OS map.

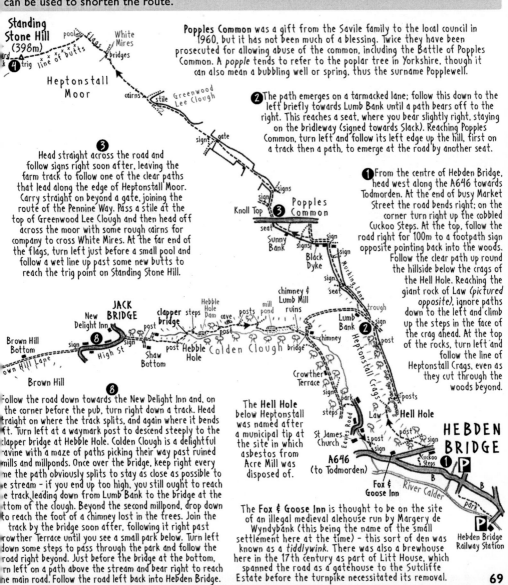

Popples Common was a gift from the Savile family to the local council in 1960, but it has not been much of a blessing. Twice they have been prosecuted for allowing abuse of the common, including the Battle of Popples Common. A *popple* tends to refer to the poplar tree in Yorkshire, though it can also mean a bubbling well or spring, thus the surname Popplewell.

2 The path emerges on a tarmacked lane; follow this down to the left briefly towards Lumb Bank until a path bears off to the right. This reaches a seat, where you bear slightly right, staying on the bridleway (signed towards Slack). Reaching Popples Common, turn left and follow its left edge up the hill, first on a track then a path, to emerge at the road by another seat.

3 Head straight across the road and follow signs right soon after, leaving the farm track to follow one of the clear paths that lead along the edge of Heptonstall Moor. Carry straight on beyond a gate, joining the route of the Pennine Way. Pass a stile at the top of Greenwood Lee Clough and then head off across the moor with some rough cairns for company to cross White Mires. At the far end of the flags, turn left just before a small pool and follow a wet line up past some new butts to reach the trig point on Standing Stone Hill.

1 From the centre of Hebden Bridge, head west along the A646 towards Todmorden. At the end of busy Market Street the road bends right; on the corner turn right up the cobbled Cuckoo Steps. At the top, follow the road right for 100m to a footpath sign opposite pointing back into the woods. Follow the clear path up round the hillside below the crags of the Hell Hole. Reaching the giant rock of Law (*pictured opposite*), ignore paths down to the left and climb up the steps in the face of the crag ahead. At the top of the rocks, turn left and follow the line of Heptonstall Crags, even as they cut through the woods beyond.

8 Follow the road down towards the New Delight Inn and, on the corner before the pub, turn right down a track. Head straight on where the track splits, and again where it bends left. Turn left at a waymark post to descend steeply to the clapper bridge at Hebble Hole. Colden Clough is a delightful ravine with a maze of paths picking their way past ruined mills and millponds. Once over the bridge, keep right every time the path obviously splits to stay as close as possible to the stream – if you end up too high, you still ought to reach the track leading down from Lumb Bank to the bridge at the bottom of the clough. Beyond the second millpond, drop down to reach the foot of a chimney lost in the trees. Join the track by the bridge soon after, following it right past Crowther Terrace until you see a small park below. Turn left down some steps to pass through the park and follow the road right beyond. Just before the bridge at the bottom, turn left on a path above the stream and bear right to reach the main road. Follow the road left back into Hebden Bridge.

The Hell Hole below Heptonstall was named after a municipal tip at the site in which asbestos from Acre Mill was disposed of.

The Fox & Goose Inn is thought to be on the site of an illegal medieval alehouse run by Margery de Wyndybank (this being the name of the small settlement here at the time) – this sort of den was known as a *tiddlywink*. There was also a brewhouse here in the 17th century as part of Litt House, which spanned the road as a gatehouse to the Sutcliffe Estate before the turnpike necessitated its removal.

69

⑤ Follow the road right for 50m to a stile on the left, from where a clear path follows a line of stakes up to the drained basin of Redmires Dam. Turn left here and follow a further line of stakes to pick up the line of a broken-down wall. The stakes lead to a stile at the back of the Hawks Stones (worthy of a brief detour), but the onward route follows a feint path along the fenceline. Cross a stile near its end and continue along the opposite side past the scattered Jack Stones, the high point of this walk. The path beyond is intermittent, but largely sticks close to the fenceline until it jags left; cut diagonally left here towards a gap in the wall and a better path along its top side. This path reaches the road at a barbed wire fence, but if needed there is a gate 150m to the right.

The Sportsmans Ar
at Keb Cote is bet
known as the Kebs.
served as both pub a
farm for many years, a
hosted an annual cat
fair until the 1920s.
keb is a dialect word f
a knackered old ew

Alternative Route: A possible shortcut avoids the rough ground above Hawks Stones by turning left at a stile shortly before the road. Emerging from the forest, follow a path diagonally right down across two fields to reach a gate and track leading right up to the signed crossroads east of Lower Intake.

④ From the trig point, follow either of the paths north-west in the directio of distant wind farms. They rejoin at waymark post, the first in a line acros the short bog leading to the further rocky outcrops of Fast Ends. The path above them descends to a stile and a track leading up to the moorland road

⑥ Turn left along the Long Causeway road for a short way, then turn right down Mount Lane (towards Shore). Beyond Higher Mount Farm, turn left on a signed track past Mount Cross, which stands in the field above. Keep to the left of Lower Intake and continue to a clear signed junction, where you turn right.

⑦ Descend the track to the bottom and turn left towards Hartley Royd. Just before the farm, go left through a gate and then bear right down another walled track to Hudson Bridge. Over the bridge, turn right and cross Hudson Moor to reach a gate just beyond a second quarry delf. Stay left here and climb up onto Orchan Rocks, from where a clearer path leads steeply down the other side to a gate. Go straight across the main track and pass through a small gate by Lower Hartley to stay to its right. Turn left into a long field beyond and cross the top of the field to enter Well Wood.

Whirlaw Stones dominate the hillside north of Todmorden, yet reveal little on closer inspection and are slightly awkward to access. A feint path leads onto the top from the walled lane to the north or you can scramble up the rocky hillside from the track above East Whirlaw. The hill was traditionally used for May Day meetings and celebrating victories. There are a couple of faces carved in the rocks, thought to have been created in the 1960s, and the name Whirlaw is thought to refer to a boundary mound.

⑧ The simplest descent crosses the bridge at the top of Stannally Clough and turns right on a track down t far side that eventually emerges on Stoney Royd Lane The alternative is to turn right immediately upon entering the wood and follow a magical but precariou path along the top of the wood. At one point it looks be blocked off by the steep terrain, but drops down a continues its remarkable journey through the beech trees to join a track down towards Lydgate. Beyond th first building on the left, turn left down a rough roa At the bottom, go straight on across a bridge and tur immediately right along the side of the stream. The pa circles the playing field to join Stoney Royd Lane.

Mount Cross

Mount Cross is a well-preserved medieval wayside cross with a calvary cross carved into its head. Also known as the Idol Cross, it is thought to date from the 10th or 11th century, and may have replaced an earlier wooden Paulinus Cross at which travelling priests preached. St Paulinus was a 7th Century missionary who travelled extensively across the North before becoming the first Bishop of York.

the Bottleneck Brid

ROUTE 11: THE BRIDE STONES & OTHER ROCKS FROM TODMORDEN

Distance: 7½ miles (12.5km)

Ascent: 350m

Difficulty: Moderate

Parking: At the railway station, or the car park just off Stansfield Road.

Public Transport: Todmorden is on the main Caldervale train & bus routes.

Character: A very satisfying route that climbs straight out of Todmorden to the various rocky outcrops that fringe the hills to the north. It is largely easy walking on clear paths and tracks, except for the rough section along Hawks Stones and Jack Stones, which can be avoided by a shortcut if necessary.

❸ A line of causey leads past the ruins of West Whirlaw and on round the foot of Whirlaw Stones. At a second gate, it joins the walled track of Stony Lane. Beyond another gate, the track splits and a rough track leads up through a gate to the right. Follow this, continuing straight ahead where the track turns sharply right towards some quarry delfs. This sheeptrack climbs across the hillside towards a stile with the Bride Stones laid out above. Stay on the path, following the fenceline until it jags right; bear right with it towards a prominent quiff-like balanced rock. Feint paths lead from Elvis Rock towards the trig point, and the famous Bottleneck Bride stands shortly beyond.

❷ The path climbs around the edge of Hole Bottom Delf; keep left to head towards the walk's first prominent rocky outcrop, the Butt Stones. You can climb up to the rocks, but the onward route follows the path round to the left, joining the walled track of Broad Gate. After descending slightly, continue straight on, following the track up the side of Bents Clough. At a sharp bend just beyond East Whirlaw Farm, turn left and follow a path above the farm. Again you can scramble up onto Whirlaw Stones, but the route continues straight on below the rocks.

Springs Farm, now a ruin, was renowned for selling stingo, a crude and strong beer.

Stony Lane was a packhorse route across the side of the moor between Cross Stone and Mount Cross. Lines of causey are visible on several sections and are particularly well preserved below Whirlaw Stones. A Packhorse Inn existed at either East or West Whirlaw until the packhorse routes were usurped by the turnpikes.

❶ From the centre of Todmorden, head out towards Burnley on the A646. Beyond the railway arches, turn right at a mini-roundabout into Stansfield Road and follow it to the top. Turn right to cross a bridge over the other railway line, then turn left down Stansfield Hall Road. At the corner, turn right up Meadow Bottom Road. Soon after the prominent Chimney House, the track splits; curve round to the right, and follow a path into the woods.

Golden Stones · delfs · stile · Springs (ruin) · Stony Lane · gate · gate · gate · gate · causey · Whirlaw Stones · gate · post · West Whirlaw (ruin) · East Whirlaw · Scrapers Lane · Bents Clough · post · Wickenberry Clough · Broad Gate · Butt Stones · sign · Hole Bottom Delf · sign · Chimney House · ❷ · dam · Meadow Bottom Rd · The Fountain (former inn) · Stannally Clough · Stannally Farm · railway · Well Wood · Allen Tree · Jumps Lane · bridge · sign · Church Lane · gate · ❾ · Stoney Royd La · sign · Stansfield Hall Road · railway

Bog asphodel, a deep yellow lily seen in early summer in wet areas of acid bog.

LYDGATE · to Burnley (7 miles) · A646 · Todmorden High School · P Leisure Centre · Ewood Lane · Centre Vale Park · statue · The Lucky Dog · Buckley Wood · Well Lane · Ridge Steps · Railway Station · P · Fire Station · railway · P · A646 · Stansfield Road · TODMORDEN · Town Hall · to Hebden Bridge · B (4 miles) · ❶ · A6033 · to Rochdale (5 miles)

0 — 300 metres

N

❾ Follow Stoney Royd Lane to the main road and head left for 400m, passing the school. Shortly after Ewood Lane, turn right into Centre Vale Park and follow the track round the back of the park. Reaching the statue of John Fielden, turn right and then immediately bear left up the slope into Buckley Woods. Join one of the larger paths above leading left above the church spire and emerging on Well Lane above the town centre. Follow the steep Ridge Steps down to reach the railway arches near the station.

71

HOOF STONES HEIGHT MAP - Southern Section (Bride Stones Moor)

CONTINUATION ON HOOF STONES HEIGHT (Western Section)

As well as taking in the Bride Stones themselves, the moorland area extends a long way down the hillside towards Todmorden, including both Whirlaw Common and Hudson Moor. All these areas are readily accessible from the settlements below and popular thanks to the line of dramatic rocky outcrops above the Cliviger Valley.

If you don't want to walk up from the valley, the best place to explore the Bride Stones from is the *Sportsman's Arms*. Follow either the path just above the pub or preferably the one 100m west along Long Causeway. This leads onto the scattered western tors around **Fast Ends** (the site of a farm that once stood between two of the rocks), from which it is simply a case of exploring the myriad paths between the boulders. Be aware that the forest and the area below Fast Ends is not Access Land.

The track around **Hudson Moor** is rather frustratingly fenced in all the way, making exploring freely a little awkward. Hopefully this practice is not a sign of things to come with paths through Access Land.

The **Bride Stones** consist of an array of fabulous gritstone outcrops with evocative shapes and names. Some, like the Indian's Head and Toad Rock (when seen from the right angle) have obvious names, others are given by the boulderers for whom this is a mecca. I have supplied the hedgehog stone and Elvis Rock as it's hard not to see a quiff in this overhang (though climbers prefer the Cheeseblock). The **Bottleneck Bride** (originally just the Bride), balancing perilously on a thin neck of rock, is the most famous. The stone by her side may have been the Groom, but was felled by a crowbar wielding gang; it is said the Bride narrowly avoided a similar fate. The Bride Stones name is thought to have come from the pagan goddess Brigid (known in Scotland as Bride).

The sarsens used in building Stonehenge and other circles are known as Bridestones, as are several prehistoric ritual sites.

Windy Harbour perhaps seems an odd name to find so high on a moorland. Yet the word harbour is originally thought to have come from an Old High German word *heriberga* referring to an open enclosure where an army would camp on a march, and is related to the words *auberge* and *albergue*.

Back Stone Hill is little mentioned despite possessing a far more impressive array of stones than nearby Whirlaw Stones. At its crest is an arc of rocks shaped like a crown from below, which was known as Th' Backstone. Backstone is the dialect word for a bakingstone which was used particularly in baking haverbread (a type of oat pancake) and was

Orchan Rocks are the most striking knuckles of rock seen from the valley below; jutting steeply up into a jagged crest, they offer magnificent views over Todmorden and the steep gorge of Cat Hole. It has been suggested that the name is a corruption of rocking stone, or indeed that it look like an

hedgehog-shaped rock (or perhaps the marching dog)

to Burnley (5 miles)

to Blackshaw Head (1½ miles)

to Todmorden (2 miles)

to Todmorden East

to Cornholme

to Harley Wood

to Lydgate

Windy Harbour Lane

Windy Harbour

the Wizard of Whirlaw (sculpture)

Whirlaw Stones

West Whirlaw

Whirlaw Common

Harley Wood Slack

Great Bride Stones trig (438m)

Little Bride Stones

The Bottleneck Bride

Th' Backstone

Back Stone Hill

Elvis Rock

Golden Stones

Bride Stones Farm

Gentleman's Common

Kebs Road

Keb Hill

Toad Rock

The Indian's Head

The Castle

hedgehog stone

Fast Ends

Hudson Clough Farm

Eleonora's (Georgina's) Woods

waterfall

Redmires Water

Sportsman's Arms

Eastwood Road

Stony Lane

Stoodley Lane

causey

Springs (ruin)

Stannally Stones

Rake Hey

Higher Hartley (ruin)

Lower Hartley

Speed Clough

Hudson Moor

Hudson Bridge

Millers Lowe

delfs

Clunters (quarries)

Orchan Rocks

Jump's Farm

Cat Hole

Hudson Clough

Orchan Rocks

metres

0   200

N

CHAPTER 11 - MANSHEAD HILL

Height: 417m

Grid Ref: SD997197

Map Sheet: OL21 (South Pennines)

Access: No dogs during nesting bird season (1st March to 31st July) except on permissive path along summit ridge.

Public Transport: Regular buses to Ripponden from Halifax and Littleborough. Bus 900 runs from Hebden Bridge to Ripponden via Cragg Vale. Bus C runs from Hebden Bridge to Cragg Vale.

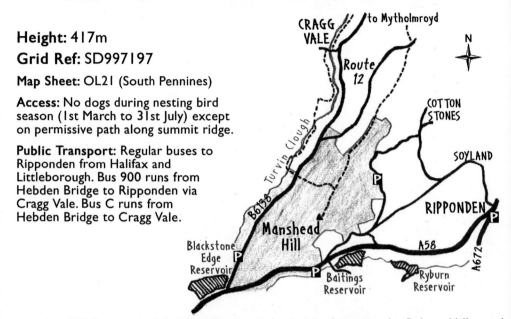

Manshead Hill is a graceful ridge of soft grassland rising between the Ryburn Valley and Cragg Vale. The trig point at Crow Hill above Sowerby village marks the culmination of this ridge of high ground jutting out eastwards from the main Pennine ridge, though it is separate from the bulk of the moor. Manshead is one of the most natural hill climbs in West Yorkshire, the summit being the only obvious target on the moor and offering great views across Calderdale. All of the ground is easily accessible from both the A58 and B6138 and there is lots of scope to create short circular walks, particularly from Baitings Reservoir or Coal Gate Road above Cotton Stones. Its name may derive from the Celtic word *maen* (meaning stone), though it is marked on some older maps as Mons Head, possibly referring to the Latin word for a mountain.

Manshead Hill from the head of Turvin Clough

Manshead Hill is a definite outlier from the main Pennine chain, and it very much looks like one. From all sides but the east it rises as one of the most shapely hills in Calderdale, a ridge with two distinctive humps. It is also remarkably smooth thanks to its covering of parched yellow-orange grass, particularly striking when compared with the rough, scarred peat the other side of the B6138. Rather than a barren moorland waste, Manshead is a gentle and welcoming hill and a pleasant walk from many directions. Interestingly this appearance is due to intensive farming across the hillsides, a process that is now in reverse. As part of the Countryside Stewardship scheme, cattle are now being put out on the moor in the early summer to help regenerate the heather and shrubs.

Manshead Hill makes a good short day's objective and is most frequently climbed from Baitings Reservoir in the south, where a permissive path allows access up Greenwood Clough, but the ridge walk from the northeast is probably the most satisfying route and allows you to take in the well-preserved World War II decoy bunker on Slate Delfs Hill.

In areas of rough, tussocky grassland like those which cover Manshead Hill, the **wheatear** is a common summer visitor. Seen between March and October, it is a small ground-dwelling bird distinguished by a black T shape on its tail and white flash on its underside - indeed the name wheatear is a corruption of 'white arse' (though locally it was known as a smattie). The sighting of a wheatear was considered in some areas to bring bad luck, especially if it was sitting on a stone.

Old Bar House Delf marks the original location of the toll bar at the top end of the Cragg Road Turnpike, which opened in 1816. Within a few years, the bar moved down the road to the marginally more secluded Mount Pleasant.

*The dry grassy slopes of Manshead Hill might appeal from the B6138 above Cragg Vale, but it is a frustrating hillside. Despite a number of lay-bys and stiles, none give access to any sort of path. In fact the only feint path leads from the eastern corner of the fence around **Wicken Hill Quarry** towards a ruin near **Liberty Gate**, but there is no stile in the vicinity and its route through the rushes is patchy at best. That leaves the path along the conduit at the top of the road, a route that links into onward paths to both Byron Edge and Blackstone Edge.*

Encircled by Black Castle Drain is an area called **Hassock**, which is a term that refers to the thick tussocks of mat-grass that cover Manshead Hill. Though gentle-looking, it is unabashed ankle-twisting ground. Other Hassocks are found near the summit of Way Stone Edge, and the word gave its name to the original kneelers used in church, which were stuffed with dried grass or straw.

Black Castle (or Black Hall as it may have previously been known) served for a few years as the Blackstone Edge Bar on the Rochdale to Halifax and Elland Turnpike. Though it was the first turnpike in the area, it was completed in stages and the cutting up Black Castle Clough was one of the last sections constructed in the 1820s. Two buildings were built on the site of a workman's house, but the toll bar soon moved back down to its original site by the car park at Baitings Gate and the stones were sold and removed by 1845.

The disused brick bunker near Slate Delfs Hill was a **World War II Starfish Bombing Decoy** control centre. Across the moor towards Manshead Hill would have been a series of decoy lights, simulated fires and shadow buildings controlled from this bunker. They utilised special effects from film studios and were designed to draw German bombers away from their intended targets - in this case, Greetland Station and Marshalling Yard, as well as the urban areas of Leeds and Manchester. It is one of the best-preserved of the 235 Starfish sites around the country; an earthern blast screen surrounds the two small rooms, the control centre on the left with an escape hatch and a generator room on the right.

The name **Collin Hill** (like Collon Flat on Wadsworth Moor) refers to *collin-bobs*, which were dead or burnt heather shoots that were gathered for kindling. Both of these locations are notably devoid of heather, but we can only assume that was not the case in the past.

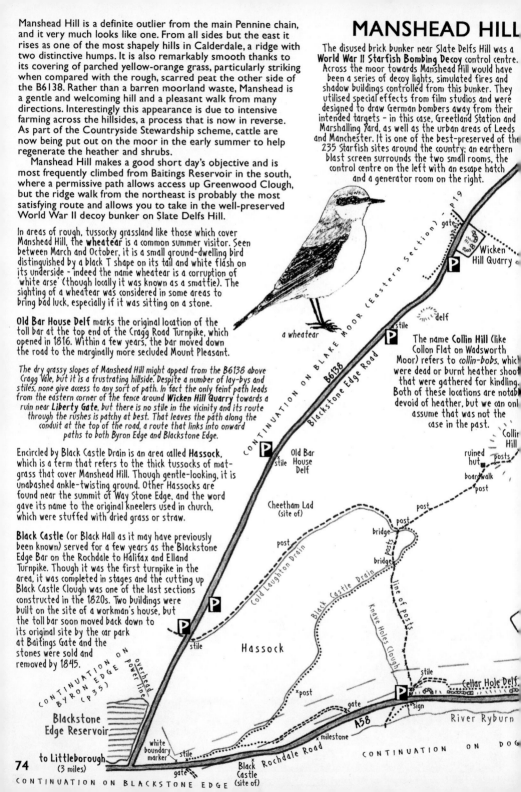

a wheatear

CONTINUATION ON BLAKE MOOR (Eastern Section) - P19

gate

Wicken Hill Quarry

delf

stile

B6138

Blackstone Edge Road

Collin Hill

ruined hut   posts

boardwalk
post

post

stile   Old Bar House Delf

Cheetham Lad (site of)

post

bridge

post

bridge

posts

Cold Laughton Drain

Black Castle Drain

line of posts

Knave Holes Clough

stile

Cellar Hole Delf

stile

CONTINUATION ON BYRON EDGE (P35)

overhead power line

Hassock

×post

gate

sign

A58

River Ryburn

CONTINUATION ON DOG

Blackstone Edge Reservoir

white boundary marker   stile

×milestone

Black Rochdale Road

74
to Littleborough (3 miles)

gate   Black Castle (site of)

MAP - Entire Moor

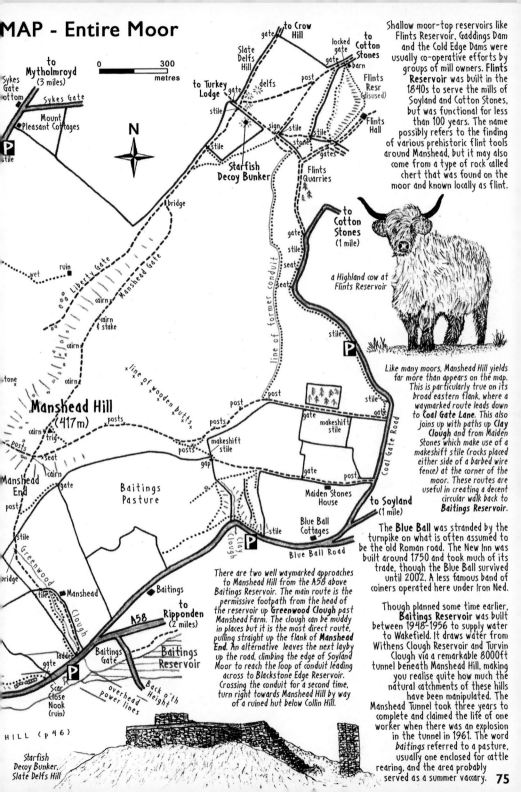

Shallow moor-top reservoirs like Flints Reservoir, Gaddings Dam and the Cold Edge Dams were usually co-operative efforts by groups of mill owners. **Flints Reservoir** was built in the 1840s to serve the mills of Soyland and Cotton Stones, but was functional for less than 100 years. The name possibly refers to the finding of various prehistoric flint tools around Manshead, but it may also come from a type of rock called chert that was found on the moor and known locally as flint.

a Highland cow at Flints Reservoir

Like many moors, Manshead Hill yields far more than appears on the map. This is particularly true on its broad eastern flank, where a waymarked route leads down to **Coal Gate Lane**. This also joins up with paths up **Clay Clough** and from Maiden Stones which make use of a makeshift stile (rocks placed either side of a barbed wire fence) at the corner of the moor. These routes are useful in creating a decent circular walk back to **Baitings Reservoir**.

The **Blue Ball** was stranded by the turnpike on what is often assumed to be the old Roman road. The New Inn was built around 1750 and took much of its trade, though the Blue Ball survived until 2002. A less famous band of coiners operated here under Iron Ned.

Though planned some time earlier, **Baitings Reservoir** was built between 1948-1956 to supply water to Wakefield. It draws water from Withens Clough Reservoir and Turvin Clough via a remarkable 8000ft tunnel beneath Manshead Hill, making you realise quite how much the natural catchments of these hills have been manipulated. The Manshead Tunnel took three years to complete and claimed the life of one worker when there was an explosion in the tunnel in 1961. The word *baitings* referred to a pasture, usually one enclosed for cattle rearing, and the area probably served as a summer vaccary.

There are two well waymarked approaches to Manshead Hill from the A58 above Baitings Reservoir. The main route is the permissive footpath from the head of the reservoir up **Greenwood Clough** past Manshead Farm. The clough can be muddy in places but it is the most direct route, pulling straight up the flank of **Manshead End**. An alternative leaves the next layby up the road, climbing the edge of Soyland Moor to reach the loop of conduit leading across to Blackstone Edge Reservoir. Crossing the conduit for a second time, turn right towards Manshead Hill by way of a ruined hut below Collin Hill.

Map labels

to Mytholmroyd (3 miles)
Sykes Gate Bottom
Sykes Gate
Mount Pleasant Cottages
stile
0   300 metres
N
to Crow Hill
gate
Slate Delfs Hill
locked gate
gate
to Cotton Stones
barn
Flints Resr (disused)
to Turkey Lodge
gate
delfs
post
stile
sign
stile
Flints Hall
stile
Starfish Decoy Bunker
stone
gates
Flints Quarries
bridge
gate
stile
to Cotton Stones (1 mile)
seat
seat
line of former conduit
Liberty Gate
Manshead Gate
wet
ruin
cairn
cairn & stake
cairn
line of wooden butts
stile
Manshead Hill (417m)
stone
cairn
posts
cairn
trig
posts
post
posts
makeshift stile
post
makeshift stile
gate
gap
makeshift stile
seat
Baitings Pasture
post
stile
to Soyland (1 mile)
Coal Gate Road
Maiden Stones House
gate
post
Manshead End
post
gate
Blue Ball Cottages
Greenwood Clough
stile
Clay Clough
stile
Blue Ball Road
bridge
stile
Manshead
Baitings
A58
to Ripponden (2 miles)
Baitings Reservoir
Baitings Gate
ladder
gate
Scar Close Nook (ruin)
overhead power lines
Back o'th Height

HILL (p46)

Starfish Decoy Bunker, Slate Delfs Hill

75

ROUTE 12: MANSHEAD HILL & CRAGG VALE FROM MYTHOLMROYD

Distance: 10 miles (16km)

Ascent: 380m

Difficulty: Moderate

Parking: Car parks at Mytholmroyd Community Centre (small charge), St Michael's Church and by White Lion.

Public Transport: Mytholmroyd is on the main Caldervale train & bus routes.

Character: A very satisfying round that combines the charming wooded valley of Cragg Vale with the broad ridge of high ground extending all the way down from Manshead Hill to Blackwood Common. Though there is a rough section at the head of Turvin Clough and up the side of Manshead, the long steady descent thereafter is very much simpler, and an alternative is provided if needed.

Nab End Quarries is a small delf surrounded by ugly walls of barbed wire. It is, however, all access land – access is via a crude stile below Nab End – and houses a surprising sculpture garden in one of its nooks. Go right to the far end from the stile to find the Lawrence Millenium Garden, where carved stone faces and stunted trees provide a surreal corner on this windswept hilltop.

1 From the main road in Mytholmroyd, head south on the B6138. Under the railway and just beyond the Shoulder of Mutton pub, turn left into Scout Road and then first right into Hall Bank Lane. Climb the hill and turn right on the bend up Stubbings Lane, at the end of which a footpath continues into the wood beyond. At a pair of stone stoops, fork right and descend to the old Hoo Hole Dye Works, where the route of the path has helpfully been painted on the ground. Bear right over the bridge and turn left onto Cragg Road.

2 Just before Dauber Bridge, follow a track off to the right (signed 'Parrock Clough & Frost Hole'). After a few hundred metres, another sign takes you left down to a bridge over Parrock Clough (also known here as Wriggles Bottom). From here a good path follows the right bank of Cragg Brook for nearly a mile. At the first road across head left for a few metres to rejoin the route, and by Cragg Spa follow the road right for a few metres. Climbing up through Paper Mill Wood, ignore routes signed off to the right and follow the top of the slope to reach Papermill Cottage. Turn left here across the bridge, then immediately right to climb up past the site of Castlegate Mill and join Castle Gate.

3 Turn right along Castle Gate and pass the mill pond (either on the track or a path that skirts around it). On the corner before New Bridge, head straight on through a gap to join a path alongside the brook. This emerges on the road by St John's Church; turn right, cross the bridge and soon after the Hinchliffe Arms turn left up a track signed towards Higher House Moor

sculpture in Nab End Quarries

9 Turn right on High Stones Road for just a few yards before following a sign left over a stile and along the side of a small wood. The fenced path soon emerges on another road. Turn right for 75m and look for an unsigned path which leads right across the heart of Blackwood Common opposite.

10 The path over Blackwood Common emerges by Nab End Quarries. Follow the flagged track left past Nab End Farm. Where it bears off into the delf, continue straight on around the perimeter fence of the quarry. Beyond a path signed off to the left, follow an open fenced avenue down off the common. Through a gate at the bottom, head straight on, joining a track down to Bent. The onward path is waymarked through the garden and down the edge of the field beyond.

11 Arriving at a stile at the top of Hollin Hey Bank, the onward path is not immediately obvious, but heads diagonally down to the right the other side of a large bush. Following yellow stakes, the path picks its way through further thickets before descending steeply to a gate into Stake Lane. Turn left down the old lane to join the newer road of Hall Bank Lane and follow it all the way back down into Mytholmroyd.

4 After 200m follow another sign left (towards Green Bank) over a stile and along a path that heads back towards the river. It doesn't matter which route you take through Higher House Wood, though the smaller path along the river may be drier at times. All routes lead to a stile at the far end of the wood. Soon after, the path reaches a gate above a lovely stone clapper bridge and turns right to climb steeply up a long set of steps. Just before reaching Higher House, double back left to climb up to a stile on the edge of the moor.

5 Once on the moor, join a path left along the edge of a drain to reach a stile over a new fenceline. The path continues down to a large new bridge in Trimming Dale and negotiates the maze of fencelines beyond via another couple of stiles. Reaching a sign by the wall, continue straight on along the higher of two grassy tracks above the clough. Through the second gate, turn right over Washfold Bridge (not as picturesque as the name sounds) and fork left immediately beyond. The obvious path angles diagonally up the slope, but a smaller path runs parallel to the stream. Beyond the piping station, you cross a small stream; look to cross the main stream soon after and head steeply up the bank opposite, following the wall to reach the road via a handy gate.

6 Cross straight over the road and climb up to the back left corner of the overgrown Wicken Hill Quarry. This side of Manshead Hill is a warren of tussocks and rushes, but a lone path strikes out from near this corner; however, all the stiles off the road are in the wrong place so you'll have to jump over the fence. Wander no more than 10 yards left from the corner and look carefully to pick up the faintest of lines heading slightly to the right of the ruin visible below Great Manshead Hill. Though it is difficult to find and follow, it's worth persevering with as it becomes more defined through the wetter rush beds. After a particularly wet section of tussock hopping, it bends left and makes straight for the lonely ruin. From here, the best bet is to head straight up the slope, a rough but short assault. Cross a feint track below the edge before joining the main track near one of the cairns along the top of Great Manshead. Follow this right for half a mile to reach the summit and trig point safe in the knowledge that the rough going is firmly behind you.

...ragg Spa is a small spring and was a 19th century attraction when its sulphurous waters were thought to have healing properties, particularly for skin ailments. On Spaw Sunday, the spa was dressed in a ceremony often linked to a religious gathering; this is a tradition that has recently been resurrected.

8 Continue straight on along the ridge to reach a walled track past Catherine Slack and up towards Little Crow Hill. Ignore a number of paths signed off in either direction and continue straight on to join the start of a surfaced track (Water Stalls Road). Beyond Little Crow Hill, follow the track through a gate and past Crow Hill Farm, where a tarmacked road is joined, dropping down to High Stones Road.

Alternative Route: To avoid the rough section at the head of Turvin Clough, a possible shortcut crosses the clapper bridge and climbs up to the road through one of the gardens of Green Bank. Follow the road right to Moorland Cottages, then turn left behind them and pick up a path up the side of the fields. Head straight across the next road and fork right where the track splits and continue up past Slate Delfs Farm to reach the moor by the Starfish bunker.

7 You may wish to wander on past the summit to Manshead End, where there is a seat and an excellent view. Otherwise, simply retrace your steps back along the ridge and begin the long steady descent. The path drops down to a small wooden bridge and follows the wall towards the prominent WW2 bunker on Slate Delfs Hill (for background information see Page 75).

The small swimming pool below **Wash Falls** was apparently created by airmen stationed at the nearby Starfish decoy airfield during World War II.

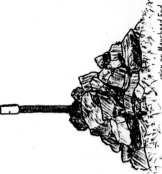

cairn on Manshead End

0 — 400 metres

Map labels: Crow Hill, Water Stalls, quarry, Little Crow Hill, Catherine Slack, Slate Delfs Hill, post, Bunker, Slate Delfs Farm, alternative route, Green Bank, Moorland Cottages, B6138, clapper bridge, Biggin, Turvin Clough, pool, Higher House Wood, Higher House, Cove Hill, Lark Hall Wood, Wash Falls, new bridge, Washfold Bridge, Piping Station, Trimming Dale, Wicken Hill Quarry, jump over fence, B6138, Great Manshead Hill, Manshead Hill (417m), trig, seat, ruin, pathless, wet

The **stonechat** is a small bird found in undisturbed vegetation, often around moorland reservoirs. It has a black head, white collar and orange breast, and is named for its call, a clack reminiscent of stones being bashed together. It is a partial migrant, generally remaining in the UK through the winter, and so is more rotund than the whinchat.

The **whinchat** is a small migratory bird that breeds on the Pennine moors in the summer months before returning to sub-Saharan Africa. It is closely related to the more common stonechat but has longer wings and a more slender body, and is most easily distinguished by its paler orange breast and distinctive white stripe above the eyes. Unlike the stonechat its presence is becoming increasingly rare, possibly because of changes in its winter habitat in Africa. It is most likely found near patches of bracken, where it prefers to nest, though its name refers to gorse.

CHAPTER 12 - NAB HILL
(aka Hollin Hill)

Height: 451m

Grid Ref: SE037323

Map Sheet: OL21 (South Pennines)

Access: No restrictions.

Public Transport: Regular bus services to Oxenhope, Denholme, Illingworth and Mixenden. Buses 502/504/505 run along A629 from Halifax through Causeway Foot. Bus 698 runs from Bradford to Oxenhope via B6141. Bus 554 runs from Halifax to Wainstalls.

The summit of **Nab Hill** stands on the boundary between Bradford and Calderdale, facing proudly to the northwest. This steep escarpment is responsible for its name, *nabbi* being Norse for a prominent hilltop. It would be easy to say that Nab Hill has been ruined; its summit is churned up by over 100 years of quarrying and the remaining plateau is dominated by the wind farms across Hollin Hill, yet the trig point perches on a satisfying crest between the two and the moor has plenty of character. Rising in the southeast from Ogden Reservoir, the southwest from Luddenden Dean, the northwest from Oxenhope and the northest from Denholme, Nab Hill provides a natural high point from all directions. Its accessibility from so many towns makes it a busy moor, yet never have I seen another soul on the summit.

Nab Hill across Warley Moor Reservoir

The northern fringe of Nab Hill is marked by a series of stone castellations, equally intriguing up close as from the hillside below. They are combination of cairns and shelters, each different from the next, formed from the leftover stone of the quarries behind. The most easterly is a Mercedes-symbol shaped shelter topped by a cairn, the next has largely crumbled. Then there is a curious mosaic tapped into the peat that appears to read A2. Beyond is the best shelter from the westerly wind, complete with seats and a chimney-like stack alongside, and finally the most compelling of all, a towering cairn that holds a shelter within in its arms like a benevolant stone monster.

Between **Leeming** and Nab Hill is a busy moorland slope that was once well populated. The coming of the reservoirs and their catchments ensured that all that remains are bare ruins and grouse-rearing enclosures. **Sawood Lane** crosses the middle of this slope but can be very muddy and wet. Better options are paths along the two conduits, the lower weaving a particularly pleasant way across the hillside from near Whitehill Farm to **Nan Scar**.

Nan Scar was home to a rifle range from the 1880s. Its name comes from the Welsh word *nant* for a small river.

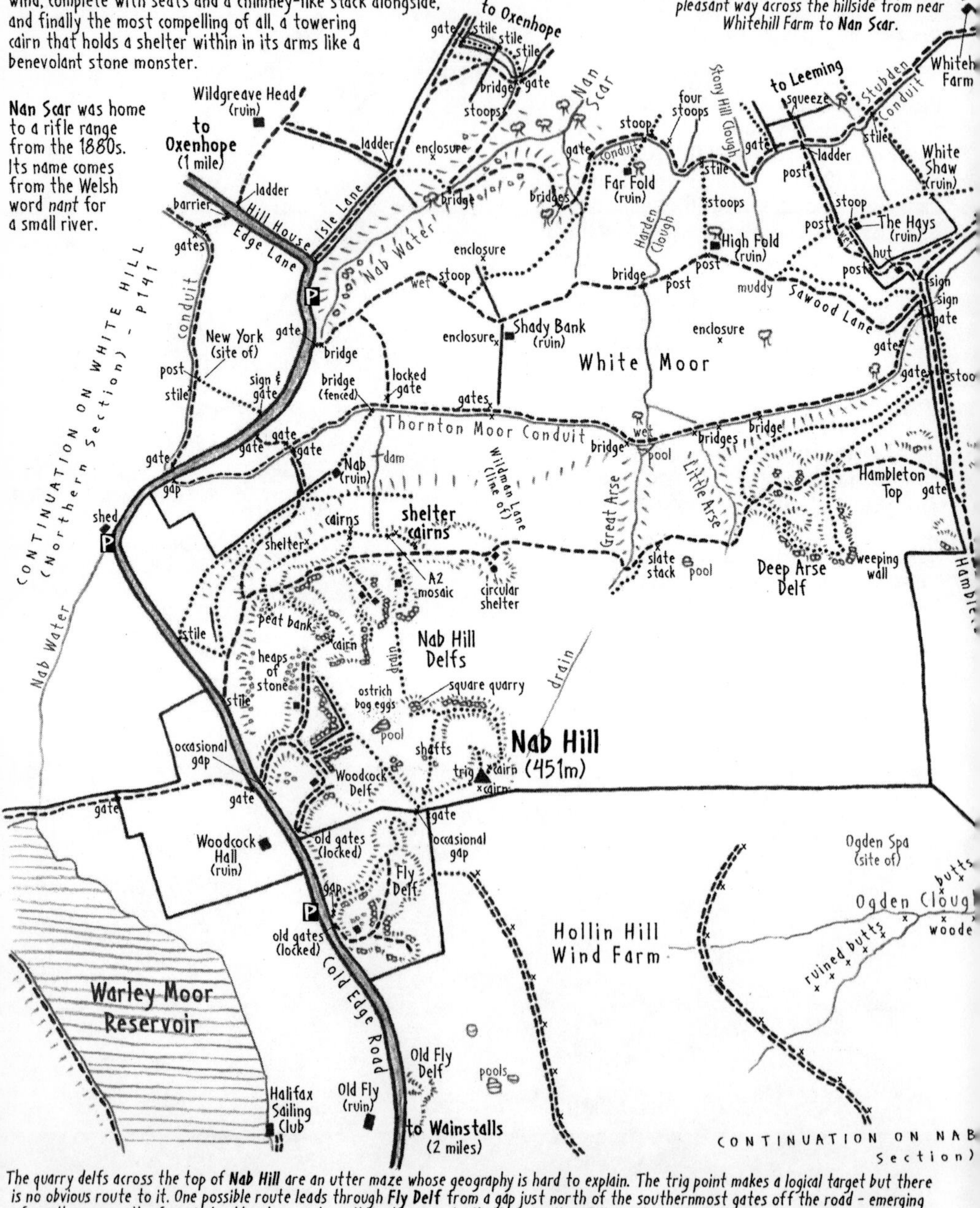

(Map labels, reading across the illustration:)

to Oxenhope · to Leeming · Whitehill Farm · White Shaw (ruin) · Stubden Conduit · squeeze · stile · Nan Scar · Story Hill Clough · four stoops · stoop · Wildgreave Head (ruin) · to Oxenhope (1 mile) · Hill House Isle Lane · Edge Lane · ladder · barrier · ladder · gates · enclosure · bridges · stoops · gate · conduit · Far Fold (ruin) · Harden Clough · stoops · High Fold (ruin) · The Hays (ruin) · hut · post · ladder · post · post · Nab Water · bridge · bridges · enclosure · post · Sawood Lane · muddy · sign · sign · gate · CONTINUATION ON WHITE HILL (Northern Section) - P141 · conduit · post · stile · New York (site of) · sign & gate · bridge · bridge (fenced) · locked gate · gates · wet · stoop · Shady Bank (ruin) · enclosure · White Moor · enclosure · gate · gate · stoop · gate · gate · gap · shed · Thornton Moor Conduit · bridge · wet pool · bridges · bridge · Great Arse · Little Arse · Hambleton Top · gate · stile · Nab (ruin) · dam · shelter · cairns · shelter · cairns · Widman Lane (line of) · drain · slate stack · pool · Deep Arse Delf · weeping wall · peat bank · cairn · A2 mosaic · circular shelter · heaps of stone · cairn · Nab Hill Delfs · square quarry · drain · ostrich bog eggs · pool · shafts · **Nab Hill** · trig · cairn · cairn · (451m) · occasional gap · gate · Woodcock Delf · gate · occasional gap · Woodcock Hall (ruin) · old gates (locked) · Fly Delf · gap · Ogden Spa (site of) · butts · Ogden Clough · wood · ruined butts · old gates (locked) · Cold Edge Road · Hollin Hill Wind Farm · Warley Moor Reservoir · Old Fly Delf · pools · Halifax Sailing Club · Old Fly (ruin) · to Wainstalls (2 miles)

CONTINUATION ON NAB Section

The quarry delfs across the top of **Nab Hill** are an utter maze whose geography is hard to explain. The trig point makes a logical target but there is no obvious route to it. One possible route leads through **Fly Delf** from a gap just north of the southernmost quarry gates off the road - emerging from the quarry, the fence is trodden down and a path leads across to the trig. Another follows the quarry track (partly filled in to dissuade motorbikes) from an occasional gap in the fence opposite the top of the track down to the reservoir, bearing right into the vast open area of **Woodcock Delf** - near the back right corner, a path leads up the peat bank leads round to the trig. Other feint tracks lead out of the northern delfs and across the short stretch of open moorland to the 'ostrich bog eggs', a distinctive area of scattered giant moorland sods that is difficult to avoid, and to cross. But probably, like me, you'll end up wandering aimlessly through the maze.

The area around **Sawood** is littered with shallow coal pits and trial holes, but the coal seams here were so fractured that little coal was ever dug.

The moorland above **Denholme** was enclosed in the 15th century as a deer park by the Tempest family. The name Denholme Gate refers to one of its entrances and parts of the boundary wall are still visible above Stubden Reservoir – the boundary roughly followed the line of Thornton Moor Road. Ultimately the estate was gambled away to the Saviles of Halifax.

Access to **Stubden Reservoir** is neither encouraged nor discouraged, but it is a tiny gem and represents the only moorland directly accessible from **Denholme**. A path runs right round the small reservoir, carved sharply from the rock of the hillside. The large path on the northern shore continues up the beck before cutting back and climbing up to **Thornton Moor Road**. The path on the southern shore is smaller, tiptoeing along a narrow shelf. A further path climbs up the rocky slope opposite a delf above the reservoir and wanders across the bracken-covered slopes to a rickety gate at the end of the dam wall.

valve tower,
Stubden
Reservoir

to Sawood &
Dog and Gun

0   300
metres

High Shaw
(ruin)

Stubden Beck

Reservoir
House

filter
beds

gate

quarry

Solomon's
Temple
(site of)

Thornton Moor
Reservoir

Thornton
Moor

dams

shaft

locked
gate

shaft

dam

delf

concrete
shaft

enclosure

enclosure

Stubden
House

gate

to Denholme
(½ mile)

stile

Stubden
Reservoir

bridge

rickety
gate

quarry

gate

locked
gate

post

post

Thornton Moor Road

stile

to Denholme
Gate
(½ mile)

Deep Arse Delf has been marked on OS maps as Deep House Delf since the 19th century, but Reg Hindley suggests its real identity lies in the folds of land along the northern edge of Nab Hill. From the hill opposite, the cloughs of Great Arse and Little Arse cleave the hill into buttocks, from which the quarry took its name. Early map-makers decided to make it less amusing.

Upper Newland
(ruins)

Lower Newland
(site of)

Newland Lane

Ash Tree Farm
(ruin)

to Denholme
Velvets

Solomon's Temple was one of a number of temporary houses for waterworks employees during the reservoir's construction, although intriguingly its name predates this by at least 50 years.

cairn

large
cairn

post

cairn

butts

Dont
Bridge
(site of)

Foreside Lane

shed &
ruin

Foreside Top
(ruin)

Thornton Moor and **Stubden Reservoirs** were built in the 1880s by the Bradford Corporation, the former acting as the city's high-level water supply. Their conduits string out across the northern slopes of Nab Hill, the higher feeding straight into Thornton Moor Reservoir, the lower passing through the hillside to Stubden Reservoir – the air shafts across the hill mark its line. There is no access to Thornton Moor Reservoir except by members of the Bradford Ornithological Group, thus it has been preserved as an important site for observing migratory birds.

quarry

gate

stile

Ogden
Kirk

post

sign

wet

post

bridge

Ogden Kirk
Quarry

stile

steps

hut

rail

bridge

gate

gate

cairn shelter,
Nab Hill

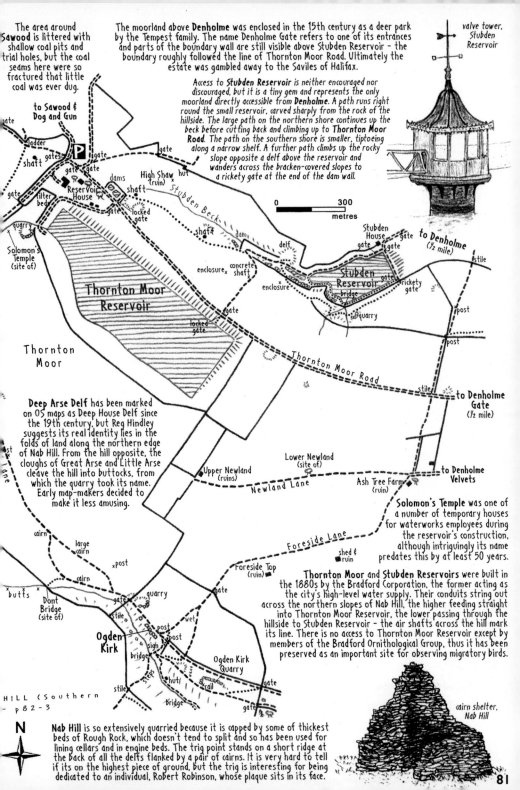

HILL (Southern
– p 82–3

N

Nab Hill is so extensively quarried because it is capped by some of thickest beds of Rough Rock, which doesn't tend to split and so has been used for lining cellars and in engine beds. The trig point stands on a short ridge at the back of all the delfs flanked by a pair of cairns. It is very hard to tell if its on the highest piece of ground, but the trig is interesting for being dedicated to an individual, Robert Robinson, whose plaque sits in its face.

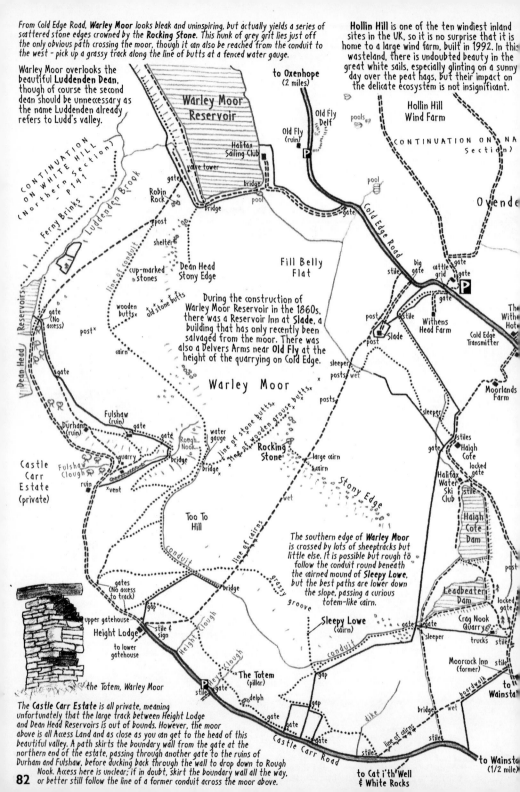

From Cold Edge Road, **Warley Moor** looks bleak and uninspiring, but actually yields a series of scattered stone edges crowned by the **Rocking Stone**. This hunk of grey grit lies just off the only obvious path crossing the moor, though it can also be reached from the conduit to the west - pick up a grassy track along the line of butts at a fenced water gauge.

Warley Moor overlooks the beautiful **Luddenden Dean**, though of course the second dean should be unnecessary as the name Luddenden already refers to Ludd's valley.

Hollin Hill is one of the ten windiest inland sites in the UK, so it is no surprise that it is home to a large wind farm, built in 1992. In this wasteland, there is undoubted beauty in the great white sails, especially glinting on a sunny day over the peat hags, but their impact on the delicate ecosystem is not insignificant.

During the construction of Warley Moor Reservoir in the 1860s, there was a Reservoir Inn at **Slade**, a building that has only recently been salvaged from the moor. There was also a Delvers Arms near **Old Fly** at the height of the quarrying on Cold Edge.

The southern edge of **Warley Moor** is crossed by lots of sheeptracks but little else. It is possible but rough to follow the conduit round beneath the cairned mound of **Sleepy Lowe**, but the best paths are lower down the slope, passing a curious totem-like cairn.

The **Castle Carr Estate** is all private, meaning unfortunately that the large track between Height Lodge and Dean Head Reservoirs is out of bounds. However, the moor above is all Access Land and as close as you can get to the head of this beautiful valley. A path skirts the boundary wall from the gate at the northern end of the estate, passing through another gate to the ruins of Durham and Fulshaw, before ducking back through the wall to drop down to Rough Nook. Access here is unclear; if in doubt, skirt the boundary wall all the way, or better still follow the line of a former conduit across the moor above.

to Oxenhope (2 miles)

NAB HILL - Southern Section (Warley & Ovenden Moors) MAP

Nab Hill's southern slopes lead down to the heads of the Luddenden and Hebble Brooks and represent the closest moorland to Halifax, rising immediately above Mixenden, Causeway Foot and Wainstalls. Ovenden Moor is dominated by the Hollin Hill Wind Farm and the country park around Ogden Water, while Warley Moor is quieter but worthy of closer inspection. The two are divided by the rough road across Cold Edge.

Halifax Golf Club lies in a pleasant green basin above Mixenden and is crossed by two well waymarked paths, the best pulling up the side of *Wamesley Scar* to Cold Edge Road. The whole course is Access Land but is probably not worth exploring off the paths for fear of flying balls. The exception is the eastern corner along the *Hebble Brook* and above, where there is an area of intriguing walled delfs and a maze of paths.

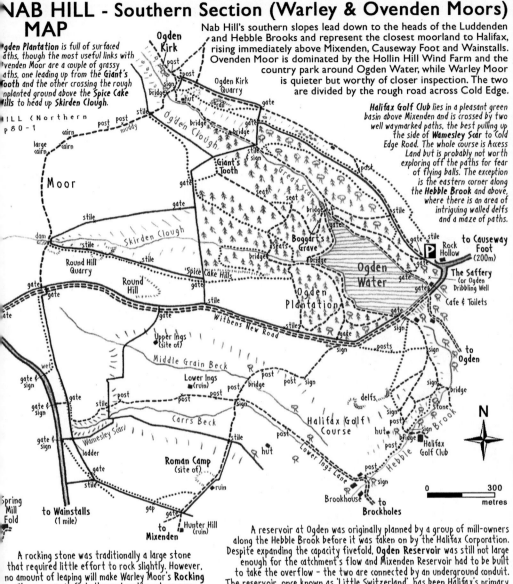

Ogden Plantation is full of surfaced paths, though the most useful links with Ovenden Moor are a couple of grassy paths, one leading up from the *Giant's Tooth* and the other crossing the rough unplanted ground above the *Spice Cake Hills* to head up *Skirden Clough*.

HILL (Northern pp 80-1

A reservoir at Ogden was originally planned by a group of mill-owners along the Hebble Brook before it was taken on by the Halifax Corporation. Despite expanding the capacity fivefold, **Ogden Reservoir** was still not large enough for the catchment's flow and Mixenden Reservoir had to be built to take the overflow - the two are connected by an underground conduit. The reservoir, once known as 'Little Switzerland', has been Halifax's primary country park for over a century, though it has recently reinvented itself, rebranding Ogden Reservoir as **Ogden Water** and restoring the Victorian Promenade. The most dubious element of this is the creation of a series of local myths whose genealogy appears very spurious. The Boggart's Grave (a stone spring that gurgles with air as it emerges), Giant's Tooth (a white stone supposedly pulled from the giant Ogden's mouth with the aid of a windmill), and Ogden Dribbling Well (another spring with alleged healing powers) are worth a look, but as little more than entertainment.

A rocking stone was traditionally a large stone that required little effort to rock slightly. However, no amount of leaping will make Warley Moor's **Rocking Stone** move. In fact, the real rocking stone was probably a short distance away from the main stone, but Revd Watson records that it was unmoveable in 1775. It has been suggested that only those with special powers could move such stones and that they were venerated by the druids. The Rocking Stone also possesses a passage that can be crawled through and may have had similar rites associated with it as Ponden Kirk on Withins Height (see Page 153).

the Rocking Stone, Warley Moor

83

ROUTE 13: NAB HILL & STAKE HILL FROM OXENHOPE

The **Waggon & Horses** was originally on the opposite side of the road, but the licence is thought to have been transferred to new premises around 1850. It remains a traditional moorland pub and serves as the start of the annual Oxenhope Straw Bale Race; every July the locals don fancy dress and run, walk or stumble the three miles into the village and up the opposite hillside while carrying a bale of straw and downing pints in every pub along the way.

2 Reaching the edge of the common, head straight across a track and follow the path along the top of Stones, a rough edge with good views over the Worth Valley. This eventually drops down to join a walled track that passes Hardnaze Farm and climbs up to the road by the Waggon & Horses.

1 From the Bay Horse pub in the middle of Oxenhope, follow the A6033 south towards Hebden Bridge. Round the corner, turn first right into Shaw Lane. After 100m, turn left on a footpath behind some houses and up the side of a field past the church. Turn right at a sign at the top and pick your way between the houses of West Croft Head.

The **Keighley & Worth Valley Railway** is a single track branch line that was extended to Oxenhope due to persistence from local mill owners as Haworth was originally planned as the terminus. The line was closed in 1962 after the Beeching Resport, but re-opened in 1968 as a volunteer-operated heritage railway specialising in the serving of real ale on-board. Its sale to the local preservation society represents the very first privatisation of British Railways, and it thrives to this day.

3 Follow a signed path above the pub to join a fenceline up onto the moor. At Thornton Moor Conduit, the simplest route is to turn left and follow the conduit right round to the foot of Nab Hill. The route up onto Stake Hill is very rough and wet in places. Head straight on across the bridge, then cross the fenceline and follow its right side up the wet slope. Veer right to avoid the worst of the wet ground and make for a small cluster of stones ahead. Follow this line of rocks right along the shallow edge to reach a fenceline. A handpost helps you to climb the fence, from which you bear diagonally left towards the prominent cairn on Stake Hill.

4 From the cairn, head back to the fenceline, aiming for the sharp corner at its end. From here, head due east diagonally across the barren moss to rejoin the fenceline again near the top of Far Peat Lane. If you reach a broken down wall you have strayed right, or a wet depression you've gone left, but it is far easier ground than simply following the fence round. Cross the stile at the top of the old walled lane and follow a path back down to the conduit.

Distance: 6 miles (9½km)

Ascent: 320m

Difficulty: Easy

Parking: Street parking along Best Lane in Oxenhope.

Public Transport: Oxenhope is on the 663, 720 & 500 bus routes from Keighley and/or Hebden Bridge. Keighley & Worth Valley Railway runs to Oxenhope station at weekends.

Character: These two hills make a natural circuit from Oxenhope, though neither of their tops are easily accessible. If the obvious alternative routes are followed, this is a very straight-forward stroll on good paths. If the tops are sought, prepare for short rough sections and an exploration of the maze that is Nab Hill Delfs.

Access: No dogs on Stake Hill between 1st March and July 31st.

the top of Nab Hill

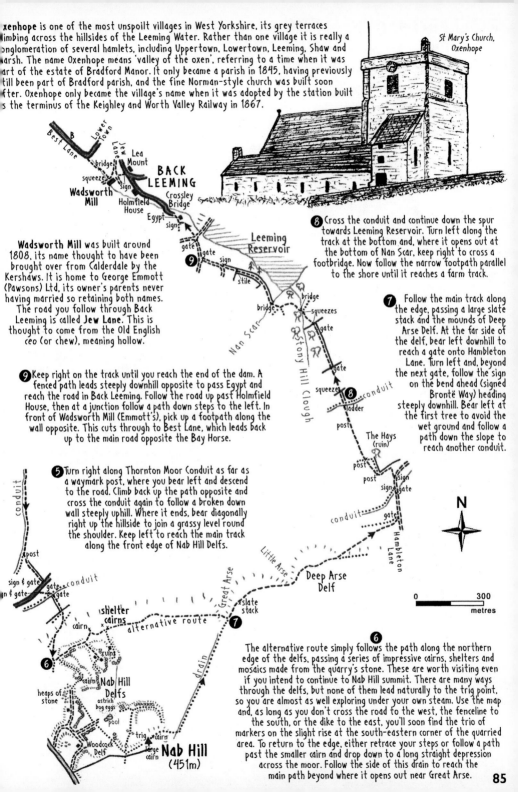

Oxenhope is one of the most unspoilt villages in West Yorkshire, its grey terraces climbing across the hillsides of the Leeming Water. Rather than one village it is really a conglomeration of several hamlets, including Uppertown, Lowertown, Leeming, Shaw and Marsh. The name Oxenhope means 'valley of the oxen', referring to a time when it was part of the estate of Bradford Manor. It only became a parish in 1845, having previously still been part of Bradford parish, and the fine Norman-style church was built soon after. Oxenhope only became the village's name when it was adopted by the station built as the terminus of the Keighley and Worth Valley Railway in 1867.

St Mary's Church, Oxenhope

Wadsworth Mill was built around 1808, its name thought to have been brought over from Calderdale by the Kershaws. It is home to George Emmott (Pawsons) Ltd, its owner's parents never having married so retaining both names. The road you follow through Back Leeming is called **Jew Lane**. This is thought to come from the Old English ceo (or chew), meaning hollow.

8 Cross the conduit and continue down the spur towards Leeming Reservoir. Turn left along the track at the bottom and, where it opens out at the bottom of Nan Scar, keep right to cross a footbridge. Now follow the narrow footpath parallel to the shore until it reaches a farm track.

7 Follow the main track along the edge, passing a large slate stack and the mounds of Deep Arse Delf. At the far side of the delf, bear left downhill to reach a gate onto Hambleton Lane. Turn left and, beyond the next gate, follow the sign on the bend ahead (signed Brontë Way) heading steeply downhill. Bear left at the first tree to avoid the wet ground and follow a path down the slope to reach another conduit.

9 Keep right on the track until you reach the end of the dam. A fenced path leads steeply downhill opposite to pass Egypt and reach the road in Back Leeming. Follow the road up past Holmfield House, then at a junction follow a path down steps to the left. In front of Wadsworth Mill (Emmott's), pick up a footpath along the wall opposite. This cuts through to Best Lane, which leads back up to the main road opposite the Bay Horse.

5 Turn right along Thornton Moor Conduit as far as a waymark post, where you bear left and descend to the road. Climb back up the path opposite and cross the conduit again to follow a broken down wall steeply uphill. Where it ends, bear diagonally right up the hillside to join a grassy level round the shoulder. Keep left to reach the main track along the front edge of Nab Hill Delfs.

6 The alternative route simply follows the path along the northern edge of the delfs, passing a series of impressive cairns, shelters and mosaics made from the quarry's stone. These are worth visiting even if you intend to continue to Nab Hill summit. There are many ways through the delfs, but none of them lead naturally to the trig point, so you are almost as well exploring under your own steam. Use the map and, as long as you don't cross the road to the west, the fenceline to the south, or the dike to the east, you'll soon find the trio of markers on the slight rise at the south-eastern corner of the quarried area. To return to the edge, either retrace your steps or follow a path past the smaller cairn and drop down to a long straight depression across the moor. Follow the side of this drain to reach the main path beyond where it opens out near Great Arse.

0 300 metres

N

Nab Hill (451m)

85

ROUTE 14: OGDEN KIRK, NAB HILL & WARLEY MOOR FROM CAUSEWAY FOOT

4 From the trig point on Nab Hill, pick up a feint path west along the high ground to a junction of fences. Bear right, away from the fenceline, and skirt round to the right of a large quarry on a rough track. Beyond, look to follow the line of a depression down to the road. Gaps in the fence (rather like paths) come and go here, so you may need to climb it to reach the layby. From the gate opposite, a clear track leads on around the head of Warley Moor Reservoir.

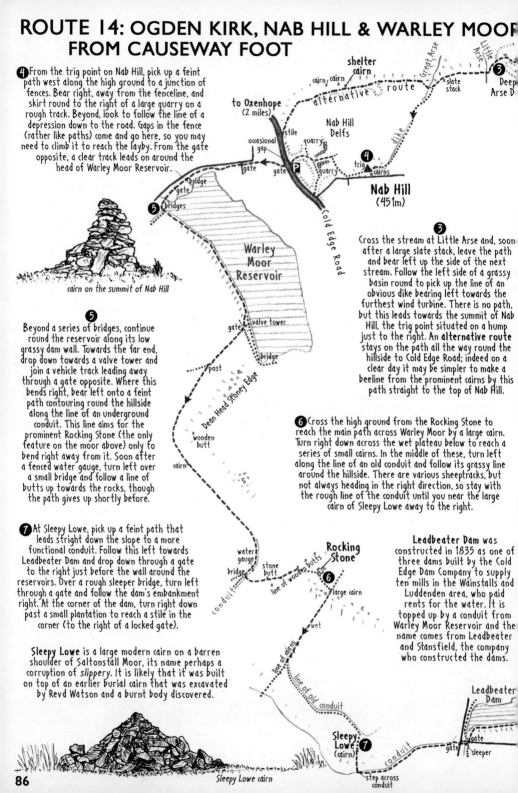

cairn on the summit of Nab Hill

to Oxenhope (2 miles)

shelter cairn

cairn cairn

alternative route

Great Arse

Little Arse

slate stack

3 Deep Arse D

Nab Hill Delfs

stile

quarry

occasional gap

gate gate

quarry

trig cairns

Nab Hill (451m)

Cold Edge Road

3 Cross the stream at Little Arse and, soon after a large slate stack, leave the path and bear left up the side of the next stream. Follow the left side of a grassy basin round to pick up the line of an obvious dike bearing left towards the furthest wind turbine. There is no path, but this leads towards the summit of Nab Hill, the trig point situated on a hump just to the right. An **alternative route** stays on the path all the way round the hillside to Cold Edge Road; indeed on a clear day it may be simpler to make a beeline from the prominent cairns by this path straight to the top of Nab Hill.

bridge gate

5 bridges

Warley Moor Reservoir

gate valve tower

bridge

post

Dean Head Stoney Edge

wooden butt

cairn

5 Beyond a series of bridges, continue round the reservoir along its low grassy dam wall. Towards the far end, drop down towards a valve tower and join a vehicle track leading away through a gate opposite. Where this bends right, bear left onto a feint path contouring round the hillside along the line of an underground conduit. This line aims for the prominent Rocking Stone (the only feature on the moor above) only to bend right away from it. Soon after a fenced water gauge, turn left over a small bridge and follow a line of butts up towards the rocks, though the path gives up shortly before.

6 Cross the high ground from the Rocking Stone to reach the main path across Warley Moor by a large cairn. Turn right down across the wet plateau below to reach a series of small cairns. In the middle of these, turn left along the line of an old conduit and follow its grassy line around the hillside. There are various sheeptracks, but not always heading in the right direction, so stay with the rough line of the conduit until you near the large cairn of Sleepy Lowe away to the right.

7 At Sleepy Lowe, pick up a feint path that leads straight down the slope to a more functional conduit. Follow this left towards Leadbeater Dam and drop down through a gate to the right just before the wall around the reservoirs. Over a rough sleeper bridge, turn left through a gate and follow the dam's embankment right. At the corner of the dam, turn right down past a small plantation to reach a stile in the corner (to the right of a locked gate).

water gauge

bridge stone butt

line of wooden butts

Rocking Stone

6

large cairn

wet

line of cairns

line of old conduit

Leadbeater Dam was constructed in 1835 as one of three dams built by the Cold Edge Dam Company to supply ten mills in the Wainstalls and Luddenden area, who paid rents for the water. It is topped up by a conduit from Warley Moor Reservoir and the name comes from Leadbeater and Stansfield, the company who constructed the dams.

Leadbeater Dam

gate

gate sleeper

Sleepy Lowe is a large modern cairn on a barren shoulder of Saltonstall Moor, its name perhaps a corruption of *slippery*. It is likely that it was built on top of an earlier burial cairn that was excavated by Revd Watson and a burnt body discovered.

conduit

Sleepy Lowe (cairn)

7

conduit

step across conduit

Sleepy Lowe cairn

Distance: 8½ miles (14km)
Ascent: 260m
Difficulty: Moderate

Parking: Car park by Ogden Water (50p)
Public Transport: Causeway Foot is on the 502, 504 & 505 bus routes between Halifax and Denholme/Keighley.

Character: A good circuit of the moorlands closest to Halifax that spends most of its time on the high ground, linking Ogden Kirk with Nab Hill and the Rocking Stone on Warley Moor. Most of the paths are good, except across Warley Moor, but the ground is not hard going. The quarries of Nab Hill take some negotiating, though they can be easily avoided by an alternative route.

1 From the A629, follow the road beside the Causeway Foot Inn down to the car park by Ogden Water. Go left through a gate at the far end of the lower car park and join a good path to the far end of the reservoir. By the bridge here, carry straight on up the right side of the stream. Once out of the plantation, ignore further bridges over the stream and follow Ogden Clough up to the crags of Ogden Kirk.

2 At the top of the steps alongside Ogden Kirk, pick up the onward track up the clough. Soon after a gate, bear right away from the stream and follow Hambleton Lane over the top of the moor. By the start of a line of wooden grouse butts, turn left through a small gate and follow a path along the edge and through the myriad depressions of Deep Arse Delf.

Boggart's Grave and **Ogden Dribbling Well** are a couple of the artificial myths invented by Ogden Water Country Park. A poem by the former suggests that the reservoir was built to drown the boggart and his 'band of evil old stoats'!

The **Roman Camp** is just about evident as a series of ditches and depressions in the rough grass above the golf course. It stands near what was a Roman road between Manchester and Ilkley that cut straight up through what is now Ogden Water; little evidence of this remains on the ground, though there is supposed to have been a well preserved section beneath the reservoir.

8 Turn left along the track towards Spring Mill Fold. Bend right to pass in front of the buildings and continue up towards Plane Trees Cottage. Keep straight on over a stile here, joining a fenced path up to the road. Head straight across the road onto a track towards the quarries by Slaughter Gap. At the first stile on the left, bear diagonally across the fields to a rough stile in the only wall still standing. Continue on the same line over the brow to reach a kissing gate leading left out onto the corner of the moor.

9 Follow a path along the wall past the site of the Roman Camp and down towards Halifax Golf Course. The path is well-waymarked as it heads straight across the fairways. Beyond the high bridge, bear right climbing the hill the other side, before bending left to reach the edge of Ogden Plantation. Turn right down the track and cross the promenade past Ogden Water to reach the café and your start point.

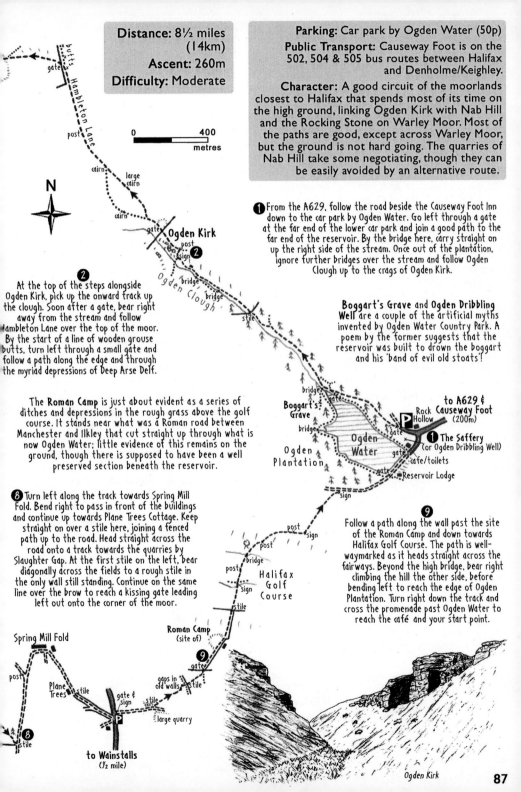

Ogden Kirk

87

DELVING IN THE QUARRIES

The quarrying of stone in the area is recorded as early as the fourteenth century, although early quarrying was generally of earthfast stones or exposed edges – pick marks can be found on some of the stones remaining on the moor. Stones gathered either from the open moor or from areas that had been cleared for grazing were used largely for building. Gritstone was only originally quarried for use as grindstones, with the Elland Flags used as crude roofing tiles. The latter occur in a narrow band east of Halifax and Keighley and were used as thackstones (thatch-stones), with moss-packs gathered from the moor then used to stuff joints and waterproof the rooves. Known as York Stone, the Elland flags had a market across the whole country and can still be seen in many London pavements.

Later, Rough Rock *(see page vii for geological background)* was used for building, with quarries appearing across the moors in ever greater number to meet the demand for stone needed for the construction of reservoirs, churches, mills, roads and houses, which reached a peak towards the end of the nineteenth century. Quarries were often dug into the sides of the moor where access was easier, and then worked steadily across the plateau, as at Nab Hill. Some of this quarrying activity decimated impressive natural features (like the Kirk Stones on Morton Moor, or Jackson Rock at Withens Gate), but others created dramatic features (at Shooters Nab, Gaddings Hole or Hell Hole Rocks near Heptonstall). As part of the enclosure acts, township delfs (quarries) were also created where people could take free stone for enclosure walls and repairing buildings, though these would usually be shallower pits dug into the poorer rock.

As well as peat, the useless broken surface stone (or rag) had to be removed to reach the workable layers, often being built into large judd walls (like those in the Shibden Valley). No explosives were used, instead steam cranes with hooks were fixed beneath a layer of the stone by the delvers (quarrymen). The stone was then dressed on site and removed by horse drawn carts. Rough Rock was used for flags, jambs and kerbs, while the older grits served as setts, building stone, pulping stones (for the paper industry) and were crushed for gravel or sand. The roughest serviceable stone was used for dry stone walling and at one time there were gangs of itinerant wallers constantly employed. Many farmers also supplemented their income by working as wallers or quarrymen.

During the nineteenth century, peat pits (those places where peat had been dug for fuel) and quarries like those across Nab Hill became popular sites for gambling activities on Sundays. Men with little else to entertain themselves gathered to bet on games like penny stone, pitch and toss, and knurr and spell. Penny stone was a boules-type game from which Penistone Hill gets its name, and knurr and spell involved striking a large marble (the knurr) with a wooden bat (the spell) as far as possible. For this, courses as long as 200 yards were marked out, so the moorland was perfect ground to play on - indeed it was invented on these moors and is often called northern spell. Lookouts were posted to keep an eye out for policemen (a possible source of the name Sentry Hill near Sawood) and there are accounts of gatherings being broken up by large operations on Nab Hill and at Widdop, following a concerted effort by Halifax, Keighley and Bradford police forces. The delfs on Nab Hill were quarried until 2000, since when they have been used only for occasional raves, keeping up the tradition of illicit activities.

CHAPTER 13 - PULE HILL

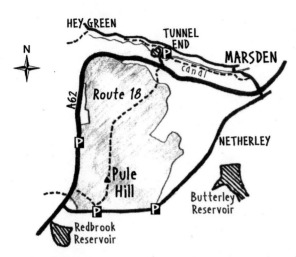

Height: 437m

Grid Ref: SE032104

Map Sheet: OL21 (South Pennines)

Access: No restrictions.

Public Transport: Regular bus and train services to Marsden from Huddersfield. Bus 184 runs from Marsden to Oldham via A62.

Pule Hill is very much unique amongst West Yorkshire summits in being a pure hill, rising steeply on all sides to a pointed peak. It is surrounded by expanses of peat moorland, yet forms a tiny oasis in their midst and a welcome view from almost any direction. Its name is a corruption or local version of *pool* (or at least the Celtic *pwll*), which once lay either on top of the hill or on its north shoulder. Pule Hill is an easy climb, criminally so from the laybys on the roads below, but even from Marsden, from where its charms are less apparent. The dramatic quarried faces of Pule Edge face west and dominate the moor along with the shafts of the Standedge Tunnel that cuts below the hillside on its way across the Pennines.

Pule Hill from Naze End

PULE HILL MAP - Entire Moor

Pule Hill covers only a very small area, squeezed between the A62 and Old Mount Road. Given its obvious aesthetic appeal and proximity to Marsden, one would expect it to be busy and covered in paths. In fact Pule Hill is surprisingly difficult to access from Marsden, its main routes climbing up from lay-bys on the roads to the west and south. Elsewhere feint paths meander across the steep flanks of the hill, leading from one large quarry delf to the next. The main attractions on Pule Hill, aside from the summit, are the Standedge Tunnels 300m below the moor. Ventilation shafts, engine houses, spoil heaps and marker stones line the route of the many tunnels as they make for nearby Tunnel End.

A site below **Worlow Quarry** has been suggested by Huddersfield & District Archeological Society to be that of a Roman fortlet or signal station. It stands on the likely earliest route of a Roman Road between Castleshaw Fort (near Delph) and Slack Fort (near Outlane), later supplanted by one further north roughly along the line of the A640. Fragments of Roman pottery similar to those at Castleshaw were found here in a series of excavations by the society in the 1980s.

*Pule Edge Quarry is easily reached from a large lay-by on the A62 and is surrounded by all manner of industrial remains. The simplest route to the edge is to pick up the main track running diagonally up past both of the ventilation shafts. It is also possible to scramble up from the loading bay at the top of the tramway incline, skirting round the edge of the quarry. Pule Edge's dramatic rock arch at **Trog 'Ole** is reached by staying on a feint track below the edge.*

The flat summit area of **Pule Hill** was the site of a Bronze Age cemetery, which was discovered and exacavated in the 1890s by George Marsden. Though there was no obvious burial mound, four urns containing human remains were found on the site set in rock cavities, along with a number of food vessels and pots. An arrowhead and other flint chippings have also been found here, thought to represent the workshops of Mesolithic hunter-gatherers who camped on the high ground of the South Pennines during the summer months. These finds are similar to dozens of others across this area's moorland (between Dean Head in the north and Rocher Moss in the south), which represent the greatest density of Mesolithic sites anywhere in the country.

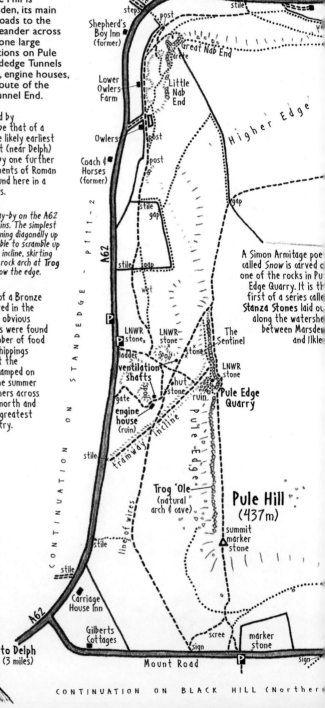

A Simon Armitage poem called *Snow* is carved on one of the rocks in Pule Edge Quarry. It is the first of a series called **Stanza Stones** laid out along the watershed between Marsden and Ilkley

the Trog 'Ole on Pule Edge

CONTINUATION ON BLACK HILL (Northern

The most direct route from Marsden to Pule Hill is via the ventilation shaft and prominent memorial cross on **Higher Edge**. These can be reached by following the wall up from a gate near Intake Head Farm and an obvious track then runs across the high ground to **Pule Edge**. An alternative is to follow the public footpath round the northern edge of the hill. The route here is not always clear, especially across the rushy ground near Intake Head Farm. From the top of the spoil heap here, a feint path contours across to **Pinglet Head Quarries**, from where the fenceline is followed above two properties. A feint grassy track can then be picked up angling across the slope towards Great Nab End.

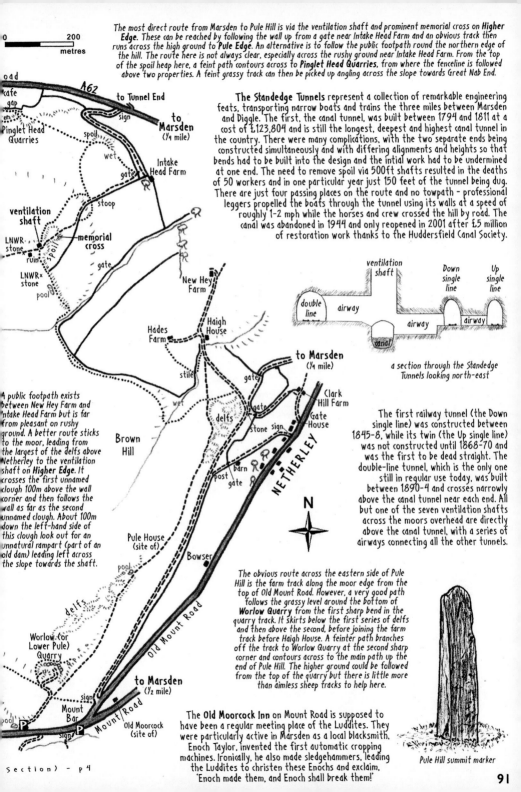

The Standedge Tunnels represent a collection of remarkable engineering feats, transporting narrow boats and trains the three miles between Marsden and Diggle. The first, the canal tunnel, was built between 1794 and 1811 at a cost of £123,804 and is still the longest, deepest and highest canal tunnel in the country. There were many complications, with the two separate ends being constructed simultaneously and with differing alignments and heights so that bends had to be built into the design and the intial work had to be undermined at one end. The need to remove spoil via 500ft shafts resulted in the deaths of 50 workers and in one particular year just 150 feet of the tunnel being dug. There are just four passing places on the route and no towpath - professional leggers propelled the boats through the tunnel using its walls at a speed of roughly 1-2 mph while the horses and crew crossed the hill by road. The canal was abandoned in 1944 and only reopened in 2001 after £5 million of restoration work thanks to the Huddersfield Canal Society.

a section through the Standedge Tunnels looking north-east

The first railway tunnel (the Down single line) was constructed between 1845-8, while its twin (the Up single line) was not constructed until 1868-70 and was the first to be dead straight. The double-line tunnel, which is the only one still in regular use today, was built between 1890-4 and crosses narrowly above the canal tunnel near each end. All but one of the seven ventilation shafts across the moors overhead are directly above the canal tunnel, with a series of airways connecting all the other tunnels.

A public footpath exists between New Hey Farm and Intake Head Farm but is far from pleasant on rushy ground. A better route sticks to the moor, leading from the largest of the delfs above Netherley to the ventilation shaft on **Higher Edge**. It crosses the first unnamed clough 100m above the wall corner and then follows the wall as far as the second unnamed clough. About 100m down the left-hand side of this clough look out for an unnatural rampart (part of an old dam) leading left across the slope towards the shaft.

The obvious route across the eastern side of Pule Hill is the farm track along the moor edge from the top of Old Mount Road. However, a very good path follows the grassy level around the bottom of **Worlow Quarry** from the first sharp bend in the quarry track. It skirts below the first series of delfs and then above the second, before joining the farm track before Haigh House. A feinter path branches off the track to Worlow Quarry at the second sharp corner and contours across to the main path up the end of Pule Hill. The higher ground could be followed from the top of the quarry but there is little more than aimless sheep tracks to help here.

The **Old Moorcock Inn** on Mount Road is supposed to have been a regular meeting place of the Luddites. They were particularly active in Marsden as a local blacksmith, Enoch Taylor, invented the first automatic cropping machines. Ironically, he also made sledgehammers, leading the Luddites to christen these Enochs and exclaim, 'Enoch made them, and Enoch shall break them!'

Pule Hill summit marker

The **Meadow Pipit** is the most common bird on the moors of the South Pennines, its familiar sharp song a soundtrack to any day out during the warmer months. It looks fairly undistinctive; small, largely brown with mottled streaks on its back and white underneath its wings. It calls when in flight, particularly during the breeding season when it performs its trademark parachute dives. Despite its prevalence here, the meadow pipit is in decline due to a loss of its winter habitats - rough pasture and broad hedgerows.

CHAPTER 14 - ROMBALDS MOOR

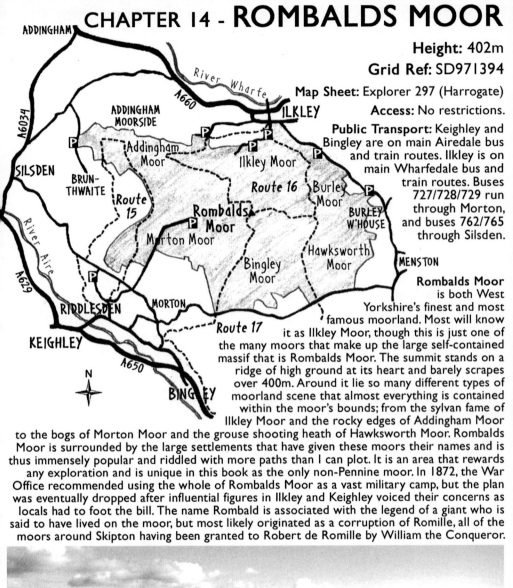

Height: 402m

Grid Ref: SD971394

Map Sheet: Explorer 297 (Harrogate)

Access: No restrictions.

Public Transport: Keighley and Bingley are on main Airedale bus and train routes. Ilkley is on main Wharfedale bus and train routes. Buses 727/728/729 run through Morton, and buses 762/765 through Silsden.

Rombalds Moor is both West Yorkshire's finest and most famous moorland. Most will know it as Ilkley Moor, though this is just one of the many moors that make up the large self-contained massif that is Rombalds Moor. The summit stands on a ridge of high ground at its heart and barely scrapes over 400m. Around it lie so many different types of moorland scene that almost everything is contained within the moor's bounds; from the sylvan fame of Ilkley Moor and the rocky edges of Addingham Moor to the bogs of Morton Moor and the grouse shooting heath of Hawksworth Moor. Rombalds Moor is surrounded by the large settlements that have given these moors their names and is thus immensely popular and riddled with more paths than I can plot. It is an area that rewards any exploration and is unique in this book as the only non-Pennine moor. In 1872, the War Office recommended using the whole of Rombalds Moor as a vast military camp, but the plan was eventually dropped after influential figures in Ilkley and Keighley voiced their concerns as locals had to foot the bill. The name Rombald is associated with the legend of a giant who is said to have lived on the moor, but most likely originated as a corruption of Romille, all of the moors around Skipton having been granted to Robert de Romille by William the Conqueror.

Rombalds Moor from Addingham Crag

ROMBALDS MOOR MAP - Northern Section (Ilkley Moor

The northern section of Rombalds Moor is the well-known Ilkley Moor, rising steeply above Ilkley and the Wharf Valley to a series of gritstone edges. Partly because the moor is quite so accessible from the town and partly because of its *baht 'at* fame, Ilkley Moor is by far the busiest hillside in West Yorkshire. It was bought by the Ilkley Local Board in 1893 for £13,500 as 'an amenity for the people of Ilkley' and is now an urban common. The moor, though, warrants this attention such is its intricacy and ability to throw up beautiful little corners amid the bracken and heather. Whether it is a stone circle or prehistoric petroglyph, a tarn, waterfall or nook of mixed woodland, Ilkley Moor is a Pandora's Box that is meant to be explored aimlessly.

*The northern slopes of Ilkley Moor are a maze of paths through the bracken, criss-crossing between rocky outcrops, tarns and pockets of woodland. It is impossible to explain particular routes, though the map attempts to simplify this remarkable warren. While lower down all routes seem to lead to **White Wells** or **The Tarn**, higher up the slopes you find yourself drawn to the large cairn on **Cranshaw Thorn Hill** (probably the best viewpoint over Ilkley) and the rocky ford across **Backstone Beck**.*

The whitewashed buildings of **White Wells** are a dominant feature of the lower slopes of Ilkley Moor. They stand on a spring that is likely to have been used since the area's first settlers and was later discovered to have medicinal properties. There was a bath here since 1703, with a local squire erecting the bath house in 1791, making it Britain's first hydropathic spa. Though initially 'the Heather Spaw' was seen as rather rustic, the rigours of the Water Cure became fashionable in the Victorian era and turned Ilkley into the attractive retreat it is today.

N

*The **Backstone Circle** is easily bypassed, its loose collection of standing stones housed within a sheepfold just above Backstone Beck. Look for the stones jutting over the skyline above you (see Page 100 for more information*

Ilkley Moor has a remarkable concentration of ancient features, by far the greatest in West Yorkshire. Other than the five stone circles, there are hundreds of **cup and ring marked stones**. These carvings are a form of sacred art associated with a late Neolithic/early Bronze Age cult that only existed for a relatively short period of time. They were particularly busy on Ilkley Moor, though, and nearly every rock on the northern side of the moor possesses some form of marking. Many are only discernible to those familiar with ancient carvings, others almost disappear in the wrong light – the rocks are best viewed when wet or in oblique (early or late) sunlight. Among the most remarkable examples (besides the renowned Swastika Stone on the western moor and the Hanging Stones near the Cow & Calf) are the Badger Stone, the Pepperpot, the Idol Stone and Haystack Rock. It is thought that many of the designs were originally coloured with pigment, but the meaning of these abstract markings is unclear, possibly relating to burials, fertility or the stars.

*The trig point at the summit of **Rombalds Moor** stands on a peaty plateau high above Ilkley and not far from the twin masts at **Whetstone Gate**. It can be reached most easily from the car park by the mast, but more satisfying approaches climb out of Ilkley. The main route across the moor climbs up **Ilkley Crags** from **White Wells** and then continues across Gill Head to reach the plateau at the **Lanshaw Lad** boundary stone. Turn right here to get to the summit. Alternatively a couple of smaller paths climb straight up the hillside, one from the **Badger Stone** and the other from the path contouring round to **Cranshaw Thorn Hill**. The latter sets off 50m to the west of a prominent boulder, from which a feinter path emerges.*

94

Map labels

ILKLEY TOWN CENTRE
ILKLEY
Wells Road
cattle grid
sign & gate
pond
water treatment
bridge
sign
shelter
lamp
shelter
lamp
The Tarn
heap of rocks
post
benches
barrier
bridges
small tarn
seat
seat
sign
post
Willy Hall's Spout
White Wells sign
seat
post
tiny pool
Willy Hall's Wood
Pepperpot
West Rock
Barmishaw Hole
C & R marked stone
delf
seats
sign
Weary Hill
Quarries
Wicken Tree Crag
posts
rock
C & R marked stones
butt x
Grainings Head
seat
Badger Stone
CONTINUATION ON ROMBALDS MOOR (western Section)
Keighley Road
Cowper's Cross
barrow
line of stone butts
butt
butt
butt
gate
stile
to Riddlesden (2 miles)
Whetstone Gate Wireless Station
flagstones
Thimble Stones
Stanza Stone (poem)
flagstones
cist
trig
Rombalds Moor (402m)
cairn
boundary stone
Ashlar Chair
gates
CONTINU

The **Hanging Stones** refers to the small crag looking north from the huge quarry west of the Cow & Calf. The top of this crag is one huge canvas of neolithic carvings, truly the most unusual of any across the moor and well worth a look. Remarkably this rock was only saved from being engulfed within the quarry by a visitor to the area who alerted the local squire to its destruction. The hole beneath the crags is known as the Fairies Parlour (or Fairies Kirk).

The **Cow & Calf** is Ilkley Moor's most distinctive landmark, a gritstone promontory from which a large chunk has fallen to lie in its lee. According to legend, the Calf was broken from The Cow when the giant Rombald fled across the valley and stood on the rock. The name is thought to have come from an ancient beltane custom of driving cattle between the old and new fires that were lit as beacons on the moor. Indeed the Cow is also known as the Inglestone (*ingle* being a fire); in it can be seen a face often called the Sphinx. There was once a giant Bull Stone too, but this was quarried to build the Crescent Hotel in Ilkley. Now the remaining rocks are covered in Victorian carvings, remarkable not for their antiquity but sheer density, covering every inch of the mammoth rocks. Never has grafitti seemed so alluring.

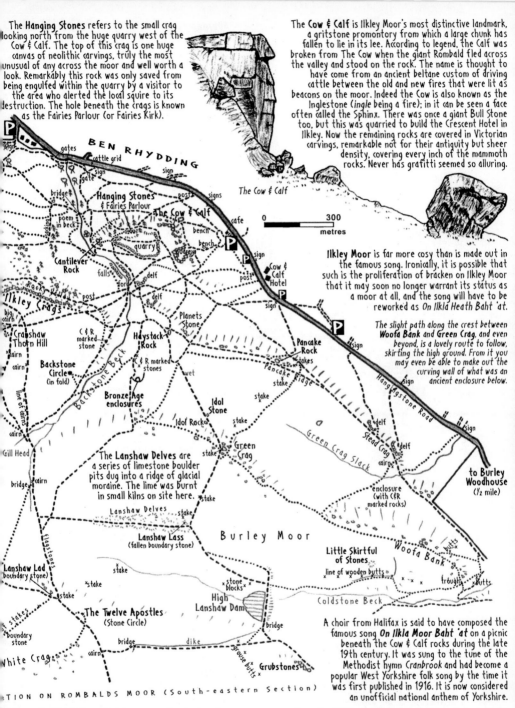

The Cow & Calf

Ilkley Moor is far more cosy than is made out in the famous song. Ironically, it is possible that such is the proliferation of bracken on Ilkley Moor that it may soon no longer warrant its status as a moor at all, and the song will have to be reworked as *On Ilkla Heath Baht 'at*.

The slight path along the crest between **Woofa Bank** and **Green Crag**, and even beyond, is a lovely route to follow, skirting the high ground. From it you may even be able to make out the curving wall of what was an ancient enclosure below.

0   300
metres

The Lanshaw Delves are a series of limestone boulder pits dug into a ridge of glacial moraine. The lime was burnt in small kilns on site here.

A choir from Halifax is said to have composed the famous song *On Ilkla Moor Baht 'at* on a picnic beneath the Cow & Calf rocks during the late 19th century. It was sung to the tune of the Methodist hymn *Cranbrook* and had become a popular West Yorkshire folk song by the time it was first published in 1916. It is now considered an unofficial national anthem of Yorkshire.

...TION ON ROMBALDS MOOR (South-eastern Section)

To the east of **Backstone Beck** is an area of **ancient enclosures**, where some Bronze Age walling and hut circles have been partially restored. During its excavation, flints and pottery were discovered, suggesting occupation since at least 2500BC. Very close to the enclosure are three impressive stones lost in the heather, each an incredible mosaic of symbols or cup marks. Another stands the opposite side of the stream, right in the middle of the path.

In December 1987, a man crossing the moor photographed a green figure with long arms near Backstone Beck. It has become known as the **Ilkley Moor Alien**, one of the most compelling extraterrestrial sightings. Philip Spencer also claims to have lost two hours and suffered flashbacks of been abducted by the domed ship he subsequently saw taking off. It has since been verified that the photo was not tampered with.

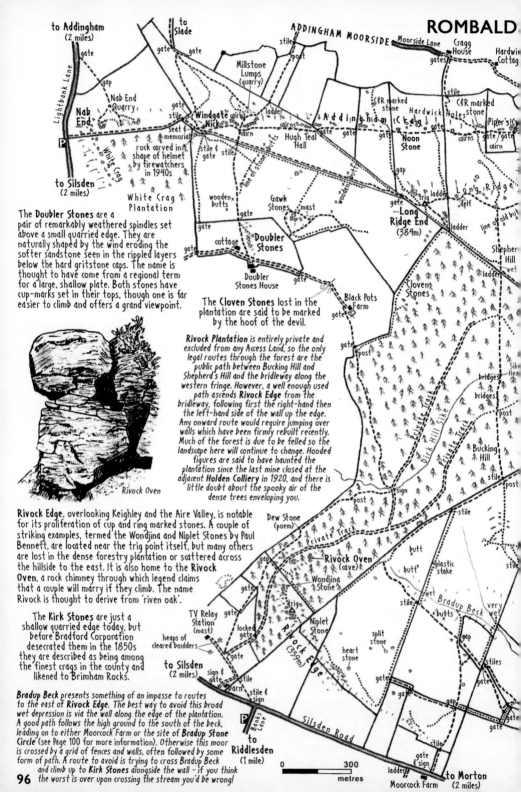

Map labels:

to Addingham (2 miles) · to Slade · ADDINGHAM MOORSIDE · Moorside Lane · Cragg House · Hardwick Cottage · gate · stile · post · gates · Lightbank Lane · gap · gate · gate · Millstone Lumps (quarry) · Nab End Quarry · Nab End · gate · stile · Windgate Nick · cairns · ladder · C&R marked stone · Hardwick Holes · C&R marked stone · Piper's Crag · A d d i n g h a m C r a g · cairn · gate · gate · gate · cairns · gate/gate · cairn · P · White Crag · seat & memorial · rock carved in shape of helmet by firewatchers in 1940s · stile & gate · stile · cairn · Hugh Teal Hall · line of stone butts · Noon Stone · to Silsden (2 miles) · White Crag Plantation · wooden butts · Gawk Stones · mast · wooden butts · gap · Long Ridge · ladder · trig · delf · gate · Long Ridge End (384m) · ladder · line of old but · gate · gate · cottage · Doubler Stones · Shepherd Hill wet · gate · Doubler Stones House · gate · Black Pots Farm · gate · Cloven Stones · ladder · gate · post · Sike Hea · bridges · bridges · post · Dirk Hill Sike · Private Track · Private Track · Bucking Hill · stile · post · sign · post · Dew Stone (poem) · Private Track · stile · butt · plastic stake · stile · Rivock Oven (cave) · butt · Wondjina Stone · wet · Bradup Beck · very wet · gap · gate · trig · butts · stile · TV Relay Station (mast) · gate · Niplet Stone · heart stone · split stone · stiles · locked gate · heaps of cleared boulders · gate · Rivock Edge (359m) · gap · to Silsden (2 miles) · sign & gate · barn · stile · stile & sign · gate · gate · gap · gate · P · Banks' Lane · Silsden Road · gate · to Riddlesden (1 mile) · gate & sign · ladder · Moorcock Farm · to Morton (2 miles)

The **Doubler Stones** are a pair of remarkably weathered spindles set above a small quarried edge. They are naturally shaped by the wind eroding the softer sandstone seen in the rippled layers below the hard gritstone caps. The name is thought to have come from a regional term for a large, shallow plate. Both stones have cup-marks set in their tops, though one is far easier to climb and offers a grand viewpoint.

Rivock Oven

The **Cloven Stones** lost in the plantation are said to be marked by the hoof of the devil.

Rivock Plantation is entirely private and excluded from any Access Land, so the only legal routes through the forest are the public path between Bucking Hill and Shepherd's Hill and the bridleway along the western fringe. However, a well enough used path ascends **Rivock Edge** from the bridleway, following first the right-hand then the left-hand side of the wall up the edge. Any onward route would require jumping over walls which have been firmly rebuilt recently. Much of the forest is due to be felled so the landscape here will continue to change. Hooded figures are said to have haunted the plantation since the last mine closed at the adjacent **Holden Colliery** in 1920, and there is little doubt about the spooky air of the dense trees enveloping you.

Rivock Edge, overlooking Keighley and the Aire Valley, is notable for its proliferation of cup and ring marked stones. A couple of striking examples, termed the **Wondjina** and **Niplet Stones** by Paul Bennett, are located near the trig point itself, but many others are lost in the dense forestry plantation or scattered across the hillside to the east. It is also home to the **Rivock Oven**, a rock chimney through which legend claims that a couple will marry if they climb. The name Rivock is thought to derive from 'riven oak'.

The **Kirk Stones** are just a shallow quarried edge today, but before Bradford Corporation desecrated them in the 1850s they are described as being among the finest crags in the county and likened to Brimham Rocks.

Bradup Beck presents something of an impasse to routes to the east of **Rivock Edge**. The best way to avoid this broad wet depression is via the wall along the edge of the plantation. A good path follows the high ground to the south of the beck, leading on to either Moorcock Farm or the site of **Bradup Stone Circle** (see Page 100 for more information). Otherwise this moor is crossed by a grid of fences and walls, often followed by some form of path. A route to avoid is trying to cross Bradup Beck and climb up to **Kirk Stones** alongside the wall – if you think the worst is over upon crossing the stream you'd be wrong!

96

0   300
metres

Rombalds Moor sprawls westwards almost as far as Silsden, displaying a distinctive scarp to the north throughout and stretching down to the forested Rivock Edge overlooking Keighley. The further you get from Ilkley, the quieter the moor gets, even though there is still plenty to see. Beyond the caged and famed Swastika Stone carving, there are the remarkable Doubler Stones, the Buck Stones, and the cup and ring marked stones littered around Rivock Edge. The southern flank is flatter and less trodden, but even here the moor throws up surprises.

Between **Cowper's Cross** and the top of Spicey Gill there is no route off the Keighley Road, a pattern that continues across **Heber Moss** and Crawshaw Moss. A feint path follows the bottom of this slope, but there is no clear path up towards the enticing **Buck Stones**. When the heather is low it is not too difficult to follow Black Beck up towards the stones. The only other possible route heads south from the prominent boundary stone perched on the edge east of **High Crag** and then skirts round the bog itself.

Cowper's Cross stands near the top of one of the main historic tracks across the moor and may have been erected to replace the nearby Badger Stone as a place for gatherings and markets. The cross is a likely replacement for an original monolithic marker or memorial - there is a tale that a man named Cowper (or Cawper, the cross's alternative name) perished at this spot. The cross has been restored again having split when struck by lightning.

Neb Stone, a large flat slab of rock, probably gets its name not from neb as in nose but another dialect word referring to a kiss. Lovers apparently met secretly here.

The portion of **Morton Moor** east of the road is largely cut off (intentionally so by those shooting there). Low Moor is rather wet and barren, but High Moor is worth exploring. The only access point is next to a gate from the car park at Whetstone Gate. The most obvious path from here runs down to an edge above Lay Thorn Hill. Another path runs south-east to a gap in the wall and gives access to **The Two Eggs**. **Thimble Stones** and broken cross base on **Black Knoll**, a remarkably prominent lump in the hillside from anywhere across Bingley Moor. This high heathery ground is not too hard to cross, but the only path runs along the wall and sections of the drain to the south. It runs out in reeds just short of the shooters track from Bingley Moor, but the ground is not as wet as it looks here.

Cowper's Cross

The back side of Rombalds Moor reveals itself to be rather empty, both of people and the rocks that draw them to Ilkley Moor. Bingley and Hawksworth Moors are broad sweeps of heather crossed by just a few obvious paths, but they are home to most of the cairn circles on the moor and the remarkable collection of cup and ring marked rocks on Stanbury Hill. Only the steep bracken-covered sides of Coldstone Beck suggest any proximity to Ilkley Moor's hordes.

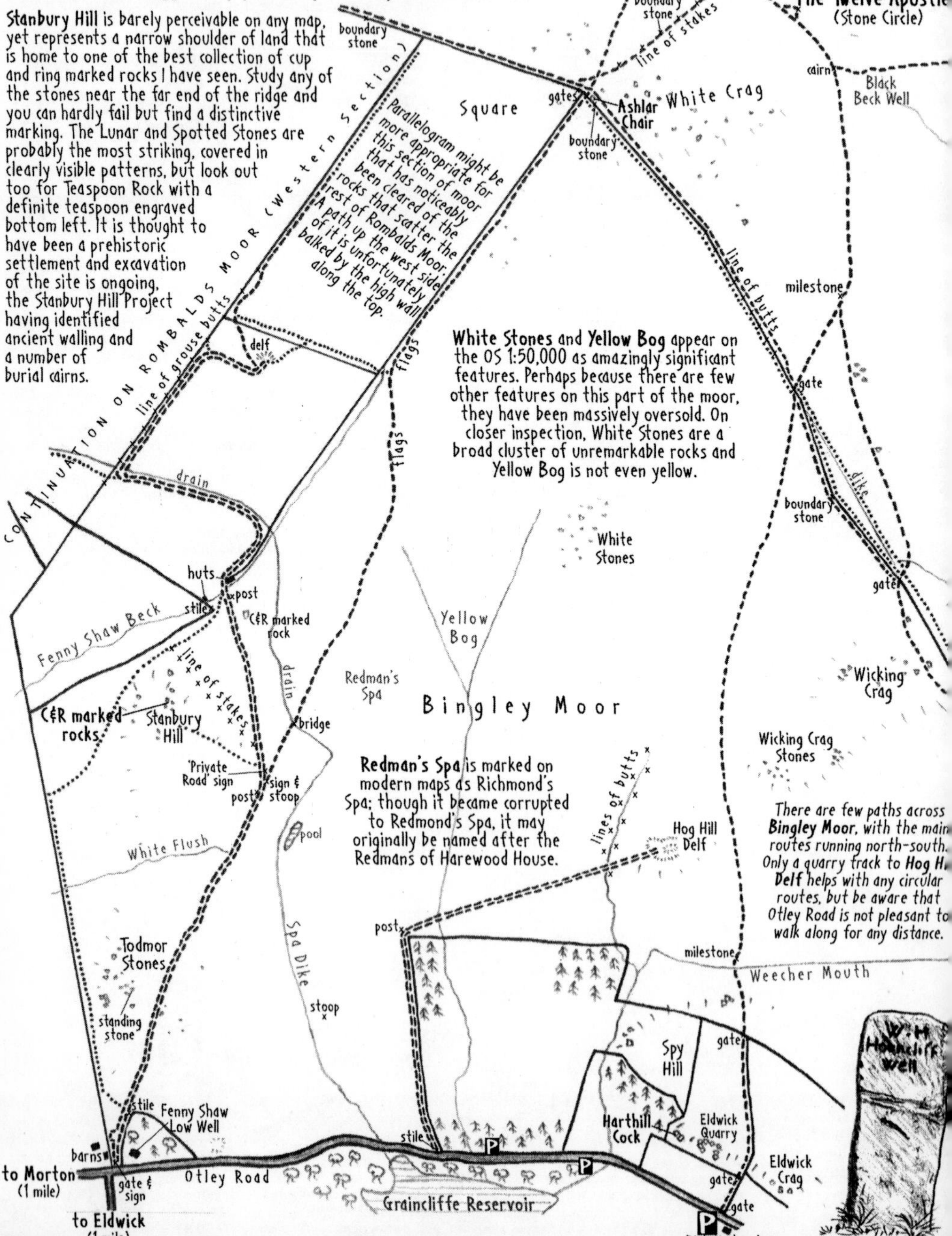

Stanbury Hill is barely perceivable on any map, yet represents a narrow shoulder of land that is home to one of the best collection of cup and ring marked rocks I have seen. Study any of the stones near the far end of the ridge and you can hardly fail but find a distinctive marking. The Lunar and Spotted Stones are probably the most striking, covered in clearly visible patterns, but look out too for Teaspoon Rock with a definite teaspoon engraved bottom left. It is thought to have been a prehistoric settlement and excavation of the site is ongoing, the Stanbury Hill Project having identified ancient walling and a number of burial cairns.

Parallelogram might be more appropriate for this section of moor that has noticeably been cleared of the rocks that scatter the rest of Rombalds Moor. A path up the west side of it is unfortunately balked by the high wall along the top.

White Stones and Yellow Bog appear on the OS 1:50,000 as amazingly significant features. Perhaps because there are few other features on this part of the moor, they have been massively oversold. On closer inspection, White Stones are a broad cluster of unremarkable rocks and Yellow Bog is not even yellow.

Redman's Spa is marked on modern maps as Richmond's Spa; though it became corrupted to Redmond's Spa, it may originally be named after the Redmans of Harewood House.

There are few paths across Bingley Moor, with the main routes running north-south. Only a quarry track to Hog Hill Delf helps with any circular routes, but be aware that Otley Road is not pleasant to walk along for any distance.

CONTINUATION ON ROMBALDS

CONTINUATION ON ROMBALDS MOOR (Western Section)

cairn
Lanshaw Lad (boundary stone)
stake
The Twelve Apostles (Stone Circle)
boundary stone
line of stakes
cairn
boundary stone
Square
gates
Ashlar Chair
White Crag
boundary stone
Black Beck Well
line of butts
milestone
gate
delf
flags
boundary stone
gate
line of grouse butts
drain
White Stones
huts
post
stile
C&R marked rock
Yellow Bog
Wicking Crag
Fenny Shaw Beck
line of stakes
drain
Bingley Moor
Wicking Crag Stones
C&R marked rocks
Stanbury Hill
bridge
Redman's Spa
'Private Road' sign
sign & post/stoop
pool
lines of butts
Hog Hill Delf
White Flush
Spa Dike
post
milestone
Weecher Mouth
Todmor Stones
stoop
standing stone
Spy Hill
gate
stile Fenny Shaw Low Well
Harthill Cock
Eldwick Quarry
Eldwick Crag
barns
stile
to Morton (1 mile)
gate & sign
Otley Road
P
P
P
to Eldwick (1 mile)
Graincliffe Reservoir
P
Dick Hudson's (inn)
Horncliffe Well Stoop

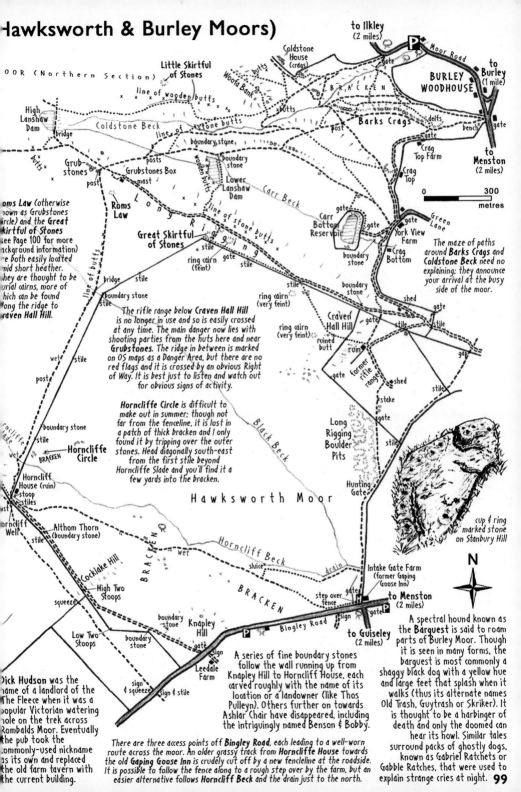

...OOR (Northern Section)

to Ilkley (2 miles)

Coldstone House (crags)

Moor Road

to Burley (1 mile)

BURLEY WOODHOUSE

Little Skirtful of Stones

line of wooden butts

Woofa Bank

B R A C K E N

butts

gate

High Lanshaw Dam

Coldstone Beck

line of stone butts

Barks Crags

delts

to Menston (2 miles)

bridge

line of boundary stone

post

bench

gate

Crag Top Farm

Grub-stones

Grubstones Box

boundary stone

Crag Top

butts

post

mast

Lower Lanshaw Dam

Carr Beck

Crag Top

oms Law (otherwise ...nown as Grubstones ...ircle) and the **Great ...kirtful of Stones** ...see Page 100 for more ...ackground information) ...e both easily located ...mid short heather. ...hey are thought to be ...urial cairns, more of ...hich can be found ...long the ridge to ...raven Hall Hill.

Roms Law

Long Rigging

Great Skirtful of Stones

line of stone butts

stile

gate

stile

ring cairn (feint)

Carr Bottom Reservoir

gate

gate

York View Farm

Green Lane

Crag Bottom

boundary stone

gate

The maze of paths around **Barks Crags** and **Coldstone Beck** need no explaining; they announce your arrival at the busy side of the moor.

line of butts

bridge

stile

boundary stone

stile

ring cairn (very feint)

boundary stone

shed

gate

The rifle range below **Craven Hall Hill** is no longer in use and so is easily crossed at any time. The main danger now lies with shooting parties from the huts here and near **Grubstones**. The ridge in between is marked on OS maps as a Danger Area, but there are no red flags and it is crossed by an obvious Right of Way. It is best just to listen and watch out for obvious signs of activity.

ring cairn (very feint)

Craven Hall Hill

ruined butt

ruin

gate

gap

wet

stile

posts

former rifle range

shed

stile

Horncliffe Circle is difficult to make out in summer; though not far from the fenceline, it is lost in a patch of thick bracken and I only found it by tripping over the outer stones. Head diagonally south-east from the first stile beyond Horncliffe Slade and you'll find it a few yards into the bracken.

Black Beck

stake

gate

Long Rigging Boulder Pits

stile

...rncliffe ...ade

boundary stone

stile

wet

BRACKEN

Horncliffe Circle

Hunting Gate

Horncliff House (ruin)

stoop

stiles

Hawksworth Moor

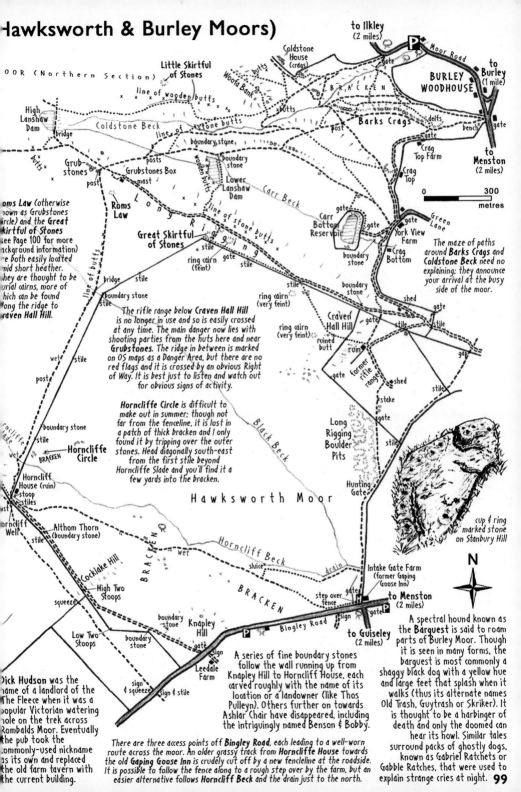

cup & ring marked stone on Stanbury Hill

...st

...rncliff Well

stile

Althom Thorn (boundary stone)

Horncliff Beck

wet

sluice

drain

N

Cocklake Hill

BRACKEN

High Two Stoops

BRACKEN

Intake Gate Farm (former Gaping Goose Inn)

to Menston (2 miles)

squeeze

step over fence

gate

boundary stone

Knapley Hill

Bingley Road

sign

gate

to Guiseley (2 miles)

Low Two Stoops

boundary stone

gate

sign

...ick Hudson was the ...name of a landlord of ...he Fleece when it was a ...opular Victorian watering ...ole on the trek across ...ombalds Moor. Eventually ...he pub took the ...ommonly-used nickname ...s its own and replaced ...he old farm tavern with ...he current building.

Leedale Farm

sign

sign & squeeze

sign & stile

A series of fine boundary stones follow the wall running up from Knapley Hill to Horncliff House, each carved roughly with the name of its location or a landowner (like Thos Pulleyn). Others further on towards Ashlar Chair have disappeared, including the intriguingly named **Benson & Bobby**.

A spectral hound known as the **Barguest** is said to roam parts of Burley Moor. Though it is seen in many forms, the barguest is most commonly a shaggy black dog with a yellow hue and large feet that splash when it walks (thus its alternate names Old Trash, Guytrash or Skriker). It is thought to be a harbinger of death and only the doomed can hear its howl. Similar tales surround packs of ghostly dogs, known as Gabriel Ratchets or Gabble Ratches, that were used to explain strange cries at night.

There are three access points off **Bingley Road**, each leading to a well-worn route across the moor. An older grassy track from **Horncliffe House** towards the old **Gaping Goose Inn** is crudely cut off by a new fenceline at the roadside. It is possible to follow the fence along to a rough step over by the farm, but an easier alternative follows **Horncliff Beck** and the drain just to the north.

0 — 300 metres

THE STONE CIRCLES & BURIAL

Stone circles are thought to have formed an important part of mid-Bronze Age ceremonial culture subsequent to that which created the cup and ring markings across the moor. However, many of those referred to as stone circles on Rombalds Moor are actually burial cairns, while some of its greatest ritual circles are now long gone.

BACKSTONE CIRCLE

Only rediscovered in 1994, the nature, and even authenticity, of this circle is very much unknown. Some have suggested it is a Victorian folly, others that is part of a greater complex, and it has become associated with ghostly sightings over recent years.

BRADUP STONE CIRCLE

The story of Bradup Stone Circle (also known as Brass Castle or Kirkstones Circle) is unremittingly sad. Though like others on Ilkley Moor it was most likely a burial cairn and not a stone circle, it was once referred to as 'Riddlesden's Stonehenge'. In 1885 there were apparently eighteen stones before the construction of Bradup Bridge used some of the stones. In 1929 it was recorded by Arthur Rastrick as having twelve stones left standing and he thought it the finest stone circle in the West Riding. These are said to have been present as late as the 1960s, but the laying of a gas pipeline in 1971 further disturbed the circle. Certainly by the 1990s all that remained was a solitary stone and an embankment clearly evident from above. However, it was declassified as a Scheduled Ancient Monument by English Heritage in 1994 and the field was ploughed up in 2004. Apparently, the archeologist mistook the collection of boulders on the other side of the fence for the stone circle, with the consequence that any remaining stones are now among those heaped along the roadside. In just over a hundred years, human folly has completely obliterated this prehistoric site, leaving nothing but an empty field in its place.

THE GREAT SKIRTFUL OF STONES & ROMS LAW

Roms Law (or Rumbles Law) is a circle of around twenty small stones on Hawksworth Moor. It is recorded on OS maps as Grubstones Circle (this appears to be a corruption of Rum Stones) but is actually thought to represent the kerb of a ring cairn. Cairns were built over Bronze or Iron Age burial chambers, originally a stone cist but later an urn once cremation became standard. It is recorded as an assembly place, particularly for freemasons - indeed the Grand Lodge of All England is believed to have met here. Paul Bennett suggests it was used for burial rituals, associated with a stone avenue running along the ridge to the nearby Great Skirtful of Stones; Roms Law would have been used as a resting place for bodies on the way to the graveyard at the Great Skirtful. This giant

CAIRNS OF ROMBALDS MOOR

ring of stones visible on the horizon surrounds a central tomb that was excavated in the nineteenth century to reveal human bones. Legend has it that a Norse giant called Rawmr was buried here after being killed by the people of Elmet. Another suggests that the giant Rombald's wife dropped some of the stones she was carrying in her apron (thus the alternative name of the Great Apronful of Stones). A large stone lies in the middle of the Great Skirtful, a significant boundary marker that proclaims 'This is Rumbles Law'. For centuries it stood at Roms Law and the Rogation Day perambulation around the parish boundary of Hawksworth ended there with the declaration 'This is Rumbles Law'. However, after an eighteenth-century dispute, the boundary moved to the Great Skirtful of Stones and the stone presumably went with it.

HORNCLIFFE CIRCLE

This is a rough double circle of stones on Hawksworth Moor that may be either a ring cairn with a central cist, but more likely an enclosure with a hearth – it was excavated in the nineteenth century and no bones or burial urn were found.

TWELVE APOSTLES STONE CIRCLE

The Twelve Apostles of Ilkley Moor is West Yorkshire's finest stone circle. Alone on the edge of a high ridge of heather moor, it is quiet, windswept and a fantastic vantage point. The twelve stones that usually (though not always) make up the circle are continually being re-erected by unknown locals. I very much like this idea of a constantly changing circle, a living entity as well as a remarkable part of the distant past, although the result is that none of the stones remains in its original position. The circle is thought to have had twenty or so stones orginally set within a rubble bank, possibly with a single central stone, but its function is disputed. Eric Cowling suggested it was a symbolic neutral ground at the junction of two ancient trackways for trading between tribes; Paul Bennett asserts it was used as a druidical dial circle to observe the movement of celestial bodies; and others that it was a more straightforward burial cairn. On the summer solstice the sun rises directly above Kilburn White Horse on the edge of the North York Moors, though oddly this figure was only created in the nineteenth century.

WEECHER CIRCLE

A stone circle was removed or destroyed during the construction of Weecher Reservoir in the 1890s, though it stood just to the south of the reservoir. Although little is known about it, in 1905 Butler Wood spoke of it as 'the finest stone circle in the Rombald's Moor area' with a diameter of around 25m.

Twelve Apostles Stone Circle

ROUTE 15: THE PREHISTORIC STONES OF ILKLEY MOO

Distance: 8½ miles (14km)

Ascent: 430m

Difficulty: Moderate

Parking: Wells Road car park (free), and street parking elsewhere in Ilkley.

Public Transport: Ilkley is the terminus for the Wharfedale train line. Buses also run regularly to Bradford and Leeds.

Character: A route that takes in the full array of Ilkley Moor's charms, combining the most impressive prehistoric markings and the trig point atop Rombalds Moor. Once descending from Haystack Rock, you may well want to pick your own route through the maze of paths back down to Ilkley, though the Hanging Stones is well worth a visit.

Swastika carving from the south

2 Queens Drive becomes a rough track as it enters Panorama Woods. Continue straight on past the top of Hollingwood Rise and join a path parallel to the track soon after. Through the woods, fork le up through the bracken. Re-entering the woods, carry straight on reach the first of a series of bridges over Heber Ghyll. The path climbs up the stream to a shelter; turn right here, then immediate left to reach a gate onto the moor. Turn right to pass through another gate, then bear slightly left to head for the crag ahead. The enclosure on the crag houses the famous Swastika Stone.

One of the reasons the mo extends so far down into Ilkl is the sheep rakes that allow access to the river for t commoners grazing the moo The rest of the lower slop were covered by **ridding** or enclosed clearing

3 Continue along the top of Wood House Crag, crossing two stiles to reach the bulky Sepulchre Stone amid a glade of windswept pine trees. Continue through one of the gaps in the next wall, before following the wall back to the left. You soon pick up a feint path through another gap; bear right beyond to ascend to a gate in the wall above. A couple of obvious shortcuts skip the Sepulchre Stone if you wish. Continue climbing from the gate to join a path along High Crag until it drops down to cross Black Beck. Bear right here, then keep left along Coarse Stone Edge to reach Neb Stone (in whose lee lovers used to kiss).

The **Swastika Stone** is the most famous carving on the whole of Rombalds Moor, though it is often very hard to make out. It is towards the bottom left of the stone within the enclosure on Wood House Crag, above the more obvious Victorian imitation. Though it possesses the usual cup marks, its intricate design has set it apart - indeed most consider it to be more recent than the other prehistoric carvings. The swastika symbol related to the sun in many ancient cultures and the design is similar to a number of Celtic sites across Northern Europe, athough unique in the British Isles. It is closest in form to the Camunian Rose, which was carved prolifically across the Val Camonica region of northern Italy. There have been suggestions that members of the Lingones tribe who were stationed at the Roman fort in Ilkley in the 2nd century may have brought the design with them and created the carving.

The design also occurs on the Badger Stone and on a stone in Willy Hall's Wood.

4 Continue through the gate above the Neb Stone and join another track to cross Keighley Road. Skirt around the top of Spicey Gill and take one of the first two feint paths off to the right to reach the lonely Badger Stone. Head straight on (the second feint path right of the seat) towards the high ground of Rombalds Moor. The path climbs the edge and passes close by what is thought to be a large unexcavated barrow (burial mound). Turn sharp left along the edge to an obvious junction; turn right here to reach the trig point.

The impressively cup and ring-marked **Badger Stone** is thought to stand on an ancient route, its name referring to the roaming corn traders who may have met or held harvest festivities here. On its right-hand side, you may be able to pick out a copy of the swastika design.

the Badge Stone

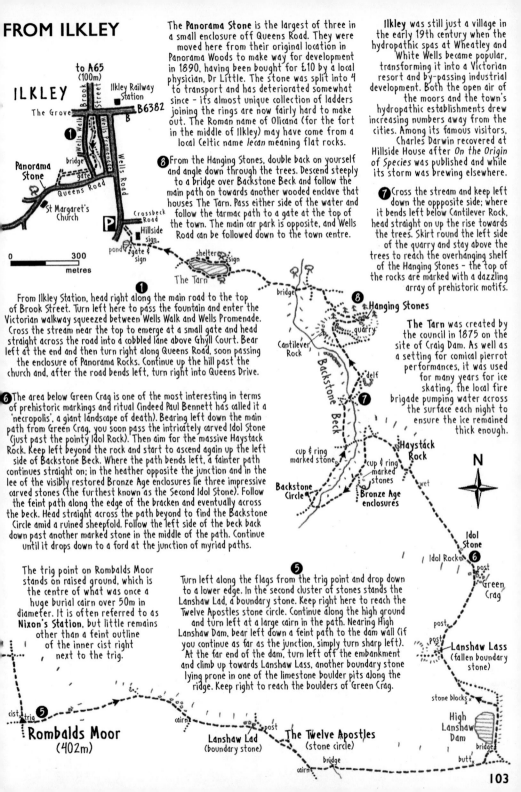

FROM ILKLEY

ILKLEY

to A65 (100m)

Brook Street

Ilkley Railway Station

B6382

The Grove

Wells Walk

Wells Promenade

Wells Road

bridge

gate

Panorama Stone

Queens Road

St Margaret's Church

Crossbeck Road

P

Hillside sign.

pond

gate & sign

0 — 300 metres

shelter & sign

The Tarn

The **Panorama Stone** is the largest of three in a small enclosure off Queens Road. They were moved here from their original location in Panorama Woods to make way for development in 1890, having been bought for £10 by a local physician, Dr Little. The stone was split into 4 to transport and has deteriorated somewhat since – its almost unique collection of ladders joining the rings are now fairly hard to make out. The Roman name of Olicana (for the fort in the middle of Ilkley) may have come from a local Celtic name *lecan* meaning flat rocks.

8 From the Hanging Stones, double back on yourself and angle down through the trees. Descend steeply to a bridge over Backstone Beck and follow the main path on towards another wooded enclave that houses The Tarn. Pass either side of the water and follow the tarmac path to a gate at the top of the town. The main car park is opposite, and Wells Road can be followed down to the town centre.

Ilkley was still just a village in the early 19th century when the hydropathic spas at Wheatley and White Wells became popular, transforming it into a Victorian resort and by-passing industrial development. Both the open air of the moors and the town's hydropathic establishments drew increasing numbers away from the cities. Among its famous visitors, Charles Darwin recovered at Hillside House after *On the Origin of Species* was published and while its storm was brewing elsewhere.

7 Cross the stream and keep left down the opposite side; where it bends left below Cantilever Rock, head straight on up the rise towards the trees. Skirt round the left side of the quarry and stay above the trees to reach the overhanging shelf of the Hanging Stones – the top of the rocks are marked with a dazzling array of prehistoric motifs.

1 From Ilkley Station, head right along the main road to the top of Brook Street. Turn left here to pass the fountain and enter the Victorian walkway squeezed between Wells Walk and Wells Promenade. Cross the stream near the top to emerge at a small gate and head straight across the road into a cobbled lane above Ghyll Court. Bear left at the end and then turn right along Queens Road, soon passing the enclosure of Panorama Rocks. Continue up the hill past the church and, after the road bends left, turn right into Queens Drive.

6 The area below Green Crag is one of the most interesting in terms of prehistoric markings and ritual (indeed Paul Bennett has called it a 'necropolis', a giant landscape of death). Bearing left down the main path from Green Crag, you soon pass the intricately carved Idol Stone (just past the pointy Idol Rock). Then aim for the massive Haystack Rock. Keep left beyond the rock and start to ascend again up the left side of Backstone Beck. Where the path bends left, a fainter path continues straight on; in the heather opposite the junction and in the lee of the visibly restored Bronze Age enclosures lie three impressive carved stones (the furthest known as the Second Idol Stone). Follow the feint path along the edge of the bracken and eventually across the beck. Head straight across the path beyond to find the Backstone Circle amid a ruined sheepfold. Follow the left side of the beck back down past another marked stone in the middle of the path. Continue until it drops down to a ford at the junction of myriad paths.

8 Hanging Stones

quarry

Cantilever Rock

Backstone Beck

delf

7

The Tarn was created by the council in 1875 on the site of Craig Dam. As well as a setting for comical pierrot performances, it was used for many years for ice skating, the local fire brigade pumping water across the surface each night to ensure the ice remained thick enough.

Haystack Rock

cup & ring marked stone

cup & ring marked stones

wet

N

Backstone Circle

Bronze Age enclosures

Idol Stone

Idol Rock **6**

post

Green Crag

post

post

Lanshaw Lass (fallen boundary stone)

The trig point on Rombalds Moor stands on raised ground, which is the centre of what was once a huge burial cairn over 50m in diameter. It is often referred to as **Nixon's Station**, but little remains other than a feint outline of the inner cist right next to the trig.

5 Turn left along the flags from the trig point and drop down to a lower edge. In the second cluster of stones stands the Lanshaw Lad, a boundary stone. Keep right here to reach the Twelve Apostles stone circle. Continue along the high ground and turn left at a large cairn in the path. Nearing High Lanshaw Dam, bear left down a feint path to the dam wall (if you continue as far as the junction, simply turn sharp left). At the far end of the dam, turn left off the embankment and climb up towards Lanshaw Lass, another boundary stone lying prone in one of the limestone boulder pits along the ridge. Keep right to reach the boulders of Green Crag.

cist, trig **5**

Rombalds Moor (402m)

cairns

post

Lanshaw Lad (boundary stone)

The Twelve Apostles (stone circle)

cairn

bridge

stone blocks

High Lanshaw Dam

bridge

butt

ROUTE 16: RIVOCK EDGE AND ADDINGHAM CRAG FROM KEIGHLEY OR RIDDLESDEN

Distance: 10 miles (16km)

Ascent: 430m

Difficulty: Moderate

Parking: Keighley town centre car parks, or various street parking in Riddlesden (including lay-by adjacent to Willow Tree pub).

Public Transport: Keighley is on major Airedale bus and train routes. Stockbridge Co-op is on buses 662 (from Keighley, Bingley & Bradford) and 760 (Keighley, Bingley and Leeds). The route can be shortened by using the 708 Keighley to Riddlesden bus service.

Character: Rivock Edge overlooks Keighley and this is the only natural moorland walk from this part of the Aire Valley. Starting in Riddlesden saves a tedious mile of main road walking at either end, but otherwise this is a very pleasant stroll with the manifold delights of the Leeds and Liverpool Canal, Rivock Plantation, Doubler Stones and Addingham Crag.

Follow Silsden Road right up to the crest and turn left onto a bridleway, following the track past a large barn round towards the TV relay mast. Leave the track where it splits, passing through a gate and aiming for the left corner of Rivock Plantation. A worn grassy line leads into the spooky plantation, where there is a potential diversion to the trig point on Rivock Edge. Where an old wall crosses the path, turn right and follow it up to a forestry track. Head left on this for a few metres to pick up a feint line up the rough edge to the left of the wall. Cross the wall again at the top and follow the edge round to the trig, almost immediately walking over the impressively cup and ring marked Wondjina Stone. There is no onward route, so retrace your steps back to the lower track, or go in search of Rivock Oven lost in the dense trees further along the forestry track *(for more information see Page 96).*

The dark track through Rivock Plantation is gloomy in places (and possibly haunted), but very clear. Where it reaches a forestry track, turn left straight back into the forest. Follow the track past the farm and onto the open ground on which stand the impressive weathered monuments of the Doubler Stones *(for more information see Page 96).* Follow the track to the front of Doubler Stones House, where a footpath notionally turns right past a bungalow and beneath the stones. The path does soon materialise, passing through a gate and climbing up onto the moor. Head straight on over a stone stile to reach the large cairn on the rocky edge of the moor by Millstone Lumps quarry.

Follow the well-cairned path right along the top of Addingham Crag, overlooking Ilkley and the Wharfe Valley. Just before the third gate (beyond which stands the large boulder of the Noon Stone), turn right up a feint path parallel to the wall. Pass through a broken section and then continue up the other side onto Long Ridge End, keeping to the right of the rocks. You may lose the feint path, but dim for the high ground to reach the trig point.

Head straight on at the trig point, staying on the high ground towards the top of the plantation. Join the boundary wall by a ladder stile and follow it all the way along to West Buck Stones, heading left only to skirt a couple of wet patches. Turn right above the stones and cross a stile to continue following the edge of the plantation (now felled in places).

Keep right along the plantation edge at the first wall heading off left. Beyond a junction, a second boundary is met in a slight depression; turn left before the stile and follow the feint path adjacent to the fence. It crosses the wet hollow of Bradup Beck (best to follow the base of the wall here) and climbs back up to reach a stile. Turn left here and, before a broken down wall, fork right across the open ground. Through a gap in the next wall, bear left to reach a stile leading down to the road.

plantation

Black Pots Farm

Doubler Stones

bungalow
Doubler Stones House

Millstone Lumps (quarry)

line of cairns gate

line of cairns

line of shafts

gate

Addingham Crag

Noon Stone

gap

trig

Long Ridge End (384m)

Shepherd's Hill

ladder

boundary stone

flags

East Buck Stones

stile

West Buck Stones

stile post

Rombalds Moor

N

Dirk Hill Stile

sign

post

Rivock Plantation

private track

Dew Stone (poem)

Wondjina Stone

Rivock Oven (cave)

Rivock Edge (250m)

gate

gap

gate

stile

white stake

Bradup Beck

butts

0   300
metres

a snow bunting in flight

3 Follow the track left up the hill to Low Wood Head and, at its end, go through a wooden gate marked The Mistal Bungalow. A path leads along the right side of the garden and across the field beyond. Climb to a gate and join the higher track above High Wood Head. Where it bends left by Wood Head Lodge head straight on to a green gate. Climb diagonally right across the field beyond to a stone stile by a large boulder in the wall. Continue along the same line, crossing a series of stone stiles to reach the road at another green gate by Holden Gate.

In the late 18th century, this moor was the haunt of a hermit known as **Rough Robin of Rumbles Moor**. Supposed to be able to see into both past and future, he was regularly consulted as a soothsayer and said to earn more than many a mill-worker. His fame spread as far Cumberland and when he arrived in Leeds in 1806, the Mercury ran an editorial warning to him. Less revered was the Ilkley Hermit, **Job Senior**, who lived in a hole on the moor after his wife died. He grew potatoes there, but was most renowned as a drunken rogue. The Hermit pub in Burley Woodhouse is named after him.

Follow the road right past Moorcock Farm and turn left at a ladder stile beyond. Hug the wall as far as a sleeper across the adjacent drain, then follow the field edge down to Heights Farm. Pass through a couple of rough squeezes in the corner of the field to stay right of the farm and follow a wall across the slope to Rivock Farm. Through a messy gate and after the farm buildings, turn left and follow the right edge of another field down to Riddlesden. At a gate, join a track that reaches the road by Ilkley Road Methodist Church.

West Riddlesden Hall is a Grade I listed manor house hidden from the canal by its ancient wooded garden. The building is dated 1687 when it was rebuilt, though features like the stained glass were retained. It is thought to have been the seat of the Maude (or Montalt) family from around 1400, when the Riddlesden estate was split, there being no male heirs. The manor house at East Riddlesden Hall is now a well-known National Trust property, but West Riddlesden remains privately owned.

10 Go briefly right along Ilkley Road to a path leading steeply down opposite the Willow Tree pub (just beyond is a large lay-by that may be the best place to park on the route). Follow the steps straight across Banks Lane and down to Scott Lane. Turn left, then first right to recross the canal on another swing bridge by Stockbridge Wharf. Follow Bar Lane to the end and rejoin the B6265 into Keighley or simply as far as Grange Road.

The **snow bunting** is a small bird that is usually seen in flight, baring its striking white underside - it is nicknamed the 'snowflake' as small flocks give an impression of falling snow. It breeds in the Arctic before wintering in Europe and may be seen anywhere on the higher moors, usually in October or November, though it is not common.

2 Soon after Arnside Avenue, turn right off Grange Road at a signed path between the houses of Stockbridge. Pass through a pair of cycle barriers to reach the Leeds and Liverpool Canal and follow it left as far as the first bridge. Cross Leache's Swing Bridge and join Leach Road heading left along the opposite bank. Reaching the houses, bear right of the track up into the woods. Cross one track and ascend towards the right corner of the woodland to reach a second track via some steps. Follow this briefly left and turn right at a sign before the houses, following the path up the side of the field above to reach a lane above Dunkirk.

The **Leeds and Liverpool Canal**, at 127 miles long, is the longest canal in the country. This was part of the first section of the canal to be constructed, with not a single lock between Bingley and Skipton. The canal was better known for its numerous swing bridges, originally timber but replaced post-war by metal structures. It is broader than the other Trans-Pennine canals and, despite the fact that it took nearly half a century to complete, it consequently survived far longer.

1 Head out of the centre of Keighley on the A6035, passing the railway station and Asda to reach the large roundabout on the A650. Bear slightly right to follow the B6265 towards Riddlesden. After half a mile, cross the River Aire and turn left opposite Co-op into Grange Road, where the circular route from Riddlesden begins.

one of the Doubler Stones

105

ROUTE 17: ROMBALDS MOOR AND SHIPLEY GLEN FROM BINGLEY

Distance: 11½ miles (19km)

Ascent: 350m

Difficulty: Strenuous

Parking: Bingley town centre car parks, or various street parking in Bingley and Crossflatts. Various car parks and lay-bys on Glen Road above Shipley Glen.

Public Transport: Bingley is on major Airedale bus and train routes.

Character: This is a long route, but follows good paths throughout and has an easy 3½ mile section along the Leeds and Liverpool Canal. The climb to Bingley Moor is a long but steady one, following Shipley Glen up from the edge of Saltaire, and the descent via Micklethwaite is far more direct. In between, the route takes in most of the interesting prehistoric sites on the south side of Rombalds Moor (three stone circles and the cup and ring marked rocks on Stanbury Hill).

❽ Reaching Otley Road again, head straight on into Heights Lane. After 100m, turn right at a stile and descend across the field to the first of a series of stiles. The path keeps descending parallel to the wall and joins a track below Whins Cottage. Drop down to the road and turn left into Micklethwaite village. At a junction below the zig zags, bear right into Beck Road. Turn left almost immediately into a cobbled yard, then bear right down a hedged track. Reaching Morton Beck, turn left down a field to its left.

❽ Reaching Otley Road onto a path climbing steadily onto the moor. At a junction below a slight scarp, turn right through the wall by Horncliffe Well and cross the fence beyond to join a path along its left side. After a couple of wet patches, this climbs towards a shooting hut on the shoulder above. Where it bends left, Roms Law (aka Grubstones Circle) can be found in the rough heather some 50m dead ahead. This is easier to locate than Horncliffe Circle, lost in the bracken over a stile back by Horncliffe Slade. Both are thought to be burial cairns (see Page 101 for background information).

Ashlar Chair, which has also been known as the Etching Stone or the Druid's Chair, is a large deeply-weathered boulder at the junction of four lines of boundary stones, many of which are now lost. It was noted for its ancient markings along the top and was said to be whitewashed at one time. Ashlar is a type of squared building stone, as well as having important Masonic ritual connotations, Paul Bennett suggesting its name was given it by the Grand Lodge of All England, who may have convened at this site.

❼ Turn left at the trig and follow a small path south off the top to reach a wall. Turn left along the wall as far as the second (smaller) gate by the scattered rocks at Ashlar Chair. Go right through the gate and follow the clear, partially flagged, path across the heather expanse of Bingley Moor. Reaching a large track by a signpost, you may wish to divert to the array of cup and ring marked rocks on Stanbury Hill (see Page 99 for more information). Otherwise follow the track left down to the edge of the moor.

❻ Past the outcrop of the Grubstones, turn left onto a major track climbing the shoulder above High Lanshaw Dam. This bears right to pass the very obvious Twelve Apostles Stone Circle (see Page 101 for background information). Fork left at a post by Lanshaw Lad to follow the edge and climb steadily up towards the trig point on top of Rombalds Moor.

The shooting hut of Grubstones Box was used as a school during the summer months in the 19th century. Horncliff House also served as a shooting house after the cottage there was abandoned in the 1870s.

Rombalds Moor (402m)

The Twelve Apostles (stone circle)

Lanshaw Lad (boundary stone)

Ashlar Chair

Bingley Moor

boundary stone

cairns

gate

flags

flags

Bridge

Cup & Ring marked rocks

Stanbury Hill

line of stakes

"Private Road" sign

Sign

Ferry Shaw Low Well

stile

gate & sign

Sign & stile

Heights Lane

Todmor Stones

barns

to Morton (½ mile)

stile

stile

stile

stile

Whins Cottage

gate

sign

MICKLETHWAITE

Methodist church

sign

gates

Beck Road

Morton Beck

High Lanshaw Dam

post

Grubstones Box

❻ Grubstones

Roms Law

bridge

Black Beck

line of butts

boundary stones

boundary stone

wet

post

stile

Horncliffe House (ruin)

Althorn Thorn (boundary stone)

Horncliffe Circle

Horncliffe Slade

stiles

stoop

post

Horncliffe Well

Hawksworth Moor

❺

to Menston (2 miles)

sign & squeeze & stile

squeeze

Otley Road

sign & squeeze

gate

squeeze & bridge

post

Birch Close

Weecheck Reservoir

gallops

N

0   400 metres

Loadpit Beck is named after some Bronze Age iron ore (or lode) workings.

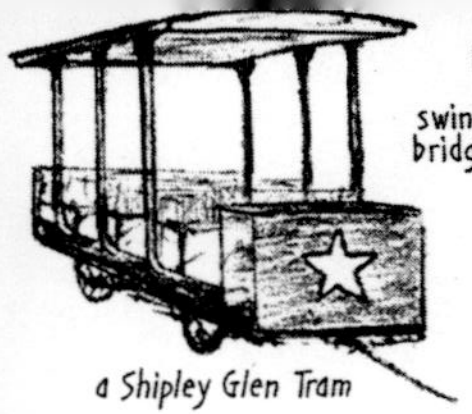

⑤ The paths along Bracken Hall Crag run parallel to Glen Road past a sign on the bend; shortly after, follow the right hand fork, climbing slightly above a quarry. Cross another track and gate leading into a narrow path up the side of Loadpit Beck. Head straight across the road at the end and follow the farm track up to Golar Farm. Do not follow the signed Dales Way Link round the farm, but head straight on.

The **Higher Coach Road** led from Salts' Mill in Saltaire to the family's mansion at Milner Field. Built by Titus Salt Junior, Milner Field was demolished in the 1950s, though the drive, lodges and walled garden still remain.

② Follow the River Aire as far as a boat house, where you join a track that curves round to the left. Turn right at the end and briefly join the estate road on the edge of Saltaire. Turn left by a noticeboard up a bridleway, then turn left into the woods of Shipley Glen. Follow the main path through the woods to climb steadily up to join a maze of paths along the top of Bracken Hall Crag. The Iron Age enclosure at Soldiers' Trench can be found by heading back along the edge for 200m (it has a lone tree in the centre of it).

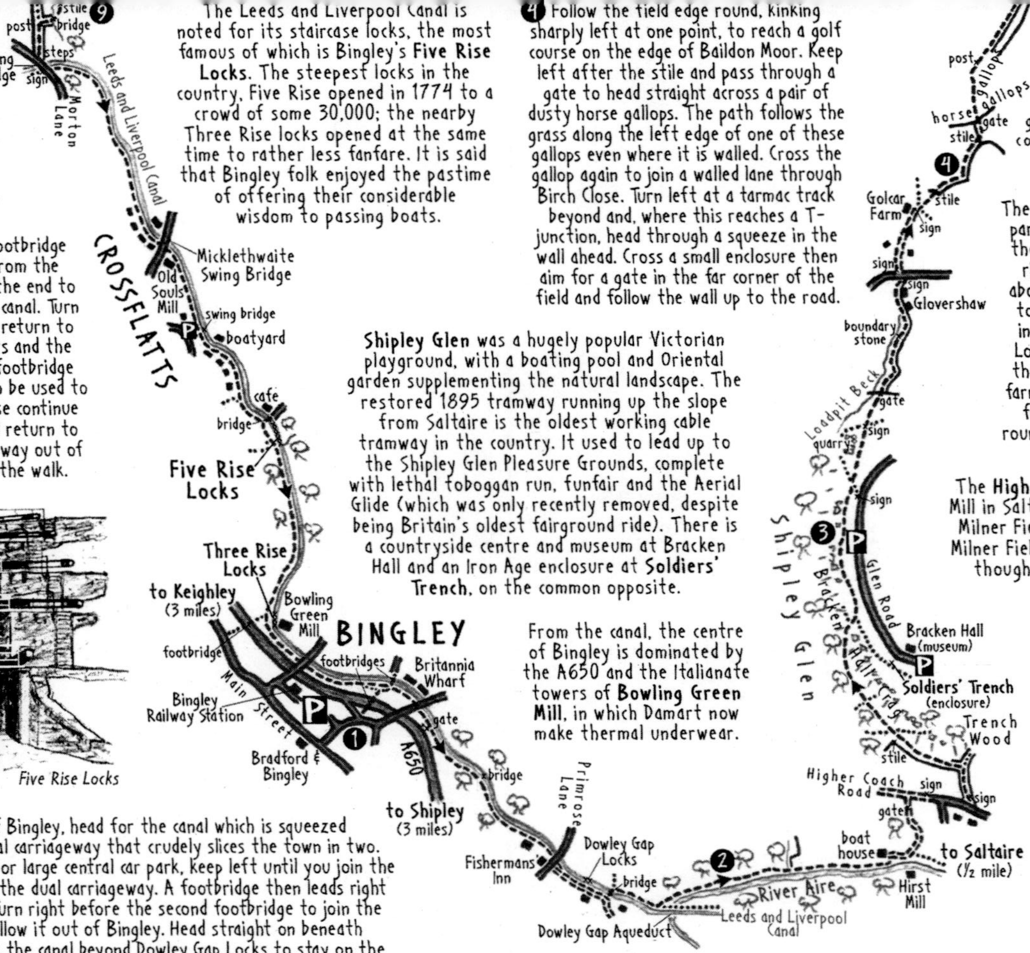

④ Follow the field edge round, kinking sharply left at one point, to reach a golf course on the edge of Baildon Moor. Keep left after the stile and pass through a gate to head straight across a pair of dusty horse gallops. The path follows the grass along the left edge of one of these gallops even where it is walled. Cross the gallop again to join a walled lane through Birch Close. Turn left at a tarmac track beyond and, where this reaches a T-junction, head through a squeeze in the wall ahead. Cross a small enclosure then aim for a gate in the far corner of the field and follow the wall up to the road.

Shipley Glen was a hugely popular Victorian playground, with a boating pool and Oriental garden supplementing the natural landscape. The restored 1895 tramway running up the slope from Saltaire is the oldest working cable tramway in the country. It used to lead up to the Shipley Glen Pleasure Grounds, complete with lethal toboggan run, funfair and the Aerial Glide (which was only recently removed, despite being Britain's oldest fairground ride). There is a countryside centre and museum at Bracken Hall and an Iron Age enclosure at Soldiers' Trench, on the common opposite.

From the canal, the centre of **Bingley** is dominated by the A650 and the Italianate towers of Bowling Green Mill, in which Damart now make thermal underwear.

Bingley was known as the Throstle-nest of England because of its sheltered location surrounded by protecting hills.

The **Leeds and Liverpool Canal** is noted for its staircase locks, the most famous of which is Bingley's **Five Rise Locks**. The steepest locks in the country, Five Rise opened in 1774 to a crowd of some 30,000; the nearby Three Rise locks opened at the same time to rather less fanfare. It is said that Bingley folk enjoyed the pastime of offering their considerable wisdom to passing boats.

⑨ Cross Morton Beck at a footbridge and follow a path away from the stream, then turn left at the end to reach Morton Lane and the canal. Turn left along the towpath to return to Bingley, passing Crossflatts and the famous Five Rise Locks. A footbridge next to Three Rise Locks can be used to reach Main Street. Otherwise continue past Bowling Green Mill and return to the footbridge used on the way out of town at the beginning of the walk.

① From the centre of Bingley, head for the canal which is squeezed in beyond the A650 dual carriageway that crudely slices the town in two. From the railway station or large central car park, keep left until you join the top of a feeder lane to the dual carriageway. A footbridge then leads right across the main road. Turn right before the second footbridge to join the canal towpath and follow it out of Bingley. Head straight on beneath Primrose Lane and cross the canal beyond Dowley Gap Locks to stay on the towpath. Soon after, the canal crosses the River Aire via the Dowley Gap Aqueduct; bear left just before this to drop down to the wooded river bank.

Map labels: post golf, dollops, horsegate golf course, stile, Glovershaw, Golar Farm, Glen Road, Bracken Hall (museum), Soldiers' Trench (enclosure), Trench Wood, to Saltaire (½ mile), quarry, Loadpit Beck, Bracken Hall Crag, Shipley Glen, boundary stone, Higher Coach Road, boat house, Hirst Mill, River Aire, Leeds and Liverpool Canal, Dowley Gap Locks, Dowley Gap Aqueduct, Primrose Lane, bridge, Fishermans Inn, to Shipley (3 miles), A650, Britannia Wharf, Bowling Green Mill, footbridges, BINGLEY, Main Street, Bingley Railway Station, Bradford & Bingley, to Keighley (3 miles), footbridge, Five Rise Locks, Three Rise Locks, café, bridge, boatyard, swing bridge, Mickelthwaite Swing Bridge, Old Salts Mill, CROSSFLATTS, Morton Lane, swing bridge sign, post bridge, swing bridge sign

a Shipley Glen Tram

Five Rise Locks

Chickweed wintergreen is a delicate small white flower found in woodland or areas that once were woodland. It was first discovered by the naturalist John Ray on Ilkley Moor in the seventeenth century, and this is now the only place it can be found in West Yorkshire.

CHAPTER 15 - STANDEDGE
(aka Millstone Edge)

Height: 448m

Grid Ref: SE012104

Map Sheet: OL21 (South Pennines)

Access: No restrictions.

Public Transport: Regular bus and train services to Marsden from Huddersfield. Bus 184 runs from Marsden to Oldham via A62.

Standedge was originally 'stone edge' (the same as Stanage in the Peak District) and refers to the long rocky escarpment that stretches most of the way between the A62 and A640. Standedge straddles the county boundary, its face lifted west towards Greater Manchester. On its Yorkshire side, it is somewhat overshadowed by Pule Hill, its lower but sleeker cousin. Hidden from Marsden, Standedge is only revealed from the A62 as a vast peat massif, though on closer inspection it is riven by a series of attractive ravines. The Pennine Way runs north along the edge from Millstone Edge, where there is a trig point, but the true summit lies a short distance to the north. I've used the name Standedge for this whole area of moorland, but it is also often used to refer to the cutting where the A62 crosses the tops, as well as the canal and railway tunnels cut deep beneath the moor. It is just outside the Peak District National Park but part of the National Trust's Marsden Moor estate.

Haigh Clough and March Hill

STANDEDGE MAP - Entire Moor

Standedge has a simple topography and its paths follow suit; hugging the escarpment in the west and following ancient highways down towards Marsden at both its north and south ends. In between, the great waste of Close Moss repels most visitors, though its peat surface covers the greater part of this moor. It hides in its belly, though, some enticing cloughs, whose rocky courses are worth exploring if you're seeking a quiet day out on the Marsden Moors. Redbrook Clough is a particular favourite with the impressive engine house looming at its head.

Redbrook Clough is one of the finest ravines in the South Pennines, richly rewarding the intrepid explorer. Though a clear path follows it south from Eastergate Bridge, it becomes harder to follow as the ravine closes in. Criss-cross the stream as necessary to reach a point where the wall on your left first allows you to clamber up the bank. A feint track can be picked up the other side of the wall, which eventually drops back down to the ravine below Far Owlers. Through a gap in the wall, climb immediately back up the bank on your left to follow the top of the ravine the rest of the way – the track here is feint but persists to reach the spoil heaps. The route is more obvious in descent once you have picked it up heading towards the scattered rocks just north of the spoil heaps.

The main route from Marsden to Oldgate Nick (or Badger Slack) follows a former packhorse road called Rapes Highway. It is marked with a series of stones engraved 'PH Road', erected in 1907 by Marsden Urban District Council after improving the whole route. This resulted in the Lord of the Manor bringing a court case against the council, during which the right of way was established but the improvements deemed to be trespass. Prior to this, the landowners had threatened users and tried to assert that the route over Oldgate had never existed despite obvious evidence to the contrary.

The gently sloping eastern flank of Standedge is referred to as Close Moss and is broken up by a series of narrow cloughs and spurs (known as lees). The terrain is largely tortuous going through tussocky grass and uneven heather. However, some remarkably insistent little paths work their way across the moor (and it is quite possible I haven't found them all). Most useful is a feint vehicle track that zigzags up Redmire Lee from Eastergate Bridge and follows this broad shoulder all the way up to Oldgate Moss. Some rough walking is still needed to reach the Pennine Way or the ruins of Short Grain House. An old road, referred to on 19th century maps as Bridle Road, crossed Close Moss and passed this house and some nearby stepping stones, but is traceable only as a line rather than as any sort of route.

110

CONTINUATION ON WAY STONE EDGE (Western Section) - p 127

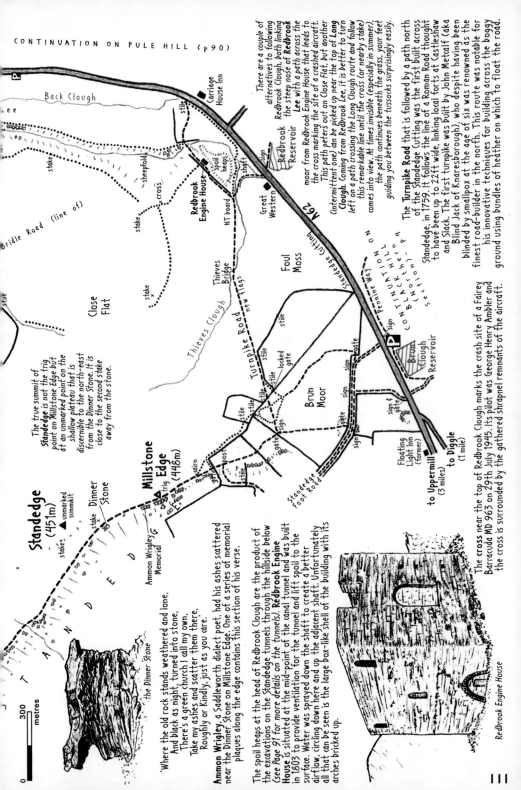

There are a couple of alternatives to following Redbrook Clough, both linking the steep nose of **Redbrook Lee** with a path across the moor from Redbrook Engine House that leads to the cross marking the site of a crashed aircraft. This path peters out on Close Flat, but another (intermittent one) can be picked up near the top of **Long Clough**. Coming from Redbrook Lee, it is better to turn left on a path crossing the Long Clough route and follow this remarkable line until the cross (or nearby stake) comes into view. At times invisible (especially in summer), the path continues beneath the grass, your feet guiding you between the tussocks surprisingly easily.

The **Turnpike Road** that is followed by a path north of the Standedge cutting was the first built across Standedge, in 1759. It follows the line of a Roman Road thought to have been up to 22ft wide, linking local forts at Castleshaw and Slack. The first turnpike was built by John Metcalf (aka Blind Jack of Knaresborough), who despite having been blinded by smallpox at the age of six was renowned as the finest road-builder in the north. This route was notable for his innovative techniques for building across the boggy ground using bundles of heather on which to float the road.

Back Clough

Carriage House Inn

stile

Redbrook Reservoir

Redbrook Engine House

spoil heaps

shaft

sign

Great Western

NT board

Bridle Road (line of)

sheepfold

cross

stake

stake

stake

Thieves Clough

Thieves Bridge

new flags

Close Flat

Foul Moss

A62

Standedge (cutting)

Pennine Way

sign

CONTINUATION ON BLACKHEATH (NORTH) P94 section

Brun Clough Reservoir

Turnpike Road

stile

stile

stile

locked gate

gate

stile

stile

sign

sign

gate

Brun Moor

gate

sign

sign

gate

sign & gate

gate

cairn

post

gate

stile

stile

Floating Light Inn (former)

sign

gate

Standedge Foot Road

to Uppermill (3 miles)

to Diggle (1 mile)

The cross near the top of Redbrook Clough marks the crash site of a Fairey Barracuda MD 963 on 29th July 1945. Its pilot was George Henry Ambler and the cross is surrounded by the gathered shrapnel remnants of the aircraft.

Standedge (451m)

The true summit of **Standedge** is not the trig point on Millstone Edge but at an unmarked point on the shallow plateau that is discernible to the north-east from the Dinner Stone. It is close to the second stake away from the stone.

stake, unmarked summit

Dinner Stone

stake

Millstone Edge (448m)

trig

cairn

S T A N D E D G E

Ammon Wrigley Memorial

the Dinner Stone

300 metres

0

'Where the old rock stands weathered and lone,
And black as night, turned into stone,
There's a green church I call my own.
Take my ashes and scatter them there,
Roughly or Kindly, just as you are.'

Ammon Wrigley, a Saddleworth dialect poet, had his ashes scattered near the Dinner Stone on Millstone Edge. One of a series of memorial plaques along the edge contains this section of his verse.

The spoil heaps at the head of Redbrook Clough are the product of the excavations on the Standedge tunnels through the hillside below (see Page 91 for more details on the tunnels). **Redbrook Engine House** is situated at the mid-point of the canal tunnel and was built in 1803 to provide ventilation for the tunnel and lift spoil to the surface. Water was sprayed down the shaft to create a better airflow, circling down here and up the adjacent shaft. Unfortunately all that can be seen is the large box-like shell of the building with its arches bricked up.

Redbrook Engine House

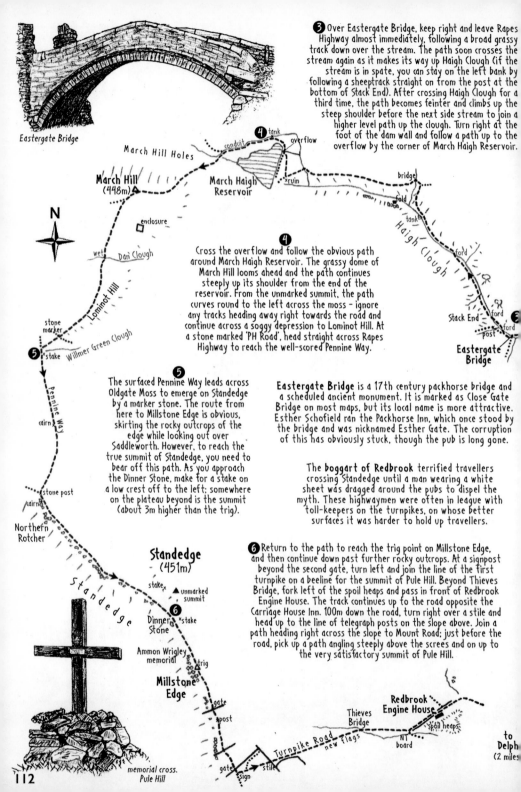

3 Over Eastergate Bridge, keep right and leave Rapes Highway almost immediately, following a broad grassy track down over the stream. The path soon crosses the stream again as it makes its way up Haigh Clough (if the stream is in spate, you can stay on the left bank by following a sheeptrack straight on from the post at the bottom of Stack End). After crossing Haigh Clough for a third time, the path becomes feinter and climbs up the steep shoulder before the next side stream to join a higher level path up the clough. Turn right at the foot of the dam wall and follow a path up to the overflow by the corner of March Haigh Reservoir.

Eastergate Bridge

March Hill Holes

4 tank
conduit
overflow

March Hill
(448m)

March Haigh
Reservoir

ruin

bridge

fold

crag

tank

Haigh Clough

N

enclosure

ford

wet   Dan Clough

Lominot Hill

4 Cross the overflow and follow the obvious path around March Haigh Reservoir. The grassy dome of March Hill looms ahead and the path continues steeply up its shoulder from the end of the reservoir. From the unmarked summit, the path curves round to the left across the moss – ignore any tracks heading away right towards the road and continue across a soggy depression to Lominot Hill. At a stone marked 'PH Road', head straight across Rapes Highway to reach the well-scored Pennine Way.

Stack End   ford

post

ford

**Eastergate
Bridge**

stone
marker

5 stake   Willmer Green Clough

Pennine Way

5 The surfaced Pennine Way leads across Oldgate Moss to emerge on Standedge by a marker stone. The route from here to Millstone Edge is obvious, skirting the rocky outcrops of the edge while looking out over Saddleworth. However, to reach the true summit of Standedge, you need to bear off this path. As you approach the Dinner Stone, make for a stake on a low crest off to the left; somewhere on the plateau beyond is the summit (about 3m higher than the trig).

Eastergate Bridge is a 17th century packhorse bridge and a scheduled ancient monument. It is marked as Close Gate Bridge on most maps, but its local name is more attractive. Esther Schofield ran the Packhorse Inn, which once stood by the bridge and was nicknamed Esther Gate. The corruption of this has obviously stuck, though the pub is long gone.

cairn

The **boggart of Redbrook** terrified travellers crossing Standedge until a man wearing a white sheet was dragged around the pubs to dispel the myth. These highwaymen were often in league with toll-keepers on the turnpikes, on whose better surfaces it was harder to hold up travellers.

stone post

cairn

**Northern
Rotcher**

Standedge
– 451m)

stake
▲ unmarked
summit

6 Return to the path to reach the trig point on Millstone Edge, and then continue down past further rocky outcrops. At a signpost beyond the second gate, turn left and join the line of the first turnpike on a beeline for the summit of Pule Hill. Beyond Thieves Bridge, fork left of the spoil heaps and pass in front of Redbrook Engine House. The track continues up to the road opposite the Carriage House Inn. 100m down the road, turn right over a stile and head up to the line of telegraph posts on the slope above. Join a path heading right across the slope to Mount Road; just before the road, pick up a path angling steeply above the screes and on up to the very satisfactory summit of Pule Hill.

Standedge

6
Dinner   ×stake
Stone

Ammon Wrigley
memorial   ▲ trig

**Millstone
Edge**

gate

post

Redbrook
Engine House

Thieves
Bridge   spoil heaps

NT
board

to
Delph
(2 miles

Turnpike Road   new flags

gate   stile

sign

*memorial cross.
Pule Hill*

112

Distance: 8 miles (12.5km)

Ascent: 430m

Difficulty: Moderate

Parking: Small free car park at Standedge Visitor Centre. Various on-street parking in Marsden (free) or at far end of Waters Lane.

Public Transport: Marsden is on the main Huddersfield Line between Leeds & Manchester, the 182, 183, 185 & 186 bus routes up the Colne Valley, and the 184 bus route between Huddersfield and Oldham/Manchester.

Character: A lovely route up the valley from Marsden that takes in the three tops of March Hill, Standedge and Pule Hill and avoids the long trudge of Rapes Highway. It follows clear paths throughout so is not difficult in bad weather, though it would be a shame to miss the impressive views both east and west.

The terrace at **Lower Hey Green** was originally built as a coach house and stables, thus the filled-in arches in the middle, with living quarters for ostler and grooms at either end. A large corn mill stood opposite with the millpond in the woods alongside and the large mill-owner's house at what is now Hey Green Hotel. It was owned at one time by Joseph Crowther, who built the nearby **Hey Green Generator** in the late 19th century to provide the house with water-powered electricity. It was the first in the area to have electricity and people used to walk up from Marsden to watch the lights being turned on. It is also said he used it to heat the water in the pond for his Polynesian wife to swim in - the cast iron gate depicting an aquatic goddess refer to this.

1 The Mechanics Hall dominates the centre of Marsden; go down the street opposite (Market Place) and over the bridge at the end. Then follow the river round to the right; reaching a road, head straight across into Clough Lea. After 100m, cross Mellor's Bridge and turn left to reach a footway leading up the hill. At the top, turn right to reach a gap in the fence opposite and join the canal heading back to the left. The small railway station is situated just beyond the lock here. Now simply follow the towpath to Tunnel End.

2 The towpath ends by a bridge shortly before the canal disappears into the Standedge Tunnel. From the small car park on the other side, look for a path leading right up the grassy slope. Cross the road at the top and follow the path alongside Waters Road. This eventually joins the road near Lower Hey Green. Continue past Hey Green Hotel and turn left just before Eastergate Cottage, following a bridleway along the river to Eastergate Bridge.

8 Follow the A62 right for 50m, then turn sharply left down Ainsley Lane to return to Tunnel End. The main road could be followed into Marsden, but it is preferable and little further to rejoin the canal back into town. Turn right off Ainsley Lane before Tunnel End Reservoir to drop down to the car park by the end of the canal.

7 Follow the path along the edge of the crags from the top of Pule Hill. Well beyond the quarries the path bends right through a broken down wall to reach a square ventilation shaft for the Standedge Tunnels. A memorial cross stands on the crest beyond and the path descends to its left to join the line of a wall down the hillside. Where the ground becomes wet above Intake Head Farm, head for a gate in the fence below and follow the track left down to the road.

The **Mechanics Hall** was built by the Marsden Mechanics Institution in 1861 as an educational centre. In the days before universal education, volunteers from such institutions offered elementary education to young working men.

Tunnel End is self-explanatory, being where the Standedge Tunnels disappear into Pule Hill (for more information on the Standedge Tunnels, see Page 91). An aquaduct carries the River Colne over the railway and canal from Tunnel End Reservoir, which used to be much larger, but has silted up and is generally kept low due to weaknesses in the dam wall. This was the case with many of those built to supply the canals, and Tunnel End Reservoir burst in 1799 flooding Marsden and beyond. A large warehouse has been restored as the Standedge Visitor Centre (free entry, but only open on the first Saturday of the month, when boat trips are also possible into the canal tunnel). There is also a cafe in Tunnel End Cottages, which were built to house the tunnel-keepers. The large stone blocks alongside were used to weigh down unladen boats going into the tunnel to make sure they fitted through.

0   400 metres

113

Bogbean (or buckbean) is found in particularly wet areas of bog, its star-like white flowers growing on long stems from the water. It has groups of three shiny leaves whose similarity to those of various beans has given the plant its common name. The bitter leaves have long been held to have medicinal properties, traditionally being used to cure ailments like rheumatism, tuberculosis, ague and scurvy. In times of hardship its roots were also used in many places to form a flour to make missen bread (famine bread). It is still prescribed by modern herbalists and has also been known as bog hop because of its occasional use in brewing.

CHAPTER 16 - STOODLEY PIKE

Height: 402m

Grid Ref: SD973241

Map Sheet: OL21 (South Pennines)

Access: No restrictions.

Public Transport: Hebden Bridge and Mytholmroyd are on Caldervale routes. Bus C runs from Hebden Bridge to Cragg Vale, and buses T6/T8 run from Todmorden to Mankinholes & Harvelin Park.

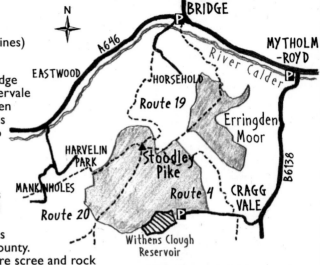

Stoodley Pike is probably the most instantly recogniseable hill in the South Pennines. This has little to do with its natural geography, but rather the 121-foot monument that stares grimly out across half of the county. This marks the fine edge of bare scree and rock that overlooks the Upper Calder Valley, but the true summit of Stoodley Pike stands some 200m south on the flat moorland behind. Without the monument, one imagines Stoodley Pike being no more remarkable than Langfield Edge, but its hold on the consciousness of the valley is unparalleled. Stoodley Pike looks out over Todmorden, Hebden Bridge and Cragg Vale and makes a popular target for walks from each, so is rarely quiet. The outlying Erringden Moor is quieter, partly thanks to be quite so soggy, and is separated from Stoodley Pike only by a quirk of the Access Land boundaries.

The source of the name Stoodley is unclear; it has been suggested it comes from a 13th century landowner called Harrie de Stoodley, yet his surname is likely to have been taken from a place itself. It may also derive from the Old English *stod leah* (meaning horse stud farm) and have been related to the functions of Erringden Deer Park, which covered the bulk of this moor in the Middle Ages.

Stoodley Pike Monument from High Stones

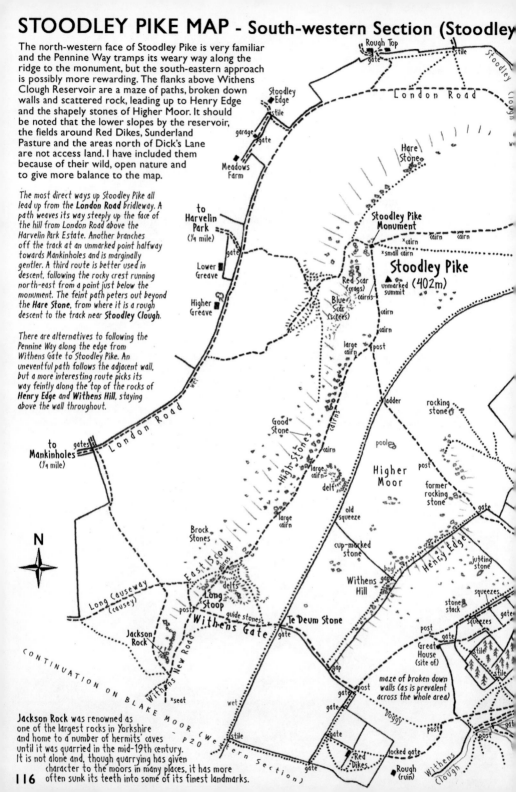

STOODLEY PIKE MAP – South-western Section (Stoodley

The north-western face of Stoodley Pike is very familiar and the Pennine Way tramps its weary way along the ridge to the monument, but the south-eastern approach is possibly more rewarding. The flanks above Withens Clough Reservoir are a maze of paths, broken down walls and scattered rock, leading up to Henry Edge and the shapely stones of Higher Moor. It should be noted that the lower slopes by the reservoir, the fields around Red Dikes, Sunderland Pasture and the areas north of Dick's Lane are not access land. I have included them because of their wild, open nature and to give more balance to the map.

The most direct ways up Stoodley Pike all lead up from the **London Road** bridleway. A path weaves its way steeply up the face of the hill from London Road above the Harvelin Park Estate. Another branches off the track at an unmarked point halfway towards Mankinholes and is marginally gentler. A third route is better used in descent, following the rocky crest running north-east from a point just below the monument. The feint path peters out beyond the **Hare Stone**, from where it is a rough descent to the track near **Stoodley Clough**.

There are alternatives to following the Pennine Way along the edge from Withens Gate to Stoodley Pike. An uneventful path follows the adjacent wall, but a more interesting route picks its way feintly along the top of the rocks of **Henry Edge** and **Withens Hill**, staying above the wall throughout.

Jackson Rock was renowned as one of the largest rocks in Yorkshire and home to a number of hermits' caves until it was quarried in the mid-19th century. It is not alone and, though quarrying has given character to the moors in many places, it has more often sunk its teeth into some of its finest landmarks.

116

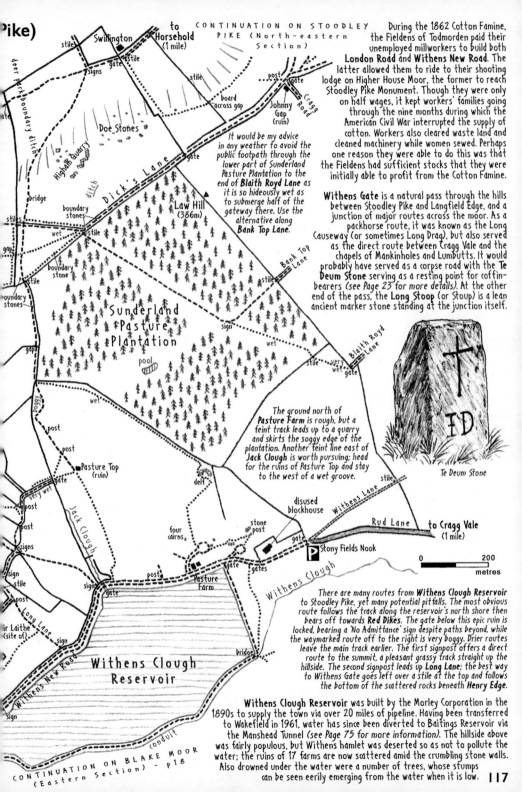

(Pike)

CONTINUATION ON STOODLEY PIKE (North-eastern Section)

to Horsehold (1 mile)

During the 1862 Cotton Famine, the Fieldens of Todmorden paid their unemployed millworkers to build both **London Road** and **Withens New Road**. The latter allowed them to ride to their shooting lodge on Higher House Moor, the former to reach Stoodley Pike Monument. Though they were only on half wages, it kept workers' families going through the nine months during which the American Civil War interrupted the supply of cotton. Workers also cleared waste land and cleaned machinery while women sewed. Perhaps one reason they were able to do this was that the Fieldens had sufficient stocks that they were initially able to profit from the Cotton Famine.

Withens Gate is a natural pass through the hills between Stoodley Pike and Langfield Edge, and a junction of major routes across the moor. As a packhorse route, it was known as the Long Causeway (or sometimes Long Drag), but also served as the direct route between Cragg Vale and the chapels of Mankinholes and Lumbutts. It would probably have served as a corpse road with the **Te Deum Stone** serving as a resting point for coffin-bearers (see Page 23 for more details). At the other end of the pass, the **Long Stoop** (or Stoup) is a lean ancient marker stone standing at the junction itself.

Te Deum Stone

It would be my advice in any weather to avoid the public footpath through the lower part of Sunderland Pasture Plantation to the end of Blaith Royd Lane as it is so hideously wet as to submerge half of the gateway there. Use the alternative along Bank Top Lane.

The ground north of Pasture Farm is rough, but a feint track leads up to a quarry and skirts the soggy edge of the plantation. Another feint line east of Jack Clough is worth pursuing; head for the ruins of Pasture Top and stay to the west of a wet groove.

to Cragg Vale (1 mile)

0   200
metres

There are many routes from **Withens Clough Reservoir** to Stoodley Pike, yet many potential pitfalls. The most obvious route follows the track along the reservoir's north shore then bears off towards **Red Dikes**. The gate below this epic ruin is locked, bearing a 'No Admittance' sign despite paths beyond, while the waymarked route off to the right is very boggy. Drier routes leave the main track earlier. The first signpost offers a direct route to the summit, a pleasant grassy track straight up the hillside. The second signpost leads up **Long Lane**; the best way to Withens Gate goes left over a stile at the top and follows the bottom of the scattered rocks beneath **Henry Edge**.

Withens Clough Reservoir was built by the Morley Corporation in the 1890s to supply the town via over 20 miles of pipeline. Having been transferred to Wakefield in 1961, water has since been diverted to Baitings Reservoir via the Manshead Tunnel (see Page 75 for more information). The hillside above was fairly populous, but Withens hamlet was deserted so as not to pollute the water; the ruins of 17 farms are now scattered amid the crumbling stone walls. Also drowned under the water were a number of trees, whose stumps can be seen eerily emerging from the water when it is low.

CONTINUATION ON BLAKE MOOR (Eastern Section) - P18

117

Map labels: Swillington, stile, signs, gate, stile, board across gap, post, gate, Johnny Gap (ruin), Cragg Road, stile, Doe Stones, Higham Quarry, Dick's Lane, ditch, Law Hill (386m), bridge, boundary stones, stiles, wet, gap, boundary stone, boundary stones, gap, Sunderland Pasture Plantation, pool, Bank Top Lane, stile, sign, wet, stile, very wet gate, Blaith Royd Lane, deer park boundary ditch, wet, boggy, post, post, Pasture Top (ruin), gate, very wet, post, post, signs, Jack Clough, delf, four cairns, stone post, disused blockhouse, Withens Lane, stile, Rud Lane, gate, Stony Fields Nook, P, gate, gates, Pasture Farm, Withens Clough, sign, stile, post, signs, gate, Long Lane, ir Laithe (site of), sign, Withens New Road, Withens Clough Reservoir, bridge, conduit

STOODLEY PIKE MAP - North-eastern Section (Erringden Moor)

Erringden Moor is a relatively small wedge of grassy moorland between Mytholmroyd, Hebden Bridge and Cragg Vale. It is easily accessible from each and consequently there are plenty of paths, too many at times to map satisfactorily. The rough grassland is also busy with cattle, sheep and birds, predominantly skylark and curlew. The moor slopes gently down from the southwest, except for the steep wooded basin of Broadhead Clough, and is notoriously wet in places. It is also worth noting that this is another moor where the useful paths differ greatly from those marked on the OS map. Erringden Moor was part of a twelfth century Norman deer park used as a hunting ground by the lords of the manor; the Earls of Warren. It formed part of the Forest of Sowerby, to which the S's on the numerous boundary stones across the moor refer. It was also home to David Hartley, leader of the Cragg Vale Coiners, who operated his counterfeiting business from Bell House until hanged in Halifax in 1770. The name Erringden is thought to refer to Eric's valley.

The woodcock is an ungainly-looking wading bird that lives in damp woodland like the one in Broadhead Clough. It is a nocturnal bird and so most likely seen at dawn or dusk, when they give impressive displays known as rodings. It spends the winters in Finland and Russia.

There are several wet areas on the north-eastern fringe of the moor, just before it starts to descend steeply into the Calder Valley. The driest route across the moor follows a broken down wall southwest to the head of Broadhead Clough. Otherwise try skirting the edge of the moor and following the boundary wall along its western side.

a woodcock

Brock Holes Wood near Broad Head End refers to badger holes.

Broadhead Clough (or Bell Hole as it is known locally) is a charming nature reserve, comprising birch and oak woodland and distinctive woodland bogs. In the 19th century it was a commercial plantation, but the ancient woodland has since regenerated and is now home to fox and roe deer, blackcap, redpoll and a number of breeding woodcock.

The heart of Erringden Moor is a complete maze of tracks that is hard to fathom and nearly impossible to map. Sheeptracks run off in every direction, some more obvious than others – and it is these I have tried to convey. The main navigational markers are the steep edges of Broadhead Clough and the long line of boundary stones running SW-NE across the middle of the moor. Numerous tracks link these, the most obvious leaving the edge just to the south of the waymark post at the head of Broadhead Clough and joining the boundary near a fallen marker stone. Another sets off from a gate stoop north of the edge and links up with the most prominent boundary stone, which marks the five-way junction at the heart of the moor.

to Mytholmroyd (1 mile)

Tower Hill

Brock Holes Wood

Broad Head End

to Hebden Bridge (1 mile)

Moorside Farm

Great Jumps

Cuckoo Stone

Buckley Stone

Cock Hill Moor

Rake Head

Wood Hey Clough

Old Harry Lane

deer park boundary ditch

Broad Head

broken down wall

boundary stone

larger boundary stone

Erringden Moor

Whittaker Road

Lumb Stone

stile · ladder · gate · post · posts · sign · muddy · wet · very wet · hollow · stoop

200 metres

0

N

118

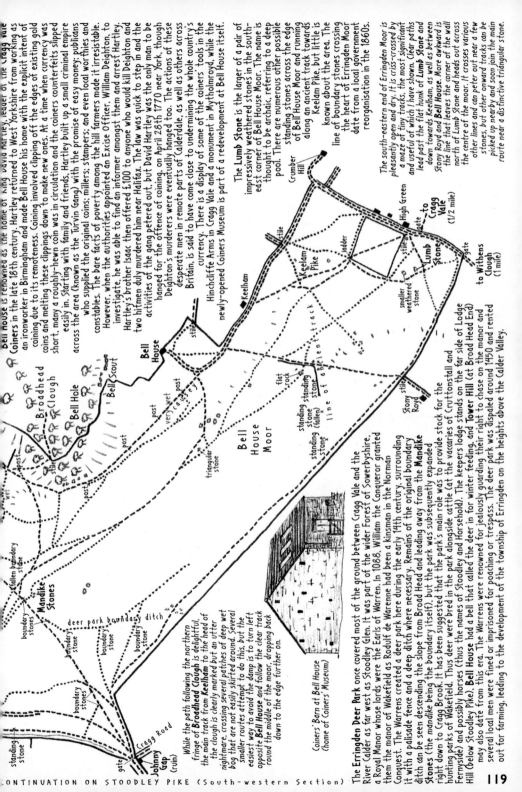

BELL HOUSE is renowned as the home of King David Hartley, leader of the Cragg Vale Coiners in the late 18th century. Hartley returned to West Yorkshire from working as an ironworker in Birmingham and made Bell House his home with the explicit intent of coining due to its remoteness. Coining involved clipping off the edges of existing gold coins and melting these clippings down to make new ones. At a time when currency was short, many a roughly-hewn coin was in circulation and the coiners counterfeits slipped easily in. Starting with family and friends, Hartley built up a small criminal empire across the area (known as the Turvin Gang) with the promise of easy money: publicans who supplied the original coins; millers; stampers; and even local worthies and constables. The bare facts of poverty among the hill farmers made it irresistible. However, when the authorities appointed an Excise Officer, William Deighton, to investigate, he was able to find an informer amongst them and arrest Hartley. Hartley's brother Isaac then offered £100 to anyone who would kill Deighton and two hitmen duly murdered him near Halifax. The law was quick to step in and the activities of the gang petered out, but David Hartley was the only man to be hanged for the offence of coining, on April 28th 1770 near York, though Deighton's murderers were eventually hanged too. The actions of these desperate men in remote parts of Calderdale, as well as others across Britain, is said to have come close to undermining the whole country's currency. There is a display of some of the coiners' tools in the Hinchliffe Arms in Cragg Vale and a monument in Mytholmroyd, while the newly-opened Coiners Museum is part of a redevelopment at Bell House itself.

The **Lumb Stone** is the larger of a pair of impressively weathered stones in the south-east corner of Bell House Moor. The name is thought to be archaic, referring to a deep pool. There are numerous other possible standing stones across the edge of Bell House Moor and running along an ancient track towards Keelam Pike, but little is known about the area. The line of boundary stones crossing the heart of Erringden Moor date from a local government reorganisation in the 1860s.

The south-eastern end of Erringden Moor is pleasantly open and dry. It is criss-crossed by a maze of tiny tracks, the most significant and useful of which I have shown. Clear paths lead past the flat hunk of **Lumb Stone** and down towards Keelham, as well as between **Stony Royd** and **Bell House**. More awkward is the line that leaves the corner of the wall north of Lumb Stone and heads out across the centre of the moor. It crosses various other lines and can peter out near a few stones, but other onward tracks can be picked up nearby and soon join the main route near a distinctive triangular stone.

While the path following the northern fringe of **Broadhead Clough** is delightful, the main track from **Keelam** to the head of the clough is clearly marked but an utter nightmare, crossing several patches of deep wet bog that are not easily skirted around. Several smaller routes attempt to do this, but the easiest way to avoid the damp is to turn left opposite **Bell House** and follow the clear track round the middle of the moor, dropping back down to the edge further on.

Coiners' Barn at Bell House
(home of Coiners' Museum)

The **Erringden Deer Park** once covered most of the ground between Cragg Vale and the River Calder as far west as Stoodley Glen. It was part of the wider Forest of Sowerbyshire, a Royal Manor whose lords were the Earls of Warren. In 1068, William the Conqueror granted them the manor of Wakefield as Rodulf de Warenne had been a kinsman in the Norman Conquest. The Warrens created a deer park here during the early 14th century, surrounding it with a palisade fence and a deep ditch where necessary. Remains of the original boundary ditch can be seen descending the slope from Broad Head and leading away from the **Mandike Stones** (the mandike being the boundary itself), but the park was subsequently expanded right down to Cragg Brook. It has been suggested that the park's main role was to provide stock for the hunting parks of Wakefield. Thus deer were bred in the park alongside cattle (at the vaccaries of Cruttonstall and Fermyside) and possibly horses (thus the names of Stoodley and Horsehold). The keepers lodge stands on the far side of Lodge Hill (below Stoodley Pike). **Bell House** had a bell that called the deer in for winter feeding, and **Tower Hill** (at Broad Head End) may also date from this era. The Warrens were renowned for jealously guarding their right to chase on the manor and several local men were fined or imprisoned for poaching or trespass. The deer park was dispaled around 1450 and rented out for farming, leading to the development of the township of Erringden on the heights above the Calder Valley.

CONTINUATION ON STOODLEY PIKE (South-western Section)

119

ROUTE 19: STOODLEY PIKE & ERRINGDEN MOOR FROM HEBDEN BRIDGE

Distance: 6½ miles (11km)

Ascent: 330m

Difficulty: Easy

Parking: Pay & display car parks and street parking in Hebden Bridge.

Public Transport: Hebden Bridge is on the main Caldervale train & bus routes.

Character: Although Stoodley Pike is hidden from the centre of Hebden Bridge, its familiar monument makes a natural target for a day's walk. There are dozens of possible routes up, but my favourite is the one used here in descent, skirting round Lodge Hill and Edge End Moor, while the ascent via Wood Hey and Erringden Moor allows for a decent tramp across the moor immediately above the town.

1 From the traffic lights in the centre of Hebden Bridge, go down Holme Street past the post office. At the end, cross the canal and turn right, following a path up some steps to Palace House Road. Turn left, cross the railway and take a signed track up to the right. Bear left after 200m where this path forks around a house, and skirt the back of the houses before climbing gently up through Crow Nest Wood. Beyond Wood Top Delf, a good view opens out to the left before the path curves round to Wood Top.

Palace House Road is named after the palisade fence that ran around Erringden Deer Park in the 14th century (see Page 119 for more information).

2 Keep to the right of the buildings at Wood Top, joining a large track, then turn left into Wood Hey Lane as this splits. The lane descends into a wood and, just before it crosses a stream, go right over a stile and climb through youthful woodland. This reaches a track at another stile; follow it just a few metres right to a signed path up the right-hand side of a gully to a stile that marks the edge of Erringden Moor.

Like many of the hilltop hamlets, **Wood Top** was a handloom weaver's hamlet with its own cotton mill and mill pond. It made fustian, a hard-wearing cotton material that Hebden Bridge was renowned for producing.

Beaumont Clough was said to be used during World War II for secretive pig slaughtering. Since all livestock had to be registered for redistribution, occasional animals were killed for personal use away from prying eyes.

Though the impressive ruin at Cruttonstall is only from the 17th century, it is included in the Domesday Book as Crubetonestun and was the site of a medieval vaccary (indeed in this area the suffix – tonstall indicates the existence of a cattle ranch). Cattle was enclosed during the winter by crude hedges and stock-proof ditches, the remains of which may be picked out around the fringe of Edge End Moor.

7 Keep right again as you near the elegant ruins of Cruttonstall; this brings you to a gate above the farm. Follow the path along the wall beyond until it drops down to the track up Beaumont Clough. An interesting alternative route drops down through Cruttonstall itself and crosses the meadows to reach a stile at the top of Callis Woods. Immediately beyond, bear right on a rough path hugging the fence at the top of the woods; this scrambles along to the dramatic cantilever of Foster's Stone and continues along the fenceline to join the same track up Beaumont Clough.

8 Drop straight down to Beaumont Clough Bridge and follow the path left up to a gate. This leads into a long walled track that emerges at the top of Horsehold Road. Follow the road left as it drops down steeply into Hebden Bridge – near the top, a short detour to Horsehold Scout offers a magnificent view of the Calder Valley. The road emerges at a bridge over the canal at Hebble End; join the towpath on the far bank to get back to Holme Street or the railway station.

HEBDEN BRIDGE

to Mytholmroyd (1 mile)

to Keighley (11 miles)

A6033

to Todmorden (4 miles)

A646

Holme Street

post office

Hebble End

Steps

bridge

railway

Rochdale Canal

Cat Scout

Horsehold Road

Calder Holmes Park

Palace House Road

Hebden Bridge Railway Station

Crow Nest Wood

Wood Top Delf

Wood Top Delf

Wood Top

Wood signpost

2 signpost

Wood Hey Lane

Shroggs

Wood Hey

Wood Hey Clough

Wood Hey Cottage

stile signpost

Erringden Pinfold (site of)

Horsehold Scout (viewpoint)

gate

Horsehold

Horse Hold Wood

gate

Beaumont (Clough Road)

gate

Callis Woods

Beaumont Clough

Beaumont Clough Bridge

8 signpost

Foster's Stone

Cruttonstall (ruin)

stile

stoops

gate

gate

7

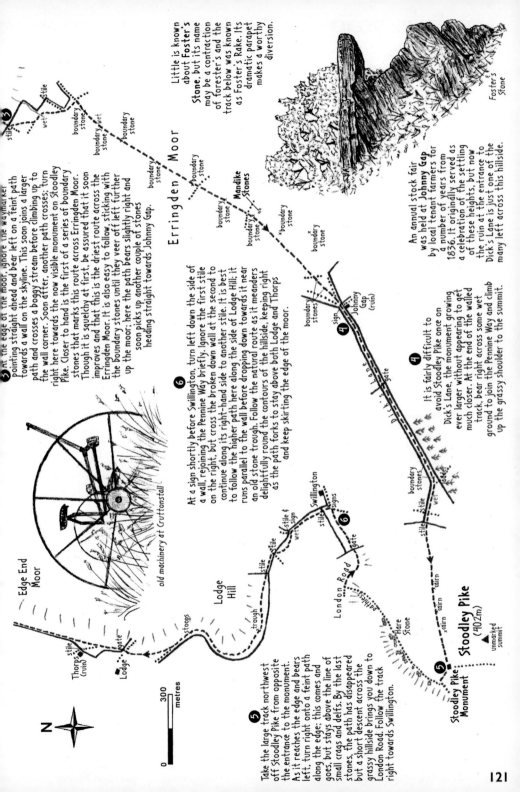

3 At the edge of the moor, ignore the waymarker pointing straight ahead and bear left on a feint path towards a wall on the skyline. This soon joins a larger path and crosses a boggy stream before climbing up to the wall corner. Soon after, another path crosses; turn right here towards the now visible monument on Stoodley Pike. Closer to hand is the first of a series of boundary stones that marks this route across Erringden Moor. Though it is squelchy at first, be assured that it soon improves and that this is the driest route across the Erringden Moor. It is also easy to follow, sticking with the boundary stones until they veer off left further up the moor; here the path bears slightly right and soon picks up another couple of stones heading straight towards Johnny Gap.

Erringden Moor

Little is known about **Foster's Stone**, but its name may be a contraction of forester's and the track below was known as Foster's Rake. Its dramatic parapet makes a worthy diversion.

Foster's Stone

An annual stock fair was held at **Johnny Gap** by local tenant farmers for a number of years from 1836. It originally served as a celebration of the settling of these heights, but now the ruin at the entrance to Dick's Lane is just one of the many left across this hillside.

6 At a sign shortly before Swillington, turn left down the side of a wall, rejoining the Pennine Way briefly. Ignore the first stile on the right, but cross the broken down wall at the second to continue along its right-hand side to another stile. It is best to follow the higher path here along the side of Lodge Hill; it runs parallel to the wall before dropping down towards it near an old stone trough. Follow the natural route as it meanders delightfully round the contours of the hillside, keeping right as the path forks to stay above both Lodge and Thorps and keep skirting the edge of the moor.

4 It is fairly difficult to avoid Stoodley Pike once on Dick's Lane, the monument growing ever larger without appearing to get much closer. At the end of the walled track, bear right across some wet ground to join the Pennine Way and climb up the grassy shoulder to the summit.

old machinery at Cruttonstall

5 Take the large track northwest off Stoodley Pike from opposite the entrance to the monument. As it reaches the edge and bears left, turn right onto a feint path along the edge; this comes and goes, but stays above the line of small crags and delfs. By the last stones, the path has disappeared but a short descent across the grassy hillside brings you down to London Road. Follow the track right towards Swillington.

Edge End Moor

Lodge Hill

Thorps (ruin)
Lodge

stile
gate

trough
stoops
stile
stile
stile & wet sign
signs
stile
gate

Swillington

6

London Road

Flare Stone
pathless

Stoodley Pike Monument

5

× cairn
cairn
cairn
× cairn

Stoodley Pike (402m)

▲ unmarked summit

boundary stone
boundary stone
boundary stone

Mandike Stones

× boundary stone
× boundary stone
× boundary stone

boundary stones

sign
4
Johnny Gap (ruin)

Dick's Lane

gate
boundary stones
adder
stile
wet
stile

boundary stone
boundary stone
boundary stone

stile
wet
boundary stone

wet
stile

3

N

0   300
metres

121

ROUTE 20: STOODLEY PIKE AND LANGFIELD EDGE FROM TODMORDEN

Distance: 8 miles (12.5km)

Ascent: 270m

Difficulty: Moderate

Parking: Various town centre car parks in Todmorden, including those on Lever Street and Oxford Street, and at the railway station.

Public Transport: Todmorden is on the main Caldervale train and bus routes.

Character: Stoodley Pike is a prominent landmark from the centre of Todmorden and, along with Langfield Edge, dominates the town's southern aspect. This route makes a beeline for the towering monument, passing Lumbutts and Mankinholes, before hugging the edge on its return. The route is clear and on good paths throughout.

2 Continue straight on through the hamlet of Oldroyd and then turn right just before a collection of sheds and caravans. A path skirts above the sheds and along the edge of the field to a stile into Bird Bank Wood. Continue straight on through the wood on a path that eventually drops down the road. Follow it right briefly, then turn left onto a path down into Lumbutts Clough. Keep right to cross bridge and follow the clough up to Lumbutts.

1 From the centre of Todmorden, pick up the Rochdale Canal heading east either directly from the Lever Street or Oxford Street car parks, or via a tunnel under the A6033 from the lock adjacent to the road. The towpath leads beneath Baltimore Bridge to reach Kilnhurst Bridge, where you join the road crossing the canal. Follow Kilnhurst Road all the way up to Kilnhurst Old Hall, from where a track leads on past the old Toll Bar.

Kilnhurst Old Hall was the home of the author William Holt, who wrote *Trigger in Europe*. Billy sold his books by loading them on his famous white horse, Trigger, who outlived him by a year and is buried just off the track to Oldroyd.

8 Follow Moor Lane down to Top o' Rough and turn right just before the farm. A narrow path skirts the property and follows the wall down to Lumbutts Road. Head straight across and follow the edge of the field to a squeeze that leads to the top of Shoebroad Lane. The track heads down to Todmorden past the Quaker burial ground and the attractive greenery of Honey Hole. Where the road (now tarmacked) bends sharps right, head straight on into the graveyard of Todmorden Unitarian Church and follow a path down to the bottom entrance. Honey Hole Road leads into Fielden Square, from where the main road can be followed back over the canal to the town centre.

7 Follow the dam wall right, passing the full Gaddings Dam, and descend the first set of steps at the far end. Bear left at the bottom on the feinter of two paths and cross the grassy ground behind the edge. Join the main path down to a large cairn by the junction on Rake End. Head straight across and follow the track as it bends round to the right and drops down to a gate at the top of Moor Lane.

The **Shewbread Quaker Burial Ground** is not at first apparent, simply a small tidy enclosure off Shoebroad Lane. Its first burials took place around the 1680s at a time when Quakers were not allowed to mark their burial places; the few stones present are more recent additions and there are in fact dozens of Quakers buried here, including many of the Fieldens. A meeting house stood down the lane at Shoebroad, a direct result of the 1689 Toleration Act, which allowed freedom of Christian worship for the first time. Shoebroad may be a corruption of Shewbread, which refers to the Old Testament *showbread* that was prepared for God at all times on a specially dedicated table, but it is also a dialect word for a narrow strip of land.

The prominent Gothic building of **Todmorden Unitarian Church** was built in the 1860s by the Fieldens, who had become involved in this relatively small non-conformist movement which believed in one God rather than the Trinity.

Lumbutts Mill wheel tower

The **Harvelin Park Estate** is beautifully situated, standing on the site of the old **Todmorden Union Workhouse** that unfortunately had to be torn down to make way for its development. Latterly converted into Stansfield View Hospital for the mentally handicapped, the workhouse was built like a great house for some 100 paupers from the various townships of Todmorden. When it was built in 1878, Todmorden was the last Union in the country to build a workhouse due to its vehement opposition to the 1834 Poor Law Amendment Act. In an earlier forebear of modern welfare issues, this sought to force people to work by making care for paupers harsher and more rigid. It led to the formation of the Todmorden Working Men's Association, who vowed to fight the Todmorden Union with demonstrations and boycotts, supported by local notables like John Fielden. The townships refused to pay centralized poor rates and so bailiffs arrived from Halifax on 16th November 1838 to collect taxes in Lumbutts. A large mob descended from Fielden's mill and proceeded to burn their cart and strip them. A few days later, another mob went on a rampage through Todmorden and Gauxholme, smashing windows, destroying furniture, and setting properties alight. Guardians of the Union, or even just supporters of the act, were targeted, with Hare Hill House and Todmorden Hall faring particularly badly. The 5th Light Dragoons cavalry were summoned from Burnley, soon followed by infantry troops from Manchester, who became permanently stationed in the town for a while. Despite forty arrests, only one man was convicted and no-one could be found to testify against John Fielden for inciting the riot. People came to Todmorden to view the destruction and the centralized workhouse was only forced upon the people of the town forty years later.

4 Turn left to follow London Road along the bottom edge of the moor. The track bends left and passes a braided wet section (with a path alongside); soon after, and some way before the building at Higher Greave, take a path climbing up the bank to the right with Stoodley Pike towering above. This fine path climbs steadily towards the monument before joining the main track up to the summit.

All that remains of **Lumbutts Mill** is the water wheel tower and chimney which stands proudly over the hamlet. This was built in the early nineteenth century, but there was a corn mill on the site from the 16th century.

3 Follow the road left and, on the bend opposite the tower of Lumbutts Mill, turn left up the Pennine Bridleway. Turn right at the top to climb some steps to the right of the Top Brink Inn and follow the edge of the field up to Mankinholes. Head straight across the road here, following a good track (Sisley Lane) across the hillside to Spencer House. Turn right at the junction beyond to reach the edge of the moor.

5 Follow the well-cairned Pennine Way south from the opposite side of the monument to its entrance – the true summit of Stoodley Pike is on the slight rise above the first cairn. Follow the cairns and stay with the edge to reach Withens Gate, marked by the massive guidestone of Long Stoop. Head straight on and climb up towards Coldwell Hill. By some stones on a slight crest (that marks the start of a line of flagstones), bear right off the main track. A path crosses the boggy ground adjacent to the flat top of Coldwell Hill, marked by a collection of huge flat stones.

6 Follow the obvious path along the edge of the high ground, the start of Langfield Edge. Across Black Clough, the path bends round towards the quarried faces of Gaddings Hole; bear left by a small cairn to stay above edge and join the line of a dry drain leading to the old dam wall of Gaddings Dam East.

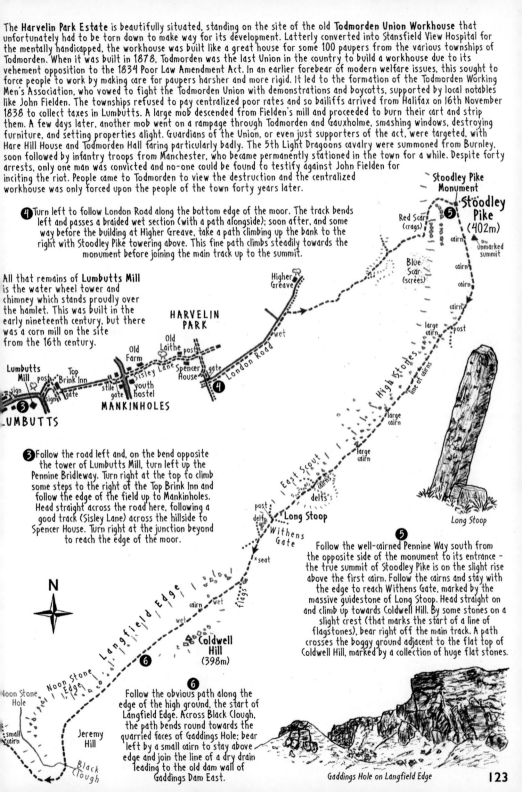

Long Stoop

Gaddings Hole on Langfield Edge

123

STOODLEY PIKE MONUMENT

If there is an image that symbolises the West Yorkshire moors then it must be that of Stoodley Pike Monument, the great black obelisk in the sky that confronts you across every corner of Calderdale. It rears its head over every horizon and muscles in on every photograph. My friends call it 'the evil one', a menacing presence that appears to emanate dark forces. Everything else on these moors is well proportioned, but Stoodley's monument is a gross imposition, too big and unwieldy to make sense of in a landscape where every small rock seems important.

Its prominent site on Stoodley Pike has probably been important for as long as people have been living in the Calder Valley. Both bones and stones were discovered when digging foundations for the first monument, possibly part of a Bronze Age burial ground. It has been suggested that a tribal chieftain was buried here with a cairn circle to mark the ground; according to legend, the owner of Stoodley Pike had to keep the cairn in perfect order otherwise everyone in the area would be unable to sleep.

Though it looks every bit the war memorial, Stoodley Pike Monument is actually a monument to peace. The foundation stone was laid in 1814 to celebrate the surrender of Paris and the defeat of Napoleon. It would, however, take two years to complete as work had to be suspended when Napoleon briefly escaped from Elba. That early model was a rather plain cylindrical tower; though marginally lower than the later model, it had a room at the top with a fireplace in it and its stairwell was said to climb all the way up the hollow tower without any handrail. However, having been earlier weakened by a lightning strike, the monument collapsed on 8th February 1854 at the same time as the Russian Ambassador left London and the outbreak of the Crimean War was declared. Peace, it seemed, was reliant on the monument standing.

When peace was proclaimed in 1856, the monument was rebuilt, once again largely by public subscription and at a cost of £812. It was moved a few yards back from the edge and a design by local architect, James Green, was chosen by a committee. Thus, it became vulgarly Victorian and the entrance covered with masonic symbolism, probably at the behest of the Fieldens who subsidised the building and provided the inscription above the entrance. The 39 steps up to the viewing platform were originally climbed in complete darkness, a ritual in itself, and the Freemasons conducted various other activities around the monument and the nearby public slake trough, as they had at the opening of the original tower.

Along with other repairs, a grill allowing some light into the stairwell and a lightning conductor were added in 1889. Another problem associated with the monument was that of vandalism. The first model was already blocked up before it collapsed and the CND symbol still evident was daubed high on the monument in 1962. As for the monument itself, it has withstood the Pennine wind for over 150 years and one suspects will take some unsettling - if only our peace had been as well founded as James Green's structure.

Stoodley Pike Monument

CHAPTER 17 - WAY STONE EDGE

Height: 482m

Grid Ref: SE001140

Map Sheet: OL21 (South Pennines)

Access: No restrictions.

Public Transport: Regular bus and train services to Marsden and Slaithwaite from Huddersfield. Bus 184 runs from Marsden to Oldham via A62. Bus 559 runs from Halifax to Deanhead.

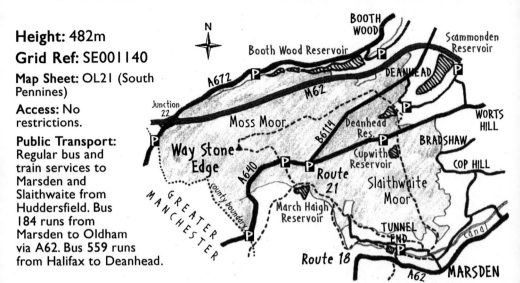

Way Stone Edge is the highest point in Calderdale, and stands on a striking shelf overlooking the M62. The unheralded summit plateau is bypassed by the Pennine Way and A640 Buckstones Road and could equally go by the name of Moss Moor, Buckstones Moss or White Hassocks (the latter is the first recorded name on Jefferys' map but has shifted south on maps in the intervening years). Though the moor is dominated by the motorway on its northern flanks, it retains a sense of barren solitude especially when the cloud descends (which in my experience is fairly often). Apart from the busy basin around March Haigh Reservoir, Way Stone Edge often feels like a forgotten moor and it is rare to meet another soul. Even Deanhead's charming basin is overlooked, but is just one of the corners of this moor that it is worth seeking out.

Way Stone Edge from Castle Dean Clough

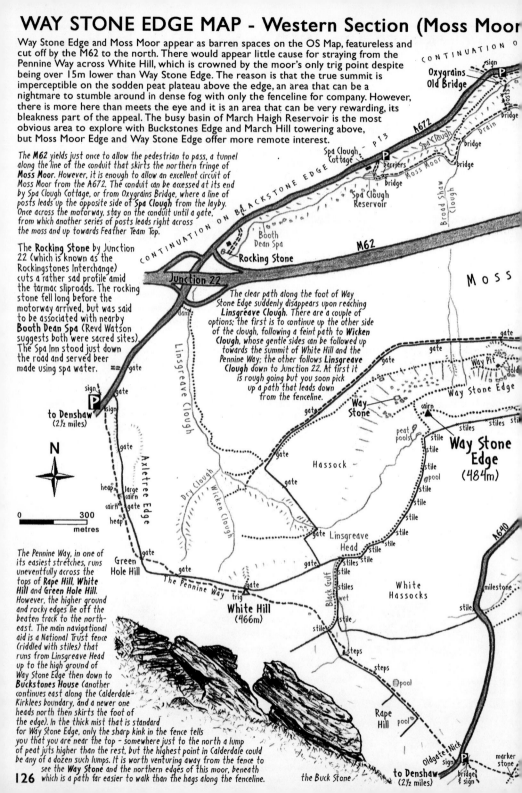

Way Stone Edge and Moss Moor appear as barren spaces on the OS Map, featureless and cut off by the M62 to the north. There would appear little cause for straying from the Pennine Way across White Hill, which is crowned by the moor's only trig point despite being over 15m lower than Way Stone Edge. The reason is that the true summit is imperceptible on the sodden peat plateau above the edge, an area that can be a nightmare to stumble around in dense fog with only the fenceline for company. However, there is more here than meets the eye and it is an area that can be very rewarding, its bleakness part of the appeal. The busy basin of March Haigh Reservoir is the most obvious area to explore with Buckstones Edge and March Hill towering above, but Moss Moor Edge and Way Stone Edge offer more remote interest.

The M62 yields just once to allow the pedestrian to pass, a tunnel along the line of the conduit that skirts the northern fringe of **Moss Moor**. However, it is enough to allow an excellent circuit of Moss Moor from the A672. The conduit can be accessed at its end by Spa Clough Cottage, or from Oxygrains Bridge, where a line of posts leads up the opposite side of **Spa Clough** from the layby. Once across the motorway, stay on the conduit until a gate, from which another series of posts leads right across the moss and up towards Feather Team Top.

The **Rocking Stone** by Junction 22 (which is known as the Rockingstones Interchange) cuts a rather sad profile amid the tarmac sliproads. The rocking stone fell long before the motorway arrived, but was said to be associated with nearby **Booth Dean Spa** (Revd Watson suggests both were sacred sites). The Spa Inn stood just down the road and served beer made using spa water.

The clear path along the foot of Way Stone Edge suddenly disappears upon reaching **Linsgreave Clough**. There are a couple of options; the first is to continue up the other side of the clough, following a feint path to **Wicken Clough**, whose gentle sides can be followed up towards the summit of White Hill and the Pennine Way; the other follows **Linsgreave Clough** down to Junction 22. At first it is rough going but you soon pick up a path that leads down from the fenceline.

The Pennine Way, in one of its easiest stretches, runs uneventfully across the tops of **Rape Hill, White Hill** and **Green Hole Hill**. However, the higher ground and rocky edges lie off the beaten track to the north-east. The main navigational aid is a National Trust fence (riddled with stiles) that runs from Linsgreave Head up to the high ground of Way Stone Edge then down to **Buckstones House** (another continues east along the Calderdale-Kirklees boundary, and a newer one heads north then skirts the foot of the edge). In the thick mist that is standard for Way Stone Edge, only the sharp kink in the fence tells you that you are near the top - somewhere just to the north a lump of peat juts higher than the rest, but the highest point in Calderdale could be any of a dozen such lumps. It is worth venturing away from the fence to see the **Way Stone** and the northern edges of this moor, beneath which is a path far easier to walk than the hags along the fenceline.

Map labels

CONTINUATION O

Oxygrains Old Bridge

sign · P

posts · bridge

A672

Spa Clough · P13

Drain · bridge

Spa Clough Cottage · P · Barriers

bridge

Moss Moor · bridge

Spa Clough Reservoir

Broad Shaw Clough

CONTINUATION ON BLACKSTONE EDGE

Booth Dean Spa

M62

MOSS

Rocking Stone

Junction 22 · dam

gate

gate · Way Pit · fold

Way Stone Edge

to Denshaw (2½ miles) · P · sign

Linsgreave Clough

Way Stone · cairn

peat pools · stile · stiles · stiles · sti

Way Stone Edge (484m)

gate · Hassock · pool · stile

Axletree Edge

heap · large cairn · cairn · gate

Dry Clough · Wicken Clough

gate · Linsgreave Head

stile · stiles

0   300   metres

N

heap

gate · Black Gulf · White Hassocks

Green Hole Hill · gate

The Pennine Way · trig

White Hill (466m)

stiles · wet · stile

A640 · milestone · stile

steps · steps · pool

Rape Hill · pool

Oldgate Nick · sign · P · bridge & sign · marker stone

to Denshaw (2½ miles)

the Buck Stone

& Buckstones)

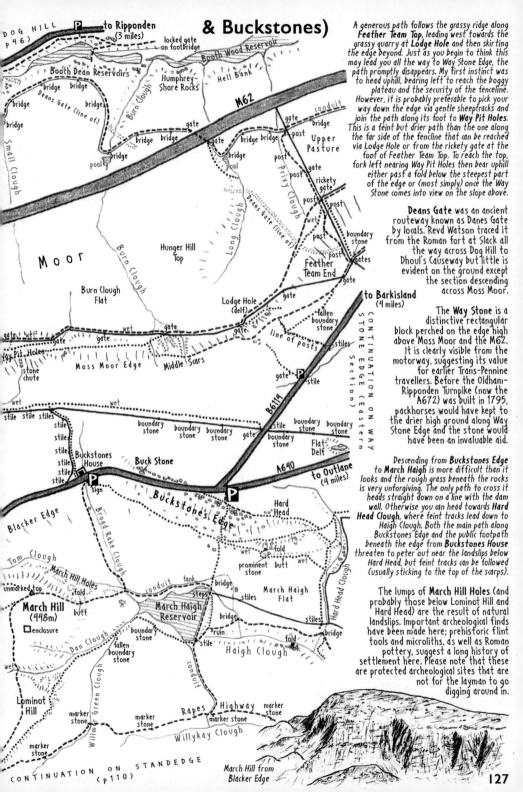

A generous path follows the grassy ridge along **Feather Team Top**, leading west towards the grassy quarry at **Lodge Hole** and then skirting the edge beyond. Just as you begin to think this may lead you all the way to Way Stone Edge, the path promptly disappears. My first instinct was to head uphill, bearing left to reach the boggy plateau and the security of the fenceline. However, it is probably preferable to pick your way down the edge via gentle sheeptracks and join the path along its foot to **Way Pit Holes**. This is a feint but drier path than the one along the far side of the fenceline that can be reached via Lodge Hole or from the rickety gate at the foot of Feather Team Top. To reach the top, fork left nearing Way Pit Holes then bear uphill either past a fold below the steepest part of the edge or (most simply) once the **Way Stone** comes into view on the slope above.

Deans Gate was an ancient routeway known as Danes Gate by locals. Revd Watson traced it from the Roman fort at Slack all the way across Dog Hill to Dhoul's Causeway but little is evident on the ground except the section descending across Moss Moor.

The **Way Stone** is a distinctive rectangular block perched on the edge high above Moss Moor and the M62. It is clearly visible from the motorway, suggesting its value for earlier Trans-Pennine travellers. Before the Oldham-Ripponden Turnpike (now the A672) was built in 1795, packhorses would have kept to the drier high ground along Way Stone Edge and the stone would have been an invaluable aid.

Descending from **Buckstones Edge** to **March Haigh** is more difficult than it looks and the rough grass beneath the rocks is very unforgiving. The only path to cross it heads straight down on a line with the dam wall. Otherwise you can head towards **Hard Head Clough**, where feint tracks lead down to Haigh Clough. Both the main path along Buckstones Edge and the public footpath beneath the edge from **Buckstones House** threaten to peter out near the landslips below Hard Head, but feint tracks can be followed (usually sticking to the top of the scarps).

The lumps of **March Hill Holes** (and probably those below Lominot Hill and Hard Head) are the result of natural landslips. Important archeological finds have been made here; prehistoric flint tools and microliths, as well as Roman pottery, suggest a long history of settlement here. Please note that these are protected archeological sites that are not for the layman to go digging around in.

March Hill from Blacker Edge

CONTINUATION ON STANDEDGE (p110)

127

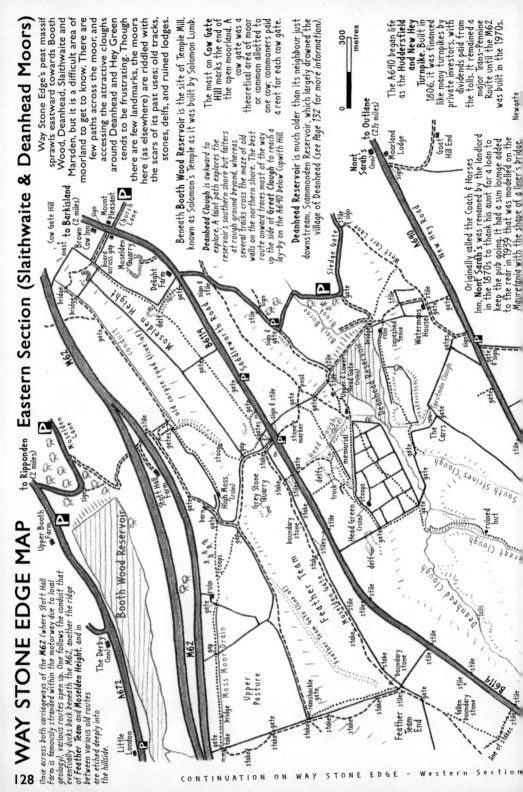

WAY STONE EDGE MAP — Eastern Section (Slaithwaite & Deanhead Moors)

Way Stone Edge's peat massif sprawls eastward towards Booth Wood, Deanhead, Slaithwaite and Marsden, but it is a difficult area of moorland to get to know. There are few paths across the moor, and accessing the attractive cloughs around Deanhead and Hey Green tends to be frustrating. Though there are few landmarks, the moors here (as elsewhere) are riddled with the scars of its past uses; old tracks, stones, delfs, and ruined lodges.

Beneath **Booth Wood Reservoir** is the site of Temple Mill, known as Solomon's Temple as it was built by Solomon Lumb.

Deanhead Clough is awkward to explore. A faint path explores the reservoir's southern shore but falters at rough ground beyond, whereas several tracks cross the maze of old walls on the northern shore. The best route onward traces most of the way up the side of Great Clough to reach a lay-by on the A640 below Cupwith Hill.

The mast on **Cow Gate Hill** marks the end of the open moorland. A cow gate was a theoretical area of moor or common allotted to one cow: commoners paid a rent for each cow gate.

Deanhead Reservoir is much older than its neighbour just downstream, Scammonden Reservoir, which largely drowned the village of Deanhead (See Page 132 for more information).

The A640 began life as the **Huddersfield** and **New Hey** Turnpike. Built in 1806, it was financed like many turnpikes by private investors, with dividends paid from the tolls. It remained a major Trans-Pennine Route until the M62 was built in the 1970s.

Originally called the Coach & Horses Inn, **Nont Sarah's** was renamed by the landlord in the 1870s to thank his aunt for a loan to keep the pub going. It had a sun lounge added to the rear in 1939 that was modelled on the *Mauretania* with the shape of a liner's bridge.

Once across both carriageways of the **M62** (where Stott Hall Farm is famously stranded within the motorway due to local geology), various routes open up. One follows the conduit that eventually ducks back beneath the M62, another the ridge of **Feather Team** and **Moselden Height**, and in between various old routes are etched deeply into the hillside.

300 metres

0

to Ripponden (2 miles)

to Barkisland (2 miles)

Nont Sarah's (½ mile) to Outlane (2½ miles)

Newgate

Labels on map
Cow Gate Hill · mast · Brown Cow Inn · sign · Mount Pleasant · Church Lane · board across gap · Moselden Quarry · Delight Farm · Moselden Height · delf · conduit · B6114 · old corpse road · Saddleworth Road · Moselden Lane · Upper Booth Farm · The Derby (Inn) · Little London · A672 · Booth Wood Reservoir · Stott Hall Farm · M62 · Moss Moor Drain · Upper Pasture · barn · gate · ruin · stoops · High Moss (ruin) · Grey Stone Quarry · Feather Team · boundary stone · ramshackle gate · Feather Team gate · stake · Feather Team End · fallen boundary stone · line of stakes · stile · sign & stile · post · stile · stone marker · Buck Burne Brook · West Carr Lane · Sledge Gate · New Hey Road · A640 · Goat Moorland Lodge · Goat Hill End · Hill · Watermans House · squashed fence · ruin · The Carr's gate · Deanhead Reservoir · Upper & Lower Head Gate · Head Clough · memorial · delfs · Head Green (ruin) · stoops · truck · South Strines Clough · ruined hut · Great Clough · Deanhead Clough · Sprotham Clough · falls

128

CONTINUATION ON WAY STONE EDGE — Western Section

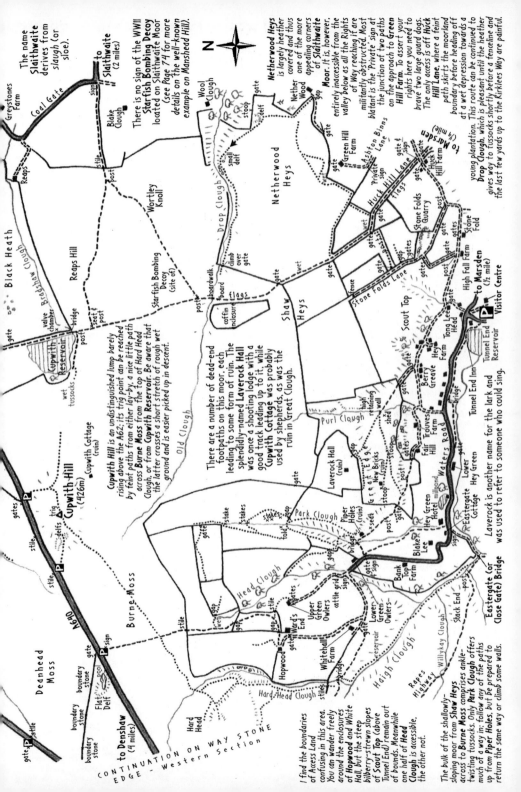

The name Slaithwaite derives from *slaugh* (or sloe).

to Slaithwaite (2 miles)

Greystones Farm

Coal Gate

Reaps

Blake Clough

sign

stile

post

Wortley Knoll

There is no sign of the WWII Starfish Bombing Decoy located on Slaithwaite Moor (see Page 74 for more details on the well-known example on Manshead Hill).

Wool Clough

stoop

Nether Wood

delf

Netherwood Heys is largely heather covered and thus one of the more appealing corners of Slaithwaite Moor. It is, however, entirely inaccessible from the valley below as all the Rights of Way reaching it are militantly obstructed. Most blatant is the Private sign at the junction of two paths on the approach to Green Hill Farm. To assert your rights here you need to brave two large guard dogs. The only access is off Huck Hill Lane, where a faint path skirts the moorland boundary before heading off across a wet depression towards a young plantation. This route can be continued to Drop Clough, which is pleasant until the heather gives way to tussocks shortly before a fenceline and the last few yards up to the Kirklees Way are painful.

Green Hill Farm

Ashton Binns

Private sign

to Marsden (¼ mile)

Huck Hill Lane

gate & sign

gate

flags

Huck Hill Farm

gate

Stone Folds Quarry

post

gate

Stone Fold

gates

Netherwood Heys

Drop Clough

small delf

post

climb over gate

board

boardwalk

Shaw Heys

wet

fence

Stone Folds Lane

gate

coffin enclosure

flags

seat & post

Scout Top

Tong Lee Head

Hey Farm

Berry Greave

High Fall Farm

gate

post

to Marsden (½ mile)

Tunnel End Reservoir

P Visitor Centre

Cupwith Hill is an undistinguished lump barely rising above the A62; its trig point can be reached by feint paths from either lay-by, a nice little path across Burne Moss from the top of Hard Head Clough, or from Cupwith Reservoir. Be aware that the latter crosses a short stretch of rough wet ground and is easier picked up in descent.

Cupwith Cottage (ruin)

There are a number of dead-end footpaths on this moor, each leading to some form of ruin. The splendidly-named Laverock Hall was once a shooting lodge with a good track leading up to it, while Cupwith Cottage was probably used by shepherds, as was the ruin in Great Clough.

Black Heath

Bradshaw Clough

valve chamber

gate

bridge

Cupwith Reservoir

seat & post

post

wet tussocks

Reaps Hill

Starfish Bombing Decoy (site of)

Old Clough

Cupwith Hill (412m)

trig

delfs

P

gates

stile

Burne Moss

stile

P sign

Deanhead Moss

boundary stone

Flat Delf

pool

boundary stone

boundary stone

gate

stile

P

gate

A640

to Densham (4 miles)

Purl Clough

high retaining wall

shed

Laverock Hall (ruin)

Great Edge

stoop

New Bricks (ruin)

gap

post

gate

gates

Fair Trouves Hill Farm

stoop

Waters Road

millpond

Hey Green Hotel

Lower Hey Green

Eastgate Cottage

Laverock is another name for the lark and was used to refer to someone who could sing.

Park Clough

stakes

fold

post

gate

Head Clough

gap

stile

stile

Ward's End

Upper Green Owlers

cattle grid

Blake Lee

sign

gate

sign

Bank Top Farm

Lower Green Owlers

reservoir

Whitehall Farm

bridge

Hopwood

stile

Eastgate (or Close Gate) Bridge

Stack End

Willykay Clough

Haigh Clough

Ropes Highway

Hard Head Clough

Hard Head

I find the boundaries of Access Land confusing in this area. You can wander freely across to Burne Moss around the enclosures of Hopwood and White Hall, but the steep bilberry-strewn slopes of Scout Top (above Tunnel End) remain out of bounds. Meanwhile one half of Head Clough is accessible, the other not.

The bulk of the shallowly-sloping moor from Shaw Heys across to Burne Moss comprises ankle-twisting tussocks. Only Park Clough offers much of a way in: follow any of the paths up from Piper Holes, but be prepared to return the same way or climb some walls.

Piper Holes (ruin)

stakes

stake

CONTINUATION ON WAY STONE EDGE – Western Section

ROUTE 21: WAY STONE EDGE & DEANHEAD RESERVOIR

Distance: 8 miles (12.5km)

Ascent: 470m

Difficulty: Moderate

Parking: Various street parking in Marsden. Lay-bys on A640 at Buckstones House or Cupwith Reservoir, or along B6114 above Deanhead Reservoir.

Public Transport: Marsden is on the main Huddersfield Line between Leeds & Manchester and the 182, 183 & 184 bus routes. Buses 185 & 186 up the Colne Valley go to Dirker (by the station)

Character: Way Stone Edge is awkward to reach, but this route provides a satisfactory yomp across the moors north of Marsden. The section across the summit is necessarily rough and pathless, but thanks to the various fences navigation is never too complicated. Elsewhere i've resisted the temptation to stray too far from the clearer paths around March Haigh, Deanhead and Cupwith Reservoirs.

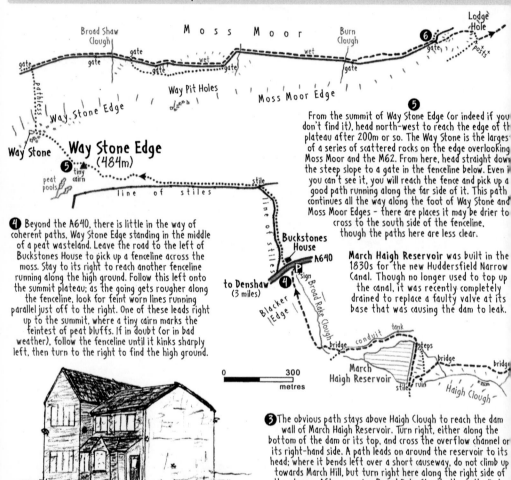

5 From the summit of Way Stone Edge (or indeed if you don't find it), head north-west to reach the edge of the plateau after 200m or so. The Way Stone is the largest of a series of scattered rocks on the edge overlooking Moss Moor and the M62. From here, head straight down the steep slope to a gate in the fenceline below. Even if you can't see it, you will reach the fence and pick up a good path running along the far side of it. This path continues all the way along the foot of Way Stone and Moss Moor Edges - there are places it may be drier to cross to the south side of the fenceline, though the paths here are less clear.

March Haigh Reservoir was built in the 1830s for the new Huddersfield Narrow Canal. Though no longer used to top up the canal, it was recently completely drained to replace a faulty valve at its base that was causing the dam to leak.

4 Beyond the A640, there is little in the way of coherent paths, Way Stone Edge standing in the middle of a peat wasteland. Leave the road to the left of Buckstones House to pick up a fenceline across the moss. Stay to its right to reach another fenceline running along the high ground. Follow this left onto the summit plateau; as the going gets rougher along the fenceline, look for feint worn lines running parallel just off to the right. One of these leads right up to the summit, where a tiny cairn marks the feintest of peat bluffs. If in doubt (or in bad weather), follow the fenceline until it kinks sharply left, then turn to the right to find the high ground.

3 The obvious path stays above Haigh Clough to reach the dam wall of March Haigh Reservoir. Turn right, either along the bottom of the dam or its top, and cross the overflow channel or its right-hand side. A path leads on around the reservoir to its head; where it bends left over a short causeway, do not climb up towards March Hill, but turn right here along the right side of the stream. After crossing Broad Rake Clough, the path climbs steeply up towards the dark silhouette of Buckstones House.

Buckstones House

Buckstones House served as both the Buckstones Inn and earlier the Buck Inn on the Huddersfield and New Hey Turnpike; indeed, the Saddleworth side of the packhorse road had been known as the Buck Road. In the early 19th century, it was home to a gang of thieves who held up coaches and travellers and raided villages in the area (perhaps this is the source of the name Thieves Bridge across Close Moss). When one of their number informed, they were arrested and many were transported for their crimes. Since then it served as a gamekeeper's house.

the Way Stone

FROM MARSDEN

N

to Barkisland (3 miles)

7 Head straight across the B6114 and follow the path down through a narrow gate. Reaching a post, turn sharply right to reach another gate – you can continue zigzagging, but it is easiest to descend straight down the near side of the wall to the end of Deanhead Reservoir. Cross a stile and follow a path along the dam wall, then climb straight up the slope beyond. The path bends left to reach a stile; follow the wall up to join another path leading right over a stile. In front of Watermans House, join a track that leads up to the road.

6 Reaching a gate where the fenceline kinks for a second time, turn right through the gate and skirt along the slope. You should pick up a feint path around the left-hand edge of Lodge Hole (a grassy quarry delf) and climb up the slope away from the fenceline. Cross a few yards of rough ground above to reach a clear track along the edge (it is possible to climb straight up the rough slope from the gate to reach this). The track passes through a couple of gates before running along the top of Feather Team. Turn right at the far end to reach the B6114.

Huck Hill Lane was once Heck Hill Lane and was one of a number of new tracks created at the time of the private enclosure of Dirker and **Shaw Heys** in the mid-19th century. As Marsden grew, areas of moorland common land were increasingly enclosed by the Lords of the Manor for cattle grazing. Plots were allocated to those with grazing rights and the ground had to be cleared of stones, drained, limed and walled using stone from the public quarry. Much of the walling never materialised (thus the irregular boxes evident on this moorland) and most of the land has long since returned to rough pasture.

2 The track kinks above Berry Greave and then passes a couple of sheds; turn right on the bend beyond. Pass in front of Troaves Farm and behind Fair Hill as you are led into a narrow walled path. The path soon opens out and climbs steadily ahead; beyond a gate, it drops over a bridge and bends right to reach the jumble of stone that used to be Piper Holes. A newly flagged path then leads across Park Clough and up to the road. Turn right, passing Lower Green Owlers, then fork left in Green Owlers Clough. Keep left of Whitehall Farm and, opposite the building, turn left through a gate onto the moor.

The *owler* (as in Green Owlers) is a word used across the Pennines for the alder tree.

Cuckoo Day is celebrated in Marsden every April. It refers to a legend that the townsfolk tried to trap a cuckoo (and therefore the spring it brought with it) by building a wall around it, only for it to fly away as they finished. At which they exclaimed, 'it were nobbut just wun course too low' and set about building it higher.

1 From Marsden Railway Station, cross the canal and railway and turn left along Reddisher Road. If heading from the centre of Marsden, follow Peel Street out past the Swan to get to the station (*see Page 113 for map*). Turn right off Reddisher Road at a sign before Rough Lea Farm and follow a track up to the right of the buildings. Where it bends off to the right, head straight on up the side of a wall. Reaching a track, turn left and skirt along the hillside, passing a number of farms and hamlets.

to Outlane (3 miles)

Cottongrass is particularly fond of very wet ground and thus serves a useful dual function. As well as brightening many a moorland scene with their wispy white heads, they warn the walker of impending sqeuelchy doom. Technically it is not a grass, but rather a sedge.

8 Follow the A640 right for 100m, then turn left onto a good track past Cupwith Reservoir. Continue straight on across Drop Clough and over Shaw Heys. Beyond a gate, it follows the line of a wall before leading into Huck Hill Lane, which runs steeply down to Huck Hill Farm.

9 Head straight across the track by Huck Hill Farm, then fork right below the farm, following the higher of two walled paths down to Ingle Nook. Join a track at the buildings that leads down to Dirker, emerging opposite Marsden Railway Station again.

Marsden was first referred to as Marchdene in the 12th century, *march* being a territorial boundary of tribes. At the time it served as a hunting forest for the Lords of Pontefract and the oak was so dense that it was said a squirrel could reach Huddersfield without touching the ground.

MARSDEN

131

THE M62 & SCAMMONDEN RESERVOIR

Plans for a trans-Pennine motorway had been discussed since the 1930s, but the first route was not proposed until 1952. Questions were raised about its high altitude crossing and the fact that it did not cater for many of the major towns in the area. Although it now reaches 1220ft at its highest point, the motorway would have been 150ft higher had it run along the exposed height of Buckstones Edge as was initially suggested. A new route was devised in 1961 and became known as the Lancashire-Yorkshire motorway (the name's order being decided by a coin toss on Windy Hill by the two surveyors). A full scale mock-up of a half-mile stretch of the motorway was constructed near the Brown Cow to see how it coped with the elements, and various other blasting, fencing and vegetation tests took place.

Construction began in 1964 by cutting through 150ft of hillside near Dean Head and dumping it in the adjacent valley to form the 200ft-high dam for Scammonden Reservoir. This feat of engineering had never been tried before, nor indeed since. The motorway severed the Blackburn valley in two and the reservoir drowned much of the village of Dean Head, leaving its church stranded on the hillside. Scammonden Cotton Mill is the only mill whose ruins remain (just below the dam), ironic given this is 'the mill that never was' (the six-storey building was built in the 1860s just before the Cotton Famine and never made a stitch).

Work on the Moss Moor section began in 1966, but there were notable problems. The weather was hideous - even the summers were some of the wettest on record - and, once vegetation was removed from the peat, the surface became impassable. A horse called Peggy was initially used to lay out the line of the road, yet she too sank into the peat; a frame had to be erected around her and Peggy was heaved out using a sling. In all, 500,000 cubic metres of peat was excavated to allow this section of the road to be laid; the peat was dumped on the adjacent moor and material from the Windy Hill cutting used to form the embankment across Moss Moor.

The M62 opened to traffic on December 20th 1970 and was officially inaugurated by the Queen the following year. When it was built, the bridge carrying the A6025 was the longest single span in Europe at 625ft, and Scammonden Dam is still the largest earth-filled dam in Europe. The motorway used mesh fencing and a wire central reservation designed to prevent snow drifts building up and was claimed never to be closed as a result of snow. Closures in the past have been blamed on gritters' strikes or incompetency (e.g. both Yorkshire and Lancashire gritters turning round on Junction 21, but neither gritting the junction), but it succumbed to the weather for the first time in April 2012.

It is sometimes suggested that the road divides around Stott Hill Farm because of its owner's objections, but it was actually due to the underlying geology that the carriageway had to be split as it wouldn't take the weight of the whole road. The eighteenth century farmhouse has since earned the nicknames 'The Island' and 'Little House on the Prairie'. In truth, individuals in these communities had little power to hinder development due to powers of compulsory purchase. Just ask Wilfred Dyson, whose farm was lost beneath Scammonden Reservoir; he challenged the compensation he was being offered, even as the bulldozers were moving in on his land, and was nearly buried in clay.

M62 Summit

Highest motorway in England 372m (1221 feet)

CHAPTER 18 - WEST NAB
(including Shooters Nab)

Height: 500m

Grid Ref: SE077088

Map Sheet: OL1 (The Dark Peak) / OL21 (South Pennines)

Access: No public access to shooting range and large Danger Area around Shooters Nab *(see Page 138 for more details)*. No dogs east of fenceline around summit of West Nab.

Public Transport: Regular bus and/or train services to Marsden, Slaithwaite and Meltham from Huddersfield. Buses 182/183 continue to Hard End, with 182 going via Blackmoorfoot. Buses 335/389 run from Slaithwaite to Meltham via Holt Head, with 335 continuing to Holmfirth.

West Nab and Shooters Nab form a distinctive anvil-shaped hunk of moorland jutting out north-eastwards from the Black Hill massif. It stands out from across most of Huddersfield, with the sharp peak of West Nab becoming more pronounced as you near Meltham, and Shooters Nab dominating the southern skyline of Marsden and Slaithwaite. Both are peaks in their own right, but are dealt with here as one because of the issues surrounding access to the summit of Shooters Nab (which is very rarely legally possible) and half of the moorland in between the two. The Danger Area sadly rips the heart out of the moor and means it is explored far less than it deserves. Other than the busy moorland fringes, West Nab is usually only accessed from the road immediately below (a route that heardly does the peak justice). Yet far more access is possible and, given that most of the moor is surrounded by rocky ramparts, it rarely disappoints the ambitious moorland tramper.

West Nab from Raven Rocks

The lower slopes of Shooters Nab are well trodden and provide the easiest moorland access from Marsden. Two paths lead up from Carrs Road; one from the top of Peel Street to Crowther, the other to Scout from opposite the park. The hillside above is riddled with tracks, with obvious targets being the scarred face of **Top of Scout** and the clustered **Piper Stones**. Other paths lead off Meltham Road across moorland pleasantly pockmarked with old quarries. All paths descend or later meet one of the two conduits leading around **Shooters Nab**: the higher of these marks the limit to the popularly explored section of the moor.

When the danger area is accessible (see Page 136 for details), **Shooters Nab** is easily reached. The obvious route leads up through the quarries via the incline heading up from Deer Hill Conduit. A feint path also leads across the summit plateau from the flagpole at the corner of the wall to the east. The summit is on the grassy lump at the corner of the quarry above the Shuttle Stone.

The danger area is marked to the east by a wall running uphill from the ranges to a flagpole on the top and then a series of signs across the mosses beyond. Outside this, a couple of paths lead up **Deer Hill** from the gate at the south-east corner of the reservoir. The easiest follows the fenceline steeply up to the wall at the top and continues beside the fence along Deer Hill Brow. The path eventually peters out near **Muddy Brook** but another climbs diagonally out of the clough to reach a fenced plantation. Following the fence leads along the edge that can be followed roughly all the way to West Nab. This side of the moor can be accessed by any of the broad straight tracks leading west from Meltham. **Red Lane** leads directly up the slope, while **Brow Grains Road** has a shooting path heading up from the end of it (though the gate is usually locked).

Meltham Road is another part of the turnpike, and was previously known as both Chain Road (referring to the chains that were put across the turnpike to deter those who hadn't paid the tolls) and Badger Gate. Badgers were licensed corn-hawkers who would have traded along the turnpike.

The name **Shooters Nab** may seem rather appropriate for a hill whose top is out of bounds due to a rifle range, but it predates the existing ownership. On older maps, it is Shorter Nab, shorter being a dialect word for an archer.

Wham (as in **Wham Head**) is a dialect word for a swamp or wet hollow.

The area below **West Nab's** summit was known as Millstone Hill and grindstones have been quarried from the exposed rocks here since the Middle Ages. A couple of millstones can still be found in the grass.

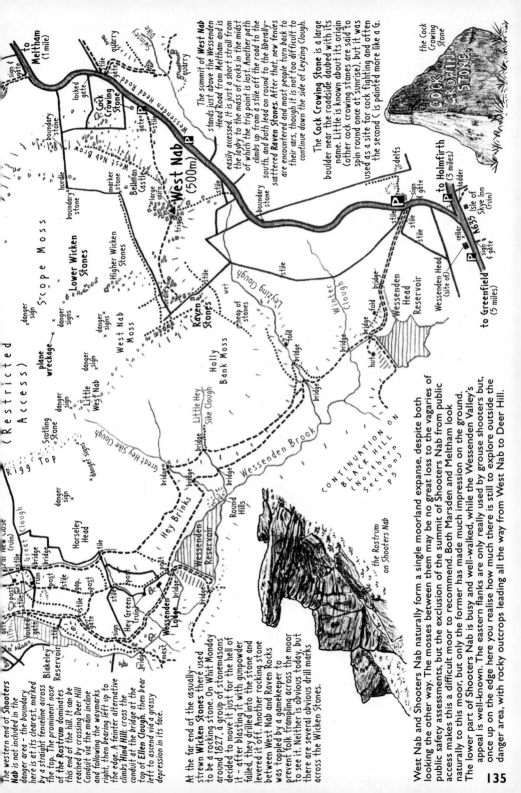

the Cock Crowing Stone

COCK CROWING STONE

Map labels:

to Meltham (1 mile) · quarry · quarry · Swinsey Dike · locked gate · stile · gate · Cock Crowing Stone · Wessenden Head Road · boundary stone · West Nab Brow · P · gate · stile · hurdle · marker stone · boundary stone · Bellman Castle · large cairn · West Nab (500m) · trig · stile · boundary stone · P · Scope Moss · (Restricted Access) · Lower Wicken Stones · Higher Wicken Stones · stile · stile · Leyzing Clough · stile · wet · P · sign & gate · to Holmfirth (3 miles) · delfs · ladder · stile · P · Isle of Skye Inn (ruin) · A635 · cellar · P · sign & gate · Wessenden Head (site of) · to Greenfield (5 miles) · stile · danger sign · danger signs · Raven Stones · plane wreckage · danger sign · danger signs · West Nab Moss · heap of stones · Holly Bank Moss · Winter Clough · Wessenden Head Reservoir · fold · bridge · hut · bridge · bridge · fold · bridge · bridge · Little West Nab · danger sign · Little Hey Sike Clough · bridge · bridge · Wessenden Brook · Scoting Stone · Rigg Top · danger sign · Great Hey Sike Clough · danger signs · bridge · bridge · bridge · Hey Brinks · Round Hills · CONTINUATION ON BLACK HILL (Northern Section - P5) · Horseley Head · stile · Far New Close (ruin) · Great Clough (ruin) · stile · post · bridge · ruin · post · Blakeley Reservoir · locked gate · gate · post · stile · ruin · stile · post · sign · gate · Hey Green (ruin) · Wessenden Lodge · bridge · Wessenden Reservoir · the Rostrum on Shooters Nab

---

The summit of **West Nab** stands just above the Wessenden Head Road from Meltham and is easily accessed. It is just a short stroll from the layby to the mass of rocks in the midst of which the trig point is lost. Another path climbs up from a stile off the road to the south, and both lead on round to the liberally-scattered **Raven Stones**. After that, new fences are encountered and most people turn back to their cars, though it is not too difficult to continue down the side of Leyzing Clough.

The **Cock Crowing Stone** is a large boulder near the roadside daubed with its name. Little is known about its origin (other cock crowing stones are said to spin round once at sunrise), but it was used as a site for cock fighting and often the second C is painted more like a G.

The western end of **Shooters Nab** is not included in the danger area – the boundary here is at its clearest, marked by a straight fenceline across the top. The prominent nose of the **Rostrum** dominates this end of the hill. It can be reached by crossing Deer Hill Conduit via the main incline and following the waymarks right, then bearing left up to the edge. A feinter alternative climbs Hind Hill, cross the conduit at the bridge at the top of Ellen Clough, then bear left to ascend via a grassy depression in its face.

At the far end of the casually-strewn **Wicken Stones** there used to be a rocking stone. On Whit Monday around 1827, a group of stonemasons decided to move it just for the hell of it – after blasting it with gunpowder failed, they drilled into the stone and levered it off. Another rocking stone between West Nab and Raven Rocks was toppled by a gamekeeper to prevent folk trampling across the moor to see it. Neither is obvious today, but there are several obvious drill marks across the Wicken Stones.

West Nab and Shooters Nab naturally form a single moorland expanse, despite both looking the other way. The mosses between them may be no great loss to the vagaries of public safety assessments, but the exclusion of the summit of Shooters Nab from public access makes this a difficult moor to recommend. Both Marsden and Meltham look naturally to this moor, but only the former has made much impression on the ground. The lower part of Shooters Nab is busy and well-walked, while the Wessenden Valley's appeal is well-known. The eastern flanks are only really used by grouse shooters but, once up on the edge here you realise how much there is still to explore outside the danger area, with rocky outcrops leading all the way from West Nab to Deer Hill.

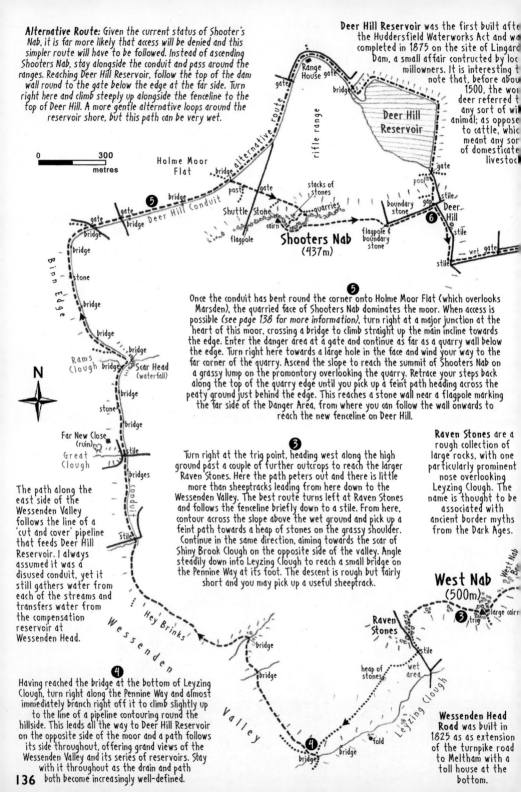

Alternative Route: Given the current status of Shooter's Nab, it is far more likely that access will be denied and this simpler route will have to be followed. Instead of ascending Shooters Nab, stay alongside the conduit and pass around the ranges. Reaching Deer Hill Reservoir, follow the top of the dam wall round to the gate below the edge at the far side. Turn right here and climb steeply up alongside the fenceline to the top of Deer Hill. A more gentle alternative loops around the reservoir shore, but this path can be very wet.

Deer Hill Reservoir was the first built after the Huddersfield Waterworks Act and was completed in 1875 on the site of Lingard Dam, a small affair contructed by local millowners. It is interesting to note that, before about 1500, the word deer referred to any sort of wild animal; as opposed to cattle, which meant any sort of domesticated livestock.

⑤ Once the conduit has bent round the corner onto Holme Moor Flat (which overlooks Marsden), the quarried face of Shooters Nab dominates the moor. When access is possible (see page 138 for more information), turn right at a major junction at the heart of this moor, crossing a bridge to climb straight up the main incline towards the edge. Enter the danger area at a gate and continue as far as a quarry wall below the edge. Turn right here towards a large hole in the face and wind your way to the far corner of the quarry. Ascend the slope to reach the summit of Shooters Nab on a grassy lump on the promontory overlooking the quarry. Retrace your steps back along the top of the quarry edge until you pick up a feint path heading across the peaty ground just behind the edge. This reaches a stone wall near a flagpole marking the far side of the Danger Area, from where you can follow the wall onwards to reach the new fenceline on Deer Hill.

Raven Stones are a rough collection of large rocks, with one particularly prominent nose overlooking Leyzing Clough. The name is thought to be associated with ancient border myths from the Dark Ages.

③ Turn right at the trig point, heading west along the high ground past a couple of further outcrops to reach the larger Raven Stones. Here the path peters out and there is little more than sheeptracks leading from here down to the Wessenden Valley. The best route turns left at Raven Stones and follows the fenceline briefly down to a stile. From here, contour across the slope above the wet ground and pick up a feint path towards a heap of stones on the grassy shoulder. Continue in the same direction, aiming towards the scar of Shiny Brook Clough on the opposite side of the valley. Angle steadily down into Leyzing Clough to reach a small bridge on the Pennine Way at its foot. The descent is rough but fairly short and you may pick up a useful sheeptrack.

The path along the east side of the Wessenden Valley follows the line of a 'cut and cover' pipeline that feeds Deer Hill Reservoir. I always assumed it was a disused conduit, yet it still gathers water from each of the streams and transfers water from the compensation reservoir at Wessenden Head.

④ Having reached the bridge at the bottom of Leyzing Clough, turn right along the Pennine Way and almost immediately branch right off it to climb slightly up to the line of a pipeline contouring round the hillside. This leads all the way to Deer Hill Reservoir on the opposite side of the moor and a path follows its side throughout, offering grand views of the Wessenden Valley and its series of reservoirs. Stay with it throughout as the drain and path both become increasingly well-defined.

Wessenden Head Road was built in 1825 as as extension of the turnpike road to Meltham with a toll house at the bottom.

West Nab (500m)

0   300
metres

136

ROUTE 22: WEST NAB & SHOOTERS NAB FROM MELTHAM

Distance: 9 miles (15km)

Ascent: 410m

Difficulty: Moderate

Parking: Clarke Lane & Carlisle Street car parks and other street parking in Meltham, or lay-by on Wessenden Head Road.

Public Transport: Buses 321/324/335 run from Huddersfield to Meltham.

Access: No dogs on this route.

Character: West Nab is a fine rocky summit, particularly when seen from Meltham, and makes a pleasing ascent from the town. The route then encircles Shooters Nab, which can only be crossed on certain days or evenings. The short descent from West Nab to the Wessenden Valley is rough and largely pathless, but enables a circuit of a beautiful moor scarred by its large danger area *(see page 138 for more details).*

8 Turn right down the road, before turning first left into Leygards Lane. Almost immediately turn right down Colders Lane and follow the grassy track into Meltham, passing a couple of terraces before it turns into a tarmac road. Continue to the end, turning right by a small green and skirting round St Bartholomew's Church to reach the crossroads at the heart of Meltham again.

7 Through the gate by the Borehole, turn left and cross the large conduit. Immediately over the bridge, turn right across a sluice and drop down a short metal ladder to continue along the conduit's side. Cross Brow Grains Road, rejoining the conduit over a stile and continuing alongside it until you reach the road. At the second farm bridge, look right to see the outline of an Iron Age enclosure on Oldfield Hill.

6 Turn right alongside the fence on top of Deer Hill, following a path past a large unnamed stone and on along the edge. Where the fence bends sharply left, cross a stile and follow the fence steeply down to a gate at the end of Red Lane. Follow the walled path down until it reaches a track, where you turn right to reach the red brick building at Brow Grains Road Borehole.

The remains of two **Iron Age enclosures** are evident above Meltham, one on Royd Edge and the other on Oldfield Hill. Evidence of smelting has been unearthed and the earthen ramparts are particular clear at the latter, which was originally mistaken for a Roman camp.

1 From the crossroads at the centre of Meltham (by the Swan), head out along Holmfirth Road. Pass the post office and fire station, before turning second right up Tinker Lane. Turn left on the bend onto a footpath between houses; after crossing Heather Road, this reaches Calmlands Road. Turn right up past the cemetery and continue straight on along the top of Royd Edge. Reaching a gate and stile, bear right over a second stile and follow the wall up the hill to the right of the barn. Over the wall is the feint outline of an Iron Age enclosure.

2 Continue along the field edge past Orleans Lodge, where the moorland is met, to eventually reach Wessenden Head Road. Turn left for 250m, passing the painted Cock Crowing Stone (of which little is known), then turn right opposite a lay-by. Follow the path diagonally up towards the ridge, crossing the fenceline via a stile (not the nearby gate) and following the obvious line to the summit of West Nab.

Meltham was recorded as Meltha in the Domesday Book, its name thought to be Scandinavian in origin, possibly referring to a bog covered in cloudberry. Alternatively, Joseph Hughes suggested it meant honey hamlet, referring to a practice of laying beehives brought from around the country across the moorland when the heather was in bloom. The Yorkshire tradition of Collop Monday is still celebrated in Meltham, with sweets handed out to local children on the monday before Ash Wednesday. Originally collops were slices of meat (usually bacon) given to children by farmers on the last day on which meat could be cooked before Lent.

the summit of West Nab

137

SHOOTERS NAB ACCESS RESTRICTIONS

paint daubed on a rock near West Nab

The quarried face of Shooters Nab constitutes one of the higher tops in West Yorkshire; at 437m, it should warrant a chapter of its own. However, the presence of the rifle range on Deer Hill Moss and its associated danger area means the opportunity to access it is rare. Even on West Nab at the opposite end of the moor, paint is daubed on rocks like the one illustrated above. Though the entire moor is now CROW Access Land and these warnings no longer carry any weight, the message is received loud and clear.

The range is home to the Lydgate Rifle and Pistol Club, but it is the MOD who licence them, having set the range up in the 1930s. They paid compensation to farmers, but still allowed grazing around the range. The extent of the current access land exclusion zone revolves around the potential 'fall of shot' based on the calibre and velocity of the firearms used on the range, something that is reassessed with each new set of regulations. No-one has ever been harmed by stray shot on the moor, but the club are required to stop shooting if they are aware of anyone within the exclusion zone, even though its stretches over a mile over the top of Shooters Nab. The current boundary is clearly marked by a new fence along its western edge and a series of danger signs to the south and east. Access is permitted to the western end of Shooters Nab (around the overhanging rock of the Rostrum), but not the summit itself.

The matter is complicated by the existence of Public Rights of Way alongside the range and up into the quarries beneath Shooters Nab. While there has been talk of deleting these, they remain on Ordnance Survey maps to lure the unwitting walker up the crag. Though the legal right of access exists here, these routes are probably best avoided when the crackle of gunfire abounds.

The British Mountaineering Council have negotiated a number of weekend days each year when climbing is permitted on the whole crag, along with Friday evenings after 6pm. It would be safe to assume that the moor is fully accessible at these times, but it is recommended to check up-to-date details first with the BMC. All these agreements are fragile and at the behest of the club; access was withdrawn in 2006 when a shooting competition was interrupted by a group of climbers. Very occasional walks on Shooters Nab may also be organised by the Ramblers Association and Peak District National Park, but it is unlikely that individual groups will be able to negotiate access with the club.

one of the danger signs on Shooters Nab

CHAPTER 19 - WHITE HILL
(aka High Brown Knoll)

Height: 446m

Grid Ref: SE007313

Map Sheet: OL21 (South Pennines)

Access Points: No dogs on Oxenhope Moor during nesting bird season (1st March to 31st July).

Public Transport: Bus 593 runs from Hebden Bridge to Old Town. Useful bus services include Halifax to Midgley (573, 574, 575), Halifax to Old Town via Hebden Bridge (593), Hebden Bridge to Old Town (MetroConnect A, B), and Hebden Bridge/Keighley to Oxenhope (500).

White Hill is the true summit of the expanse of moor that stretches north from the Calder Valley above Hebden Bridge, Mytholmroyd and Luddendenfoot, all the way over to Oxenhope and Warley Moor Reservoir. There are more natural hilltops at High Brown Knoll, Sheep Stones Edge and Crow Hill, but the broad grassy ridge above the A6033 outflanks them all. I have split the moor into three sections north to south. Both Midgley Moor and Wadsworth Moor are well trodden with good networks of tracks, whereas most of Oxenhope Moor is infinitely wilder and devoid of well-used paths. Each yields its own delights, whether the ancient burial mounds or imposing boundary stones of Midgley Moor, or the weathered rock caps and peat groughs of Oxenhope Moor.

Sheep on the top of White Hill

The high moor north of High Brown Knoll and White Hill is a particularly bleak plateau of rough grass and peat bog. It is an extension of White Hill's demeanour and the only area from which one looks to the moor's summit as a natural high point. Even then, the Winny Stone steals the limelight on the tramp south from Cock Hill - it is a natural rampart, crested by beautifully weathered hunks of gritstone, and is part of the same lump of land as White Hill and barely a foot or two lower. To add to the sense of isolation, not a single path crosses the moor usefully. The solitary fenceline between Warley Moor Reservoir and the laboratories on Cock Hill, and a few rock outcrops are really the only landmarks to go by. Yet it is an area worth exploring; feint sheeptracks appear and disappear readily, especially around the moor's fringes, where paths along the catchwater drains also offer solace from the undulating tussocks of the high moor. It is worth considering just how different this moor may have looked had the Flaight Hill wind farm been built covering most of the high ground north of High Brown Knoll with turbines and tracks.

Oxenhope Moor Laboratories have been steadily dismantled since the University of Bradford abandoned them to the elements. The curious collection of buildings and satellite dishes there were built as RAF Oxenhope Moor, serving as a navigational aid station during World War II.

the Winny Stone

The **Winny Stone** is one of the most striking features across the whole of White Hill, especially as it sits amid the most barren stretch of the moor. It was previously known as the **Hoyning Stone**, which is referred to as 'ancient' in 1594. It has been optimistically suggested Winny is a mispronunciation of Honing, yet *whin* is gorse and the Whinny Moor in Yorkshire is traditionally the thorn-covered land across which the soul must travel after death. Whinstone is also a quarrying term describing a hard rock that makes a particular sound when struck with a hammer, particularly chert which is found in erratics on these moors and used for some of the earliest flints. The rock itself is invisible from most angles; only from Cock Hill or Nab Hill is this cap of rock an obvious landmark in a sea of tufty grass and bog.

The A6033 over **Cock Hill** was built as the Hebden Bridge to Lees Turnpike in 1814, replacing the older route over Stairs. It was a notoriously dangerous route in bad weather – in 1831, Ben Foster, a yarn manufacturer from Denholme, lost his way on Cock Hill in a blizzard and stumbled across the moor to his frozen death. Subsequently 185 whitewashed stone stoops (with black tops that were visible in snow) lined the roadside, some of which (minus paint) can still be seen across the top today.

*The path that skirts the edge of the moor above the A6033 is feint but invaluable. It becomes steadily more difficult to follow as you leave **Clattering Edge**, but do not despair if you lose it – be assured that it does soldier on to the top of Cock Hill. At a small basin of short grass below **Leaning Grooves Edge**, you should head down towards a stile to pick up the ongoing path. It also links up with the track up from the wonderfully-named **Bedlam**.*

Map labels

- gate
- Sun Hill Clough
- Stubde
- CONTINUATION ON WITHINS HEIGHT – P155
- dam
- Thornton Moor Conduit
- CONTINUATION ON WITHINS (Southern Section) – HEIGHT
- Sun Hill
- dike
- stones
- Yeoman's Stoop x (boundary stone)
- Yeoman Hill
- Gold Dike
- Red Dike Clough
- A small standing stone, wedged upright between two others sits just below a slight crest on Roms Hill.
- Cock Hill Stoop (boundary stone)
- line of sto
- Oxenhope Moor Laboratories
- gate, stile
- sti
- to Stairs Lane
- bridge
- Roms Hill
- Rom's Greave (ruin)
- gate
- ix standing stone
- bog
- stile
- Granny Hill
- post
- Roms Clough
- stile
- ditch
- post
- Leaning Grooves Edge
- pool
- wet
- Bedlam Knoll
- old gate
- bog
- A6033
- barn
- Cross Ends Lane
- gate
- gate
- Bedlam
- gates
- Bedlam Hill
- bog
- Winny Stone (or Hoyning Stone)
- to Pecket Well (1½ miles)
- stile
- stile
- stile
- boulder
- Clattering Edge
- Bare Clough
- ditch
- **White Hill** (446m)
- unmarked summit
- to Hebden Bridge (2½ miles)

CONTINUATION ON WHITE

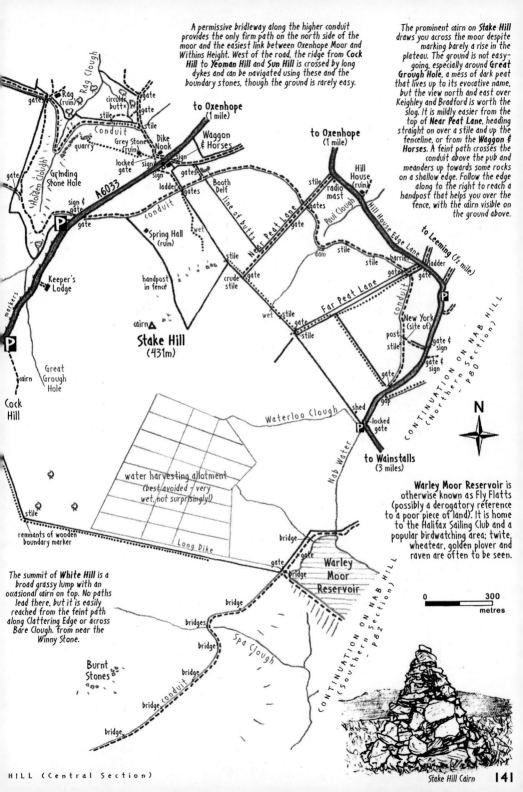

A permissive bridleway along the higher conduit provides the only firm path on the north side of the moor and the easiest link between Oxenhope Moor and Withins Height. West of the road, the ridge from **Cock Hill** to **Yeoman Hill** and **Sun Hill** is crossed by long dykes and can be navigated using these and the boundary stones, though the ground is rarely easy.

The prominent cairn on **Stake Hill** draws you across the moor despite marking barely a rise in the plateau. The ground is not easy-going, especially around **Great Grough Hole**, a mess of dark peat that lives up to its evocative name, but the view north and east over Keighley and Bradford is worth the slog. It is mildly easier from the top of **Near Peat Lane**, heading straight on over a stile and up the fenceline, or from the **Waggon & Horses**. A feint path crosses the conduit above the pub and meanders up towards some rocks on a shallow edge. Follow the edge along to the right to reach a handpost that helps you over the fence, with the cairn visible on the ground above.

Rag Clough

Rag (ruin)

gates

circular butt

gate

gate

stile

to Oxenhope (1 mile)

Dike Nook

Waggon & Horses

Conduit

Grey Stones (ruin)

quarry

locked gate

sign

sign

sign

sign

gates

ladders

gates

Booth Delf

to Oxenhope (1 mile)

Hill House (ruin)

stile

radio mast

gates

Paul Clough

gate

Hill House Edge Lane

to Leeming (½ mile)

Holden Clough

gate

A6033

Grinding Stone Hole

sign & gate

gate

P

Spring Hall (ruin)

wet

line of butts

Near Peat Lane

stile

stile

gate

dam

stile

stile

barrier

gate

ladder

gate

P

Keeper's Lodge

handpost in fence

crude stile

gate

wet

stile

Far Peat Lane

conduit

markers

P

Great Grough Hole

cairn

Stake Hill (431m)

wet

stile

gate

stile

stile

gate

New York (site of)

post stile

gate & sign

gate & sign

CONTINUATION ON NAB HILL (Northern Section) p80

Cock Hill

cairn

gate

Waterloo Clough

shed

locked gate

gap

P

N

to Wainstalls (3 miles)

Nab Water

Warley Moor Reservoir is otherwise known as Fly Flatts (possibly a derogatory reference to a poor piece of land). It is home to the Halifax Sailing Club and a popular birdwatching area; twite, wheatear, golden plover and raven are often to be seen.

water harvesting allotment (best avoided - very wet, not surprisingly!)

stile

remnants of wooden boundary marker

Long Dike

bridge

gate

gate

bridge

Warley Moor Reservoir

The summit of **White Hill** is a broad grassy lump with an occasional cairn on top. No paths lead there, but it is easily reached from the feint path along Clattering Edge or across Bare Clough, from near the Winny Stone.

bridge

bridges

bridge

Spa Clough

CONTINUATION ON NAB HILL (Southern Section) p82

Burnt Stones

bridge

bridge

conduit

bridge

0   300
metres

Stake Hill Cairn

WHITE HILL MAP - Central Section (Wadsworth Moor)

Wadsworth Moor is the busy midrift between the barren grassy heights of Oxenhope Moor and the lower heather-clad Midgley Moor; the change in vegetation is pronounced, occurring between the knolls of Tom Tittiman Hill and Low Brown Knoll and the climb up to High Brown Knoll. The shallow edge of High Brown Knoll is the dominant feature of the moor, its trigpoint standing at a junction of major routes and surrounded by flat, weathered rocks. Higher, more forbidding ground rises to the north of Limers Gate, where the summit of White Hill stands lonely and unrecognised. This moor is easily accessible from Hebden Bridge and fringed on the west by the settlements of Pecket Well, Old Town and Chiserley, so it has plenty of well-worn routes and a plethora of tiny tracks. Dimmin Dale, the narrowest point of the moor, is a particularly disorientating maze, especially if trying to make sense of the rights of way on the OS map. Unfortunately the beautiful head of Luddenden Dean (below the Dean Head Reservoirs) can only be admired from afar as it is part of the Castle Carr Estate (see Page 150 for more information) and excluded from any access land. Signs at the boundary make this clear, but be aware of estate workers across the rest of the moor asserting that there is no access off the rights of way.

CONTINUATION ON NAB HILL (Southern Section) - p 82

CONTINUATION ON WHITE HILL (Northern Section)

The easiest way up *White Hill* is from the lay-by opposite the bus turning circle. Follow a feint track straight up onto *Naze Hill* and pick up a path heading left along the edge. Reaching some stones by the first stream, branch right up to the slight depression and head straight on to the summit where this bends right.

There is no easy route to *White Hill*, but the highest point of the moor offers a taste of the bleak spaces further north. From the waymark post on *Limers Gate*, follow the line of an old track across the rough ground to the top of *Bare Clough*, from where you can branch off north-west to the summit. Alternatively follow another old track from the depression before Flaight Hill towards *White Hill Rocks*.

A useful (though wet in places) path drops down from the conduit to pick up an older track above *Upper Dean Head Reservoir*.

The Greenwood Stone, Lad of Law and Wadsworth Lowe were all boundary stones between the manors of Wadsworth and Midgley. It has been suggested Lad of Law (originally recorded as a boundary lad or

Limers Gate was a packhorse route between Luddenden and the limestone hushings of Boulsworth Hill. Trains of 20-30 ponies, led by a packman (or jagger), carried lime that was needed to neutralise the acidic Pennine soils. Packhorse routes kept to the higher ground, initially to avoid the marshes of the valley bottoms and later to avoid any potential levies.

Upper Dean Head Reservoir

Lower Dean Head Reservoir

Ferny Brink

delf

Castle Carr Estate

bridge

bridge

bridge

bridge

conduit

mud

Horse Pasture Clough

bridge

bridge

wet

Burnt Stones

Bare Clough

bridge

standing stone

Wadsworth Lowe (boundary stone)

conduit

bridge

post, post

post

post

post

post

post

post

line of wooden butts

Cousins Spring

High Brown Knoll (443m)
trig

Black Gate

wet

Summer Rake Edge

White Hill Rocks

depression

(boggy)

unmarked summit

White Hill (446m)

wet

Limers Gate

clay gate

cairn

tiny cairn

Flaight Hill

Naze Hill

Naze End

to Oxenhope (3 miles)

Robin Delf

P

gate

bus turning circle

sign & gate

sign & gate

gate

gate

gate

line of ditch

Pecket Well Clough

Aberdeen Flat

Spinks Hill

stile

stile

stile

gate

wet

dam

gate

locked gate

South

A6033

Old Road

P

Gibraltar Farm

sign & gate

gate

Upper Small Shaw

Middle Small Shaw

pole

Spinks Hill Farm

to Lumb Falls

Lumb Falls

to Hebden Bridge (2 miles)

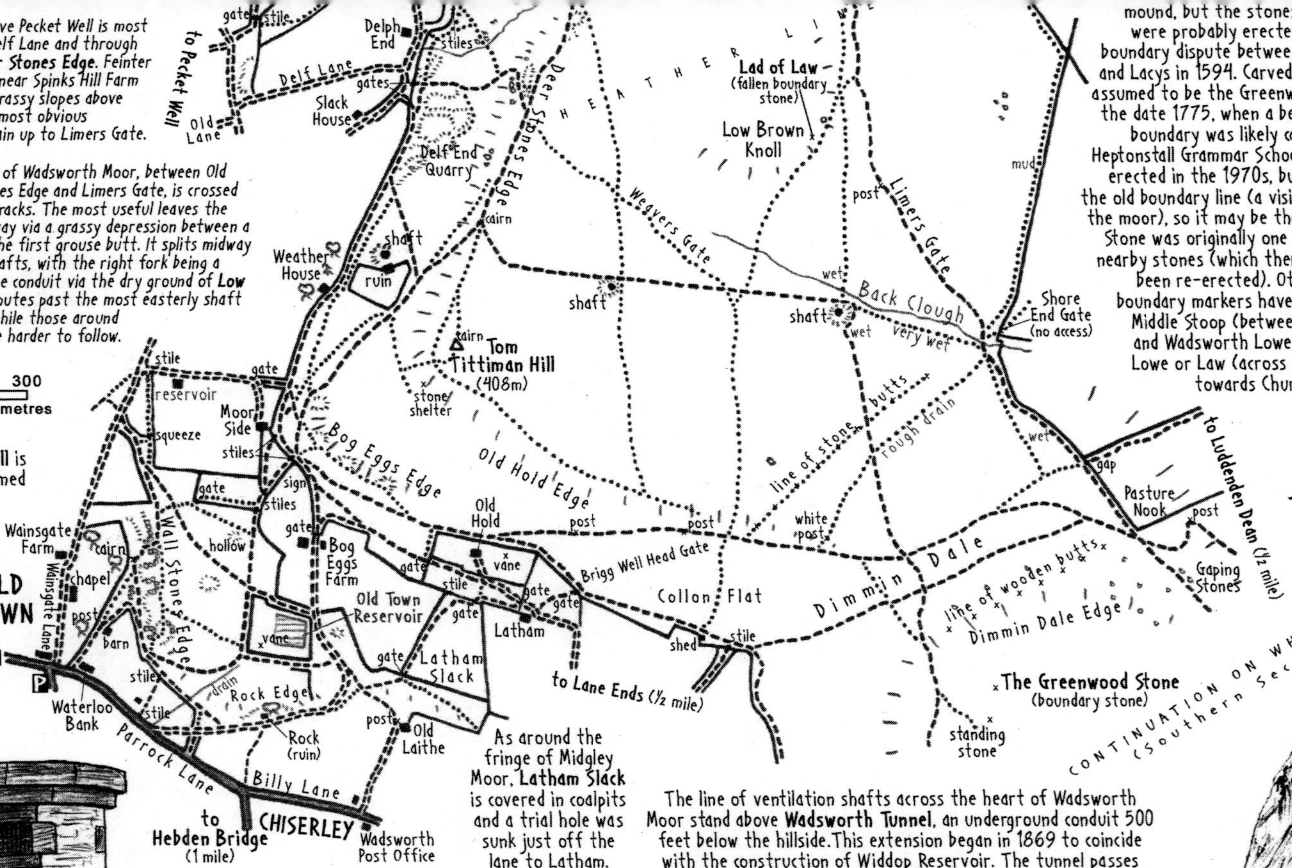

mound, but the stones themselves were probably erected to settle a boundary dispute between the Saviles and Lacys in 1594. Carved into what is assumed to be the Greenwood Stone is the date 1775, when a beating of the boundary was likely carried out by Heptonstall Grammar School. It was re-erected in the 1970s, but stands off the old boundary line (a visible groove in the moor), so it may be the Greenwood Stone was originally one of the other nearby stones (which themselves have been re-erected). Other recorded boundary markers have disappeared: Middle Stoop (between Lad of Law and Wadsworth Lowe) and Savile's Lowe or Law (across Midgley Moor towards Churn Milk Joan).

the Greenwood Stone

The line of ventilation shafts across the heart of Wadsworth Moor stand above **Wadsworth Tunnel**, an underground conduit 500 feet below the hillside. This extension began in 1869 to coincide with the construction of Widdop Reservoir. The tunnel passes from Well Holes (near the Packhorse Inn) to Alcomden Water and from there round Shackleton along the line of the tramway. It was originally planned to cross Crimsworth Dean by a large aqueduct, but it was never built and the route actually climbs two hills on its way to the treatment works in Halifax. Momentum carries the water uphill as air is pushed out of these vents - if you put your ear to the grill you can hear the water far below.

As around the fringe of Midgley Moor, **Latham Slack** is covered in coalpits and a trial hole was sunk just off the lane to Latham.

Bog Eggs Edge.
If you look closely at the ground around **Bog Eggs Edge**, moss gathers in a series of small lumps where the grass is short. I like to think of these as bog eggs, though John Billingsley has suggested it most likely referred to the bog edge, or even witches and demons that sucked children's blood because of its closeness to boggart and hegges.

The arc of moor above Pecket Well is most easily accessed via *Delf Lane* and through the delfs below *Deer Stones Edge*. Fainter tracks lead up from near Spinks Hill Farm and cross the bare grassy slopes above *South Shields*, the most obvious following a rough drain up the moor.

The heathery heart of Wadsworth Moor, between *Old Hold Edge*, *Deer Stones Edge* and *Limers Gate*, is crossed by numerous small tracks. The most useful leaves the *Dimmin Dale* bridleway via a grassy depression between a waymark post and the first grouse butt. It splits midway between the two shafts, with the right fork being a good route up to the conduit via the dry ground of *Low Brown Knoll*. The routes past the most easterly shaft are invariable wet, while those around the higher shaft are harder to follow.

Tom Tittiman Hill is thought to be named after an owner of the quarries on its slopes.

ventilation shaft near Tom Tittiman Hill

Map labels:

to Luddenden Dean (½ mile) · Gaping Stones · Pasture Nook · post · gap · Shore End Gate (no access) · mud · Limers Gate · Back Clough · wet · very wet · shaft · line of wooden butts · Dimmin Dale Edge · Dimmin Dale · **The Greenwood Stone** (boundary stone) · standing stone · line of stone butts · trough drain · white post · **Lad of Law** (fallen boundary stone) · Low Brown Knoll · HEATHER · Weavers Gate · shaft · Collon Flat · stile · Brigg Well Head Gate · shed · to Lane Ends (½ mile) · Deer Stones Edge · cairn · Delf End Quarry · cairn **Tom Tittiman Hill** (408m) · Old Hold Edge · vane · Old Hold · gate · Latham · stile · Latham Slack · Old Loathe · post · Delph End · stiles · Slack House · Delf Lane · Old Lane · to Pecket Well · Weather House · ruin · shaft · stone shelter · Bog Eggs Edge · Old Town Reservoir · Bog Eggs Farm · Rock Edge · Rock (ruin) · Billy Lane · to CHISERLEY · Wadsworth Post Office · Moor Side · sign · stiles · gate · vane · Parrock Lane · to Hebden Bridge (1 mile) · reservoir · squeeze · stile · hollow · Wall Stones Edge · barn · Wainsgate Farm · chapel · Waterloo Bank · Wainsgate Lane · OLD TOWN · to Pecket Well (½ mile)

CONTINUATION (SOUTHERN SECTION) WHITE HILL

0 300 metres

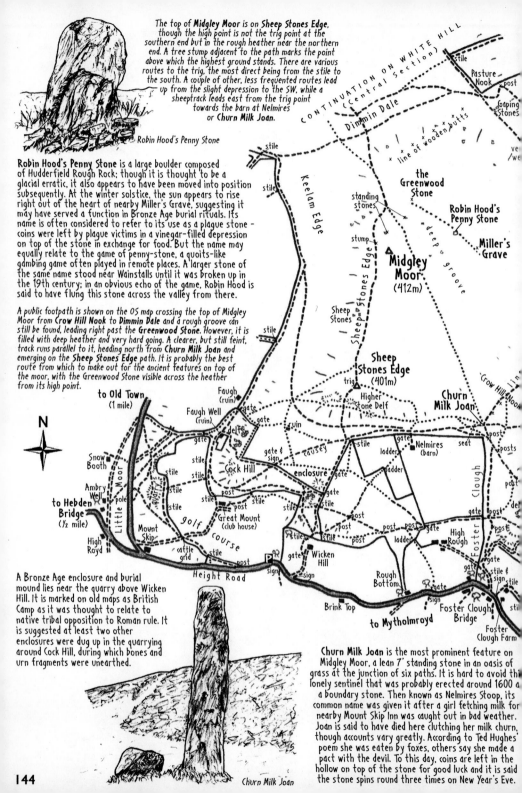

The top of **Midgley Moor** is on **Sheep Stones Edge**, though the high point is not the trig point at the southern end but in the rough heather near the northern end. A tree stump adjacent to the path marks the point above which the highest ground stands. There are various routes to the trig, the most direct being from the stile to the south. A couple of other, less frequented routes lead up from the slight depression to the SW, while a sheeptrack leads east from the trig point towards the barn at Nelmires or **Churn Milk Joan.**

Robin Hood's Penny Stone

Robin Hood's Penny Stone is a large boulder composed of Hudderfield Rough Rock; though it is thought to be a glacial erratic, it also appears to have been moved into position subsequently. At the winter solstice, the sun appears to rise right out of the heart of nearby Miller's Grave, suggesting it may have served a function in Bronze Age burial rituals. Its name is often considered to refer to its use as a plague stone - coins were left by plague victims in a vinegar-filled depression on top of the stone in exchange for food. But the name may equally relate to the game of penny-stone, a quoits-like gambing game often played in remote places. A larger stone of the same name stood near Wainstalls until it was broken up in the 19th century; in an obvious echo of this, Robin Hood is said to have flung this stone across the valley from there.

A public footpath is shown on the OS map crossing the top of Midgley Moor from **Crow Hill Nook** to **Dimmin Dale** and a rough groove can still be found, leading right past the **Greenwood Stone**. However, it is filled with deep heather and very hard going. A clearer, but still feint, track runs parallel to it, heading north from **Churn Milk Joan** and emerging on the **Sheep Stones Edge** path. It is probably the best route from which to make out for the ancient features on top of the moor, with the Greenwood Stone visible across the heather from its high point.

A Bronze Age enclosure and burial mound lies near the quarry above Wicken Hill. It is marked on old maps as British Camp as it was thought to relate to native tribal opposition to Roman rule. It is suggested at least two other enclosures were dug up in the quarrying around Cock Hill, during which bones and urn fragments were unearthed.

Churn Milk Joan is the most prominent feature on Midgley Moor, a lean 7' standing stone in an oasis of grass at the junction of six paths. It is hard to avoid thi lonely sentinel that was probably erected around 1600 a a boundary stone. Then known as Nelmires Stoop, its common name was given it after a girl fetching milk for nearby Mount Skip Inn was caught out in bad weather. Joan is said to have died here clutching her milk churn, though accounts vary greatly. According to Ted Hughes' poem she was eaten by foxes, others say she made a pact with the devil. To this day, coins are left in the hollow on top of the stone for good luck and it is said the stone spins round three times on New Year's Eve.

Churn Milk Joan

WHITE HILL MAP - Southern Section (Midgley Moor)

Midgley Moor is one of the most fascinating areas of moorland in West Yorkshire, surrounded on all sides by the hillside villages of Chiserley, Midgley and Booth as well as the larger valley towns. As a result it bears the scars of human impact, from numerous prehistoric sites to large areas of disused quarries and lines of shooting butts. It remains heavily used today and the southern fringe in particular has a very dense network of paths, making it a great area to explore. Amid the moor's heather tracts are two natural high points, the small knoll of Crow Hill and the trigpoint on Sheep Stones Edge. Both are easily reached and have good views over the Calder Valley. At the meeting of the main paths across the moor stands Churn Milk Joan, a tall boundary stone steeped in local folklore. Further north, other boundary markers like the Greenwood Stone and Robin Hood's Penny Stone have historical significance and, along with the burial mound at Miller's Grave and numerous other cairns and enclosures lost in the heather, make Midgley Moor an important archaeological site.

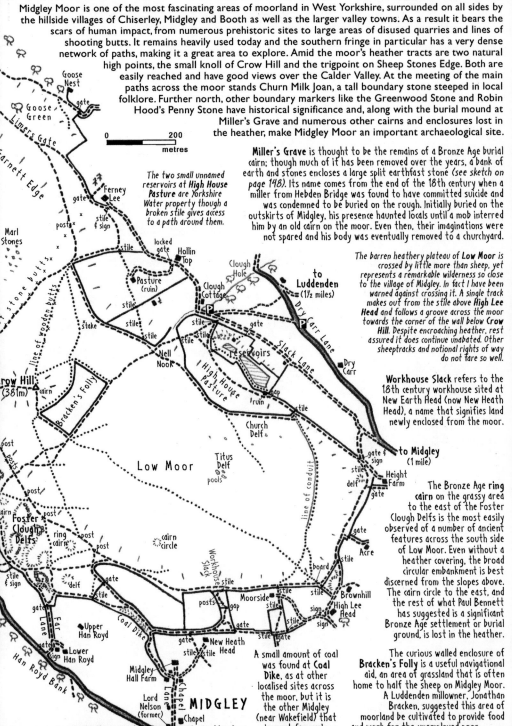

The two small unnamed reservoirs at **High House Pasture** are Yorkshire Water property though a broken stile gives access to a path around them.

Miller's Grave is thought to be the remains of a Bronze Age burial cairn; though much of it has been removed over the years, a bank of earth and stones encloses a large split earthfast stone (see sketch on page 148). Its name comes from the end of the 18th century when a miller from Hebden Bridge was found to have committed suicide and was condemned to be buried on the rough. Initially buried on the outskirts of Midgley, his presence haunted locals until a mob interred him by an old cairn on the moor. Even then, their imaginations were not spared and his body was eventually removed to a churchyard.

The barren heathery plateau of **Low Moor** is crossed by little more than sheep, yet represents a remarkable wilderness so close to the village of Midgley. In fact I have been warned against crossing it. A single track makes out from the stile above **High Lee Head** and follows a groove across the moor towards the corner of the wall below **Crow Hill**. Despite encroaching heather, rest assured it does continue unabated. Other sheeptracks and notional rights of way do not fare so well.

Workhouse Slack refers to the 18th century workhouse sited at New Earth Head (now New Heath Head), a name that signifies land newly enclosed from the moor.

The Bronze Age **ring cairn** on the grassy area to the east of the Foster Clough Delfs is the most easily observed of a number of ancient features across the south side of Low Moor. Even without a heather covering, the broad circular embankment is best discerned from the slopes above. The cairn circle to the east, and the rest of what Paul Bennett has suggested is a significant Bronze Age settlement or burial ground, is lost in the heather.

The curious walled enclosure of **Bracken's Folly** is a useful navigational aid, an area of grassland that is often home to half the sheep on Midgley Moor. A Luddenden millowner, Jonathan Bracken, suggested this area of moorland be cultivated to provide food and work for the unemployed poor, but its failure seems inevitable.

A small amount of coal was found at **Coal Dike**, as at other localised sites across the moor, but it is the other Midgley (near Wakefield) that is most famously linked to coal.

145

ROUTE 23: HIGH BROWN KNOLL, WHITE HILL & CRIMSWORTH DEAN FROM HEBDEN BRIDGE

Distance: 7 miles (11 km)

Ascent: 420m

Difficulty: Moderate

Parking: Pay & display car parks in Hebden Bridge town centre, or National Trust car park at Hardcastle Crags.

Public Transport: Hebden Bridge is on the main Caldervale train & bus routes.

Character: High Brown Knoll is Hebden Bridge's natural vantage point and this route makes straight for its trig point via Nutclough Woods. It returns via Lumb Hole waterfall and the beautiful valley of Crimsworth Dean. The true summit of White Hill is only a short roam from Limers Gate, though this additional loop is largely untrodden; otherwise the paths are all obvious and generally easy-going.

Lumb Bridge is an 18th century packhorse bridge on the Limers Gate route that is followed right over High Brown Knoll; in fact it used to be known as Horse Bridge and the valley Horse-bridge Clough. The word *lumb* refers to a small wooded section of a clough. On a misty night, Lumb Bridge is supposedly haunted by a White Lady, the ghost of a woman who committed suicide by jumping from the bridge into the falls. Ignoring the fact that it is impossible to reach the falls from the bridge, you only have to watch the kids jumping into the pool from the rocks high above **Lumb Hole** to know that this is hardly a way to certain death.

5 At Naze End, the moor drops steeply down to the main road. Follow the road left for 100m before taking a bridleway right, signed towards Haworth Old Road. This drops down to another gate and a narrow path that emerges on Old Road. Follow the road right past Gibraltar Farm to another bridleway leading down to the left. The cobbles of Lumb Lane emerge by the waterfall at Lumb Hole, a perfect opportunity for a dip on a hot day.

4 Head NNW along the high ground from the trig point on High Brown Knoll. To stay on the beaten track, follow the old packhorse route of Limers Gate all the way to Naze End. To reach the true summit of White Hill, bear right on a feint path 50m before an obvious waymark post. This becomes clearer, following the line of Black Gate towards the outcrop of the Winny Stone. After crossing a wet area, turn left off the path and climb through short grass onto the unmarked high ground of White Hill. From the top, aim due east (towards the Gorple Reservoirs) to reach the rock-strewn edge of Naze Hill. Pick up another feint path above the edge to rejoin the main route at Naze End.

Flaight Hill was the planned site for a 44 turbine wind farm in 1993 which would have covered most of Oxenhope Moor. It was eventually dropped on ecological grounds after significant local opposition. *Flaight* (or *flait*) is a dialect word for a thin piece of peat for burning – it was cut with a flait-spade, which was also used for removing the surface turf

6 Cross Lumb Bridge and follow the track round. Where it starts to climb steeply up a walled lane, follow a waymarker left to pick up a path through the bracken. This stays above Crimsworth Dean to reach a high stone stile behind Outwood. Skirt to the right of the building and then head straight across the track leading away from it. Before the gate, a path leads down to a stile at the edge of Abel Cote Wood and continues through the wood to Wheat Ing Bridge.

7 Cross Wheat Ing Bridge and turn right through a gate above the house. Follow the clear path across three fields and into Purprise Wood. Fork right at the first waymark post and follow the splodges of yellow paint on the trees, staying above the mill ponds and drains. Follow further posts through Middle Dean Wood to emerge at a gate in the corner of a field. Descend to join the packhorse route of Jockey Gate, which winds down past Lane End to the road and public toilets at Midgehole.

Hirst Bridge, Nutclough

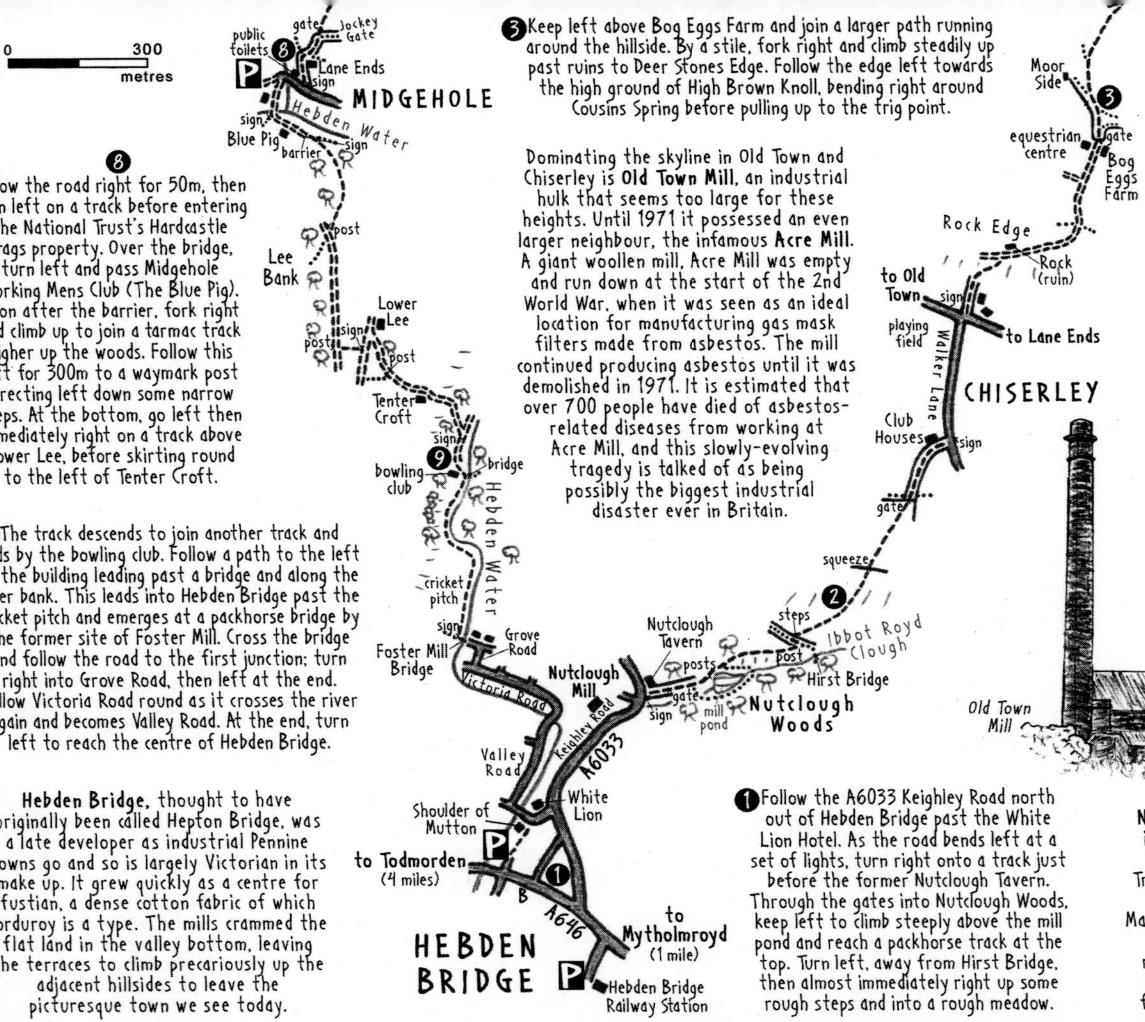

Nutclough Woods is named after the hazel nut as the woods were used for traditional hazel coppicing until the industrial revolution. It was then an ancient oak woodland, but the planting of fast-growing beech and sycamore to power the mills in Hebden Bridge led to a decline in biodiversity and left the dingy, litter-strewn hole that remained until recently. Since 2003, the area has been managed as a Local Nature Reserve by a volunteer organisation. Friends of Nutclough Woods, and has quickly become a pleasant sanctuary close to the town.

2 Climb steeply across fields to join a walled track by an old gate. This leads to the road up through the village of Chiserley. At the T-junction at the top, go straight across following a walled path up towards Rock Edge. This bends right to join a larger track, which curves around the hill and leads up to Bog Eggs Farm and a gate onto the edge of the moor.

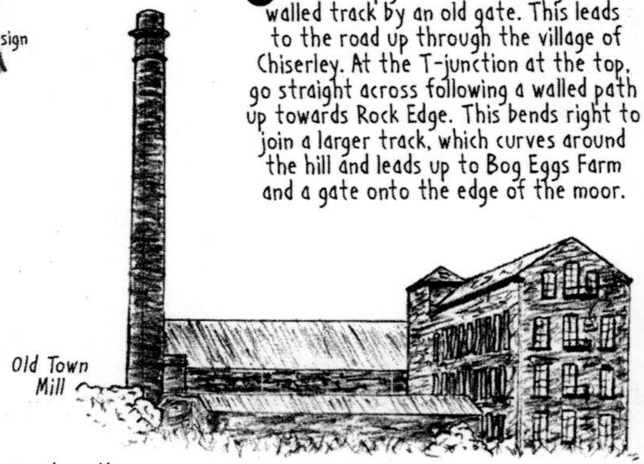

Nutclough Mill is the largest remaining mill in Hebden Bridge, though its only remaining due to its restoration by the Pennine Heritage Trust. Built in the late 18th century, it was home to the Nutclough Fustian Manufacturing Society, a notable workers co-operative with as many as 356 workers receiving a share of the profits. One of its members, Robert Halstead, went on to co-found the Workers Educational Association.

3 Keep left above Bog Eggs Farm and join a larger path running around the hillside. By a stile, fork right and climb steadily up past ruins to Deer Stones Edge. Follow the edge left towards the high ground of High Brown Knoll, bending right around Cousins Spring before pulling up to the trig point.

Dominating the skyline in Old Town and Chiserley is Old Town Mill, an industrial hulk that seems too large for these heights. Until 1971 it possessed an even larger neighbour, the infamous Acre Mill. A giant woollen mill, Acre Mill was empty and run down at the start of the 2nd World War, when it was seen as an ideal location for manufacturing gas mask filters made from asbestos. The mill continued producing asbestos until it was demolished in 1971. It is estimated that over 700 people have died of asbestos-related diseases from working at Acre Mill, and this slowly-evolving tragedy is talked of as being possibly the biggest industrial disaster ever in Britain.

1 Follow the A6033 Keighley Road north out of Hebden Bridge past the White Lion Hotel. As the road bends left at a set of lights, turn right onto a track just before the former Nutclough Tavern. Through the gates into Nutclough Woods, keep left to climb steeply above the mill pond and reach a packhorse track at the top. Turn left, away from Hirst Bridge, then almost immediately right up some rough steps and into a rough meadow.

9 The track descends to join another track and ends by the bowling club. Follow a path to the left of the building leading past a bridge and along the river bank. This leads into Hebden Bridge past the cricket pitch and emerges at a packhorse bridge by the former site of Foster Mill. Cross the bridge and follow the road to the first junction; turn right into Grove Road, then left at the end. Follow Victoria Road round as it crosses the river again and becomes Valley Road. At the end, turn left to reach the centre of Hebden Bridge.

8 Follow the road right for 50m, then turn left on a track before entering the National Trust's Hardcastle Crags property. Over the bridge, turn left and pass Midgehole Working Mens Club (The Blue Pig). Soon after the barrier, fork right and climb up to join a tarmac track higher up the woods. Follow this left for 300m to a waymark post directing left down some narrow steps. At the bottom, go left then immediately right on a track above Lower Lee, before skirting round to the left of Tenter Croft.

Hebden Bridge, thought to have originally been called Hepton Bridge, was a late developer as industrial Pennine towns go and so is largely Victorian in its make up. It grew quickly as a centre for fustian, a dense cotton fabric of which corduroy is a type. The mills crammed the flat land in the valley bottom, leaving the terraces to climb precariously up the adjacent hillsides to leave the picturesque town we see today.

Map labels: MIDGEHOLE · CHISERLEY · HEBDEN BRIDGE · Bog Eggs Farm · Moor Side · equestrian centre · Rock Edge · Rock (ruin) · to Lane Ends · to Old Town · Walker Lane · playing field · Club Houses · Ibbot Royd Clough · Hirst Bridge · Nutclough Woods · steps · squeeze · Nutclough Tavern · mill pond · posts · sign · Keighley Road · A6033 · Nutclough Mill · White Lion · Valley Road · Victoria Road · Grove Road · Shoulder of Mutton · P · to Todmorden (4 miles) · A646 · B · to Mytholmroyd (1 mile) · Hebden Bridge Railway Station · Foster Mill Bridge · cricket pitch · bowling club · Hebden Water · Tenter Croft · Lower Lee · Lee Bank · Blue Pig · Lane Ends sign · jockey gate · public toilets · Old Town Mill · 300 metres · 0

ROUTE 24: MIDGLEY MOOR FROM MYTHOLMROYD & MIDGLEY

Distance: 6½ miles (10km)

Ascent: 330m

Difficulty: Easy

Parking: Car parks at Mytholmroyd Community Centre (small charge), St Michael's Church and by the White Lion.

Public Transport: Mytholmroyd is on the main Caldervale train & bus routes.

Character: This is a fairly short and straightforward walk such is the proximity of Midgley Moor to Mytholmroyd. Having climbed steeply up the hillside straight out of the town, the route takes in the two natural summits of Sheep Stones Edge and Crow Hill while exploring the various sites of interest scattered across the moor. The walking is largely easy apart from a brief optional diversion to Miller's Grave.

The **Northern Eggar** is the northern form of the Oak Eggar moth. It eats heather and bilberry and is associated with heath and bog, thus it is often seen on Midgley Moor. It has a two-year life cycle and is most likely seen as this large hairy caterpillar during July and August before it pupates in September. The moth itself is large, brown and with a distinctive yellow line and single white spot on each wing.

a Northern Eggar caterpillar

6 Rejoin the main track and descend to Dimmin Dale, a broad saddle between Midgley and Wadsworth Moors. Keep right, turning towards the Luddenden Valley and descending to Pasture Nook. Turn right again here to contour along the hillside below Garnett Edge. Beyond a very wet section, the path forks either side of a reedy ditch – turn right here on a smaller path which soon climbs across the hillside. If you reach a wall corner or the buildings of Ferney Lee, you have gone too far and missed this junction.

7 Reaching another wall corner bear right up through Crow Hill Nook (another shallow saddle), joining a line of butts to reach Churn Milk Joan. Turn sharp left at this famous marker stone (*see Page 145 for more information*) and ascend the gentle knoll of Crow Hill. Turn right at the cairn and follow a feint path down to the corner of broken walls. Continue straight on here; the feint path soon bends left and picks up the line of a grassy groove through the heather. This groove can be followed all the way down to a post on the Calderdale Way, ignoring a couple of larger paths crossing its line.

Miller's Grave

5 If you have the time, it is worth making a diversion from the main route to have a look at the Greenwood Stone and Miller's Grave. The former is a prominent boundary stone visible just off the junction of paths on Keelam Edge – climb the brow to your right to see it. From the Greenwood Stone, the large glacial boulder of Robin Hood's Penny Stone is just visible across the heather with a feint track leading part of the way. The burial cairn of Miller's Grave is then clearly evident shortly beyond (*see Pages 143-5 for more background information*). Tempting as it may be to drop straight down to the onward route below Garnett Edge, the ground is far easier going if you retrace your steps.

4 Follow a path along the fenceline, through a gate and up to a wall corner below Sheep Stones Edge. Continue straight across the Calderdale Way here, bearing slightly left to pick up a clear path to reach the trig point. The path continues straight on along the lovely heather-clad slope to the far end of Keelam Edge.

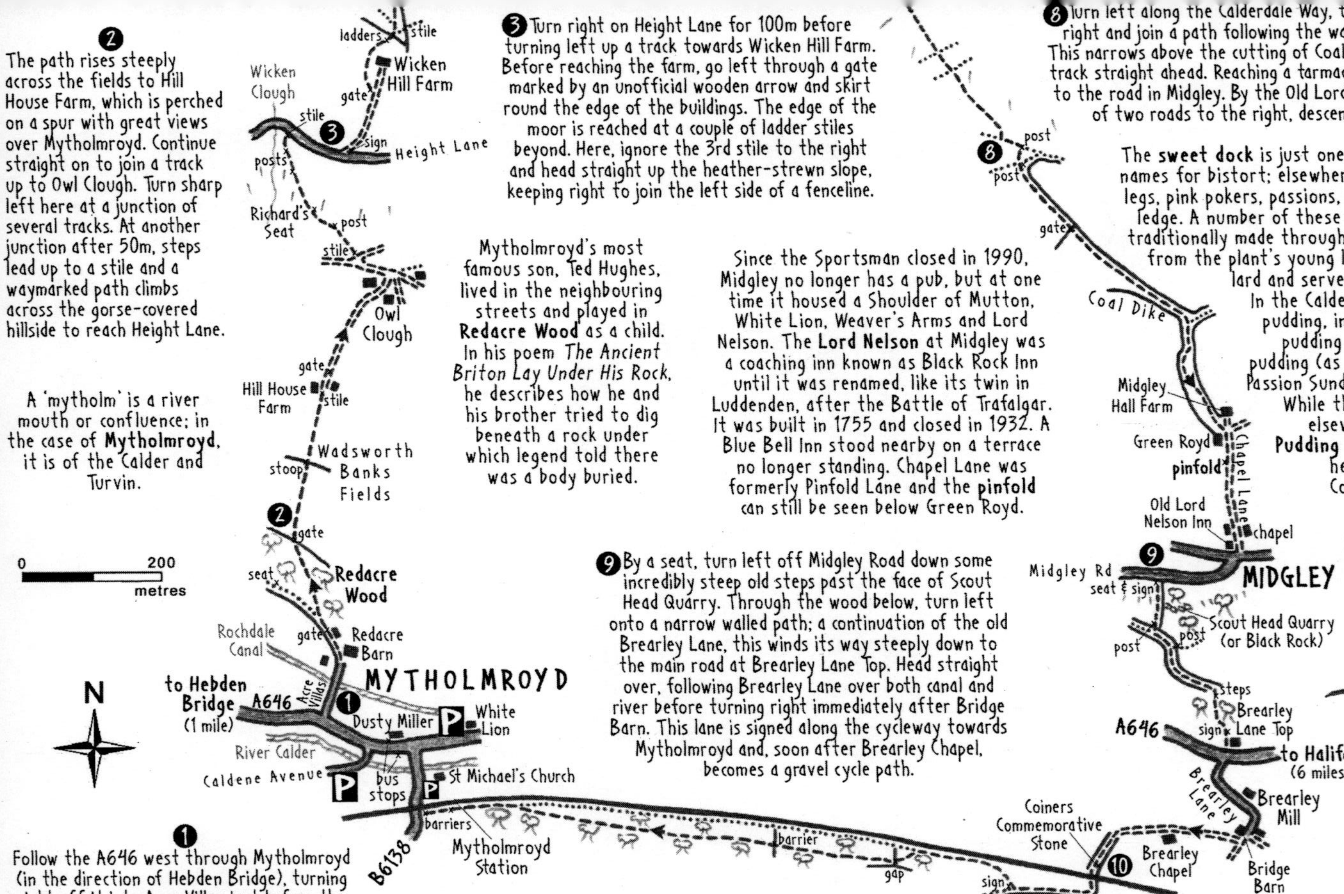

8 Turn left along the Calderdale Way, then fork immediately right and join a path following the wall down off the moor. This narrows above the cutting of Coal Dike, then joins a larger track straight ahead. Reaching a tarmacked lane, follow it down to the road in Midgley. By the Old Lord Nelson, take the lower of two roads to the right, descending Midgley Road.

The **sweet dock** is just one of many (often local) names for bistort; elsewhere it is snakeweed, red legs, pink pokers, passions, dragonwort or easter ledge. A number of these refer to the puddings traditionally made throughout Northern England from the plant's young leaves, usually fried in lard and served with bacon and eggs. In the Calder Valley, this was dock pudding, in Cumbria easter-ledge pudding and elsewhere passion pudding (as the dish was eaten on Passion Sunday, the fifth in Lent). While the tradition has lapsed elsewhere, the **World Dock Pudding Competition** has been held in the Mytholmroyd Community Centre every March since 1971.

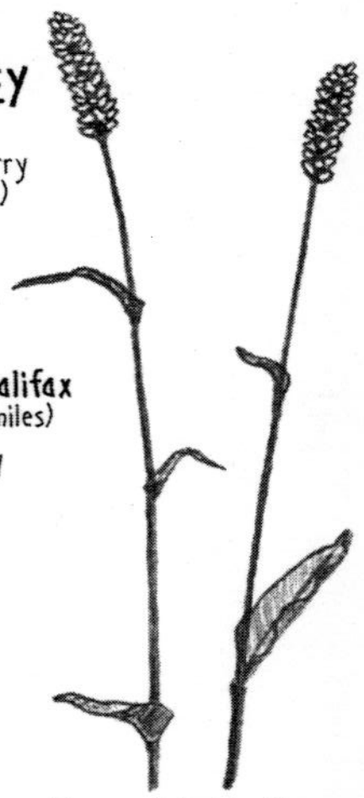

the sweet dock in flower

3 Turn right on Height Lane for 100m before turning left up a track towards Wicken Hill Farm. Before reaching the farm, go left through a gate marked by an unofficial wooden arrow and skirt round the edge of the buildings. The edge of the moor is reached at a couple of ladder stiles beyond. Here, ignore the 3rd stile to the right and head straight up the heather-strewn slope, keeping right to join the left side of a fenceline.

Since the Sportsman closed in 1990, Midgley no longer has a pub, but at one time it housed a Shoulder of Mutton, White Lion, Weaver's Arms and Lord Nelson. The **Lord Nelson** at Midgley was a coaching inn known as Black Rock Inn until it was renamed, like its twin in Luddenden, after the Battle of Trafalgar. It was built in 1755 and closed in 1932. A Blue Bell Inn stood nearby on a terrace no longer standing. Chapel Lane was formerly Pinfold Lane and the pinfold can still be seen below Green Royd.

2 The path rises steeply across the fields to Hill House Farm, which is perched on a spur with great views over Mytholmroyd. Continue straight on to join a track up to Owl Clough. Turn sharp left here at a junction of several tracks. At another junction after 50m, steps lead up to a stile and a waymarked path climbs across the gorse-covered hillside to reach Height Lane.

A *mytholm* is a river mouth or confluence; in the case of Mytholmroyd, it is of the Calder and Turvin.

Mytholmroyd's most famous son, Ted Hughes, lived in the neighbouring streets and played in Redacre Wood as a child. In his poem *The Ancient Briton Lay Under His Rock*, he describes how he and his brother tried to dig beneath a rock under which legend told there was a body buried.

9 By a seat, turn left off Midgley Road down some incredibly steep old steps past the face of Scout Head Quarry. Through the wood below, turn left onto a narrow walled path; a continuation of the old Brearley Lane, this winds its way steeply down to the main road at Brearley Lane Top. Head straight over, following Brearley Lane over both canal and river before turning right immediately after Bridge Barn. This lane is signed along the cycleway towards Mytholmroyd and, soon after Brearley Chapel, becomes a gravel cycle path.

1 Follow the A646 west through Mytholmroyd (in the direction of Hebden Bridge), turning right off it into Acre Villas just before the junior school. Over the canal bridge, follow the track round to the left of Redacre Barn. Through the gate into Redacre Wood, fork right to climb steeply up to a gate out of the top of the woods.

10 Follow the cycle path over the railway and right at another signed junction, but bear left off it upon entering the woods. This path goes through a gap in the concrete barrier before opening out on a pleasant grassy avenue through the trees. This is a far nicer route than sticking to the cycle path throughout, but rejoins it shortly before Mytholmroyd Railway Station. Descend to the B6138 and follow it right to get back to the main road.

Map labels: MIDGLEY · Chapel Lane · Chapel · Green Lane · pinfold · Old Lord Nelson Inn · Midgley Hall Farm · Coal Dike · post · gate · post · Midgley Rd · seat & sign · post · steps · Scout Head Quarry (or Black Rock) · Brearley signs · Brearley Lane Top · Brearley Lane · to Halifax (6 miles) · Brearley Mill · Bridge Barn · Brearley Chapel · Coiners Commemorative Stone · signs · gap · barrier · Mytholmroyd Station · St Michael's Church · barriers · White Lion · Dusty Miller · bus stops · MYTHOLMROYD · Redacre Wood · Redacre Barn · Acre Villas · B6138 · Rochdale Canal · River Calder · Caldene Avenue · A646 · to Hebden Bridge (1 mile) · Wicken Hill Farm · Wicken Clough · ladders · stile · gate · sign · Height Lane · posts · Richard's Seat · post · Owl Clough · stiles · Hill House Farm · stoop · Wadsworth Banks Fields · gate · seat

N

0 — 200 metres

149

THE CASTLE CARR ESTATE

The **Castle Carr Estate** is a sealed private enclave at the head of Luddenden Dean, possibly the most picturesque valley in the county. The name Castle Carr existed before there was ever a castle on the site and possibly refers to an ancient burial mound that may have existed beneath one of the reservoirs. The area was part of the grazing land of the Saltonstall vaccaries (cattle ranches) in the thirteenth century, as evidenced by buildings called Winter Booth Lee and Summer Booth Fold within the estate (*booths* were the farmers' temporary seasonal shelters). There were 21 farms in the area by the time the estate was assembled in the nineteenth century, first by George Bischoff and then by Captain Joseph Priestley Edwards. 'A gentleman of independent means', Edwards previously rented a shooting estate in Scotland and decided to replicate it closer to home. He acquired much of the moorland wastes in the Warley Enclosure Act of 1852 and was subsequently granted the right to hunt, fish and hawk across the moors and reservoirs of Warley, Saltonstall and Oxenhope (which extended right up to the edge of the village).

The castle itself was built from 1859 on the site of an earlier house and took over twelve years to complete, employing as many as a hundred people on the site. Built from local stone, the castle is a mix of Norman and Elizabethan styles, complete with battlements, towers and a courtyard with a grand fountain flanked by talbot hounds in the centre. Inside, it housed a grand hall, banqueting hall, gallery, ante hall, billiard room, and library, and featured paved corridors, giant arches and a sprung oak floor for dancing. In the park, there was a croquet lawn, pheasantry, kennels and plantations, overseen by the Castle Carr Commissioner of the Woods and Forests. Captain Priestley never saw the castle completed as he died in the Abergele rail disaster in 1868, though one of his sons oversaw its completion. Its primary purpose had been as a shooting lodge and retreat, but it was only briefly in use. Through a succession of owners, it fell into ruin and was largely dismantled due to dry rot and its component parts sold off in 1962. The fountain ended up in Trevelyan Square in Leeds and the remains that are visible from Midgley Moor and Warley Moor are part of the crumbling gatehouse and adjacent heaps of embellished stone.

When land within the estate was acquired by Halifax Corporation to build the Dean Head and Castle Carr Reservoirs in the 1860s, a fountain and ornamental water garden were created by way of compensating the owners. The gravity-powered fountain was over 100ft high and renowned for being higher than those in Versailles. It functions to this day and occasionally the estate is opened to the public for a display. Otherwise access is vigorously opposed and has been since the two roads up the valley were closed in 1868. Following legal disputes in the 1890s, a London judge ruled that the current right of way across Warley Moor to Slade was sufficient compensation for the routes lost through the estate. And that was that. Until 2000, you couldn't get anywhere near the estate; now you can peer in from the moorsides and bemoan the lack of access to this exclusive enclave slowly rotting in its damp glade.

the ruined gatehouse at Castle Carr today

CHAPTER 20 - WITHINS HEIGHT
(aka Stanbury Moor)

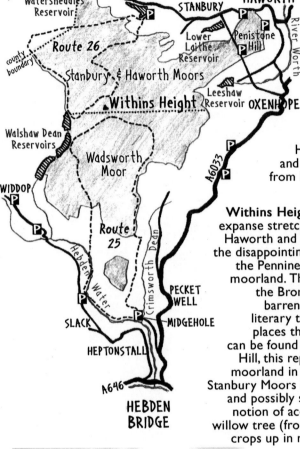

Height: 457m

Grid Ref: SD978350

Map Sheet: OL21 (South Pennines)

Access: No dogs at any time on Wadsworth Moor (except Walshaw Dean Reservoirs & Public Rights of Way). Dogs on lead on Stanbury Moor in shooting season (1st August to 10th December).

Public Transport: Bus 906 runs from Midgehole to Widdop via Hebden Bridge on summer weekends and Bank Holidays. Buses 500 & 663 run from Keighley to Haworth and Oxenhope, and 664 to Haworth and Stanbury.

Withins Height is the high point of the moorland expanse stretching north from Hardcastle Crags to Haworth and Stanbury. Though the summit sits on the disappointing tussocky top of Round Hill just off the Pennine Way, it is a fascinating and evocative moorland. The northern section is well known as the Brontë Moors, sheltering in the lee of its barren heights various notable sites for the literary tourist. Yet it is away from these busy places that the real character of these moors can be found - indeed, combined with Boulsworth Hill, this represents the largest expanse of open moorland in the county. Much of Wadsworth and Stanbury Moors is still dominated by grouse shooting and possibly struggling to come to terms with the notion of access land. A withen (or within) was a willow tree (from the Anglo-Saxon word *withig*) and crops up in numerous places across these moors.

Withins Height seen above the Walsaw Dean Reservoirs from Alcomden

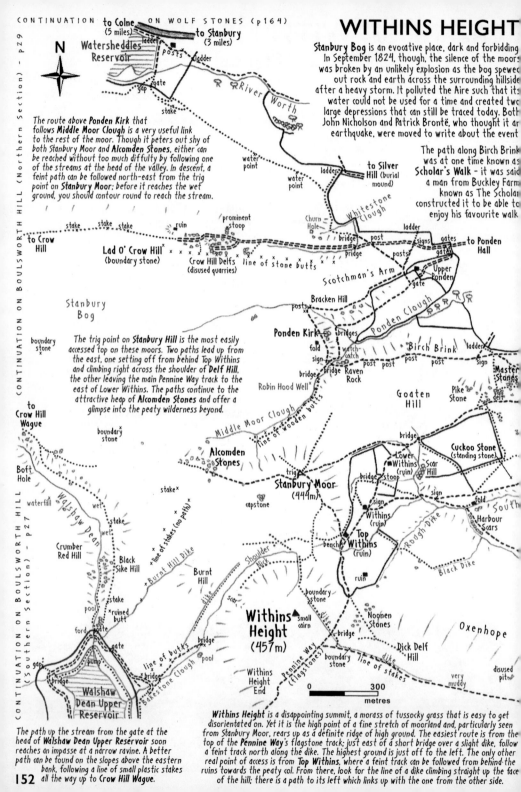

CONTINUATION ON WOLF STONES (p164)

CONTINUATION ON BOULSWORTH HILL (Northern Section) – p29

CONTINUATION ON BOULSWORTH HILL (Southern Section) – p27

WITHINS HEIGHT

Stanbury Bog is an evocative place, dark and forbidding. In September 1824, though, the silence of the moors was broken by an unlikely explosion as the bog spewed out rock and earth across the surrounding hillside after a heavy storm. It polluted the Aire such that its water could not be used for a time and created two large depressions that can still be traced today. Both John Nicholson and Patrick Brontë, who thought it an earthquake, were moved to write about the event.

The path along Birch Brink was at one time known as Scholar's Walk – it was said a man from Buckley Farm known as The Scholar constructed it to be able to enjoy his favourite walk.

The route above Ponden Kirk that follows Middle Moor Clough is a very useful link to the rest of the moor. Though it peters out shy of both Stanbury Moor and Alcomden Stones, either can be reached without too much difficulty by following one of the streams at the head of the valley. In descent, a feint path can be followed north-east from the trig point on Stanbury Moor; before it reaches the wet ground, you should contour round to reach the stream.

The trig point on Stanbury Hill is the most easily accessed top on these moors. Two paths lead up from the east, one setting off from behind Top Withins and climbing right across the shoulder of Delf Hill, the other leaving the main Pennine Way track to the east of Lower Withins. The paths continue to the attractive heap of Alcomden Stones and offer a glimpse into the peaty wilderness beyond.

The path up the stream from the gate at the head of Walshaw Dean Upper Reservoir soon reaches an impasse at a narrow ravine. A better path can be found on the slopes above the eastern bank, following a line of small plastic stakes all the way up to Crow Hill Wague.

Withins Height is a disappointing summit, a morass of tussocky grass that is easy to get disorientated on. Yet it is the high point of a fine stretch of moorland and, particularly seen from Stanbury Moor, rears up as a definite ridge of high ground. The easiest route is from the top of the Pennine Way's flagstone track; just east of a short bridge over a slight dike, follow a feint track north along the dike. The highest ground is just off to the left. The only other real point of access is from Top Withins, where a feint track can be followed from behind the ruins towards the peaty col. From there, look for the line of a dike climbing straight up the face of the hill; there is a path to its left which links up with the one from the other side.

MAP - Northern Section (Haworth & Stanbury Moors)

Above Ponden Clough stands a dramatic arc of cliffs cutting the valley off prematurely. Streams cascade steeply down from both corners, while straight ahead rears the vertical crag of **Ponden Kirk**. Sheltering beneath it is a small gap in the rock long associated with marriage rituals. It was said that if a maiden crawled through she would be married before the year is out, while other versions have it that a couple passing through together are either deemed married or destined to be. There were also suggestions of sexual rituals, Halliwell Sutcliffe writing of 'This dark kirk of the wilderness, at which Pagan mothers once worshipped lustily'. Ponden Kirk is thought to be the Peniston Crag in Emily Brontë's *Wuthering Heights*.

'The wild moor' had a tendency to swallow people, but the deaths of two children in the nineteenth century are curiously conincidental. In 1801 two-year old Joseph Helliwell tried to follow his father across Haworth Moor, but became lost and froze to death near **Harbour Lodge**. In 1849, another Joseph Helliwell, this time four-years old, was lost for three days and his body discovered further up Haworth Moor by the Harbour Lodge gamekeeper.

The **Brontë Chair** is a distinctively-shaped hunk of rock that the young Brontë sisters apparently used to take turns to sit on to tell each other stories, stories that would later become part of their famous books. Such is the crazy world of Brontë tourism, you can now buy a Brontë Chair for your office, described as a 'sturdy modern design'. If the nearby **Brontë Bridge** comes as a disappointment it is because the original stone clapper bridge was washed away by a flash flood in 1989.

There was a smallpox isolation hospital at **Upper Heights** in the late 19th century.

Solitary and interesting looking stones are scattered across Flaight Hill, but only the **Cuckoo Stone** is thought a monolith. It stands in the heather above South Dean Beck and has a cross carved in one side. It is so-called because it is thought of as being out of place. It is said the stone represents the petrified body of a giant who prowled these moors, and that hoarded somewhere nearby is the treasure he stole.

There was a tiny stamp mill near **Forks House** in the early 19th century, used for crushing and washing minerals. It may have been used to extract what farmers thought was gold during a gold rush in Sladen Beck in the 1860s.

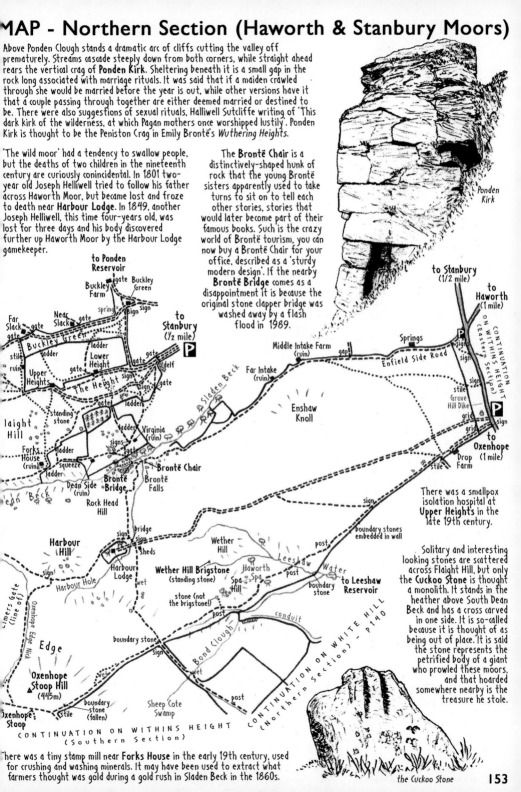

the Cuckoo Stone

WITHINS HEIGHT MAP - Southern Section

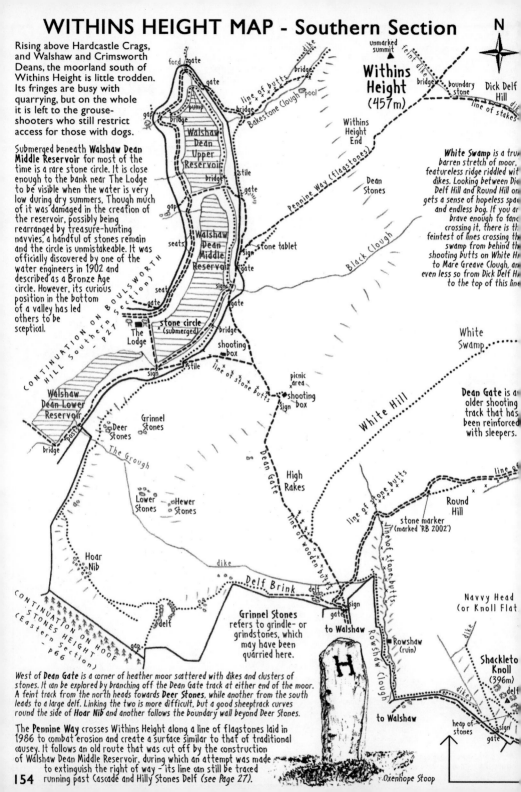

N

Rising above Hardcastle Crags, and Walshaw and Crimsworth Deans, the moorland south of Withins Height is little trodden. Its fringes are busy with quarrying, but on the whole it is left to the grouse-shooters who still restrict access for those with dogs.

Submerged beneath **Walshaw Dean Middle Reservoir** for most of the time is a rare stone circle. It is close enough to the bank near The Lodge to be visible when the water is very low during dry summers, Though much of it was damaged in the creation of the reservoir, possibly being rearranged by treasure-hunting navvies, a handful of stones remain and the circle is unmistakable. It was officially discovered by one of the water engineers in 1902 and described as a Bronze Age circle. However, its curious position in the bottom of a valley has led others to be sceptical.

White Swamp is a tru barren stretch of moor, featureless ridge riddled wit dikes. Looking between Di Delf Hill and Round Hill on gets a sense of hopeless spa and endless bog. If you ar brave enough to fanc crossing it, there is th feintest of lines crossing th swamp from behind th shooting butts on White H to Mare Greave Clough, an even less so from Dick Delf H to the top of this line

Dean Gate is a older shooting track that has been reinforced with sleepers.

Grinnel Stones refers to grindle- or grindstones, which may have been quarried here.

West of **Dean Gate** is a corner of heather moor scattered with dikes and clusters of stones. It can be explored by branching off the Dean Gate track at either end of the moor. A feint track from the north heads towards **Deer Stones**, while another from the south leads to a large delf. Linking the two is more difficult, but a good sheeptrack curves round the side of **Hoar Nib** and another follows the boundary wall beyond Deer Stones.

The **Pennine Way** crosses Withins Height along a line of flagstones laid in 1986 to combat erosion and create a surface similar to that of traditional causey. It follows an old route that was cut off by the construction of Walshaw Dean Middle Reservoir, during which an attempt was made to extinguish the right of way – its line can still be traced running past Cascade and Hilly Stones Delf (see Page 27).

Map labels

- ford
- gate
- gate
- dike
- bridge
- line of butts
- pool
- bridge
- pump
- gap
- bridge
- **Walshaw Dean Upper Reservoir**
- Bakestone Clough
- **Withins Height (457m)**
- unmarked summit
- feint dike
- bridge
- boundary stone
- **Dick Delf Hill**
- line of stakes
- Withins Height End
- Dean Stones
- Pennine Way (flagstones)
- Black Clough
- tile
- bridge
- gate
- gap
- **Walshaw Dean Middle Reservoir**
- seats
- stone tablet
- sign
- gate
- seat
- signs
- gate
- gate
- stone circle (submerged)
- **The Lodge**
- bridge
- shooting box
- sign
- stile
- line of stone butts
- picnic area
- shooting box
- sign
- White Hill
- White Swamp
- **CONTINUATION ON BOULSWORTH HILL Southern Section – P27**
- **Walshaw Dean Lower Reservoir**
- bridge
- posts
- Deer Stones
- Grinnel Stones
- The Grough
- Dean Gate
- High Rakes
- line of stone butts
- Round Hill
- stone marker (marked 'RB 2002')
- line o
- Lower Stones
- Hewer Stones
- line of wooden butts
- Hoar Nib
- dike
- delf
- **CONTINUATION ON HOOF STONES HEIGHT (Eastern Section) – P66**
- gap
- delf
- **Delf Brink**
- delf
- sign
- gate
- to Walshaw
- line of stone butts
- Navvy Head (or Knoll Flat)
- dike
- Rowshaw (ruin)
- Rowshaw Clough
- to Walshaw
- **Shackleto Knoll (396m)**
- delf
- H
- heap of stones
- sign
- gate
- Oxenhope Stoop

154

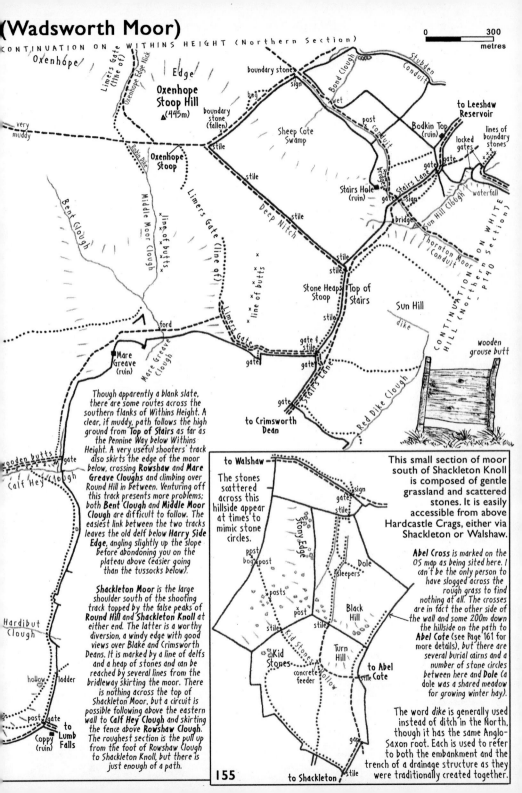

300 metres

Oxenhope

Edge

Oxenhope Stoop Hill
▲(445m)

Limers Gate (line of)
Oxenhope Edge Nick

very muddy

Delfs Dike

Oxenhope Stoop

Bent Clough

Middle Moor Clough

line of butts

Limers Gate (line of)

ford

Mare Greave (ruin)

Mare Greave Clough

boundary stones
sign
bog

boundary stone (fallen)

stile

stile

Sheep Cote Swamp

Deep Nitch

stile

stile

line of butts

x x x x

line of butts

Limers Gate

gate

gate & stile

gate

gate

Stairs Lane

to Crimsworth Dean

Bond Clough

wet

post & conduit

bridges

Stairs Hole (ruin)

gate

bridge

Stone Heaps Stoop

stile

stile

stile

Top of Stairs

Stubden Conduit

to Leeshaw Reservoir

Bodkin Top (ruin)

locked gates

lines of boundary stones

gate gate

gate sign

waterfall

Sun Hill Clough

Thornton Moor Conduit

Sun Hill

dike

Red Dike Clough

CONTINUATION ON WHITE HILL (Northern Section) — PT140

wooden grouse butt

Though apparently a blank slate, there are some routes across the southern flanks of Withins Height. A clear, if muddy, path follows the high ground from **Top of Stairs** as far as the Pennine Way below Withins Height. A very useful shooters' track also skirts the edge of the moor below, crossing **Rowshaw** and **Mare Greave Cloughs** and climbing over Round Hill in between. Venturing off this track presents more problems; both **Bent Clough** and **Middle Moor Clough** are difficult to follow. The easiest link between the two tracks leaves the old delf below **Harry Side Edge**, angling slightly up the slope before abandoning you on the plateau above (easier going than the tussocks below).

Shackleton Moor is the large shoulder south of the shooting track topped by the false peaks of **Round Hill** and **Shackleton Knoll** at either end. The latter is a worthy diversion, a windy edge with good views over Blake and Crimsworth Deans. It is marked by a line of delfs and a heap of stones and can be reached by several lines from the bridleway skirting the moor. There is nothing across the top of Shackleton Moor, but a circuit is possible following above the eastern wall to **Calf Hey Clough** and skirting the fence above **Rowshaw Clough**. The roughest section is the pull up from the foot of Rowshaw Clough to Shackleton Knoll, but there is just enough of a path.

wooden butts

gate

Calf Hey Clough

Hardibut Clough

hollow   ladder

post   gate

to Lumb Falls

Coppy (ruin)

to Walshaw

The stones scattered across this hillside appear at times to mimic stone circles.

Stony Edge

post
bog post

posts

stile

Kid Stones

sign
gate
stile

Dole
sleepers

post

Black Hill

Kid Stones Hollow

stile

Turn Hill

concrete feeder

to Abel Cote
stile

gap

stile

to Shackleton

This small section of moor south of Shackleton Knoll is composed of gentle grassland and scattered stones. It is easily accessible from above Hardcastle Crags, either via Shackleton or Walshaw.

Abel Cross is marked on the OS map as being sited here. I can't be the only person to have slogged across the rough grass to find nothing at all. The crosses are in fact the other side of the wall and some 200m down the hillside on the path to **Abel Cote** (see Page 161 for more details), but there are several burial cairns and a number of stone circles between here and **Dole** (a dole was a shared meadow for growing winter hay).

The word dike is generally used instead of ditch in the North, though it has the same Anglo-Saxon root. Each is used to refer to both the embankment and the trench of a drainage structure as they were traditionally created together.

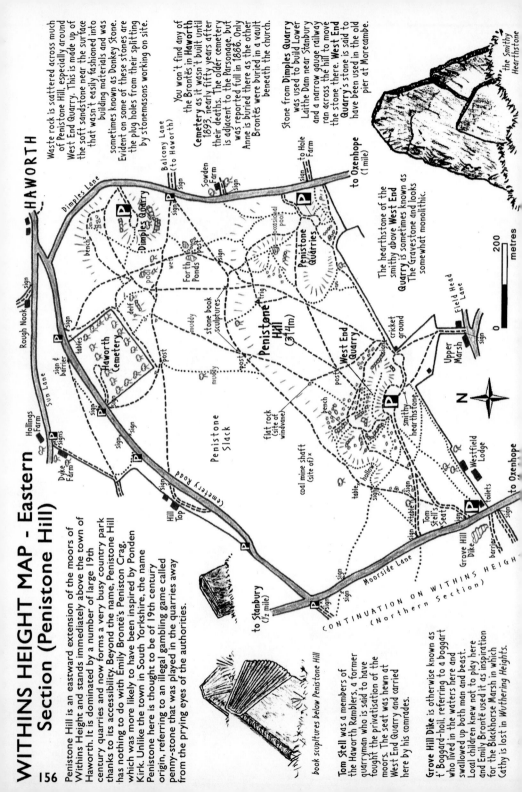

HAWORTH

Penistone Hill is an eastward extension of the moors of Withins Height and stands immediately above the town of Haworth. It is dominated by a number of large 19th century quarries and now forms a very busy country park thanks to its accessibility. Beyond the name, Penistone Hill has nothing to do with Emily Brontë's Peniston Crag, which was more likely to have been inspired by Ponden Kirk. Unlike the town in South Yorkshire, the name Penistone here is thought to be of 19th century origin, referring to an illegal gambling game called penny-stone that was played in the quarries away from the prying eyes of the authorities.

Waste rock is scattered across much of Penistone Hill, especially around West End Quarry. This is made up of the soft sandstone near the surface that wasn't easily fashioned into building materials and was sometimes known as Donkey Stone. Evident on some of these stones are the plug holes from their splitting by stonemasons working on site.

You won't find any of the Brontës in Haworth Cemetery as it wasn't built until 1893, nearly fifty years after their deaths. The older cemetery is adjacent to the Parsonage, but was reported full in 1856. Only Anne is buried there as the other Brontës were buried in a vault beneath the church.

Stone from Dimples Quarry was used to build Lower Laithe Dam near Stanbury and a narrow gauge railway ran across the hill to move the stone there. West End Quarry's stone is said to have been used in the old pier at Morecambe.

The hearthstone of the smithy above West End Quarry is sometimes known as The Gravestone and looks somewhat monolithic.

the Smithy Hearthstone

Tom Stell was a members of the Haworth Ramblers, a former quarryman who is said to have fought the privatisation of the moors. The seat was hewn at West End Quarry and carried here by his comrades.

book sculptures below Penistone Hill

Grove Hill Dike is otherwise known as t' Boggard-hoil, referring to a boggart who lived in the waters here and swallowed up both man and beast. Local children knew not to play here and Emily Brontë used it as inspiration for the Blackhorse Marsh in which Cathy is lost in *Wuthering Heights*.

CONTINUATION ON WITHINS HEIGHT
(Northern Section)

TOP WITHINS & THE BRONTËS

It is impossible to ignore the Brontës' influence on Haworth and its surrounding moors. They are surely the single biggest reason that people venture out onto the West Yorkshire Moors, and they are bound up with our vision of these wild spaces. It has been suggested that the Brontës' associations with the eastern slopes of Withins Height was one of the reasons why pylons were not erected here and why there is still a footpath across Walshaw Dean, which now carries the Pennine Way but which the water board attempted to close with the construction of the reservoirs.

By all accounts the Brontë family were a rather sickly bunch who died too young, but their ill health didn't stop them walking the moors above Haworth, most frequently visiting the bridge and falls on West Dean Beck to read and write each other stories. Their poetry is laden with images of the moorland and *Wuthering Heights* is the most famous description of life on the edge of the Pennine wilderness.

Top Withins is a proper Brontë pilgrimage site, so much so that the signs leading up there are marked in both Japanese and English. When the pilgrims reach their destination, they are faced with a concrete-reinforced shack and a plaque explaining that the building bears no resemblance to that described in *Wuthering Heights*. It is widely held that Emily Brontë took the Jacobean mansion at High Sunderland (near Halifax) and transported it here to the location of Top Withins to create her *Wuthering Heights*, home of the Earnshaws. Sure enough, wind howls through the walls and the wild moor presses closely in on Top Withins. However, there the romance ends.

There has been a building at Top Withins since the fourteenth century, though the current ruins are those of a seventeenth-century farmhouse. Top Withins was last lived in by a Haworth man, Ernest Roddy, who was advised by doctors to move to the country after being gassed in the war. He farmed poultry here until 1926, when he returned to Haworth. Yorkshire Water acquired Top Withins by chance as part of the catchwater for Lower Laithe Reservoir, and it has slowly decomposed since. It was listed as a historical building by English Heritage in 1974, apparently in error, but the concrete botch job on its restoration sealed its fate as little more than a remote picnic spot. Now de-listed, it is the least glorious ruin in all of the Pennines and one of the few places where it is hard to find solitude. Go to Coolam, Red Dikes, Rastrick Greave, or even Lower Withins, and imagine how atmospheric this spot might have been.

A far better Brontë pilgrimage is to wander the empty moorland spaces of Oxenhope Edge, Withins Height and Stanbury Moor, where the landscape will impress a far more convincing Wuthering Heights on your imagination, as it did for Emily Brontë. If you're very lucky you'll see her ghost wandering the moor as so many others have claimed, causing *The Yorkshire Post* to mischievously claim there was a need for 'a first-aid post to be set on the edge of the moors to revive people'.

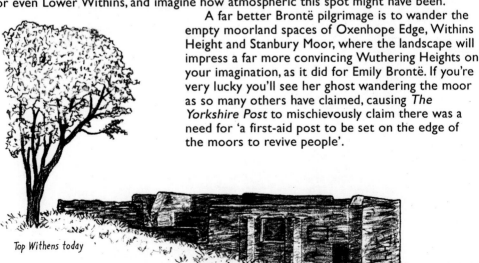

Top Withens today

ROUTE 25: WITHINS HEIGHT, CROW HILL & PONDEN KIRK FROM PONDEN

Distance: 7½ miles (12.5km)
Ascent: 370m
Difficulty: Strenuous

Parking: Along track around Ponden Reservoir.
Public Transport: Bus 812 from Haworth to Ponden or Bus 664 from Keighley to Stanbury.

3 The path continues off Crow Hill, bending left before dropping down towards the depression below (Crow Hill Wague). A stake here marks the top of a line leading all the way up from Walshaw Dean; turn left and make a beeline for a white plastic stake (on a bearing of 345°). This line continues past further stakes towards Crow Hill Beck. Either follow the line of the stream or the stakes across the heather to the left to reach a confluence at the top of Walshaw Dean. A surprising path appears here along the line of plastic stakes and follows the top of the slope on the north side of the valley. In the bracken above Boft Hole, fork right and drop down the slope, staying with the stakes – if you reach a cluster of rocks, you've gone slightly too far.

2 Keep right through Crow Hill Delfs and, when the track ends, head straight on, passing the Lad O' Crow Hill to the left. Aim for the first of a series of wooden stakes and pick up a feint path following the high ground steadily up towards Crow Hill. The stakes have become more intermittent and a new line runs parallel at first, but the path becomes clearer as it pulls up the shoulder to the summit.

Lad o' Crow Hill

Robin Hood Well is just one of three adjacent springs in Middle Moor Clough, the others being known as Little John Well and Will Scarlett Well. Haworth Spring is another well, at the head of Leeshaw Water, and was the site of an annual church pilgrimage from Haworth on Spa Sunday with a band playing sacred music.

Alcomden Stones (also known as Oakenden Stones) stand on the brink of the wilderness; though a cosy path leads here from Stanbury Moor, it deposits you amid these ancient stones. Despite suggestions of druidical sacrifices and the presence of a dolmen (with a capstone forming a small room), it is now widely acknowledged that these are entirely natural features. However, this is not to belittle their wonderful sense of isolation and craggy splendour.

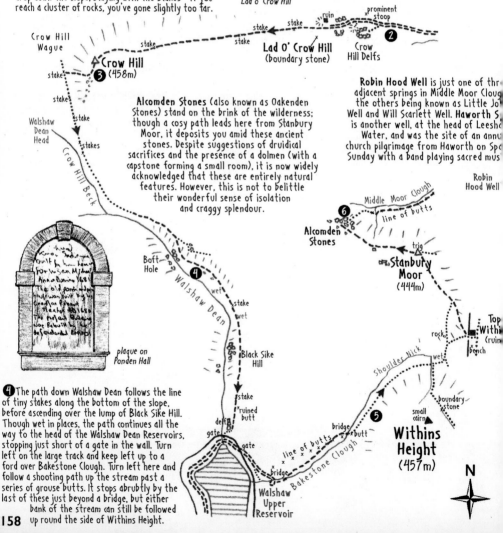

plaque on Ponden Hall

4 The path down Walshaw Dean follows the line of tiny stakes along the bottom of the slope, before ascending over the lump of Black Sike Hill. Though wet in places, the path continues all the way to the head of the Walshaw Dean Reservoirs, stopping just short of a gate in the wall. Turn left on the large track and keep left up to a ford over Bakestone Clough. Turn left here and follow a shooting path up the stream past a series of grouse butts. It stops abruptly by the last of these just beyond a bridge, but either bank of the stream can still be followed

up round the side of Withins Height.

Character: This is a short but strenuous walk very much off the beaten track. Apart from the start and finish around Ponden, all the walking is on feint paths and across rough pathless ground. It is also quite likely you will lose the path once or twice, but the route is such that there are enough landmarks (streams and often stakes) to navigate and most of the ground underfoot is not too hard going. What the route does allow is a wonderful exploration of the wild moor north of Withins Height and the upper reaches of Walshaw Dean, as well as some of the more familiar landmarks of Ponden Kirk and Top Withins. Until the CROW Act was enforced, almost all of this area was out of bounds, so it is a treat to be able to wander freely into one of the wildest parts of West Yorkshire.

In the 1880s, a railway was proposed to link the Worth Valley with Colne; the initial route went via Watersheddles, but was amended to cut through Crow Hill via tunnel. After numerous public meetings, the bill was passed in Parliament in 1890 and money raised for the project. Yet the line never materialised, as was the case with a similar proposal from Oxenhope to Hebden Bridge, possibly because the railway era was beginning to run out of steam.

1 The route starts and finishes on the south shore of Ponden Reservoir, where there is plenty of parking along the track. If on the bus or walking from Stanbury, a track leads up to the reservoir from Ponden Mill and the Stanbury Road. Continue along the track, bending right at the far end of the reservoir to climb up past Ponden Hall. Turn left at a junction soon after and follow the signs up to the edge of the moor beyond Height Laithe. Keep straight ahead on the quarry track, climbing steadily up Whitestone Clough with a series of grouse butts on your left.

Ponden Reservoir was built in the 1870s as a compensation reservoir for the mill-owners in the valley below as all the water from Middle Moor Clough and Stanbury Bog is taken via an underground conduit to Watersheddles Reservoir.

6 The path goes no further than Alcomden Stones, but in Middle Moor Clough below a good path leads down to Ponden. The last rough section is a descent from the stones to pick up the rich green line of the stream - the path begins above its right bank near the first of a line of wooden grouse butts. Cross a bridge and keep right as the ravine tightens above Ponden Kirk. To reach the kirk, fork left at the next junction; otherwise, turn right here and cross a second bridge to follow Scholar's Walk along Birch Bank. As the ground flattens, follow a sign left to a ladder stile and then follow the wall down the hill. Where this bends right, pick up a grassy line across the fields towards Lower Slack Farm. Go through a small gate and skirt the top side of the farm to reach the large entrance gates, from where the track leads back down to Ponden Reservoir.

5 If heading for the top of Withins Height, you're best following the right bank up Shoulder Nick, staying on the drier ground until sheep-tracks appear. At the top of Shoulder Nick, the stream takes a sharp and unnatural kink up to the right. To reach the summit of Withins Height, follow this drain up and fork left; the tussock-covered summit is off to the right near a boundary stone. The onward route from Shoulder Nick heads across the broad depression, where you may pick up a feint path heading up the slight slope and on towards Stanbury Moor trig. If in doubt, though, follow the depression right towards the large tree by the ruins of Top Withins. You need not even cross the wall into Brontë-ville as the onward path turns left before the building and climbs the shoulder towards the trig point on Stanbury Moor. Turn left here to reach Alcomden Stones, the quietest place around here to take a breather.

The large boundary stone known as **Lad o' Crow Hill** (or Lancashire Lad) marks a corner of the county boundary on the ridge between Crow Hill Delfs and the hill's summit. It is inscribed 'lad or scarr on crow hill' and is said to mark the place where a young lad died having been caught in a storm. Though he was Lancastrian, the authorities there disputed that he had perished on Yorkshire soil and, when eventually they did bury him in Trawden, Lancashire claimed this chunk of the moor as their own. Hence both the words *lad* and *scar* are taken to mean boundary stone. However, it was also known as Laddock Royle, which suggests it may have been an older site with Lad coming from the celtic word *lladd* meaning to destroy or slaughter.

Ponden Hall is an Elizabethan farmhouse that is usually cited as the model for Thrushcross Grange in Emily Brontë's *Wuthering Heights*. The lower section is thought to have been built around 1634 with the upper half added in 1801. Until 1898 it belonged to the Heaton Family, who owned Ponden Mill and Crow Hill Quarries and were friends of the Brontë family, who regularly visited its extensive library. The adjacent building called the Bunkhouse served as a stopping point on the Pennine Way for a number of years, but was originally built as a peat store and cow shed in 1680.

the dolmen at Alcomden Stones

159

ROUTE 26: WITHINS HEIGHT FROM MIDGEHOLE

Distance: 10 miles (16.5km)

Ascent: 450m

Difficulty: Strenuous

Parking: National Trust pay car park at Midgehole.

Public Transport: Midgehole is the terminus of the 906 bus service, which runs from Hebden Bridge six times a day on weekends and Bank Holidays from April to September.

Character: This route combines the relatively twee delights of the National Trust woodlands at Hardcastle Crags with some of the more remote corners of the moorlands above Hebden Bridge. While most of the navigation is straight-forward, the section between Shackleton Knoll and Oxenhope Stoop Hill is less trodden and needs care. It is, however, I think a more satisfying route than the traditional traipse up Stairs and along the dreaded Deep Nitch. The return route follows the well-used Hebden Bridge to Haworth walk in large part, but drops down to the top of the Hebden Water, where the valley is at its most impressive.

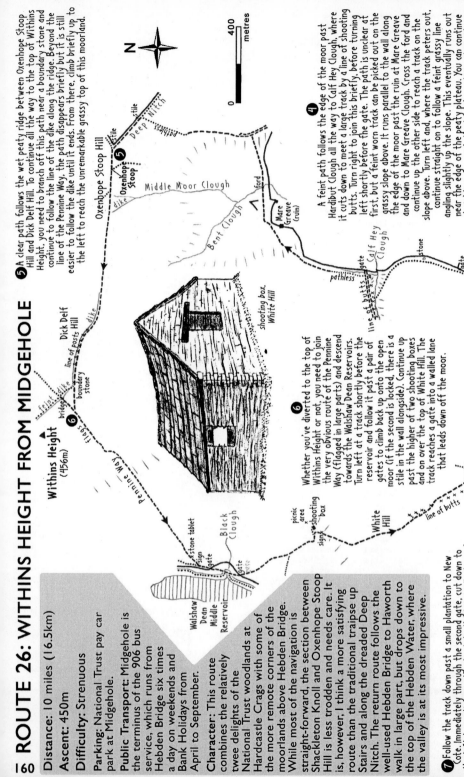

⑤ A clear path follows the wet peaty ridge between Oxenhope Stoop Hill and Dick Delf Hill. To continue all the way to the top of Withins Height, you need to branch off this path near a boundary stone and continue to follow the line of the dike along the ridge. Beyond the line of the Pennine Way, the path disappears briefly but it is still easier to follow the dike until it ends. From there, climb briefly up to the left to reach the unremarkable grassy top of this moorland.

④ A feint path follows the edge of the moor past Hardibut Clough all the way to Calf Hey Clough, where it cuts down to meet a large track by a line of shooting butts. Turn right to join this briefly, before turning left shortly before the gate. The path is unclear at first, but a feint worn track can be picked out on the grassy slope above. It runs parallel to the wall along the edge of the moor past the ruin at Mare Greave and down to Mare Greave Clough. Cross the ford and continue up the other side to reach a track on the slope above. Turn left and, where the track peters out, continue straight on to follow a feint grassy line angling slightly up the slope. This eventually runs out near the edge of the peaty plateau. You can continue straight on to reach the boundary stone at Oxenhope Stoop, but a safer bet is to head slightly right and contour across to Deep Nitch (a bearing of 15° if necessary). Pick up a good path heading left here and keep left at the wall corner to reach Oxenhope Stoop.

⑥ Whether you've diverted to the top of Withins Height or not, you need to join the very obvious route of the Pennine Way (flagged in large parts) and descend towards the Walshaw Dean Reservoirs. Turn left at a track shortly before the reservoir and follow it past a pair of gates to climb back up onto the open moor (if the second is locked, there is a stile in the wall alongside). Continue up past the higher of two shooting boxes and on over the top of White Hill. The track reaches a gate into a walled lane that leads down off the moor.

⑦ Follow the track down past a small plantation to New Cote. Immediately through the second gate, cut down to the left to continue on the track to the large collection of buildings at Walshaw Lodge. Head straight across the junction and look for a stile in the wall to the left leading out into the field beyond. Head straight on down the field to reach a stile and re-enter the National Trust woodland.

Access: no dogs on this route.

3 The track descends slightly from Abel Cote to pass Abel Cross and reach the main track up from Hollin Hall. Turn left, passing Laithe and the path down towards Lumb Bridge, before turning left up a clear walled lane by the ruined farm at Nook. Reaching the edge of the moor at the next gate, turn immediately right on a feint path that hugs the wall. Upon reaching a ladder stile over the wall, ignore it and climb diagonally left for a few yards to reach another feint path continuing along the wall in the same direction.

2 Turn right into the cluster of farmhouses that make up Shackleton and look for a stile to the left-hand side of the far building. The path from here keeps the wall to its right then crosses an open field to aim for a gateway on the right side of the boundary dead ahead. Keep this fence to your left as you contour across the hillside with great views over Crimsworth Dean, until a stile deposits you on the opposite side close to Abel Cote. Pass to the left of the farm and join the track immediately in front of it.

1 From the end of the road at Midgehole, take the bridleway signed from the entrance to the National Trust property. Where this reaches a track, continue straight across to follow a smaller path along the edge of the woods. After 100m, this turns right into a narrow walled walkway. Follow this and bear left as it opens out into woodland again, climbing past several boulders to reach the top of the woods. A stile leads into another narrow walled route up to the track by Shackleton.

Sitting outside the Blue Pig on a summer evening, it's hard to imagine **Midgehole** isn't named after the midges gnawing on you. However, it probably refers to a hollow where there was a manure dump or a boggy site. The **Blue Pig** itself is thought to have taken its name from the original colour of the Liberal Party in the 19th century, when pigs were a nickname for working men's clubs.

Abel Cross is actually a pair of stone crosses, nicknamed Cain & Abel or Mourning & Vanity. They probably served as wayside markers but legend says they mark the graves of two rivals who fought over a lady. She subsequently killed herself at nearby Lumb Falls, the White Lady who is said to haunt the spot to this day.

Walshaw Lodge was transformed from a small hamlet into the Savile's shooting retreat in 1850 and has since become the family home.

The **Hardcastle Crags** (or Hills) themselves are hard to find, further up the track from Gibson Mill and not worth the effort. The river and the woods hold the real charm here, the latter being partially planted as a verdant entrance to the Savile's shooting estate in the 19th century. The woods were given to the National Trust in 1950.

Slurring Rock stands at the top of the woods below Shackleton and is marked with grooves where children slid (or slurred) down the rock.

8 From the stile, head straight on briefly before a path leads steeply down the right side of Rowshaw Clough to reach a forest track. Cross the bridge and turn immediately right on a large path down to the river, which is followed the rest of the way. At first the valley is steep and rocky and the path crosses the river several times to avoid rock faces until it reaches the café at Gibson Mill.

Gibson Mill was an early 19th century cotton mill, originally called Lord Holme Mill. These days it is prided by the National Trust as a low-energy sustainable restoration, housing a café and museum. Yet, even in the early part of the 20th century, it was used as a leisure facility with a dancing hall, roller skating rink, restaurants, boating lake and refreshments kiosks.

9 Having crossed the bridge to reach Gibson Mill, you now stay on the left bank of the river the rest of the way. Ignore the main vehicle track heading away from the mill and descend a few steps to pick up the path right beside the river. In places the path is narrow and rocky, in others it opens out in sparse woodland. Level with the stepping stones over to Hebden Hey, the path briefly climbs away from the river; take the first path off to the right and then ignore other routes off to the left to stay with the river all the way to Midgehole. Through a gap in the wall, turn left on the track here to return to the car parks.

MIDGEHOLE

to Hebden Bridge

Blue Pig

to Hebden Bridge (1 mile)

Hebden Water

Hebden Water

Shackleton

Slurring Rock

Hardcastle Crags (National Trust Woodland)

stepping stones

steps

steps

mill pond

bridge

Gibson Mill (museum & café)

stepping stones

flags

Rom Hole

Hardcastle Hills

Walshaw Lodge

Hebden Water

Rowshaw Clough

New Cote

Lane

8

9

2

3

Abel Cote

Abel Cross

Shackleton Knoll

Coppy

Nook

Laithe

to Lumb Falls

ladder

post gate

gate & sign

gates

gate

stile

gate

gap

gate

stile & sign

post

gate & sign

stile

gate

Abel Cross

THE RESERVOIRS OF WEST YORKSHIRE

Reservoirs are such an important part of the Pennine moorland landscape it is hard to imagine the scene without them. Yet, until the nineteenth century, drinking water came from the natural springs and wells that abounded in the area. The earliest dams on the moorland were usually small affairs constructed by groups of mill-owners who wanted to ensure a steady supply of water to their mills when the streams were low. Some of these can still be seen (Gaddings Dams, the Cold Edge Dams, Noah Dale Dam and Flints Reservoir), others were later buried under other reservoirs (Wessenden Old Reservoir, and Lingards Dam beneath Deer Hill Reservoir). The construction of the Rochdale and Huddersfield Narrow Canals in the 1790s required a number of reservoirs to be built to keep the water levels topped up, though most of these were still fairly small (indeed sometimes too small, as Thomas Telford commented on Brun Clough Reservoir).

From the mid-19th century, towns became responsible for their own drinking water. Victoria Reservoir in Halifax was one of the first constructed by a water corporation, in 1848, and was known as 'the people's reservoir', though it was insufficient to meet the needs of the growing town. The corporations held powers of compulsory land purchase and set about clearing entire catchments in the hills to provide clean and safe drinking water. So paranoid were they about the possibility of pollution (and particularly the spread of typhoid), that they often sought to extinguish footpaths and remove de facto access agreements.

In the late 1890s and 1900s, the demand for water increased dramatically and many reservoir projects were initiated. For the first time, experienced labour was in short demand and navvies were known to move from project to project depending on weather, pay and conditions. Small wooden huts or alternative lodgings, often in mills that were due to be drowned, were usually provided and led to small shanties for a couple of hundred men springing up for a few years. The Navvy Mission Society was established in 1877 and built mission rooms at every site, and there was even a small church at the navvy settlement for Green Withens Reservoir above Oxygrains Bridge. There was usually a store and occasionally other facilities existed, such as a library, workshop, sports team or hospital. The latter was usually forced upon the contractor after a spate of accidents, as it was at Dawson City near Heptonstall, probably the largest and most notorious shanty, accommodating up to 540 men.

Tramways were often built around reservoir sites to move materials and men. Though stone could usually be quarried close by (think of the excavated faces above Blakeley and Deer Hill dams), puddle clay was often harder to come by. This watertight material was needed to fill the cut offs at the foot of the dam and necessitated the construction of many of these tramways and often steep inclines into or out of the valley bottoms. Initially trams were pulled by horses (as at Widdop) or even by hand (at Shiny Brook Clough), but steam locomotives were available by the time the Walshaw Dean Reservoirs were constructed in the 1900s, providing the most spectacular tramway of all as it crossed high above Blake Dean on a 100ft-high trestle bridge (see Page 66 for more information).

Dams regularly leaked when they were first filled, necessitating further work by the contractors. Enoch Tempest was bankrupted by leaks on Walshaw Dean Lower and Middle Reservoirs and died of a stroke shortly after, meaning the work took nearly thirteen years to complete. Bilberry Reservoir never stopped leaking and burst in 1852, flooding Holmfirth and killing eighty-one people, and the collapse of Swellands' dam killed six people in Marsden in 1810.

Over the years the natural flow of water has been so altered by human intervention that it is often hard to work out where it ends up. As well as layer upon layer of reservoirs, their catchwaters, regulating drains and conduits take water from one side of a hill round (or sometimes through) to the other. Many reservoirs simply serve as compensation reservoirs for others, ensuring that as much water as possible can be stored for a dry spell, and there is such a maze of drains and culverts left over from the industrial boom that tracing any watercourse can often prove impossible.

CHAPTER 21 - **WOLF STONES**

Height: 443m

Grid Ref: SD971394

Map Sheet: OL21 (South Pennines)

Access: No dogs permitted at any time south of fenceline on Wolf Stones (basin overlooking Watersheddles).

Public Transport: Regular bus services to Cowling, Sutton and Oakworth from Keighley.

Wolf Stones crowns a vast moor that is split between West Yorkshire, Lancashire and North Yorkshire. I have included a large chunk of the latter in my survey as a natural northward continuation of the county's peat moorland. Beyond Cowling, the landscape changes quickly and the Pennine backbone disappears into the limestone of the Dales. Wolves were present in England until around the turn of the 16th century, but it may be simply the shape of the rocks which inspired the name. The Pennine Way crosses the moor near the summit outcrop, but much of the moor is left to shooting parties and peat-cutters. Only Earl Crag and its twin sentinels (recognisable to travellers up the Aire Valley) command any real attention.

Wainman's Pinnacle on Earl Crag

WOLF STONES MAP - Southern Section (Oakworth

The summit of Wolf Stones stands on a rocky crest overlooking the Keighley to Colne road, from where it has a definite hilltop appearance. From all other sides, it presents broad shoulders of heather. The southern part of the moor centres around Keighley Moor Reservoir and is well trodden away from the ridge that runs from Maw Stones to Combe Hill.

Heath rush, or juncus squarrosus, is one of the most common plants across the South Pennines, its hardy tussocks thriving in the wettest areas of acidic moorland. Its stems are circular and spongy inside, and have brown clusters of flowers near their sharp tips. It is favoured by grazing livestock during the winter when there is little else on offer.

The summit trig of **Wolf Stones** stands on the undistinguished cluster of Little Wolf Stones. The real edge of Great Wolf Stones is beyond a stile to the southwest. The trig point is easily visible from the Pennine Way, though the pa to it is far from obvious. 20m north of the post on the crest look for a feintly worn line heading just right of the summit, path that soon becomes more obvious.

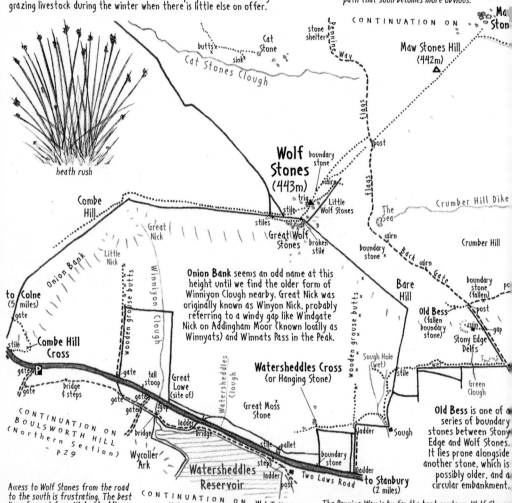

heath rush

Onion Bank seems an odd name at this height until we find the older form of Winniyon Clough. Great Nick was originally known as Winyon Nick, probably referring to a windy gap like Windgate Nick on Addingham Moor (known locally as Winnyats) and Winnats Pass in the Peak.

Watersheddles Cross (or Hanging Stone)

Old Bess is one of a series of boundary stones between Stony Edge and Wolf Stones. It lies prone alongside another stone, which is possibly older, and a circular embankment.

Access to Wolf Stones from the road to the south is frustrating. The best line of ascent from **Watersheddles Reservoir** follows a wall and then a line of wooden grouse butts towards Combe Hill. When the path peters out, bear left up the shallow hollow of Little Nick to reach the fenceline along the ridge. There are no useful stiles to reach the feint path on the other side, but the ground is reasonably easy going on both sides. The hilltop fence can also be reached via a stile and feint path up past **Combe Hill Cross.** The only other access points are via a short walled lane opposite the eastern end of the reservoir and the footpath across the field west of Sough.

The Pennine Way is by far the best route up Wolf Stones because much of the rest of its south-eastern flank is rough and wet. The path from **Highfield House** looks appealing but crosses one of the wettest hollows in the South Pennines and is best avoided unless you have a keen interest in cotton and bog grasses. The continuation of this path towards Watersheddles Cross also crosses wet ground, but the worst of this can be avoided by dropping down towards the ruin at Sough.

Combe Hill Cross is known locally as Camel Cross, a probable corruption of Gamel, the Saxon Lord who is thought to have erected it. It may have served as both a boundary stone and wayside cross along the medieval road whose straight line is still followed by the modern road. What remains is the base, inscribed 'Combe Cross', and a small stone set within the socket.

Combe Hill Cross

Moor)

As it is a quiet area of moorland, nesting birds are common across Oakworth Moor; linnets, stonechats, peregrine, golden plover, wrens and goldeneye are among those that can be seen.

The unmarked heathery top of *Maw Stones Hill* is just a metre lower than *Wolf Stones*. Its only feature is the collection of large flat rocks at **Maw Stones**, which are reached by a feint path along the ridge from the post at the top of the Pennine Way. In the heart of a sea of rough heather, there is only one satisfactory path up to Maw Stones. It follows the line of wooden grouse butts up from the corner of **Keighley Moor Reservoir**; though it threatens to peter out, the route can be traced up the right side of the grough that bears left at the end of the butts.

The enclosures around **Higher Intake** and **Clough Hey** are not included in access land, with only public footpaths to follow, but there are some attractive areas around them that are. **Blue Scar** is a dry ravine carved from an outcrop of limestone and can be reached from a gap in the wall above *Morkin Bridge*. Duck under the barbed wire and drop down across the smaller stream below to pick up a feint path following the slope above first **Morkin Beck**, then the dry valley itself. The path continues as far as the track to **Clough Hey**, though you'll have to jump the fence here.

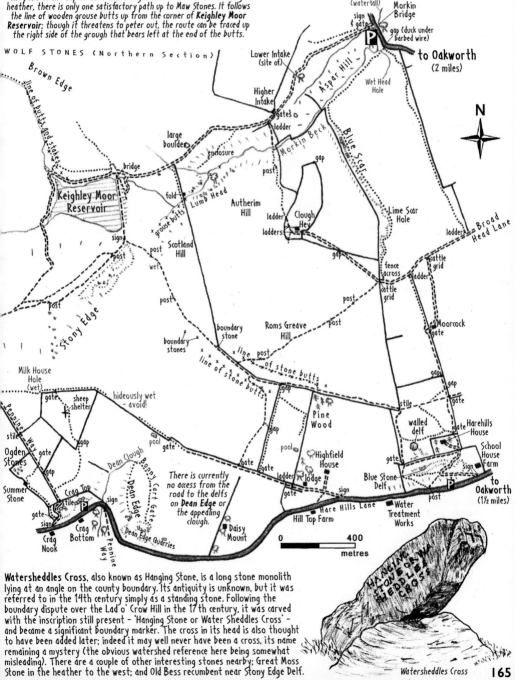

Watersheddles Cross, also known as Hanging Stone, is a long stone monolith lying at an angle on the county boundary. Its antiquity is unknown, but it was referred to in the 14th century simply as a standing stone. Following the boundary dispute over the Lad o' Crow Hill in the 17th century, it was carved with the inscription still present - 'Hanging Stone or Water Sheddles Cross' - and became a significant boundary marker. The cross in its head is also thought to have been added later; indeed it may well never have been a cross, its name remaining a mystery (the obvious watershed reference here being somewhat misleading). There are a couple of other interesting stones nearby; Great Moss Stone in the heather to the west; and Old Bess recumbent near Stony Edge Delf.

Watersheddles Cross

Most of the northern flank of Wolf Stones is actually in North Yorkshire, the giant glacial boulder of the Hitching Stone representing the north-western corner of West Yorkshire. But I have included the dramatic edge of Earl Crag and its pair of distinctive follies as a natural extension of this gritstone moorland before the limestone country of the Dales takes over. Ickornshaw and Keighley Moors are empty swathes of vibrant heather and soggy mosses with only occasional boulders for company, while Sutton Moor is far more full of interest and consequently more well trodden.

Ickornshaw Moor is common land on which freeholders still hold fiercely defended shooting and turbary (peat-cutting) rights. Peat was cut for fuel and dried in large stacks designed to repel the rain before being carted off the moors. The wooden huts found along the moorside are known as cowlings and were originally used by families when gathering peat. In some cases they were former garages carted up to the moor by villagers and used as basic holiday cottages. They remain in use largely for shooting, as does the New Stone Hut, built on the site of an older shooting hut. Villagers traditionally sleep in the hut the night before the Glorious 12th (the Quack as it is known) to ensure an early start.

The Pennine Way descends past **Further Dean Hole** to Ickornshaw, though the best route down to Cowling follows the edge of the moor round to **Moor Lodge** (which also links up with the Earl Crag part of the moor). The track up past Over Dean gives access to some feint paths along **Dean Brow** and to Mistress Moss. Heading straight up the shallow slope, you'll soon see the line of butts heading across to **Smalldn Clough** and can pick up the only path across the moor.

to Cowling (1 mile)

to Cowling (1/2 mile)

to Cowling (1/2 mile)

Builden

barn

E.a.r.l.

q.uarry

gate

gap

gate

gap

stile

Hallin Hill

sign

The Scars are remarkably weathered limestone erratics perched like imposters on the side of this gritstone moor. Unfortunately you get only glimpses of them as they sit on a chunk of private land. Similar glacial deposits of limestone at **Timothy Scaurs** and Lower Edge were mined by hushing (see Page 28).

to Cowling (1/2 mile)

Old Lane

Piper Lane

Dean Laithe

Long Hill End

Pond Hill gate

Over Fields

Moor Lodge

Over Dean (ruin)

bridge

wet

Dean Brow Clough

gate

gap

Dean Brow

Further Dean Hole (ruin)

ladder

to Ickornshaw (1 mile)

ruin

cowling

barn

Dean Hole Clough

sign

cowling

post

Dean Moss

Andrew Gutter

Lower Edge

toad rock

stake

to Ickornshaw (1 mile)

Pad Cote Lane

Pad Cote

sign

gate

stile

Wreck

gate

gate

Cowloughton

Viscount Snowden Memorial Cairn

barn

chimney

wet

stiles

gate

cowling

cowling

The Scars

cowling

Cowloughton Clough

Scar Hill

cowlings

cowling

High End Lowe

Timothy Scars (lime hushings)

pool

locked gate

stile & gate

The name **Ickornshaw** derives from an Old Norse word meaning squirrel.

Brown Hill

butt

Cowloughton Dam (site of)

The New Stone Hut (c1902)

High End Lowe Spring

The Pennine Way crosses the heart of **Ickornshaw Moor**; though there is little to the east of it, Hart Hill Moor and Cowlaughton Clough are surprisingly busy. The most obvious route up from Pad Cote goes up the long field above the ugly memorial cairn, but another leads up the sliver of moorland from a gate off the lane below Wreck. A good path then leads up the side of **Cowlaughton Clough** to join the Pennine Way.

Hart Hill Moor

butt

butt

butt

cairn

cairns

The Viscount Snowden Memorial Cairn was unveiled on 21st May 1938 before a large crowd to remember Philip Snowden, Labour's first Chancellor of the Exchequer. Viscount Snowden was born in Cowling and had his ashes scattered on Ickornshaw Moor.

butt

Cat Stone Clough

butts

sink

Cat Stone

stone shelter

The **Cat Stone** is an unremarkable boulder capped by a few stones. It can be reached by continuing on feint grooves across Hart Hill Moor from the gates on the moor edge.

Maw Stones

a cowling on Ickornshaw Moor

& Sutton Moors)

When the county boundaries were redrawn in 1974, **Cowling** was originally included in Lancashire. The incensed locals eventually succeeded in having the village returned to its rightful place in Yorkshire.

The massive **Hitching Stone** dominates the moorland expanse between Earl Crag and Wolf Stones (see *Page 171* for more details). There were at one time more large boulders across this section of moor; though the Kid Stone and Winter Hill Stone remain, others have been quarried away, including the Quicken Stone, Buck Stone and Navaxstone. The latter two were somewhere across the moss north-east from the Hitching Stone.

Reaching the **Hitching Stone** from Long Gate is not as straight-forward as it looks. The best path runs from a gate near the top of the road, passes over **Kid Stone Hill**, then skirts Quicken Hole to stop at a covered dam just short of the boulder. Another path sets off from a ladder stile further down the road and leads either up the side of **Slatesden Clough** or along the wall that leads to the stone. It is a wall that is not easily crossed in between thanks to locked gates and a new fence alongside.

The western end of **Earl Crag** is a maze of paths through the bracken, but further east there is little useful below the rocks and a couple of well-built walls obstructing progress. This leaves only the well-trodden route along the crag between the twin monuments (further information on Page 172).

The shooting path up the side of **Smallden Clough** is the only route across the broad swathe of heather north of **Maw Stones**. The path eventually peters out by the last of the butts, but the **Hitching Stone** can be reached by crossing Smallden Head at its driest point and climbing up to the obvious stone on the top of Hitching Stone Hill. Otherwise you are liable to end up in the clutches of **Mistress Moss**, which extends its soggy claws all the way round the north and west sides of Hitching Stone Hill.

Map labels

Crag Side
Dick Lane
Brush gate & sign
sign
picnic tables
gap
quarry
rough stile
gate
seat
seat
gate
Hangingstone Quarry
Lund's Tower
to Sutton -in-Craven (2 miles)
Earl Crag
Wainman's Pinnacle
trilithion
Buckstones
Crag Slack
shed
Stake Hill
Buck Stone Lane
Higher Buck Stone
to Sutton -in-Craven (2 miles)
Lanshaw Beck
air lace
gate
wet
gate
gate
gate
Winter Hill Stone (C&R marked stone)
gate
gate
Winter Hill
Hitching Stone Slack
Mistress Moss
drain
memorial
Kid Stone Hill
Kid Stone
gate
to Laycock (3 miles)
Sugar Hole (ruin)
Lund's Tower
0   300 metres
wet
wet
stake
dam
Quicken Stone
Hitching Stone
Quicken Hole
stile
Mistress Moss
grassy groove
Hitching Stone Hill
locked gate
locked gate
Green Clough
Long Gate
N
pool
Smallden Head
line of wooden grouse butts
Slatesden Clough
sign & ladder
Smallden Top
line of sunken butts
Smallden Clough
Round Hill
bridge
gate
stile
wet
stile
gate & sign
Far Slippery Ford
stile
shooting lodge
Old Ibber Dike
Old Ibber Edge
gate
gate
sign
gate
Middle Slippery Ford
Cob Stone (cup & ring marked stone)
Slitheroford Farm
signs
Brown Edge
to Oakworth (2 miles)

CONTINUATION ON WOLF STONES (Southern Section)

167

ROUTE 27: WOLF STONES AND NEWSHOLME DEAN FROM OAKWORTH

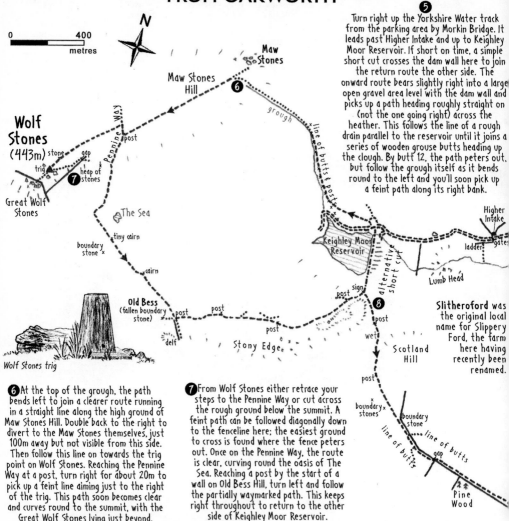

⑤ Turn right up the Yorkshire Water track from the parking area by Morkin Bridge. It leads past Higher Intake and up to Keighley Moor Reservoir. If short on time, a simple short cut crosses the dam wall here to join the return route the other side. The onward route bears slightly right into a large open gravel area level with the dam wall and picks up a path heading roughly straight on (not the one going right) across the heather. This follows the line of a rough drain parallel to the reservoir until it joins a series of wooden grouse butts heading up the clough. By butt 12, the path peters out, but follow the grough itself as it bends round to the left and you'll soon pick up a feint path along its right bank.

Slitheroford was the original local name for Slippery Ford, the farm here having recently been renamed.

⑥ At the top of the grough, the path bends left to join a clearer route running in a straight line along the high ground of Maw Stones Hill. Double back to the right to divert to the Maw Stones themselves, just 100m away but not visible from this side. Then follow this line on towards the trig point on Wolf Stones. Reaching the Pennine Way at a post, turn right for about 20m to pick up a feint line aiming just to the right of the trig. This path soon becomes clear and curves round to the summit, with the Great Wolf Stones lying just beyond.

⑦ From Wolf Stones either retrace your steps to the Pennine Way or cut across the rough ground below the summit. A feint path can be followed diagonally down to the fenceline here; the easiest ground to cross is found where the fence peters out. Once on the Pennine Way, the route is clear, curving round the oasis of The Sea. Reaching a post by the start of a wall on Old Bess Hill, turn left and follow the partially waymarked path. This keeps right throughout to return to the other side of Keighley Moor Reservoir.

⑧ Turn right at the sign before the reservoir and follow the waymark posts to join the line of wall between two files of large stone butts. Reaching another wall, the path goes through a gap to the left side of the wall and follows this past Pine Wood to a stile at the far end. Continue straight on with an old wall for company to reach a narrow gate leading off the moor. A path hugs the wall beyond, crossing one stile before bending left to reach a walled track.

Distance: 9 miles (14.5km)

Ascent: 380m

Difficulty: Moderate

Parking: Street parking in Oakworth Lane End and next to Oakworth Cemetery. Small car park at Morkin Bridge (2 miles from Oakworth).

Public Transport: Oakworth is on the 665, 717, 917 & 918 bus routes from Keighley and Haworth.

Character: There are few paths on the east side of Wolf Stones, so this is the only natural round route to the summit, though it can be shortened by parking at Morkin Bridge or skipping the moor tops. The route out of Oakworth follows the lush valley of Newsholme Dean up onto the moor, before making a loop of the high ground around Keighley Moor Reservoir and following the long ridge back down to Oakworth. The paths are generally easy to follow, except the short stretch up to Maw Stones.

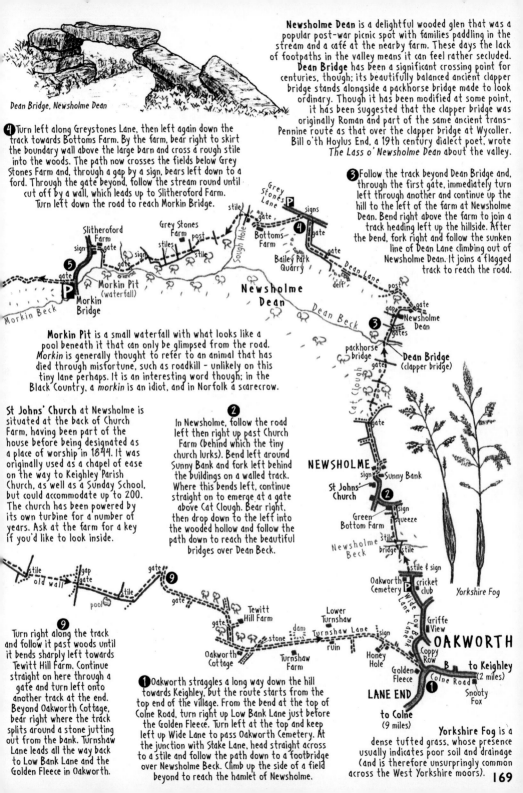

Newsholme Dean is a delightful wooded glen that was a popular post-war picnic spot with families paddling in the stream and a café at the nearby farm. These days the lack of footpaths in the valley means it can feel rather secluded.

Dean Bridge has been a significant crossing point for centuries, though; its beautifully balanced ancient clapper bridge stands alongside a packhorse bridge made to look ordinary. Though it has been modified at some point, it has been suggested that the clapper bridge was originally Roman and part of the same ancient trans-Pennine route as that over the clapper bridge at Wycoller. Bill o'th Hoylus End, a 19th century dialect poet, wrote *The Lass o' Newsholme Dean* about the valley.

Dean Bridge, Newsholme Dean

4 Turn left along Greystones Lane, then left again down the track towards Bottoms Farm. By the farm, bear right to skirt the boundary wall above the large barn and cross a rough stile into the woods. The path now crosses the fields below Grey Stones Farm and, through a gap by a sign, bears left down to a ford. Through the gate beyond, follow the stream round until cut off by a wall, which leads up to Slitheroford Farm. Turn left down the road to reach Morkin Bridge.

3 Follow the track beyond Dean Bridge and, through the first gate, immediately turn left through another and continue up the hill to the left of the farm at Newsholme Dean. Bend right above the farm to join a track heading left up the hillside. After the bend, fork right and follow the sunken line of Dean Lane climbing out of Newsholme Dean. It joins a flagged track to reach the road.

Morkin Pit is a small waterfall with what looks like a pool beneath it that can only be glimpsed from the road. *Morkin* is generally thought to refer to an animal that has died through misfortune, such as roadkill – unlikely on this tiny lane perhaps. It is an interesting word though; in the Black Country, a *morkin* is an idiot, and in Norfolk a scarecrow.

St Johns' Church at Newsholme is situated at the back of Church Farm, having been part of the house before being designated as a place of worship in 1844. It was originally used as a chapel of ease on the way to Keighley Parish Church, as well as a Sunday School, but could accommodate up to 200. The church has been powered by its own turbine for a number of years. Ask at the farm for a key if you'd like to look inside.

2 In Newsholme, follow the road left then right up past Church Farm (behind which the tiny church lurks). Bend left around Sunny Bank and fork left behind the buildings on a walled track. Where this bends left, continue straight on to emerge at a gate above Cat Clough. Bear right, then drop down to the left into the wooded hollow and follow the path down to reach the beautiful bridges over Dean Beck.

9 Turn right along the track and follow it past woods until it bends sharply left towards Tewitt Hill Farm. Continue straight on here through a gate and turn left onto another track at the end. Beyond Oakworth Cottage, bear right where the track splits around a stone jutting out from the bank. Turnshaw Lane leads all the way back to Low Bank Lane and the Golden Fleece in Oakworth.

1 Oakworth straggles a long way down the hill towards Keighley, but the route starts from the top end of the village. From the bend at the top of Colne Road, turn right up Low Bank Lane just before the Golden Fleece. Turn left at the top and keep left up Wide Lane to pass Oakworth Cemetery. At the junction with Stake Lane, head straight across to a stile and follow the path down to a footbridge over Newsholme Beck. Climb up the side of a field beyond to reach the hamlet of Newsholme.

Yorkshire Fog is a dense tufted grass, whose presence usually indicates poor soil and drainage (and is therefore unsurprisingly common across the West Yorkshire moors).

Map labels: Grey Stones Lane, signs, stile, gate, Bottoms Farm, Slitheroford Farm, sign, gate, Grey Stones Farm, post, stiles, stile, Sough Hole, Bailey Park Quarry, gate, Dean Lane, delf, post, gap, gate, Newsholme Dean, gates, packhorse bridge, Dean Bridge (clapper bridge), gate, Cat Clough, Dean Beck, Morkin Pit (waterfall), Morkin Bridge, Morkin Beck, Newsholme Dean, gate, NEWSHOLME, sign, Sunny Bank, St Johns' Church, sign, squeeze, Green Bottom Farm, stile, bridge, stile, Newsholme Beck, stile & sign, stile & sign, Oakworth Cemetery, cricket club, Yorkshire Fog, Wide Low Bank Lane, Griffe View, Coppy Row, OAKWORTH, to Keighley (2 miles), Colne Road, Honey Hole, Golden Fleece, Snooty Fox, LANE END, to Colne (9 miles), stile, old wall, gap, gate, pool, stile, gate, gate, gate, Tewitt Hill Farm, Lower Turnshaw, Turnshaw Lane, dam, stone, ruin, Oakworth Cottage, Turnshaw Farm

ROUTE 28: EARL CRAG AND THE HITCHING STONE FROM SUTTON-IN-CRAVEN

Distance: 7 miles (11.5km)

Ascent: 370m

Difficulty: Easy

Parking: Street parking in Sutton-in-Craven, though this can be awkward on some of the narrow streets.

Public Transport: Sutton is on the 65, 66, 67 & 78A bus routes between Keighley and Skipton, with further buses running through Cross Hills half a mile away.

Character: A very satisfying round that admittedly takes in more of North Yorkshire than West Yorkshire, but links the gritstone moorland features of Earl Crag, the Hitching Stone and Grey Stones Hill with the sylvan charms of the Victorian walkways in Sutton Clough. The going is generally very good, though some of the footpaths are not well marked and there is a short pathless section across Smalldin Head.

Sutton village may be in North Yorkshire, but in many ways it is a typical Pennine mill village. One of its landmarks is the Jacobethan gatehouse that you pass under on Hall Drive. Sutton Hall Lodge was built in the late 19th century as the entrance to Sutton Hall, but is all that remains of the Hartleys' short-lived gothic mansion, which was demolished in the 1940s. The Hartleys operated High Mill in Sutton Clough and later the large converted mill (known either as Hartleys Mill or Greenroyd Mill) that still dominates the centre of the village. The gates themselves were also removed and now mark the entrance to Cliffe Castle in Keighley.

1

From Sutton-in-Craven High Street (running past the giant Greenroyd Mill and the Kings Arms and Black Bull pubs), head straight on where it bends left towards the Bay Horse. Hall Drive soon passes under the gatehouse of Sutton Hall Lodge and continues as a rough track through the houses beyond. The track leads straight into the estate woods of Sutton Clough: bear left and follow the clear path all the way up the left bank of the stream. Reaching a walled track, turn right over an old clapper bridge and continue up the other side.

2

Follow the path up the right side of the clough to emerge into fields by a small waterfall. Stay with the stream and, beyond another stile, drop down to cross it and follow a path up the right edge of the fields to Gill Top. Keep left through a couple of gateways in front of the farm, then bear right beyond the barn and aim for the far corner of the field. Through a gate, follow the wall up to the steps below America Farm.

8

Follow the track downhill from Crag and, where it bends left, angle down the field to its right to a gate in the far corner. A narrow fenced path leads between houses to a road on the edge of Sutton. Head straight on, even where the road turns to the left, following a rough track called The Acres. At the far end turn left to reach the High Street and centre of the village again.

Sutton Clough and Lumb Clough are used somewhat interchangeably to refer to the ancient wooded valley running down into the village. Its walkways were laid out as a private Victorian garden by the owners of Sutton Hall, after whose demolition it was gifted to the parish. At the confluence further up Lumb Clough, there was a small lead smelting mill in the 18th century utilising ore from mines on Glusburn Moor.

7

Retrace your steps from Lund Tower and follow the path down the quarry edge to the road. 250m down the hill, turn right on a concrete track that descends steeply to High Jack Field. Skirt round right in front of the house to a small gate beyond, then follow the field edge along to a stile by a small wood. Cut diagonally down across the field to join a track to the left of the farm at Crag.

SUTTON-IN-CRAVEN

to Cross Hills (½ mile)

Kings Arms

Greenroyd Mill

The Bay Horse

High St

West La

Hall Way

Hall Drive

Sutton Hall Lodge (gatehouse)

The Acres

Long Dike

Bridge & gate

bridge

1

bridge & gate

bridges

Sutton Clough

High Mill (site of)

gate

Lumb Clough

bridge

8

Crag

Jack Field Wood

stiles

stile

High Jack Field

gate

postil gate

cattle grid

sign

7

Lund's Tower

Brush (ruin)

gate & sign

Earl Crag

gate

gate

gate

Wainman's Pinnacle

Stake Hill

gate

to Cowling (1 mile)

clapper bridge

squeeze

Wood Top

stile bridge

waterfall

2

0   300   metres

N

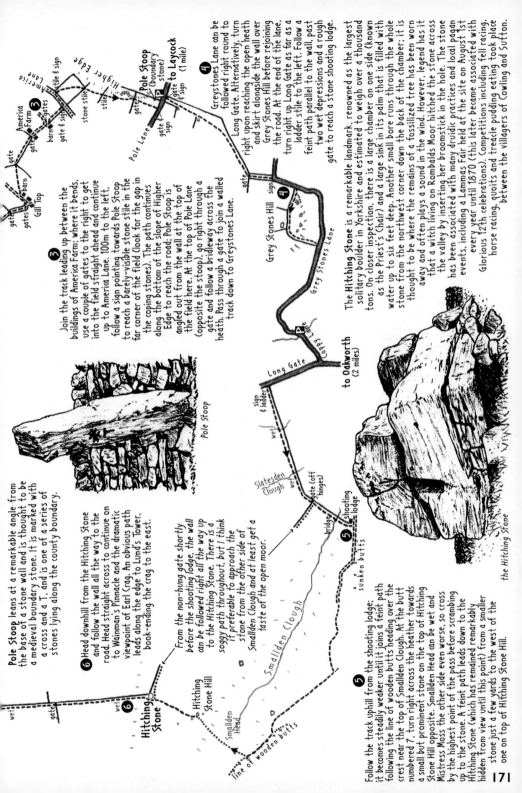

Pole Stoop leans at a remarkable angle from the base of a stone wall and is thought to be a medieval boundary stone. It is marked with a cross and a T, and is one of a series of stones lying along the county boundary.

America Lane / **Higher Edge** / **Pole Lane** / Higher Edge / **Pole Stoop** (boundary stone) / **P** / gate & sign / **to Laycock** (1 mile) / stile & sign / stone stile / **America Farm** ③ / gates / barn / gate & sign / gate / barn / gate / **Gill Top** / gates / gate

③ Join the track leading up between the buildings of America Farm; where it bends, use a couple of gates on the right to get into the field straight ahead and continue up to America Lane. 100m to the left, follow a sign pointing towards Pole Stoop to reach a barely-visible stone stile in the far corner of the field (look for the gap in the coping stones). The path continues along the bottom of the slope of Higher Edge to reach the road: Pole Stoop is angled out from the wall at the top of the field here. At the top of Pole Lane (opposite the stoop), go right through a gate and follow a bridleway across the heath. Pass through a gate to join a walled track down to Greystones Lane.

Pole Stoop

④ Greystones Lane can be followed right round to followed Grey Stones Hill. Alternatively, turn right upon reaching the open heath and skirt alongside the wall over Grey Stones Hill before rejoining the road. At the end of the lane, turn right up Long Gate as far as a ladder stile to the left. Follow a feint path parallel to the wall, past two wet depressions and a rough gate to reach a stone shooting lodge.

Grey Stones Hill sign ④

Grey Stones Lane

to Oakworth (2 miles)

Long Gate / COPPY / **P**

sign & ladder / wet / wet

Slatesden Clough / wet / gate (off hinges) / bridge / ⑤ / **shooting lodge** / x x sunken butts

Smallden Clough / *line of wooden butts* / Smallden Head

The **Hitching Stone** is a remarkable landmark, renowned as the largest solitary boulder in Yorkshire and estimated to weigh over a thousand tons. On closer inspection, there is a large chamber on one side (known as the Priest's Chair) and a large sink in its palm that is filled with water up to six feet deep. Another small bore runs through the whole stone from the northwest corner down the back of the chamber; it is thought to be where the remains of a fossilized tree has been worn away and often plays a sound in the wind. However, legend has it that a witch living on Rombalds Moor hitched the stone across the valley by inserting her broomstick in the hole. The stone has been associated with many druidic practices and local pagan events, including a Lammas Fair held at the site on August 1st every year until 1870 (this later became associated with Glorious 12th celebrations). Competitions including fell racing, horse racing, quoits and treacle pudding eating took place between the villagers of Cowling and Sutton.

the Hitching Stone

⑥ Head downhill from the Hitching Stone and follow the wall all the way to the road. Head straight across to continue on to Wainman's Pinnacle and the dramatic viewpoint of Earl Crag. An obvious path leads along the edge to Lund's Tower, book-ending the crag to the east.

From the non-hung gate shortly before the shooting lodge, the wall can be followed right all the way up to the Hitching Stone. There is a soggy path throughout, but I think it preferable to approach the stone from the other side of Smallden Clough and at least get a taste of the open moor.

wet / gate ⑥ / **Hitching Stone** / ⑥ / **Hitching Stone Hill** / Smallden Head

⑤ Follow the track uphill from the shooting lodge; it becomes steadily weaker until it joins a feint path following the line of wooden butts heading over the crest near the top of Smallden Clough. At the butt numbered 7, turn right across the heather towards a small but prominent stone on the top of Hitching Stone Hill opposite. Smallden Head can be wet and Mistress Moss the other side even worse, so cross by the highest point of the pass before scrambling up to the stone. A feint path leads down to the Hitching Stone (which has remained remarkably hidden from view until this point) from a smaller stone just a few yards to the west of the one on top of Hitching Stone Hill.

171

EARL CRAG MONUMENTS

The pair of follies at either end of Earl Crag are visible from many miles around and consequently represent fine vantage points. The two striking structures though are unrelated and carry their own stories.

WAINMAN'S PINNACLE

Wainman's Pinnacle (also known as Cowling Pinnacle or 'salt pot') is the older of the two monuments, thought to have been built shortly after Wellington's victory at Waterloo. It is not obviously a war memorial, though, and may have been erected by a member of the Wainman family for personal reasons or simply as a folly. Either Richard Wainman or his wife, Lady Amcotts, are likely to have been responsible; though the common tale is that Lady Amcotts' husband died in the Civil War, the two only married in 1809. The Wainmans owned the sizeable Carr Head Estate in Cowling from the early seventeenth century, yet built the monument on private land they had to pay ground rent on. The monument was rebuilt in 1898 after being struck by lightning and falling into disrepair and stands proudly on the highest boulder on the edge, very close to a trilithion (stone arch) possibly used in sun worship.

LUND'S TOWER

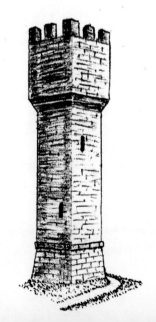

Lund's Tower (also known as Sutton Pinnacle or 'pepper pot') was built by James Lund of Malsis Hall (near Sutton) in 1897. No-one knows for sure why it was built; some have suggested to commemorate Queen Victoria's diamond jubilee, others for his daughter Ethel's 21st birthday (and indeed refer to it as Ethel's Tower). The plaque on its face is mysteriously left blank. It is a very pure folly, a crenelated viewing tower plonked on the landscape as in a fairytale, but Lund's folly can still be enjoyed as a narrow stone staircase inside leads up to the top.

BIBLIOGRAPHY

Armitage, Harry - 'Dam It! - The Building of the Halifax Reservoirs 1830-1914' in *Transactions of the Halifax Antiquarian Society* (1977)

Armitage, Harry - *Dawson City, Heptonstall* (1980)

Askwith, Richard - *Feet in the Clouds* (London: Aurum, 2004)

Baines, Edward - *History of the County Palatine and Duchy of Lancashire* (London: Fisher, Co and Son, 1836)

Barley, M.W. (ed.) - *The Buildings of the Countryside 1500-1750* (Cambridge University Press, 1990)

Baumber, Michael - *A History of Haworth from Earliest Times* (Lancaster: Carnegie, 2009)

Bennett, Paul - *The Old Stones of Elmet* (Milverton: Capall Bann, 2001)

Bibby, Andrew - *The Backbone of England* (London: Frances Lincoln, 2011)

Billingsley, John - *Folk Tales from Calderdale: Volume I* (Mytholmroyd: Northern Earth, 2007)

Bowtell, Harold D. - *Reservoir Railways of the Yorkshire Pennines* (Oakwood Press, 1979)

Brown, A.J. - *Moorland Tramping in West Yorkshire* (London: Country Life Ltd, 1931)

Brunskill, R.W. - *Houses and Cottages of Britain: Origins and Development of Traditional Buildings* (London: Orion, 1997)

Campbell, Marie - *Curious Tales of West Yorkshire* (Wilmslow: Sigma Leisure, 1999)

Clark, E. Kitson - 'Excavation at Pule Hill near Marsden' in *Yorkshire Archaeological and Topographical Journal, Vol 16* (1902)

Collins, Herbert Cecil - *The Roof of Lancashire* (London: Dent, 1950)

Cowling, Eric T. - *Rombalds Way: A Pre-history of Mid-Wharfedale* (Otley: William Walker, 1946)

Craven, Joseph - *A Brontë Moorland Village and its People: A History of Stanbury* (Keighley: The Rydal Press, 1907)

Crump, W.B. - 'Dialect on the Map - Some Calder Valley Placenames' in *Transactions of the Halifax Antiquarian Society* (1931)

Crump, W.B. - *Huddersfield Highways Down the Ages* (Huddersfield: Tolson Museum, 1949)

Dixon, Mike - *History and Guide: Ilkley* (Stroud: Tempus, 2002)

Dyson, Taylor - *The History of Huddersfield and District from the earliest times down to 1951* (Huddersfield: Alfred Jubb & Son, 1951)

Eccles, Robert. - 'Local Pinfolds' in *Transactions of the Halifax Antiquarian Society* (1936)

Ekwall, Eilert - *The Place-Names of Lancashire* (Manchester: University Press, 1922)

English, Barbara - *Yorkshire Enclosure Awards* (Hull University Press, 1985)

Faull, M.L. & Moorhouse, S.A. (eds) - *West Yorkshire: An Archaeological Survey to AD 1500* (Wakefield: West Yorkshire County Council, 1981)

Fielding, Alan & Haworth Paul F. - *Upland Habitats* (London: Routledge, 1999)

Fletcher, John C. - 'Flints Reservoir, 1834-1929' in *Transactions of the Halifax Antiquarian Society* (2004)

Folley, E.W. - *Romantic Wycoller* (Nelson: Coulton & Co., 1949)

Forrest, Charles and Grainge, William - *A Ramble on Rombalds Moor* (Wakefield: W.T. Lamb, 1868)

Gee, H.L. - *Folk Tales of Yorkshire* (Edinburgh: Thomas Nelson & Sons, 1960)

Gledhill, B. - 'Cragg Road: A Turnpike Trust' in *Transactions of the Halifax Antiquarian Society* (1987)

Goodhall, Armitage - *Place-names of South-west Yorkshire* (Cambridge University Press, 2012)

Greenough, George Bellas - *Memoir of a Geological Map of England* (London: Geological Society of London, 1840)

Haigh, Donald - 'Local History from World War II: The Starfish Sites at Cragg Vale and Clifton' in *Transactions of the Halifax Antiquarian Society* (1993)

Hannon, Paul - *Ilkley Moor* (Keighley: Hillside, 1994)

Hanson, T.W. - 'Cattle Ranches of Sowerbyshire' in *Transactions of the Halifax Antiquarian Society* (1949)

Hanson, T.W. - 'The Cragg Coiners' in *Transactions of the Halifax Antiquarian Society* (1909)

Hardwick, C. - 'Traditions' in *Yorkshire Folk-lore Journal* (1888)

Harland, John & Wilkinson, T.T. - *Lancashire Folklore* (London: Frederick Warne, 1867)

Heginbottom, J.A. - 'Fences and Fields: The Evolution of the Calderdale Rural Landscape from Prehistoric Times to the Present Day' in *Transactions of the Halifax Antiquarian Society* (1993)

Heginbottom, J.A. - 'The Landscape History of Erringden Park for the 12th to the 20th Century' in *Transactions of the Halifax Antiquarian Society* (2006)

Heginbottom, J.A. - 'The Stoodley Pike Obelisk: A Commemoration Monument' in *Transactions of the Halifax Antiquarian Society* (1995)

Hewitt, Peggy - *These Lonely Mountains: A Biography of the Brontë Moors* (Huddersfield: Springfield Books, 1985)

Heywood, Malcolm, Heywood, Freda & Jennings, Bernard - *A History of Todmorden* (Skipton: Dalesman, 1996)

Hill, Howard - *Freedom to Roam* (Ashbourne: Moorland, 1980)

Hindley, Reg - *Oxenhope: The Making of a Pennine Community* (Cleckheaton: Amadeus, 2004)

Hindley, Reg - *Exploring Oxenhope* (Cleckheaton: Amadeus, 2006)

Holden, Joshua - *A Short History of Todmorden with Some Account of the Geology and Natural History of the Neighbourhood* (Manchester: Sherratt & Hughes, 1912)

Hudson, David - *Grouse Shooting* (Shrewbury: Quiller, 2008)

Hughes, Joseph - *The History of the Township of Meltham* (Huddersfield: J. Crossley & Co, 1866)

Hughes, Ted - *Remains of Elmet* (London: Faber & Faber, 1993)

Jacobi, R.M., Tallis, J.H. & Mellars, P.A. - *The Southern Pennine Mesolithic and the ecological record* (1976)

James, T. - 'On Antiquities of the South Western Part of the County of York' in *Huddersfield Archaeological and Topographical Association Papers* (1867)

Jennings, B. - *Pennine Valley: A History of Upper Calderdale* (Skipton: Dalesman, 1992)

Jepson, Boel - *English Place-Name Elements Relating to Boundaries* (Lund University, 2011)

Keighley, William - *Keighley: Past and Present* (Keighley: A. Hey, 1879)

Kendall, H.P. - 'The Civil War as affecting Halifax and the Surrounding Towns' in *Transactions of the Halifax Antiquarian Society* (1911)

Kendall, Hugh P. - 'The Forest of Sowerbyshire' in *Transactions of the Halifax Antiquarian Society* (1926)

Langdale, Thomas - *A Topographical Dictionary of Yorkshire* (Northallerton: J. Langdale, 1809)

Lawrence, A. - *A History of Menston and Hawksworth* (Otley: Smith Settle, 1991)

Le Patourel, Jean, Long, Moira H. and Pickles, May F. - *Yorkshire Boundaries* (Leeds: Yorkshire Archaeological Society, 1993)

Lunn, Norman - *The Romans Came This Way* (Huddersfield & District Archaeological Society, 2008)

Manley, Gordon - 'Saxton's Survey of Northern England' in *The Geographical Journal Vol 83* (Blackwell Publishing, 1934)

March, Dr H.C. - *East Lancashire Nomenclature and Rochdale Names* (London: Simpkin, 1880)

Midgley History Group - *Pennine Perspectives: Aspects of the History of Midgley* (Midgley: Midgley Books, 2007)

Midgley, Samuel & Bentley, William - *A History of the Town and Parish of Halifax* (Halifax: E. Jacobs, 1789)

Minter, Gordon & Enid - *Discovering Old Huddersfield* (Huddersfield Local History Society, 2010)

Newell, Abraham - 'Primitive Iron Industry in Upper Calder Dale' in *Transactions of the Halifax Antiquarian Society* (1918)

Newell, Abraham - *A Hillside View of Industrial History* (Todmorden: Newell, 1925)

Ogden, J.H. - 'A Moorland Township: Wadsworth in Ancient Times' in *Transactions of the Halifax Antiquarian Society* (1904)

Orton, Richard - *The Story of Meltham* (Meltham Town Council, 1977)

Pearson, E. Irene - *Marsden Through the Ages* (Marsden: E. Irene Pearson, 1984)

Priestley, J.H. - 'Mills of the Ryburn Valley' in *Transactions of the Halifax Antiquarian Society* (1933-34)

Priestley, J.H. - 'The Rochdale to Halifax and Elland Turnpike' in *Transactions of the Halifax Antiquarian Society* (1952-53)

Raistrick, Dr A. - 'The Bronze Age in West Yorkshire' in *Yorkshire Archaeological Journal* (1929)

Raistrick, Arthur - *Yorkshire Maps and Map-makers* (Skipton: Dalesman, 1969)

Redmonds, Dr George - *Slaithwaite Places and Place Names* (Huddersfield: GR Books, 1988)

Samuels, David et al - *A Brief History of Oxenhope* (Keighley: Samuels, 1996)

Savage, Mrs E.M. - *Stoodley Pike* (Todmorden Antiquarian Society, 1974)

Shepherd, David - 'Prehistoric Standing Stones in the South Pennines' in *Transactions of the Halifax Antiquarian Society* (2009)

Shires, David and King, Sheila - *The Halifax Cavaliers and the Heptonstall Roundheads* (Hollis, NH: Puritan Press, 1993)

Smith, Albert Hugh - *The Place-names of the West Riding of Yorkshire* (Cambridge: The University Press, 1959)

Smith, Nigel - 'The Location and Organisation of Demesne Cattle Farms in Sowerby Graveship Circa 1300' in *Transactions of the Halifax Antiquarian Society* (2007)

Smith, Nigel - 'The Medieval Park of Erringden' in *Transactions of the Halifax Antiquarian Society* (2009/2011)

Smith, William - *Old Yorkshire Volume IV* (London: Longmans, Green, 1883)

Speight, Harry - *Chronicles and Stories of Bingley and District* (London: Elliot Stock, 1904)

Spikins, Penny - *Prehistoric People of the Pennines* (Wakefield: West Yorkshire Archaeology Service, 2002)

Stephens, J.V, Mitchell, G.H. & Edwards, Wilfrid - *Geology of the Country between Bradford and Skipton* (London: HMSO, 1953)

Stephenson, Tom - *Forbidden Land: The Struggle for Access to Moorland and Mountain* (Manchester University Press, 1989)

Sugden, John - *Slaithwaite Notes Past and Present* (Manchester: John Heywood, 1905)

Sutcliffe, Halliwell - *By Moor and Fell: Landscapes and Lang-Settle Lore from West Yorkshire* (London: T. Fisher Unwin, 1899)

Sutcliffe, T. - 'Castle Carr' in *Transactions of the Halifax Antiquarian Society* (1921)

Sykes, D.F.E. - *The History of the Colne Valley* (Slaithwaite: F. Walker, 1906)

Thompson, Dennis - *Stanbury: A Pennine Country Village* (Calgary: Two Margarets, 2002)

Thornber, Titus - *A Pennine Parish: The History of Cliviger* (Burnley: Rieve Edge Press Limited, 1987)

Toomey, J.P. - *An Iron Age Enclosure at Oldfield Hill, Meltham* (Huddersfield: Brigantian, 1976)

Trigg, W.B. - 'The Industrial Water Supply of Ovenden' in *Transactions of the Halifax Antiquarian Society* (1933)

Trueman, A.E. - *Geology and Scenery in England and Wales* (London: Pelican, 1961)

Turner, Whiteley - A *Spring-time Saunter Round and About Brontë Land* (Wakefield: S.R. Publishers, 1913)

Watson, E.W. & Gledhill, G. - 'Wadsworth Highways' in *Transactions of the Halifax Antiquarian Society* (1951-55)

Watson, Rev J. - *The History and Antiquities of Halifax* (Manchester: F.J.Morten, 1973)

Whitehead, Lewis Buckley - *Bygone Marsden* (Manchester: Percy Brothers, 1942)

Wilkinson, T.T. - 'On the Druidical Rock Basins in the Neighbourhood of Burnley', in *Transactions of the Historic Society of Lancashire and Cheshire, Volume 5* (Liverpool: Adam Holden, 1861)

Wilkinson, Tattersall - 'Local Folklore' in *Transactions of the Halifax Antiquarian Society* (1904)

Wilkinson, Tattersall & Tattersall, J.F. - *Memories of Hurstwood, Burnley, Lancashire* (Burnley: J & A Lupton, 1889)

Williams, Eileen - *Holmfirth: From Forest to Township* (Huddersfield: Advertiser Press, 1975)

Wood, Alec (ed.) - *Cowling: A Moorland Parish* (Cowling Local History Society, 1980)

Wood, Alec (ed.) - *Sutton-in-Craven: The Old Community* (Driffield: The Ridings, 1973)

Wood, Steven & Palmer, Ian - *Oxenhope and Stanbury Through Time* (Stroud: Amberley, 2009)

Woodhead, T.W. - *History of the Huddersfield Water Supplies* (Huddersfield: Tolson Museum, 1939)

Websites:

Charlestown History Group *(www.charlestownhistory.org.uk)*

Cotton Town *(www.cottontown.org)*

Countryside and Rights of Way Act 2000 *(www.legislation.gov.uk/ukpga/2000/37/contents)*

Cowling Web *(www.cowlingweb.co.uk)*

Forgotten Relics of an Enterprising Age *(www.forgottenrelics.co.uk)*

Friends of Ilkley Moor *(www.ilkleymoor.org)*

From Weaver to Web *(www.calderdale.gov.uk/wtw)*

Haworth Village *(www.haworth-village.org.uk)*

Hebden Bridge Local History Society *(www.hebdenbridgehistory.org.uk)*

Hebden Bridge Web *(www.hebdenbridge.co.uk)*

Internet Archive: Digital Library *(www.archive.org)*

Jim Jarrett *(www.jimjarratt.co.uk)*

Mytholmroyd Net *(www.mytholmroyd.net)*

One Guy From Barlick *(www.oneguyfrombarlick.co.uk)*

Pennine Prospects *(www.pennineprospects.co.uk)*

Power in the Landscape *(www.powerinthelandscape.co.uk)*

Scammonden Wardens *(www.scammondenwardens.co.uk)*

Stoodley Pike West Yorkshire *(stoodleypike.blogspot.com)*

The Cricket History of Calderdale and Kirklees *(www.ckcricketheritage.org.uk)*

The Megalithic Portal *(www.megalithic.co.uk)*

The Modern Antiquarian *(www.themodernantiquarian.com)*

The Moorland Association *(www.moorlandassociation.org)*

The Northern Antiquarian *(megalithix.wordpress.com)*

The Ramblers Association *(www.ramblers.org.uk)*

The Rombalds Moor Project *(therombaldsmoorproject.wordpress.com)*

Todmorden and Walsden History *(www.todmordenandwalsden.co.uk)*

A Vision of Britain Through Time *(www.visionofbritain.org.uk)*

Wild West Yorkshire Nature Diary *(www.wildyorkshire.co.uk)*

INDEX / GAZETTEER

Entries shown in bold refer to book chapters or sketches/background information on a particular feature.

Your feedback and any suggestions/corrections you may have would be very warmly welcomed through the book's website at:

www.westyorkshiremoors.co.uk